Research and Multicultural Education:
From the Margins to the Mainstream

Research and Multicultural Education:
From the Margins to the Mainstream

Edited by

Carl A. Grant

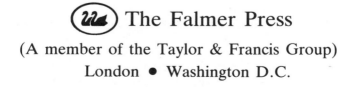

The Falmer Press

(A member of the Taylor & Francis Group)
London • Washington D.C.

USA   The Falmer Press, Taylor & Francis Inc., 1900 Frost Road,
        Suite 101, Bristol, PA 19007
UK   The Falmer Press, 4 John St, London WC1N 2ET

First published 1992

A catalogue record of this publication is available from the British Library

ISBN 1 85000 476 5 cased
ISBN 1 85000 477 3 paperback

Library of Congress Cataloging-in-Publication Data are available on request

Jacket design by Caroline Archer

Typeset in 9.5/11 pt Times by
Graphicraft Typesetters Ltd., Hong Kong

Printed in Great Britain by Burgess Science Press, Basingstoke on paper which has a specified pH value on final paper manufacture of not less than 7.5 and is therefore 'acid free'.

Contents

Contents

Introduction

Research and Multicultural Education: From the Margins to the Mainstream is
written to encourage research in multicultural education and to help scholars
think through some of the problems and issues inherent in doing research in this
area. Presently multicultural education is receiving major national and international attention, not only within the educational community, but within society
at large. Demographic changes in our society are requiring people who never
had to deal with one another seriously to work together. This contact among
and between different groups of people is taking place in political, social and
economic contexts that are dominated by an ever-widening gulf between the
'haves' and 'have nots'.

Schools now more than in the recent past are being required to respond to
the challenge of educating different groups of students about each other and to
making schooling equal and equitable for all. Educators at all levels and in all
roles are having to confront the racism, sexism and classism that they have, in a
large part, ignored but that has continued to hound them with an increasing
intensity. Quality research is needed to help educators understand and resolve
this quagmire and to help schools become portals to life opportunities and
choices for all students. *Research and Multicultural Education: From the Margins
to the Mainstream* is a volume intended to facilitate the production of this
research.

This volume is not a primer for doing multicultural research. However, it
includes discussions about many important areas that must be considered when
doing multicultural research. It responds to the felt needs of a number of
scholars, who have a serious interest in researching and writing in this area;
these researchers are often frustrated because there is a lack of discussion,
directions and support for doing multicultural research. Similarly, these scholars
have criticized the paucity of multicultural education research studies. *Research
and Multicultural Education: From the Margins to the Mainstream* is an attempt
to respond to both of these valid criticisms. It offers chapters about doing
research in multicultural education and makes contributions to the research base
in multicultural education by including chapters that are themselves studies in
multicultural education and it critiques national and state multicultural policy
initiates.

Research and Multicultural Education: From the Margins to the Mainstream
begins with a discussion by Grant and Millar of many of the barriers, needs and

1

boundaries that are inherent in doing multicultural research. These authors argue that multicultural research must be included in all areas of research on education and schools and that multicultural research has a close kinship to the equal opportunity and equity movement and therefore researchers of multicultural education have an obligation to demand to be included as part of this research cadre in leadership positions.

Gordon continues the discussion of barriers and boundaries when she discusses the marginalization of minority intellectual thought in traditional writing and teaching. She argues that at the level of curriculum development and implementation, there is a need for a triumvirate of anti-racist policies, emancipatory pedagogy and cultural consciousness that includes political action at both the school and community level.

Swartz argues that there is a critical need for multicultural education to move from its compensatory efforts to a scholarly foundation which would include more 'informed space' for its discussion. Swartz also points out to the critics the inclusion of multicultural curriculum of the hybrid origin and development of knowledge.

Weis discusses how it is to be a researcher in a multicultural environment. She discusses the importance of knowing oneself and how her gender influenced her role as a field researcher. Weis also points out how people in the field of the study influenced how she was defined. She additionally discusses the importance of being aware of one's own biography and the importance of personal integrity when doing field research.

Price provides researchers, especially those with misgivings about quantitative methodology, with reasons for using it in multicultural research. He also informs researchers of quantitative alternatives that educational researchers have rarely used. He tells those interested in doing multicultural research that it is important for them to become well grounded in the 'underlying logic and mathematics' of quantitative methods so that they can modify this method to better serve their research purpose. Price also points out and dispels some of the myths and stereotypes that exist between quantitative and qualitative methods.

Borman, Timm, El-Amin and Winston present a study of a school district facing racial tensions that exist between parents and teachers *and* African-American parents and white parents. The study includes seven recommendations to the school district to eliminate the racial tension and to affirm a multicultural environment. Borman, Timm, El-Amin and Winston also discuss why they believe these recommendations will or will not be effective. They additionally explain the use of multiple strategies to collect their data. Central to this chapter is the authors' critique of their own research efforts. They discuss research questions that they wished they had asked and offer this critique to other scholars, who may be considering similar research efforts.

Ahlquist, working within the paradigm of critical pedagogy, examines her teaching of a multicultural foundation course. She describes the forms of resistance that her students used against her anti-racist and critical teaching approach. Ahlquist also describes and critiques her response to this resistance, arguing that objectivity on the part of teacher is a myth and students' beliefs, ideologies and experiences need to be considered while teaching.

Ladson-Billings tells us that culturally relevant teaching is the key to successful multicultural education. She defines culturally relevant teaching, describing some of its characteristics as student empowerment, the use of students' culture in teaching and the importance of students having both social and cultural success. She also argues that researchers need to collect more anecdotal and ethnographic evidence from teachers who are successful with students of color.

Montero-Sieburth and Gray tell educators about the realities of collaborative inquiry, that include reflections on their entry into an urban school and their development of rapport with the teachers. They explain how the collaborative process between teachers and university professors and graduate students develops into a partnership based upon respect, support and trust. They also explain how the collaborative process informs the teachers about their own diversity as teachers and the diversity of their students. Montero-Sieburth and Gray additionally share what they learn from their collaborative inquiry and offer counsel to others contemplating collaboration.

Hernandez discusses the knowledge base for educating language minority students. She suggests a research agenda that should be considered by those interested in doing research in this area. Hernandez also offers recommendations that include a description of how teacher education and university policy can be changed to implement the agenda.

Soto, like Ladson-Billings, argues that educators need to highlight the successes of ethnically diverse learners in order to counteract the deficit philosophy inherent in the many messages that bombard families and students of color. She also argues that researchers must examine the hidden implications of their own research questions and their own theoretical frameworks.

Bloch and Swadener raise several questions regarding doing research in general, but particularly when the research focuses upon young children in their home and community. They direct their attention to research 'questions' that need to be addressed, instead of research 'results'. Fundamental to their discussion is the way in which students' ascribed characteristics impact their home, community and school experiences. Bloch and Swadener also discuss the importance of 'theory' in doing multicultural research.

Fuller, reporting the findings of a group research project, takes a look at the racial/ethnic, gender, and class make-up of the public schools and compares them to the like demographics of nineteen large teacher education programs. She describes the mismatch of these two populations and speculates as to the effects of this unequal distribution on public school students and pre-service teachers alike. Fuller also describes the dynamics, the fun and the frustration of group research and examines those factors that may influence equity research questions.

Marrett, Mizuno and Collins discuss the importance of intergroup contact, and its impact on interethnic attitudes. They describe some of the problems and issues associated with facilitating successful intergroup contacts. Marrett, Mizuno and Collins also remind advocates of multicultural education that having the opportunity for contact does not always result in contact, therefore attention must be given to making certain that the 'opportunity' is acted upon.

Gollnick discusses multicultural education policy at the national level, particularly as it relates to teacher education. She points out that policies for the inclusion of multicultural education in programs preparing teachers are found in the standards for national accreditation and the guidelines of professional organizations. Gollnick also critiques the major policies for multicultural education in teacher preparation programs.

Crumpton discusses multicultural policy at the state level and describes the characteristics of policy analysis. He discusses the nature of state policy studies in multicultural education. Crumpton also offers recommendations regarding the future direction of state policy studies in multicultural education.

Carl Grant
Madison
Wisconsin

Part 1

The Marginalization of Multicultural Discourse

Chapter 1

Research and Multicultural Education: Barriers, Needs, and Boundaries

Carl A. Grant and Susan Millar

It is slowly becoming standard for schools in the USA to take explicitly into account the ascribed characteristics (race, class, gender, and disability) of their students and the human diversity in society. The nomenclature for these aspects of education may change — as it has over the last thirty or more years — but the attention focused on student diversity in the schools and classrooms will continue to increase. This attention is a function of: the increasing number of students of color entering schools, many of whom have a primary language other than English; the demands of women who seek to have their history, culture, ideology and pedagogy fully accepted, appreciated and affirmed in every aspect of the policies and practices of the educational system; the accelerated movement of the United States population into a 'have' and 'have not' society; and the national fear that the USA is losing its technological and economic eminence to other countries.

During the late 1980s, education that deals with human diversity most commonly is referred to as 'multicultural education'. Other terms used synonymously in the past and the present for multicultural education have included, 'pluralism' or 'pluralistic', 'multiethnic', 'cross cultural', 'bi-cultural', and 'human relations'. Recently, multicultural education as an ideology and concept expressed through policies and practices has begun to make some small inroads into almost every aspect of schooling. It has also become more popularly accepted (at least with lip service attention) and thereby received a noticeable increase in status over the last ten years. However, scholarly research about multicultural education has not kept abreast of attempts to actualize the various ideas that school personnel hold about multicultural education. Teacher education (pre-service and in-service) has perhaps received the most research attention. However, Grant and Secada (1990) were able to locate only twenty-three research studies in the pre-service and in-service area of teacher education. There are a variety of reasons why research that takes into account multiculturalism is proceeding at a snail's pace. This chapter presents some of the more salient reasons, discusses the kinds of research about multicultural education that need to occur, and concludes by suggesting a set of boundaries on multi-cultural research.

Barriers to Multicultural Education

There are several reasons why research on multicultural education as well as educational research that takes multiculturalism into account have not kept pace with the discussion and debate.

1 *The demographic characteristics of higher education faculties are not conducive to the development of research on multicultural education.* In education, 93 per cent of the professors are white, and of this number, 70 per cent are male. In addition, the average age for full professors is 53, associate professors, 47, and assistant professors, 42. Given this profile, it is reasonable to assume that the great majority of education faculty have had little exposure to multiculturalism during their formative years of professional development. Examination of the bibliographies of their publications and of the syllabuses for their courses (Grant and Koskela, 1986) indicate that their working knowledge of multicultural education is very limited.

   This demographic picture is not likely to change quickly. The percentage of persons of color receiving doctorates is half of their representation in the general population. The number of African Americans receiving PhDs has declined since 1976 (McKenna, 1989, p. 11).

2 *The meaning of multicultural education has been, and very often still is, presented in an unclear manner.* Authors usually do not clearly define what they mean by the term (Banks, 1977; Grant and Sleeter, 1985; Sleeter and Grant, 1988). As a result, some educators/authors include under the rubric of multicultural education only work related in some way to students of color or to some aspect of human diversity (Grant and Sleeter, 1985; Grant, Sleeter and Anderson, 1986). This lack of definition allows critics to either ignore multicultural education or view it as an idea without meaning and structure.

3 *Monies to support multicultural research have been extraordinarily limited.* Occasionally, isolated projects with multicultural education in the title receive funding. For example, Zeichner and Grant received $30,000 per year over three years from the Department of Education to prepare pre-service students to teach effectively diverse students in multicultural settings. However, such studies are the exception in educational funding. Also, of the research studies on multicultural pre-service and in-service programs that Grant and Secada reviewed (1990), only a few were supported with additional institutional, state, or federal funds. It is important here to point out that although federal monies regularly support the Bureau for Equal Educational Opportunity and Bilingual Centers, the contractual purposes of these Bureaus and Centers are to provide training and technical assistance to schools and parents. For example, the mission of the Upper Great Lakes Multifunctional Re-

source Center — one of the sixteen regional resource centers funded by the US Department of Education — is to 'provide training and technical assistance to educators and parents in the education of students who have a limited proficiency in English (LEP)' (Secada, 1989). The Centers and the Bureaus are not budgeted to conduct general research. Furthermore, research on the effectiveness of their training and technical assistance activities is not considered primary to the scope of their mission.

4 *Academic ethnocentrism and elitism act to limit multicultural education research.* Academic ethnocentrism has been discussed recently in a number of educational publications. For example, in an issue of the *Chronicle of Higher Education* (1988) scholars of color point out that, for a variety of reasons, their work frequently is not accepted as solid scholarship. In particular, they note that the standards used to judge work in the social sciences, including education, are not sufficiently independent of the personal interests of the reviewers. In other words, the criteria used for evaluation are 'moving targets' rather than a standard understood by all ahead of time. It is significant, these scholars of color argue, that these moving targets are artifacts of the perspectives of white males.

Another form of academic ethnocentrism is expressed when reviewers hold that the work of scholars of color is only or mainly for people of color, and therefore not considered relevant for the majority of education scholars. Linda Grant (1988) has argued that patterns of 'ghettoization' exist in journal publication. She points out that articles on students of color in schools most often appear in journals that have a smaller specialized readership than mainstream journals. Staples (1984) earlier made a similar observation when referring to the general written scholarship of African-Americans. He concluded, '. . . few established white journals will publish the works of black scholars, work that generally challenges the prevailing white view of the racial situation. Most are forced to publish in black-oriented periodicals' (p. 9).

To avoid this ghettoization in journal publication, many scholars of color 'play the game', that is, abandon their desires to work from an ethnic perspective and instead work from a mainstream/traditional perspective. This point becomes doubly compounded because of the small number of scholars of color. Presently, even an informal review of conference papers and of published articles and books would point out that almost all of the research being conducted on educational problems and issues, including issues pertaining to people of color, is being conducted by white researchers.

Academic elitism is sometimes experienced by white scholars who have an interest in multicultural research. This occurs when their colleagues — both white and of color — ridicule their interest in this line of research, and suggest it should be left to people of color. As one white scholar told me, some of his white colleagues question why he works in this area and advise him that research on this topic is, 'their [people of color's] problem'. Academic elitism in the form of patriarchy also is present when women (of color and white) who employ feminist ideologies and methodologies experience barriers to their research programs (Harding, 1987; Hartsock, 1987; Raymond, 1985).

At the 1986 American Educational Research Association conference, the Sig for Examining the Application of Gender, Race, and Social Class in Educational Theory and Research was formed in part to ameliorate this academic elitism and ethnocentrism. The Sig is encouraging mainstream researchers to study the interactions between and among the actors in schools in terms of race, class, and gender issues.

5 *The ghettoization of academic conference participants who are advocates of multicultural education acts to inhibit research in this area.* At conferences or meetings, it frequently happens that only a few or no white males participate in or attend sessions that have 'multicultural', 'gender', or 'minority' in the title *unless* the work is 'done on' people of color. In other words, when researchers of color are presenting their research, relatively few white male researchers attend. However, when the session involves a white researcher discussing, for example, 'blacks', a good-sized audience of all colors attends. This ghettoization, although not documented, has become so commonplace that presenters and audience participants openly comment on it.

6 *Formal and informal socialization about research methodology and academic expectations rarely entails multicultural education.* It is well known that this kind of socialization often takes place in advanced level seminars. These seminars provide force not only for learning about research methodology and procedures. Popkewitz (1984) argues that,

> [A]s people are trained to participate in a research community, the learning involves more than the content or the field. Learning the exemplars of a field of inquiry is also to learn how to see, think about and act towards the world. An individual is taught the appropriate expectations, demands, and consistent attitudes and emotions that are involved in doing science. (p. 3)

Courses at either the undergraduate or graduate level (let alone at the advanced seminar level) in multicultural education are rarely available at colleges or universities.[1] The absence of seminars and other forums for analysis and debate about multicultural education undercuts conceptual development in this area and discourages young scholars from becoming involved in this field.

7 *A lack of leadership by scholars of color is another reason multicultural education research hasn't flourished.* It could be argued, based upon civil rights history, that until scholars of color assume prominent leadership positions in determining research directions, educational programs for students of color and *all* female students will be flawed and progress will be slow.

There are, no doubt, additional reasons why multicultural education research has not flourished. These, as well as the reasons discussed above, act as resistance, or barriers to change (Zaltman and Duncan, 1977) and are probably impeding the development of research on multicultural education in institutions. An understanding of these resistances will, according to Rubin *et al.* (1974), give valuable insights into the nature of the university, 'who it is', and what it considers valuable research.

What Multicultural Research Needs to Take Place

Multicultural research must be carried out on all areas of schooling, including school routines and interactions, teaching and learning practices, and the effects of educational policy and practices. A few illustrations of prominent research themes will help to make this clear.

Research on Teaching

The *Third Edition of the Handbook of Research on Teaching* (1986) has identified five major areas presently receiving research attention: Part I: Theory and Method of Research on Teaching; Part II: Research on Teaching and Teachers; Part III: The Social and Instructional Context of Teaching; Part IV: Adapting Teaching to Differences Among Learners; and Part V: Research on the Teaching of Subjects and Grade Levels. These five parts are divided into thirty-five chapters, each of which includes a bibliography listing the research studies reviewed. It seems logical, given the great student diversity in the nation's schools and the civic mission of schooling, that a careful study of teaching must take into account multiculturalism. For example, in Part II, Chapter 11, 'Students' Thought Processes', Whittrock, the *Handbook* editor, explains that '. . . research on students' thought processes examines how teaching and teachers influence what students think, believe, feel, say, or do that affects their achievement' (p. 297). He further explains how teachers influence student achievement: '. . . the distinctive characteristic of the research on students' thought processes is the idea that teaching affects achievement through students' processes. That is, teaching influences student thinking. Student thinking mediates learning and achievement' (p. 297). In reviewing the research in this area, his discussion includes: teacher expectations, student behavior, student self-concept, students' perception of schools, teachers, and teachers' behavior. It would be reasonable to conclude that these are important areas to study. It is also reasonable to conclude that research that takes into account multiculturalism is vital to these areas of study. For example, the educational literature is replete with accounts of students of color self-concepts' being detrimentally affected by school policies and practices (Beane and Lipka, 1987; Combs and Snygg, 1959; Kvaraceus, *et al.*, 1965; Rosenfeld, 1971). In fact, the issue that school segregation led to low self-esteem among blacks was a major argument offered by the social scientists who testified in Brown v. Board of Education. The literature is also replete with reports of how teachers' behavior has negatively affected low income students, students of color and female students (Gouldner, 1978; Rist, 1970; Grant and Sleeter, 1986a&b; Payne, 1984). Research that includes multiculturalism would make certain that students' ascribed characteristics (race, class and gender) are analyzed within the context of the above mentioned research areas, or it would address this omission if this were the case. Yet, such research studies were not included in this piece.

It can be concluded that the *Handbook* would be of greater benefit to educators if multiculturalism had been included in more of the chapters.

Teacher-student Interaction

Very closely related to teachers and teaching is the research on 'interactions' between teachers and students. For example, differences in interactions between teachers and students attributable to race/ethnicity and gender have been observed to account for differences in student performance (Brophy and Good, 1984; Fennema and Peterson, 1986; Reyes, 1981). Also, research on expectancy theory (Atkinson, 1964; Rosenthal and Jacobson, 1968) and social group theory (Rogers, 1969) argues that teachers' behavior toward students is influenced by their expectations of the students' abilities. Research that takes into account multiculturalism is important to this area because of recent demographic projections. Demographic projections suggest that interactions between and among these actors will need careful study. In 1984, 29 per cent of the total student enrollment in US schools was non-white. In the country's twenty largest school districts, students of color constituted between 60 per cent and 70 per cent (Center for Education Statistics, CES, 1987a, p. 64). It is projected that by the year 2000, students of color will comprise between 30 and 40 per cent of the total school enrollment (Hodgkinson, 1985). In contrast to the increasingly diverse student population, the teaching force in this country is becoming increasingly white and female (CES, 1987b, pp. 60, 175, 183 and 195). This contrast is compounded by socioeconomic class differences that frequently separate teachers and students. One in every four students is poor (Kennedy, Jung and Orland, 1986, p. 71) and one in every five students lives in a single-parent home (CES, 1987b, p. 21). The importance of this area is further compounded by a legacy of judicial, legislative and social inequities experienced by students of color, female students and poor students in their interactions with school officials.

All research thrusts of the Department of Education and of funding foundations such as Ford or Carnegie need to include multicultural education as an integral part of their research efforts on schooling. The Department of Education's current agenda for research on elementary and secondary schooling is fairly comprehensive, including both policy and practice initiatives. The research agenda is also fairly deep in that it includes research in the following areas: governance and finance, evaluation, student testing, writing, reading, effective secondary schools, elementary and middle schools, art, teacher evaluation, and educational technology. Research development centers are handsomely funded. The Center for School Leadership and the Center on Student Testing, Evaluation, and Standards each receive $1,000,000 for each of five years. Other centers may receive even more money annually. For example, the Center for the Study of Learning receives $1,300,000 for each of five years (The National Institute of Education, 1985).

Sometimes the focus of these research efforts is on students of color or, as the Government puts it (see, for example, FY 1989 Application for Educational Research and Development Centers Program, US Office of Education, 1988), 'Schooling of Disadvantaged Students'. This, however, is not the same as a focus on multiculutral education. For example, the bibliography (pp. 48–58) of the application package described above does not include publications on multicultural education. This omission could influence the way these research centers will operate in regards to multiculturalism.

Boundaries of Multicultural Research

Schooling can be compared to a ladder, with the first rung pre-school and the final rung undergraduate/graduate or professional school. The breadth of schooling encompasses technical training through the arts and sciences. Both the length and breadth of schooling needs to include curriculum and instruction that has multiculturalism comprehensively integrated throughout. Important to the success of this integration is research that examines this integration. In other words, it is important to actually know — not guess about — the attitudes and behaviors of the members of the educational community. Even at our institutions of higher education, it is becoming commonplace to hear or read about physical and verbal race and gender violence occurring on the campuses. According to Caldwell (1989) a report from the National Institute Against Prejudice and Violence, '174 universities reported incidents of violence against ethnic groups during the school years 1986–87 and 1987–88' (p. 32). This unrest is further exacerbated by the debate to include or not to include non-Western studies in the traditional college core curriculum.

This debate has increased tensions between and among faculty members, students, and university officials. For example, Stephen H. Balch, President of the National Association of Scholars, argues that 'ethnic and women studies are synonymous with lower standards. By and large, the emphasis is not scholarly. These courses are severely corrupting, they incorporate wrong values' (*On Campus*, 1989, p. 10). Rhetoric of this nature and actions that prevent people of color and women from seeing their history and culture in the core curriculum increase the intensity of the debate over 'whose' ideology and culture will be included in the core college curriculum. It fuels the growing tension on the campus. The boundaries of multicultural research therefore have to include all of schooling, from pre-school through professional school, and from the learning of the alphabet to appreciating and comparing the differences and similarities of the poetry of Gwendolyn Brooks to the poetry of Carl Sandburg.

Research on Policy

Research has only recently become formally associated with the formulation and evaluation of policy. It was in the 1960s that the relationship between the social sciences and public policy moved from the periphery to the mainstream (Mitchell, 1985). During the 1960s, research on equity issues, especially desegregation, influenced educational policy decisions. The Coleman Report (1966) stands out as research that significantly influenced public policy. The Westinghouse Study that reported that Head Start programs did not positively improve academic achievement can be cited as another piece of research that greatly impacted schooling for poor people and students of color. Other research studies during the 1960s and the 1970s dealt with equity issues such as class. Wise's (1967) examination of poor and wealthy schools caused some policy analysts to suggest different funding policies — policies that took into consideration the wealth of a school district. Wise argued that,

> Differences in per-pupil expenditure could not be based on the accident of location, as is now the practice in most states. Undoubtedly, this conclusion will not meet with the favor of wealthier communities. But if we are to heed the equal protection clause of the Constitution, it seems that the state cannot deny to some what it grants to others. (p. 214)

Research on Hispanic students in particular led to language policy as written in the Bilingual Act. Research on gender disparities in school programming and the lack of equal opportunities for female students led to such policies as Title IX of the Education Amendments of 1972, while research on disabled students led to policies that demand that these students be placed in less restricted environments, as stated in the 1975 Public Law 94-142 (the Education for All Handicapped).

Research since the 1960s has had a significant impact on policy related to race, class, gender, language and disability. Some of this policy has had a positive impact on race, class, gender, language and disability practices in schools, especially as it relates to equal opportunity as expressed through 'equal access'. For example, Title IX and PL 94-142 opened doors in schools to students who had been previously denied access. However, some other research has had the opposite impact, for example, the Coleman Report and the Westinghouse Study. Both of these research reports led to unwritten policy that guided the day-to-day schooling practices affecting students based on their race and class. After the Coleman Report was released and discussed, it was not uncommon for school people to argue that poor children of color could not learn because they were from homes that did not foster learning, and that school could make very little difference in their future lives. Similarly, discussions of the putatively negligible impact of Head Start programs on the achievement of poor minority students influenced unwritten day-to-day policy. White and Buka (1987) point out that 'the findings of the Westinghouse study were widely discussed and almost all the discussion centered on the measure of intellectual function' (p. 70).

Rather than critique these policies, the purpose here is to point out that policy based upon 'equity' research impacts the schooling of *all* students, and therefore needs to include multiculturalism. It is important to point out that most of the research that was and is considered 'equity' research erroneously assumes that the concept of 'equity' is synonymous with the concept of 'equal opportunity'. 'Equal opportunity', meaning having equal access is not synonymous with 'equity', which means having a fair and just opportunity. Grant (1989) and Secada (1989) have raised questions regarding this interpretation. Secada asserts 'Equity attempts to look at the justice of a given state of affairs, a justice that goes beyond acting in agreed-upon ways and seeks to look at the justice of the arrangements leading up to and resulting from those actions' (p. 81). Secada further clarifies this difference when he argues:

The fundamental difference between equity and equality is that equity is a qualitative property while equality is quantitative. Yet one of the most powerful constructs at the disposal of equity is equality, and the recognition that group inequalities may be unjust. The two terms, however, are — or at least should be — different. Work in educational equity needs to discriminate when its concerns coincide with those of equality and when they do not.

Additionally, it should be noted that 'access' into a classroom doesn't necessarily include with it an analysis of race, class, gender and disability interactions that take into account curriculum, staffing, instruction and other schooling factors that are critical to equitable education. Multicultural research would take this neglected dimension into account. Furthermore, research that reports no significant increase in student achievement (such as that reported in the Westinghouse Study), has not considered other important noncognitive outcomes such as improved home-school relationships and increased student self-esteem. In other words, the social and emotional impacts of the program on the students and their significant others were not adequately assessed and reported. Bronfenbrenner (1974; 1979) made this point when he took issue with the testing procedures in early childhood studies. He argued in 1974:

Information available across the board is limited to the cognitive area only and consists of IQ scores on the Stanford-Binet (with a few exceptions as noted) and, once the children have entered school, measures of academic achievement on standardized tests.... The restriction of available data to measures of this type sets limitations to the conclusions that can be drawn. (US Children's Bureau, Vol. 2, 1976, p. 2)

Finally, Mitchell (1985) describes four basic themes of recent educational policy research: equity, pattern of school governance, teaching and learning, and the economics of education. We already have discussed two of these themes — equity, and teaching and learning. An example related to a very popular aspect of school governance — school base management — is also instructive with regard to the matter of the boundaries of multicultural research. School base management currently is being promoted and adopted by many school districts because it is considered to be a way to give teachers, parents, and local school officials a greater role in running their school. Research in this area must seek to determine if parents are involved on the community councils, and if so, which parents. Are they mainly middle class parents? Are meetings scheduled in a manner that ensures that parents of color and 'second language' parents can attend as easily as other groups? Are they organized so that all parents can understand what is taking place? In other words, are language translators available and is the English free of jargon? Does the community council have significant decision-making responsibilities, and if so, is the decision-making understood in terms of multiculturalism? Research that is multicultural must be a part of all of these areas of educational research on policy.

Conclusion

In this chapter, it has been argued that there are numerous barriers to multicultural research, including an unclear definition, lack of money, academic ethnocentrism, and academic ghettoization. It was further pointed out that multicultural research must be included in all areas of research on education and schools and it should not be bound to any particular area of the curriculum or instructional process. This chapter has also argued that educational research would better serve its clients, especially students of color, poor students, and all female students, if multiculturalism was an integrated part of the research paradigm, design and method. In summary, this chapter has argued that barriers and boundaries should not obstruct the important need for scholars to conduct research in multicultural education.

Additionally, this chapter has challenged various educational research practices which act as barriers to people pursuing access to multicultural research. It has pointed out that serious and extensive educational research is only a few decades old and this research received a great impetus from conditions in schools as identified by the civil rights movement and the War on Poverty. Therefore, advocates of multicultural research should realize that they have a close kinship to the equal opportunity and equity movement and should not be intimidated and stopped by the barriers. In fact, they have an obligation to demand to be included as part of this research cadre in positions of leadership.

Note

1 It is unfortunate that when such courses are presented, they frequently promote what Sleeter and Grant (1988) describe as 'education for the culturally and exceptionally different'. By this they mean that the courses present an assimilationist ideology and hold traditional educational aims.

References

ATKINSON, J.W. (1964) *An Introduction to Motivation*, Princeton, NJ, Van Wostrand.
BANKS, J.A. (1977) 'The implications of multicultural education for teacher education' in KLASSEN, F.H. and GOLLNICK, D.M. (Eds) *Pluralism and the American Teacher*, Washington DC, American Association of Colleges for Teacher Education, pp. 1–34.
BEANE, J.A. and LIPKA, R.P. (1987) *When the Kids Come First: Enhancing Self Esteem*, Columbus, OH, National Middle School Association.
BLUM, D.E. (1988) 'To get ahead in research, some minority scholars choose to "Play the game"', *The Chronicle of Higher Education*, 22 June, p. A17.
BRONFENBRENNER, U. (1974) Is early intervention effective? A report on longitudinal evaluations of preschool programs. Vol. 2. Washington, D.C. Department of Health, Education and Welfare, Office of Child Development.
BRONFENBRENNER, U. (1979) *The Ecology of Human Development: Experiments by Nature and by Design*, Cambridge, MA, Harvard University Press.
BROPHY, J.E. and GOOD, T.H. (1984) *Teacher-Student Relationships: Causes and Consequences*. New York, Holt, Rinehart and Winston.
CALDWELL, J. (1989) 'The need for 'anti-racism' education', *Education Week*, 20 September, p. 32.

CENTER FOR EDUCATION STATISTICS (1987a) *The Condition of Education*, Washington DC, US Government Printing Office.

CENTER FOR EDUCATION STATISTICS (1987b) *Digest of Education Statistics*, Washington, DC, US Government Printing Office.

COLEMAN, J.S. (1966) *Equality of Educational Opportunity*, Washington, D.C. United States Government Printing Office.

COMBS, A.W. and SNYGG, D. (1959) *Individual Behavior* New York, Hayser and Brotter, pp. 190–200.

FENNEMA, E. and PETERSON, P. (1986) 'Teacher-student interaction and self-related difference in learning mathematics', *Teaching and Teacher Education*, 2(1), pp. 19–42.

GOULDNER, H. (1978) *Teachers' Pets, Troublemakers, and Nobodies: Black Children in Elementary School*, Westport, CT, Greenwood Press.

GRANT, C. (1989) 'Equity, equality, and classroom life' in SECADA, W.G. (Ed.) *Equity in Education*, London, Falmer Press, pp. 89–102.

GRANT, C. and KOSKELA, R. (1986) 'Education that is multicultural and the relationship between pre-service campus learning and field experiences', *Journal of Educational Research*, 79, 4, pp. 197–203.

GRANT, C. and SECADA, W.G. (1990) 'Preparing teachers for diversity' in HOUSTON, W.R. (Ed.) *Handbook of Research on Teacher Education*, New York, Macmillan Publishing Co.

GRANT, C. and SLEETER, C. (1985) 'The literature on multicultural education: Review and analysis', *Educational Review*, 37, 2, pp. 97–118.

GRANT, C. and SLEETER, C. (1986a) *After the School Bell Rings*, London, Falmer Press.

GRANT, C. and SLEETER, C. (1986b) 'Race, class, and gender effects in education: An argument for integrative analysis', *Review of Educational Research*, 56, pp. 195–211.

GRANT, C., SLEETER, C. and ANDERSON, J. (1986) 'The literature on multicultural education: Review and analysis', *Educational Studies*, 12, pp. 47–71.

GRANT, L. (1988) 'Introduction: Regenerating and refocusing research on minorities and education', *The Elementary School Journal*, 88, 5, pp. 441–8.

HARDING, S. (1987) 'Introduction: Is there a feminist method?' in HARDING, S. (Ed.) *Feminism and Methodology*, Bloomington and Indianapolis, IN, Indiana University Press, pp. 1–14.

HARTSOCK, N. (1987) 'The feminist standpoint: Developing the groundwork for a specifically feminist historical materialism' in HARDING, S. (Ed.) *Feminism and Methodology*, Bloomington and Indianapolis, IN, Indiana University Press, pp. 157–80.

HODGKINSON, H.W. (1985) *All one system: Demographics of education — Kindergarden through graduate school*, Washington DC, Institute for Educational Leadership.

KENNEDY, M.M., JUNG, R.K. and ORLAND, M.E. (1986) *Poverty, Achievement, and the Distribution of Compensatory Education Services* (An interim report from the National Assessment of Chapter I), Washington DC, US Government Printing Office.

KVARACEUS, W.C., GIBSON, J.S., PATTERSON, F., SEASHOLES, B. and GRAMBS, J.D. (1965) *Negro Self-concept: Implications for School and Citizenship*, the report of a conference sponsored by the Lincoln Filene Center for Citizenship and Public Affairs, New York, McGraw-Hill.

NATIONAL INSTITUTE OF EDUCATION (1985) *Application For Educational Research*, Washington DC, Government Printing Office.

McKENNA, B. (1989) 'College faculty: An endangered species?', *On Campus*, Washington DC, American Federation of Teachers, p. 10.

MIDWEST BILINGUAL EDUCATION MULTIFUNCTIONAL RESOURCE CENTER (1986) *Annual Report: 1985–1986* (Contract no. 300850188), Rosslyn, VA, InterAmerica Research Associates.

MITCHELL, D. (1985) *State Policy Strategies For Improving Teacher Quality*, San Francisco, Far West Laboratory.

PARKAY, F. (1983) *White Teacher, Black School*, New York, Praeger.

PAYNE, M. (1984) *Getting What We Ask For*, Westport, CT, Greenwood Press.

POPKEWITZ, T.S. (1984) *Paradigm and Ideology in Educational Research*, London, Falmer Press.

RAYMOND, J. (1985) 'Women's studies: A knowledge of one's own' in CULLEY, M. and PONTAGE, C. (Eds) *Gendered Subjects: The Dynamics of Feminist Teaching*, Boston, MA, Routledge and Kegan Paul, pp. 49–63.

REYES, L.N. (1981) 'Classroom process, Sex of Student and Confidence in Learning Mathematics, Unpublished doctoral dissertation, University Wisconsin-Madison.

RIST, R. (1970) 'Student Social Class and Teachers' Expectations: The Self-Fulfilling Prophecy,' *Harvard Educational Review*, **40**, p. 413.

ROGERS, C-R (1969) *Freedom To Learn*, Columbus, OH, CHARLES, E. Merrill Publishing Co.

ROSENFELD, G. (1971) *Shut Those Thick Lips!: A Study of Slum School Failure*, New York, Holt, Rinehart and Winston.

ROSENTHAL, R. and JACOBSON, W. (1968) *Pygmalion in the Classroom: Teacher Expectation and Pupils' Intellectual Performance*, New York, Holt, Rinehart and Winston.

RUBIN, I., *et al.* (1974) 'Initiating planned change in health care system', *Journal of Applied Behavorial Science*, **10**, 1, pp. 108.

RUSSELL, W.J. (1989) *Educational Researcher*, **18**, 6, August-September, p. 30.

SECADA W., (1989) *Technical Proposal Upper Great Lakes Multifunctional Resources Center*, unpublished manuscript. Madison, Wisconsin: University of Wisconsin-Madison Center for Education Research.

SECADA, W.G. (1989) 'Equity in education versus equality of education: Toward an alternative conception' in SECADA, W.G. (Ed.) *Equity in Education*, London, Falmer Press, pp. 68–88.

SLEETER, C. and GRANT, C. (1988) 'An analysis of multicultural education in the United States', *Harvard Educational Review*, **57**, pp. 421–44.

STAPLES, R. (1984) 'Racial ideology and intellectual racism: Blacks in academia', *The Black Scholar*, **15**, 2.

UNITED STATES DEPARTMENT OF EDUCATION, (1988) *FY 1989 Application for Educational Research and Development Centers Programs*, United States Government Printing Office, Washington, D.C.

WESTINGHOUSE LEARNING CORP. (1969) *The Impact of Head Start: An evaluation of the effects of Head Start on children's cognitive and affective development*. Executive summary (Report to the Office of Economic Opportunity). Washington, D.C.: Clearinghouse for Federal Scientific & Technical Information.

WHITE, H.S. and BUKA, S.L. (1987) 'Early education: Programs, traditions, and policies' in ROTHKOPP, E.Z. (Ed.) *Review of Research in Education*, Washington DC, American Educational Research Association, pp. 43–91.

WISE, A.E. (1967) *Rich Schools, Poor Schools: The Promise of Equal Education Opportunity*, Chicago, IL, University of Chicago Press.

WITTROCK, M.C. (Ed.). (1986). *Handbook of research on teaching* (3rd ed.). New York: Macmillan.

WITTROCK, M.C. (1986) Students' Thought Processes. In M.C. WITTROCK (Ed.), *Handbook of Research on Teaching* (pp. 297–314). New York: Macmillan.

ZALTMAN, G. and DUNCAN, R. (1977) *Strategies for Planned Change*, New York, John Wiley.

Chapter 2

The Marginalized Discourse of Minority Intellectual Thought in Traditional Writings on Teaching

Beverly M. Gordon

Introduction — The Lived Experience

During the Christmas holidays I watched a television program of college choirs singing a variety of Christmas carols. There was a reputed international flavor, with French, Swedish and Chinese carols included.[1] I was reminded of my own upbringing in the Episcopalian church. I recalled long choir rehearsal every Thursday night at St James in addition to the Tuesday afternoon one for elementary and junior high school members, in preparation for each Sunday Mass. Rehearsals during the Christmas season had a special anticipatory spiritual and emotional beauty, all directed towards midnight Mass on Christmas Eve. And even though I fell asleep during my earliest years in the Christmas Eve choir, preparations for the Mass, the event itself, and family traditions afterward — the meal of fried chicken, potato salad, homemade rolls, iced tea, and dessert; the opening of presents; our retiring at 5:00 am — engendered feelings that were probably similar to those of many of the television program's participants and audience.

But simultaneously, a disturbing feeling intruded on my recollections. I pondered, 'Where are they?' ('they' referring to the African-American students). My eyes scanned the youthful faces, the blue, white, and red robes; studied one close-up shot after another; grew anxious for the sight of even one face. At last, 'There she is!' and a sigh of relief. While I continued in the experience, listening to the music, and watching the expressions on the faces of the majority youth, an even more disturbing feeling began to take hold. I thought, 'No wonder, they (they now referring to the Anglo students) believe in their way of viewing the world!' Their eyes seemed to emanate a sublime acceptance of the dominant societal structure as ultimately being, regardless of its flaws, the correct, good, and beautiful one. The sounds, symbols, imagery, artifacts, indeed, all the culture (and not only at Christmas) validates, reifies, and confirms the Anglo-American rightness of being.

What did all these symbols say to me throughout my life experiences? At one point, I took for granted my sameness with the dominant society, but somewhere along the way of life I learned a different lesson. Was it in the third grade, when I had dutifully written out valentine cards for all thirty students in my class, only to receive four in return, two of which were from the only other two African-American students in the class? Or was it in the fourth grade, when walking home with an Anglo friend, and hearing another Anglo student call him a 'nigger lover'? From these and countless other incidents came a dawning awareness that I was regarded as very different from the dominant society.

Hegemony as a cultural construct is powerful, but elusive. There are difficulties in unpacking and critiquing one's own individual cultural baggage to understand how one has come to see the world. For example, in-service teachers can seemingly understand, identify with issues, critique articles,[2] and engage in graduate course dialogue, yet be stymied when trying to unpack what they are or are not doing in their own classrooms, and why they hold tenaciously to various assumptions about different segments of the student populations. They assimilated their beliefs long ago, over a period of time, not from one singular incident, perhaps when they too were singing in church choirs, and twenty or thirty years of socialization will not be altered simply by pre-service or in-service teacher education and professional development courses. Critiquing one's own assumptions about the world — especially if the world works for you and if you win or have won by the current configuration and normative structures — is a formidable task. Actualizing a new knowledge in classrooms is even more difficult because it requires a self-connectedness with a different reality.

Teachers and the teacher education field are in need of a fundamental critique of how they look at, interpret, and assist people of color in the educational process. Such a critique will require fundamental shifts in the frameworks through which teachers view themselves and others in their world, not only in the paradigms they employ and validate in their teachings, but also in a willingness to acknowledge the credibility of other perspectives, particularly those that challenge comfortable, long held assumptions.

We know that by the year 2000, one-third of the public school population will be children of color. These children seem to have less success than their Anglo counterparts, and as this population continues to grow, the blame continues to fall on the shoulders of the victims. There are popular discussions on the problems of worsening educational preparation for, and academic results among, poor students. Some critics have given higher education failing grades and proposed various curricula, – most recently a classical academic, great books response to this crisis (Bloom, 1988; see also Hirsch, 1988). Fortunately, in some cities, experiments in upgrading academic attainment and results in urban public education have taken a collaborative approach incorporating university researchers, school teachers and staff, and parental involvement (Comer, 1980). Also, in higher education, there are efforts such as experimental tuition-granting programs (for example, Gordon, 1989). However, while there are discussions on the shrinking pool of African-American school teachers and staff, the struggle to ensure future generations of black public school educators will be an uphill battle. Even with the Holmes and Carnegie Reports calling for reform in the teaching profession and indicating the need to attract more minorities into the profession,[3] realistically speaking most children who attend American public schools now and in the foreseeable future will be taught by Anglo teachers. These reports also state that schools need an infusion of more attractive curricula — especially in the sciences and in mathematics — for children of color, particularly for minority females, and that students need positive role models to bolster their self-esteem and endorse positive attitudes. Yet, there have been few reforms in the fundamental paradigms used in teacher education programs. The knowledge base is still generated from the same theoretical framework of the dominant literature, and it seems to ignore or downplay a key question: What are the results of these 'new' infused teacher education programs? Have these ideas, agendas, reforms produced any significant results in the academic achievements of black and other disenfranchised students? Allegedly, there seems to be an absence of cross-cultural studies that can give guidance to teachers. The issue, however, is not *absence* but marginalization of the ideas, agendas, perspectives, and programs produced by African-American educators and scientists.

The Necessity of Including Non-marginalized Discourse: A Black[4] Perspective in Dominant Research and Development Institutions

Is there a black perspective in educational research? Is it conducted and written by black people? And is this perspective represented in the dominant and traditional writings on teaching? First, I am assuming that the majority of African-American educational scholars who produce research studies and write in the field of education are concerned with a wide variety of issues that impact on students of color in academic institutions. Second, I am assuming that the marginalization and racism confronting African-American scholars arises from a 'quiet consensus', from unspoken but agreed upon conscious and/or unconscious baggage of Anglo scholars, which is very difficult to unpack.

There is no absence of discourse and literature produced by African-American scholars. What is produced by contemporary African-American scholars and practitioners has limited influence in the white bourgeois intellectual establishment. While there are well respected black educational scholars whose works are being published in mainstream (Anglo) journals, their ideas, theories and experience have not impacted significantly the prevailing paradigms and ideology within the scholarly community. Although African-American scholarship is given lip service under the broad rubric of multicultural and/or cross-cultural studies, dominant Anglo scholarship seems to be directing the field, and resulting in little overall improvement in the academic preparation of working and under class African-American and other at-risk groups of children.

The way in which cross-cultural/multicultural studies are clustered seems to emphasize problems or pathology — deprivation, adjustments, pluralism, interpersonal relationships, and tensions — associated with black people. Such studies seem to be grouped in three categories: teaching the culturally different; human relations; and single-case studies (Sleeter and Grant, 1987). Focusing primarily on problems distracts and detracts from the theories and paradigms and epistemology of the subjugated. Such focusing also keeps attention away from the fact that the subjugated are capable of the development of cultural knowledge, epistemology and philosophy without approval of, and in opposition to, the dominant Anglo interpretative frames of reference (Harris, 1983).

At times, work generated by African-American scholars has been set aside because it has been deemed by Anglo scholars as misguided, misdirected, or even racist. For example, discussions on the issue of learning styles of African Americans were deemed racist (Hale, 1982). The vervistic learning style argument was misconstrued to mean that the learning style repertoire of African-American students was limited to one particular and specific style to the exclusion of others. From the unfortunate example of a high-level official in New York who attempted to implement the idea of specific learning styles, we have learned that such inferences are very premature. The concern was that teachers would rationalize: If certain groups could learn only under certain conditions, teachers could not be held accountable for instructing these students. In turn, the students would be considered uneducable by teachers who could not or would not teach in a specific style. Inevitably, the learning style itself would be considered a disability. In light of this controversy, educators must be careful lest multicultural education be construed to promote an alternative (an implied less rigorous) learning style as contrasted with the dominant (an implied more rigorous) style.

Another marginalization of African-American scholarship, is that very little of it is employed in the preparation of teachers. The number of black studies libraries at universities, and the private and public collections around the country, bear witness to an enormous body of literature written by black scholars, while the academy gives little credence or visibility to their work in pre-service and in-service discussions. That pre-service and in-service teachers and administrators can complete their programs and never read classics by Horace Mann Bond, W.E.B. DuBois, Oliver C. Cox and Carter G. Woodson, or critically discuss contemporary scholars such as Asa Hilliard, Carl Grant, A. Wade Boykin, Joseph L. White, Sarah Lawrence Lightfoot, James Comer; Cornel West, Hazel Carby, Vincent Franklin, James Anderson, Jawanza Kunjufu, and countless others, says as much about the theories and paradigms embraced and disseminated by university faculty as do the resulting pedagogical and world view practices of teachers, principals and school districts.

In an effort to see what research and literature were available for education students, the author performed an ERIC search that revealed 103 citations on multicultural and teacher education topics.[5] The readings on cross-cultural studies located in RIE and CIJE deal with description, prognostication, intervention, pedagogy, and remediation. Grant and Sleeter, in their review and analysis of the literature on multicultural education, identify four general groupings of articles that constitute multicultural literature: position papers, teaching guides, project descriptions, and empirical research (Sleeter and Grant, 1987). Contemporary volumes do not exclude completely African-American scholars or materials in general concerning people of color in scholarly writing and debate.[6] Nevertheless, using Grant and Sleeter's work as a salient example of what is available, there are two questions that command attention: To what extent are African-American scholars quoted in dominant, influential scholarship? And, on the whole, what have been the implications and impact of their voices on daily practice in school classrooms, teacher preparation programs and curricula?

Part of the reason for this marginalization could be that Anglo scholars view much of the research and writing of African-American scholars as provocative but without substance. Another reason, which is more interesting, involves the emancipatory and empowering nature of serious dialogue and debate within the scholarship produced by people of color. The very nature of their work lends itself to a critique of the dominant societal structures; it tends to challenge and change societal institutions, such as schools. Scholarship that points people toward making changes and taking charge of their own destinies, is antithetical and threatening to the dominant power configurations challenging as it is to the social construction of their reality.

Clearly the Western societies (in this instance the United States) want an educated, literate work force in order to compete in a technologically advancing and changing world economy. However, it is the nature of the future roles of African-Americans that is in question. The twenty-first century will be marked by the struggles of people of color for position, credibility, and respect within Western societies, and the struggles will have global implications. The greatest battle will be for control over who educates minorities within Western societies and the nature of that education. Whose vision of the role of African-Americans, other people of color and the disenfranchised will prevail? Questions about the kinds of societal structures and assemblages, and the gradations of workers and work envisioned are directly linked to my fundamental concern: For what purposes might people of color be educated? How might education assist people of color in challenging the societal structures that maintain and reproduce inequality?

Black Intellectual Discourse and Cultural Knowledge: Variations on a Theme

Perhaps mainstream academicians have experienced difficulty with African-American intellectual thought — and its potential influence in education — because it is both eclectic and non-synchronous. It is eclectic because it is produced by scholars from a variety of fields and media in many instances not specifically in education or even in academia. It is non-synchronous because it does not share the same economic and political consciousness as the dominant culture, nor 'similar needs within it at the same point in time'.[7]

In response to racism in educational theory and practice, and in consideration of service to and within the black community, there is an emerging scholarship generated and influenced in large measure by people of color. Several traditional and non-traditional works come to mind. We shall focus our attention on four pieces, which this author believes are representative of work that has, thus far, received little application within the academic circles. The first is a PBS documentary by Ali Mazuri; the second and third are educational volumes, Madan Sarup's *The Politics of Multiracial Education* (1986) and Ranjit Arora and Carlton Duncan's *Multicultural Education: Towards Good Practice* (1986);[8] and the fourth is a biography, Sarah Lawrence Lightfoot's *Balm in Gilead* (1988).

The swirl of controversy surrounding the 1986 PBS documentary series, *The Africans*, written and directed by Ali Mazuri, is a salient example of the politics inherent in African-Americans' continuing struggle — a struggle against the imposition of the 'agreed-upon' definitions that constitute cultural meanings of daily life, cultural hegemony. The series presented a non-Western perspective of Africa and its historical relationship to the West that was far from flattering to the West, a perspective not often seen in the United States and one that met with strong criticism. Mazuri was accused of turning the PBS series into a diatribe against the West.[9] Mazuri's real crime was challenging the comfortable definitions and meanings through which US citizens have commonly viewed Africa and its historical relationship with the West. Critics implied that citizens within Western societies know their historical relationship with Africa and that taxpayers do not want to pay for a depiction of Westerners as brutal capitalist barbarians. The fact is, most Westerners do not know their nation's historic relationship in the context of the Western experience, either in Africa or in the rest of the non-Western non-white world, although it constitutes the majority world population. By making problematic the Western societies' missionary, philanthropic, altruistic, epistemic role in the world, Mazuri's documentary has made many people terribly uncomfortable.

For people of color, there are many gnawing problems relative to the control and nature of education in Western societies. Three of the more obvious problems are the reliance of people of color on the dominant society to educate their children; the diminishing numbers of black professional educators; and the marginalizing of educational practice based on theoretical models outside traditional frames of references (Gordon, 1982). The literature on multicultural education in this country reveals few theoretical models to guide classroom implementation of and education that is multicultural (Grant *et al.*, 1988). Yet, we know that within schools the dominant ideology is often rejected and that there are opportunities for contestation, challenge and change. The pernicious effects of racism, beyond the institutional dilemmas faced by students of color, are seldom alluded to. Regarding ideology and practice in schooling, the following holds true:

> [T]he hard and continuous day-to-day struggle at the level of curriculum and teaching practice is part of these larger conflicts as well. The key is linking these day-to-day struggles within the school to other action for a more progressive society in that wider arena. (Apple and Weis, 1983, p. 22)

What is needed at the level of curriculum development and implementation is a triumvirate of anti-racist policies, emancipatory pedagogy (specifically consciousness raising at the classroom level), and cultural consciousness that involves political action at both school and community levels. Emancipatory education empowers; it facilitates and encourages people to participate in activities, to take charge of their own destiny, and to shape the cultural, economic, and political foundations of their communities (Gordon, 1986). In light of the Mazuri controversy, one can appreciate Paulo Freire's cautionary note about the danger in underestimating the 'capacity and audacity of the elite' (Freire, 1985). It would be naive to believe that those who wish to maintain agreed-upon definitions, values, beliefs systems, and so forth, would not react against an education that challenges, or at least makes problematic, the current power configuration in society. Perhaps multicultural education is being viewed as cultural tolerance within a less than tolerant society. If regarded in a pejorative way, learning diversity will be seen as a disability, and diversity will become the next deficiency model.

The sixteen articles in the volume, *Multicultural Education: Towards Good Practice*, edited by Ranjit Arora and Carlton Duncan, are directed to the teaching profession. The book deals with the insidious nature of racism, which is a part of the fiber of Western society (in this case British society), and how it is reflected in the miseducation and deskilling of black children. The consensus is that education should help people play a more socially active and participatory role in society, especially in the political-economic realities of their own destiny. The organizing idea of the editors was to highlight the contested terrain of societal and curriculum discourse — language meanings and definitions; strategies for implementing multicultural education in classroom pedagogy; and professional development in pre-service and in-service teacher preparation programs. This collection of articles offers practitioners ways to provide black students with heuristic tools, concepts, and skills to analyze materials and to engage in academic preparation that ideally will empower them in the near future societies.

Overall these articles present a more realistic view of the relationships between the majority (non-white) and the minority (white) global population. Moreover, they counteract racism with definitions and meanings that challenge old assumptions and beliefs. Throughout this volume there is expressed a pervasive belief that the success of multicultural education depends on at least two conditions: first, that such education makes an analysis of the social context of the society; second, that teachers along with other interested persons who wish to have influence on the contested terrain, work within it to build conditions for change.

Another exemplary book is Madan Sarup's *The Politics of Multiracial Education*, important because his theoretical arguments are coupled with guidelines that can assist teachers in transforming consciousness-raising theory into pedagogy. Sarup's position is that unless people endeavor to change the structures that dominate, to the benefit of some and to the known or unknown detriment of others, internal contradictions will persist. Sarup asserts that consciousness raising is the ultimate threat and enemy of the power elite. Sarup's arguments are reminiscent of the 1960s Civil Rights campaign to fight racism and injustice in the United States. Now, as then, the liberation struggles of blacks to eliminate racism and its perennial ally, economic exploitation, not only assist the liberation struggles of other oppressed groups but also have the potential to raise working-class consciousness and the overall consciousness level of the society. Ironically, many of the culturally and politically conscious children of the 1960s now embrace their predecessors' conservative and patronizing views, thus perpetuating very real issues of class, power, and racism.

Sarup argues that multiracial education based on the concept of equality of opportunity places the attention on the individuals affected and away from the societal structures that create and maintain inequality. Critically reflective activities generated from this book can help teachers to think about and confront issues in very different ways from before. Sarup stresses that all discourse must include, not ignore, the social structure and its relationship with the school system. Anything less is an 'ideological diversion [serving] to deflect attention from the racist structure and practices of the ... state and obscure the real issues of power, class and racial oppression' (Sarup, 1986, p. 103). Sarup suggests that ties be developed between the community and the school and that teachers develop a political movement based outside the school. Beyond what he terms the 'contested reproduction', he argues for an examination of the contradictions and struggles in schools and careful study of its reproductive and transformative elements. The main strength of the book lies in Sarup's suggestions for reconceptualizing curriculum and the restructuring of schooling institutions.

Sarup proposes a new curriculum emphasizing that knowledge is gained through disciplined, hard work (in Gramsci's sense) and is not given by divinity to the upper classes. Such a curriculum would teach, among other subjects, courses in economics and dialectics and would integrate mental and manual labor. Sarup reminds teachers of the significant ways they counteract and/or change the curriculum by teaching, 'children the concepts and skills which would enable them to recognize the underlying assumptions in a text' (*ibid.*, p. 52) thus enabling them to learn how to critique.

One point that Sarup does not address directly involves teacher educators, and the issues facing the teaching force. If the knowledge employed in such programs continues to marginalize the voices of black scholars, teacher educators maximize their chances of disseminating the same old cultural and political baggage and the same old world views. The result will be little change in the status of knowledge provided to children of color. What may happen is that teachers will become more adept at disseminating low status knowledge and ensuring that high status empowering knowledge stays out of the reach of the majority of people of color. In regarding the current planning for expediting the Holmes plan at many institutions around the country, it remains to be seen if the pedagogy that will be disseminated in these 'new' programs will produce a different kind of professional educator and correspondingly a better student.

Unfortunately Sarup assumes that educators who would advocate such change will have sufficient power, influence, and control over pre-service and in-service teacher training to institute what he calls 'anti-racist teacher training'. For the foreseeable future, neither African-American or any other minority group educators alone will have the sufficient strength to influence teacher training; however, if their efforts are coupled with those of community action groups, local practioners, coalitions of black educators in colleges and universities, historically black institutions, and urban and suburban school practitioners, then such pressure and constant monitoring may prove to be successful in the long run.

The fourth example of black cultural knowledge, and one that is dear to me, is Sarah Lawrence Lightfoot's *Balm in Gilead — Journey of a Healer* (1988), a biography of her mother, Margaret Cornelia Morgan Lawrence. This biography is illustrative of the struggle of becoming a black scientist and of the obstacles to practicing and providing service to the black community. Reading this book I am reminded of Cornel West's argument concerning what it is to be part of the black intelligentsia — the mission is, in part, to serve the black community (West, 1985, pp. 109–124).

The chronicle of Margaret Morgan Lawrence's growing up in the south, being influenced by her Episcopalian father; traveling to Harlem for secondary school and living with her aunts; attending Cornell University and during her undergraduate years having to sleep in an attic with no heat while she worked as a maid to support her college aspirations; meeting and marrying Charles R.

Lawrence, a sociologist; fighting racism throughout her medical training; witnessing the suffering within the black community and making a commitment with her husband to build a clinic in order to serve the black community is a powerful story that would be the stuff that dreams are made of for both young black girls and boys. This biography details the social and economic, the struggles, the personal sacrifices, the scientific work and the overcoming of adversity during times that were in many respects, even more difficult for African-Americans than today.

Balm in Gilead was a catalyst for re-experiencing the passion — the emotions, triumphs, and agonies of my own life history. I empathized with Lawrence's struggle in her profession because of my own struggle against the currents within my field. Like Lawrence, I engage in a continual struggle for equitable recognition, credibility and acceptance with its full rewards and amenities. In reflecting on my own life history in the context of Lightfoot's biography and the discussions of autobiography by Pinar and Grumet (1981) and Grumet (1981) among others in the curriculum field, I have a growing awareness of the forces that worked both to support and to thwart my efforts. To have verified that one is not alone in the struggle, that we are all struggling in our own moments in history with issues that are critical to ourselves and our people, is necessary for African-American scholars to help keep perspective. And it is refreshing to have verified that the intellectual anguish we feel is not psychosis but righteous indignation about the dangers and challenges that confront people of color and/or the disenfranchised.

Supplementing the four books I have outlined above are other books that should be mandatory reading for teachers and pupils in upper elementary and middle school classrooms, and not just during Black History Month. Taulbert's *Once Upon a Time When We Were Colored* (1989) Comer's *Maggie's American Dream* (1988) and Lanker's *I Dream a World* (1989) are valuable for the entire class, and particularly for African-American children who may have aspirations, but have found few models to guide them. Such works would also be most helpful to college and university teacher educators and valuable to in-service and pre-service teachers, particularly those who do not have a sense of the heterogeneity or culture of the African-American community.

Conclusion: Black Cultural Knowledge and Its Implications for Studies in Teacher Education

Black cultural knowledge and products with implications for the education of African-American people have always been available and are continually emerging. Some products that might be useful to the educational community may not specifically focus on educational issues, but more broadly focus on understanding the culture of the African-American community beyond college course textbooks. Examples are biographical works such as those of Lightfoot and Comer, international perspectives and issues, as well as documentaries already alluded to. In the literature and art of the 1970s, 1980s and 1990s, are a generation of literacy artists such as Toni Morrison, Gloria Naylor, Ishmael Reed, and film producers such as Euzhan Palcy and Spike Lee, who takes us on forays which also illuminate various dimensions of and complexities in the culture of the African-American community. Still another example of knowledge production is West's works on the impact of African-American culture on the American way of life, and the dilemma of the black intellectual in the post-modern era.

Cornel West has identified what he considers to be organic intellectual traditions in African-American life, the black Christian tradition of preaching, and the black tradition of performance (West, 1989). He promotes collective intellectual work and critique and the creation of institutions that are infrastructures for strengthening African-American scholarship by promoting discourse and 'high quality critical habits'. To develop these critical habits, West urges African-American scholars to embrace the Foucaultian model which

> encourages an intense and incessant interrogation of power-laden discourse in the service of . . . revolt. And the kind of revolt enacted by intellectuals consists of disrupting and dismantling of prevailing 're-gimes of truth' — including their repressive effect — of present day societies. This model suits the critical, skeptical, and historical concerns of progressive black intellectuals . . . the problem is the struggle over the very status of truth and the vast institutional mechanisms which account for this status . . . the new key terms become those of 'regime of truth' 'power/knowledge', and 'discursive practices'. (West, 1985, p. 121)

There is a need for a reconceptualization of the 'specificity and complexity of Afro-American oppression' throughout educational and social theorizing in general and particularly among African-American scholars. What is needed, is

> the creation or reactivation of institutional networks that promote high quality critical habits primarily for the purpose of black insurgency. . . . The central task of post modern black intellectuals is to stimulate, hasten, and enable alternative perceptions and practices by dislodging prevailing discourses and powers. (West, 1985, p. 122)

Black people have created a body of knowledge, cultural knowledge, (cultural meaning across the disciplines, in science, social theory, art and philosophy, etc.). The marginalizing of its substance — theoretical constructs, paradigms, models of viewing and seeing the world — in the dominant body of knowledge is troublesome. It may be that pluralism is used and defended in the United States because pluralism can assist the dominant power in maintaining their structures. When we speak of a pluralistic system, part of the rationale is that everyone must fit in, however, in this instance the United States is not pluralistic, but a white-male dominated system, coupled with the specificism of racism; Anglos have defined themselves as white in relation to blacks.

The knowledge generated and products offered by African-American scholars have far reaching implications for teacher education; however, the current maginal usage of only a few categories may prove stifling and debilitating. While multicultural and cross-cultural categorizations have been useful as a way of identifying certain types or genres of work, it is problematic as to whether or not they can encompass the 'purpose of black insurgency' for African-

American and other black scholars around the world. Categories such as 'critical, emancipatory or liberatory pedagogy', may work as descriptors that not only expand the narrow frames of reference, but also move them from pejorative to self-reflection, critique and social action.

At the present time, talk about a unique learning style for black children is premature. Instead, particularly in academic research and development centers, we must focus our attention on separating content from pedagogy (Hilliard, 1989). Our research agenda must open up fields of inquiry and identify territory that needs to be explored and data that needs to be collected. Black psychologists have data on a wholistic view of black culture (White, 1984; see also Boykin *et al.*, 1979), but so far there are no ethnographic studies on black culture indicating how to infuse this view or what happens when it is infused. John Ogbu's discussion of the black citizens in the 1960s emphasized the homogeneous culture of African-American community (Ogbu, 1974). Where are the studies about what is happening within African-American communities in the 1980s and 1990s, with a diversity of students in various settings — middle-class suburbs and inner city tenements, working class and under classes, gang and drug cultures, to name a few. The charge of African-American scholars is to put such issues into the mainstream research arena.

We must also study the attitudes and techniques of teachers, black and Anglo, who are effective with African-American children. By introducing their practices in school situations we can study and document content, process and school interaction. Again, the call is for applied research. If there is such a thing as culturally compatible pedagogy, we must attempt to identify and apply it, to see whether it can be transfused into public schools. Additional research focusing on, for example, what 'regimes of truth' means for education, particularly school knowledge — its creation, production and dissemination, and/or challenges to disrupt and dismantle these 'regimes of truth', could result as a provocative litmus test for mainstream educational theory and practice from college campuses to school classrooms.

Dialogue that does not marginalize minority intellectual discourse, allows for scholarly engagement. This could result in the production of school knowledge that promotes social participation for change. Such dialogue in the writings on teaching is long overdue.

Summary Remarks

It may be that the currents of thought — notably self-help, service, economic autonomy, political power, and nationalism (see Gordon, 1985) — within African-American cultural knowledge and products are antithetical to the normative structure that the educational community has defined for people of color. The marginalization of African-American cultural knowledge — its theoretical constructs, paradigms, models of viewing and seeing the world — in the body of mainstream educational literature has limited its influence but not its continuance. The challenge for African-American scholars is to synthesize this knowledge, and incorporate it into social theorizing and educational paradigms, implement it in educational settings, and critique the interaction of children who have experienced such pedagogy.

Notes

1 *St Olaf Christmas*, 19 December 1989, Columbus, OH, WOSU.
2 This is from my own teaching experiences. I am referring to articles such as Gordon (1982) and also Anyon (1980).
3 Note that collectively less than ten pages in both reports were devoted to the declining numbers of minority educators. Elsewhere, this author has discussed this issue at length. See Gordon (1988).
4 I am using the term 'black' as inclusive of all people of color. However, throughout the discussion, I will refer specifically to African-Americans.
5 RIE and CIJE 1966-November 1988, which resulted in 103 citations. While not presented here in its entirety, the search, in part, was keyed in as follows:

  4 ('040' or '041' or '042' or '070' or '143' or '140' or '142') PT or EDUCATIONAL-RESEARCH or CLASSROOM-RESEARCH or CURRICULUM-RESEARCH Result 189681
  6 (CROSS-CULTURAL-STUDIES   MULTICULTURAL-EDUCATION BLACK-EDUCATION   AMERICAN-INDIAN-EDUCATION   AMERICAN-INDIANS HISPANIC-AMERICANS) MJ or CROSS ADJ CULTURAL ADJ ANALYSIS. TI, ID or ((BLACKS DE or BLACK-TEACHERS) and (COLLEGE-FACULTY)) Result 10526
  7 (TEACHER-EDUCATION IN-SERVICE-TEACHER-EDUCATION PRE-SERVICE-TEACHER-EDUCATION KINESTHETIC-METHODS TEACHING-METHODS TEACHING-OCCUPATION TEACHING MJ INSTRUCTION MJ) MJ
    Result 51080

Result 103

6 This would be the case using Grant and Sleeter's work as exemplary. Their 127 item list of articles and books in indicative (but not all inclusive) of scholarship circulating within educational literature.
7 I am using the term 'non-synchrony' as I understand McCarthy's (1988) use of the term.
8 An in-depth review (1987) of these two volumes by this author can be found in *Education Studies*, **18**, 3, Fall, pp. 434–43.
9 Chamberlin, W.B. Jr (1986) 'Public funding for "The Africans"', *Washington Post*, 21 October; Corry, J. (1986) 'The Africans' renews a funding fight", *The New York Times*, 14 September, TV View Section; Garment, S. (1986) 'The Africans': Public TV caught napping', *Wall Street Journal*, 19 October; Krauthammer, C. (1986) 'Africa through angry eyes', *Washington Post*, 12 December; Molotsky, I. (1986) 'US aide assails TV series on Africa', *The New York Times*, 5 September.

References

ANYON, J. (1980) 'Social class and the hidden curriculum of work', *Journal of Education*, **162**, 1, pp. 67–92.
APPLE, M.W. and WEIS, L. (Eds) (1983) *Ideology and Practice in Schooling*, Philadelphia, PA, Temple University Press.
ARORA, R. and DUNCAN, C. (Eds) (1986) *Multicultural Education: Towards Good Practice*, Boston, MA, Routledge and Kegan Paul.
BLOOM, A. (1988) *The Closing of the American Mind*, New York, Simon and Schuster.
BOYKIN, A. W. *et al.* (Eds) (1979) *Research Directions of Black Psychologists*, New York, Russell Sage Foundation.

COMER, J. (1980) *School Power: Implications of an Intervention Project*, New York, Free Press.

COMER, J. (1988) *Maggie's American Dream — The Life and Times of a Black Family*, New York, New American Library.

FREIRE, P. (1985) *The Politics of Education*, South Hadley, MA, Bergin and Garvey.

GORDON, B. (1982) 'Towards a theory of knowledge acquisition in black children', *Journal of Education*, **164**, 1, pp. 90–108.

GORDON, B. (1985) 'Toward emancipation in citizenship education: The case of African-American cultural knowledge', *Theory and Research in Social Education*, **12**, 4, pp. 1–23.

GORDON, B. (1986) 'The use of emancipatory pedagogy in teacher education', *Journal of Educational Thought/Revue de la Pensee Educative*, **20**, 2, pp. 59–66.

GORDON, B. (1988) 'Implicit assumptions of the Holmes and Carnegie reports: A view from an African-American perspective', *Journal of Negro Education*, **57**, 2, pp. 141–58.

GORDON, B. (1989) *A Longitudinal Study of the Ohio State University's Young Scholars Program, First Year Report*, Columbus, OH, Ohio State University.

GRANT, C.A., SLEETER, C.E. and ANDERSON, J.E. (1986) 'The literature on multicultural education: Review and analysis', *Educational Studies*, **12**, 1, pp. 47–71.

GRUMET, M. (1981) 'Restitution and reconstruction of educational experience: An auto-biographical method for curriculum theory' in LAWN, M. and BARTON, L. (Eds) *Rethinking Curriculum Studies*, London, Croom Helm, pp. 115–31.

HALE, J. (1982) *Black Children, Their Roots, Culture and Learning Styles*, Provo, UT, Brigham Young University Press.

HARRIS, L. (Ed.) (1983) *Philosophy Born of Struggle — Anthology of Afro-American Philosophy from 1917*, Debuque, Kendall/Hunt Publishing Co.

HICKS, E. (1981) 'Cultural Marxism: Non-synchrony and feminist practice' in SERGEANT, L. (Ed.) *Women and Revolution*, Boston, MA, South End Press, pp. 219–38.

HILLIARD, A.G. (1989) 'Teachers and cultural styles in a pluralistic society', *Rethinking Schools*, December, p. 3.

HIRSCH, E. (1988) *Cultural Literacy*, New York, Vantage Press.

LANKER, B. (1989) *I Dream a World*, New York, Stewart, Tabori and Chang.

LIGHTFOOT, S. (1988) *Balm in Gilead — Journey of a Healer*, Reading MA, Addison-Wesley.

McCARTHY, E. (1988) 'Marxist theories of education and the challenge of a cultural politics of non-synchrony' in ROMAN, L.G., CHRISTIAN-SMITH, L.K. with ELLSWORTH, E. (Eds) *Becoming Feminine: The Politics of Popular Culture*, London, Falmer Press, pp. 185–203.

OGBU, J. (1974) *The Next Generation*, New York, Academic Press.

PINAR, W. and GRUMET, M. (1981) 'Theory and practice and the reconceptualisation of curriculum studies' in LAWN, M. and BARTON, L. (Eds) *Rethinking Curriculum Studies*, London, Croom Helm, pp. 20–42.

SARUP, M. (1986) *The Politics of Multiracial Education*, Boston, MA, Roultedge and Kegan Paul.

SLEETER, C. and GRANT, C.A. (1987) 'An analysis of multicultural education in the United States', *Harvard Educational Review*, **57**, 4, pp. 421–44.

TAULBERT, C.L. (1989) *Once Upon a Time When We Were Colored*, Tulsa, OK, Council Oak Books.

WEST, C. (1985) 'The dilemma of the black intellectual', *Cultural Critique*, Fall, 1.

WEST, C. (1989) 'Black culture and postmodernism', in KRÜBER, B. and MANANI, P. (Ed.) *Remaking History*, Bay Press, pp. 87–96.

WHITE, J.L. (1984) *Psychology of Blacks: An Afro-American Perspective*, Englewood Cliffs, NJ, Prentice Hall.

Chapter 3

Multicultural Education: From a Compensatory to a Scholarly Foundation

Ellen Swartz

As the 1980s drew to a close, New York State Education Commissioner Thomas Sobol drew fire from around the country for a task force report entitled 'The Curriculum of Inclusion'. Even repeated attacks on this report did not deter the New York State Board of Regents from formally agreeing that New York needs a 'detailed plan for increasing, among all students in the elementary, middle, and secondary schools of New York State, the understanding of American history and culture, of the history and culture of diverse groups which comprise American society today, and of the history and culture of other peoples throughout the world.'[1] The action steps outlined by Commissioner Sobol repeatedly reference the need for incorporating multicultural concepts into the New York State curricula. In various forms, other states and local districts are moving in a similar direction.

In this time of curricular challenge and change, there is a critical need for a more 'informed space' within the current national debate on multicultural education. Recently, national magazines and newspapers have given voice to commentators (Leo, 1989; Schmidt, 1990; Krauthammer, 1990; Will, 1989) whose assessments of multicultural education and curriculum reform do not help to create such an informed space. Commentators, such as Charles Krauthammer (1990) and John Leo (1989), arrogantly assure the public that there is no problem worth naming, and that the issue of omission and distortion of diverse cultures and groups is so insignificant as to need no correction.[2] In order to attack multicultural education, which they see as leading to a needlessly stretched and distorted revision of history, recent commentators have framed the debate as an ongoing polemic over the relative importance of issues and events. Within this framework, traditionally omitted cultures and groups are being weighed and inspected on an information age auction block designed to maintain their subordinate position. Their subaltern state is 'confirmed' when critics of multicultural education 'set up' and 'knock down' the issue of inclusion as a misguided search for social justice and self-esteem (Ravitch, 1990; Leo, 1989; Krauthammer, 1990). Further, these same critics compare and judge the relative importance of civilizations through a culturally dominant and singular construction of knowledge which they present as 'natural' and 'factual' (Sleeter and Grant, 1990). This framework obfuscates and ignores the most fundamental and practical principles of multicultural education: the development of curriculum, instructional materials, and methodologies based upon high standards of academic integrity and scholarship, and upon the inherently multiple and eclectic origins of knowledge. Within this collective and ventilated framework, multicultural education is a vehicle for repairing systemically rooted insufficiencies in the knowledge base and its classroom applications. For example, when George Will (1989) states that 'Nothing can be done about the fact that Locke, Montesquieu ... were important and African, Latin American, and Asian philosophers were not, as sources of the American Revolution', he is obviously unaware that Locke's work was influenced by other than European sources. For example, Locke studied Jesuit accounts of the Huron's free and civil government, which he acknowledged and cited in his second treatise (Burton, 1988). In addition, colonial writers such as Benjamin Franklin and Cadwallader Colden used Iroquois government and social structure as a demonstration of the truth of Locke's philosophy that political power originated and rested in the people, not in a monarch, and in the eighteenth century, the Iroquois and other sovereign nations were written about as symbols of the developing colonial conception of 'liberty' (Venables, 1989). Generations of cultural contact, the exchange of ideas, the treaties negotiated, the Congresses jointly attended, all document that the philosophical roots of our democracy have a collective origin and include the Iroquois, as well as Greece, Rome, and the English and French philosophers (Grinde, 1988). Will fails to see that educational materials constructed with high academic standards in a culturally collective and interconnected context remove any need to force-fit or falsely impose cultures and groups on any event or era. Classroom applications, at all levels, of the continuously emerging research on the influence of indigenous and sovereign nations on the formulation of the earliest US documents and government structures, stimulate critical, open-ended thinking. These applications encourage students to 'be historians' as they explore the past (Johnson, Smith and Gearhart, 1989) and examine some of the gaps and insufficiencies so entrenched in 'standard' textbook knowledge.

Those who reject the eclectic and hybrid origin and development of knowledge seem unable to detect the faulty scholarship that lies beneath the misrepresentation and consignment of the majority of the world's cultures to the margins of curriculum and textbook knowledge. They seem unaware of the demeaning characterizations and racist stereotypes that continue to surface in children's literature. They seem unable to identify the curricular absence of the multiple voices upon which all disciplines of knowledge have been built, and to realize the restrictive effect of such an absence on the development of critical thinking skills among students. The criticisms of these detractors of a broad knowledge base reveal not only their rejection of diverse sources of knowledge, but also their resistance to, and inexperience with, threading those sources together in a comprehensive account of history and all other disciplines of cultural production.

In an educational context, this dismissal and disregard for decades of scholarly research (Weiner, 1922; Lawrence, 1962 and 1987; Kaplan, 1973; Diop, 1974; Van Sertima, 1976 and 1987; Harding, 1983; Hawkins, 1984; Badillo-Sued and Cantos-López, 1986; Grinde, 1988; Venables, 1989) nestles close to the core meaning of censorship: the restriction of knowledge through a process that discriminates what may even enter the books selected as repositories of 'standard' knowledge by school systems. As educators, we are being asked to don ethnocentric blinders, to pull down the shades on the light of ancient/medieval African, Asian, and American 'firsts', and to believe that the achievements of European civilization developed in a culturally incestuous vacuum, unlinked to the achievements of prior civilizations (Bernal, 1989). To censor or purge the knowledge base of its inherent diversity requires that we impoverish our students with curricula and instructional materials that represent a singular monological band of knowledge (McCarthy, 1990). This form of censorship maintains a hierarchy of knowledge and power in which Western culture is the master.[3]

As one commentator and educator after another march the canons of Western accomplishment before us, in order to confirm that Europeans and their white descendants are responsible for the 'truly great' accomplishments of civilization (Leo, 1989; Gagnon, 1987), I wonder what type of supremacist ideology requires that the West and only the West be revered as the source and foundation of all that is worthy? Unfortunately, these canonical marches are mirrored in the pages of most commercial textbooks and school curricula — a primary source of their validation to youngsters. Such educational practice subverts academic integrity and makes a mockery of intellectual inquiry. We would all benefit if journals, popular magazines, and newspapers encouraged more informed discussions, and if proponents of multicultural education contributed definitions of multicultural education that would link it to standard educational practice rather than allow it to wander endlessly in a compensatory space. Without clear definition, multicultural education is often perceived as a tool to compensate for social, political, and economic inequities, and is used by educators and appropriated by publishers as a means of seeking social justice and promoting higher self-esteem. Clearly, instructional materials and methodologies do play their role in the unjust educational onslaught on individual and communal self. However, in order to reduce this onslaught, we first need to construct a framework of knowledge that has the capacity to produce non-hegemonic emancipatory narratives built upon a scholarly foundation. With such a foundation, and in such a framework, social justice and the affirmation of individual/communal self are coterminous by-products.

The following definition attempts to place multicultural education solidly within the context of standard educational practice through its focus on collective representation achieved through intellectual inquiry, integrity, and high standards of academic scholarship.

Multicultural education is an education that uses methodologies and instructional materials which promote equity of information and high standards of academic scholarship in an environment that respects the potential of each student. An education that is multicultural conforms to the highest standards of educational practice: the use of well-researched content that is accurate and up-to-date; the presentation of diverse indigenous accounts and perspectives that encourage critical thinking; the avoidance of dated terminologies, stereotypes, and demeaning, distorted characterizations; the use of intellectually challenging materials presented in an environment of free and open discussion. In short, multicultural education is a restatement of sound educational pedagogy and practice that requires the collective representation of all cultures and groups as significant to the production of knoweldge.

Such a definition of multicultural education helps to clarify, for example, that the omission and misrepresentation of the ancient African, Asian, and American roots of religion, science, mathematics, art, literature, music, and philosophy, deny the longevity and inherency of these cultures in the production of knowledge. If allowed to exist, this intellectual disruption paves the way for the idea of inevitability regarding the cultural disruption and genocide that was used to conquer the societies from which these accomplishments came, and to remove and often destroy the information (books, manuscripts, sculptures, religious sacraments, etc.) that validated those accomplishments.

If multicultural education is to facilitate a movement away from this notion of the naturality and inevitability of colonialism and imperialism, we need to counteract not only attacks on the need for multicultural education, but also attacks on its language — attacks which attempt to obscure and invalidate such terms as 'cultural oppression', 'white supremacy', and 'Eurocentrism'. Disdain for use of these terms suggests a discomfort with the social conditions they signify as much as a discomfort with tired ideological jargon. Does use of these terms irritate and remind us of the intractable presence of the conditions they signify in American society, at a time when we would rather think the conditions only exist in South Africa? Cultural oppression, white supremacy, and Eurocentrism won't simply disappear by not using the words. In a great burst of intellectual inquiry, John Leo (1989) suggested that we throw out any report that merely includes the term Eurocentrism because its use means, 'The report is not really serious.' Mr. Leo apparently fails to understand the meanings of this term, and how to use those meanings to analyze and deconstruct the text and sub-text of most school curricula and instructional materials.

A more informed and less paranoid understanding of Eurocentrism is required. Eurocentrism refers to a hegemonic or dominant world view that exclusively values European culture, and denigrates and subordinates the cultures of people from all other lands and origins. Eurocentrism is a sorting and selection process used to screen out information and accounts that do not support the superiority of Western culture's social, political, economic, and spiritual manifestations. Eurocentrism segments knowledge, keeping information and action separate from their sources, causes, and effects. Thus, educational materials include benign images of slavery, but never images of the atrocities committed by its perpetrators. They include pictures of African American World War I and II heroes, but never the violent realities they faced upon returning home. They have accounts of the blowing up of the battleship Maine and Teddy Roosevelt charging up San Juan Hill, but nothing about the Cuban patriotic struggle for independence which preceded and led to the Spanish American War. Eurocentric materials regularly show and discuss a preaching, non-violent Dr Martin Luther King, Jr., rather than the violent conditions about which he preached. These separations of 'acts' from their causes and effects restrict the development of consciousness about social conditions through absorption of the 'act' into an acceptable dominant ideology. Thus, Dr King becomes acceptable as a preacher of and dreamer about American democratic values. Yet the social conditions and unequitable power relations that were the motivation for his actions are submerged. Inclusion of African American World War I and II heroes suggests that equality is at work because all Americans could fight and die for their country. The barbaric, gruesome hangings, castrations, and burnings that awaited many of these heroes are avoided because they cannot be subsumed under a dominant ideology that most educators would be willing to claim. In this way, a Eurocentric approach to curriculum not only denigrates and subordinates information about the 'other', but it also restricts knowledge about topics to that which can be made 'claimable' under supremacist ideologies, such as 'benevolent master and faithful slave', 'social and economic Darwinism', and the Western world as 'protectorate of the underdeveloped'.

Another commentator, Peter Schmidt (1990), believes that a less Eurocentric world view would mean including less about European history at a time when events in Eastern Europe suggest that students should know more. This confuses Eurocentrism with European. To remove Eurocentrism would not eliminate or suppress knowledge about Europe and its achievements. If students were to study European history and culture devoid of the supremacist ideologies that usually form the textual warp and woof of instructional materials, this knowledge would actually begin to counteract a Eurocentric world view. In other words, if the presentation of knowledge about European history and culture can eliminate continuous justification of past and present denigration and subordination of people and cultures from other lands of origin — as if it was (and still is) the natural, rightful course of events — knowledge of Europe can avoid filtration through a Eurocentric lens. The value of multicultural education is that it does not propose the replacement of European centrism with another form of centrism, but attempts to put European perspectives and accounts in a context of other significant perspectives and accounts — in other words to reconstruct our knowledge base to reflect the interconnectedness of the multiple voices who have created it.

This leads to questions about 'proportion' and 'distortion', which other commentators have recently raised. Charles Krauthammer (1990) wrote that 'American history has not been smoothly and proportionally multicultural from the beginning'. George Will (1989) fears that a multicultural curriculum tampers with historical accuracy. The assumptions beneath these positions suggest that representatives of traditionally omitted cultures and groups need to have been visible players, similar in notoriety and acceptance to known (read white) historical figures in each era and event, in order for the recording of that era or event to be multicultural; and that attempts to 'stretch' history to accommodate this need will result in distortions.

These assumptions and simplistic application of multiculturality only understand multicultural education literally and one dimensionally as the inclusion of well-known achievers — the leaders and heroes from 'many cultures'. The initial problem with this application is the 'well-known' factor, which itself is a function of cultural transmission and education in a society that has, with a few carefully chosen exceptions, suppressed and limited knowledge to a singular race/class/gender band. This misunderstanding of proportion and distortion also suggests that an alteration of the upper class, white, male dominant band of knowledge will most likely result in distortion. Even if white Americans numerically constitute the majority of the population, and dominate the identified leadership of US historical issues, events, and scholarly fields, accurate representation of these issues, events, and fields requires a collective integration of the accounts of those present, told from their own 'eyes' and experiences, i.e., from indigenous or intrinsic perspectives. The issue is one of presence, not of judgment or demographic dominance. A multicultural orientation disavows the textual dominance of any culture or group. It suspends judgment of one perspective over another and attempts to provide an equitable presence and presentation of multiple perspectives or accounts, each constructed within the context of high standards of academic scholarship.

Krauthammer's request for smooth proportionality also obscures the power struggle among groups with uneven social, political, and economic relations. These struggles in themselves have shaped history. A few examples will hopefully clarify how the removal or blocking of indigenously voiced historical struggle can result in a narrow, monocultural account, whereas the acknowledgment of groups in concert and in conflict will help to construct a collective and panoptic framework of knowledge. The following examples have a multicultural orientation because they strive for equity of information, the use of indigenous accounts of a diversified presence, and the inclusion of average group members of diverse cultures and groups along with leaders and heroes. In this way, the inherent collectivity of knowledge can emerge. Thus, for example, the Revolutionary War period and the writing of the Declaration of Independence and the Constitution can be presented multiculturally (read with accuracy, inclusivity, indigeneity, and criticality) even though no women (of any cultural group), Native Americans, African Americans, Latinos, or Asians were among the European American 'Founding Fathers'.

We can begin with the general picture we usually present to students: that for the most part, men such as George Washington, Samuel Adams, Thomas Jefferson, Patrick Henry, and Benjamin Franklin, were the founders of our country who forged a new concept of government and a new vision of freedom in the middle to late eighteenth century. This singular, heroic, and patrician characterization of the 'founding' of this country separates leaders from the people they led. It disconnects indigenous Nations who had been here for thousands of years, and the millions of representatives of African Nations who were forced here, from their own revolutionary struggle of liberation and self-determination.[4] Further, it denies the collective interdependence of these three major cultural groups, as well as each group's specific make-up, i.e., hundreds of distinct Native American Nations; colonies founded by different European colonizers for different purposes; and Africans and African Americans representing diverse African Nations.

The undeniable focus of the Revolutionary War period is that all peoples in the American colonies were struggling for freedom. Native Americans were fighting for the right to maintain their cultural traditions and preserve their ancestral homelands. Large numbers of white colonists of all classes were fighting England for the right to govern themselves. Africans and African Americans, free (of all classes) and enslaved, were fighting in various ways for their freedom from the inhuman system of slavery and for the same rights and liberties of their colonial peers. When textbooks evaporate the common struggle for survival and the singularity and interdependency of each group in forging a vision of freedom strong enough to counteract colonial domination and oppression, the result is a distorted monovocal account of the period. Following are two brief overviews that demonstrate the shared knowledge, the common needs, and the prevailing drive for self-determination among Native Americans, Africans, and Europeans.

- The Iroquois Confederacy and its Great Law of Peace influenced Benjamin Franklin, who visited the Iroquois and 'took lessons' from them about the value of confederation and of representative self-rule. This influence can be seen in the language of the 1754 Albany Plan of Union, which became a working model of Federalism and representative self government at the 1787 Constitutional Convention. The Congress that wrote the Albany Plan was attended by 150 Native Americans and twenty-five representatives from seven colonies. It was the first Congress of the colonies and was called to address issues such as confederation, common defense against the French, taxation, and alliances with Native American Nations (Burton, 1988). Following are some principles of government which colonial law makers found in the Great Law of Peace:
  - A system of checks and balances with three branches of government
  - The right to assemble
  - The right to speak freely
  - Religious freedom
  - The right to vote, including women
  - A process of impeaching leaders
  - Representative government

At the ideological level, the hundreds of years of colonial interaction with sovereign Nations in North America resulted in significant cross cultural impact (Usner, 1988) that is omitted from textbooks. If Native American values, social relations, and institutions were more accurately characterized and contextualized as having a determinant effect on the course of colonial history, their continuous efforts to retrieve full self-determination, and the impact of these efforts on colonial events, would more clearly be understood. For example, in 1763, Chief Pontiac of the Ottawa Nation tried to drive British colonists from land around the Ohio River. He captured many British forts but was defeated after England sent many more soldiers to the colonies. In an attempt to decrease conflicts between the colonies and sovereign Nations, King George III issued the Proclamation of 1763 which set aside all land west of the Appalachian Mountains for Native Americans. This, along with the Stamp Act (1765), which taxed colonists to raise money for the additional British troops stationed in the colonies to suppress Native American struggles, added fuel to the growing white colonists' desire for freedom from British control.

- African Americans used colonial laws as one way to gain freedom (Kaplan, 1973). In 1766, a group of black men in Boston filed a test case in court against slavery. They asked for freedom and damages because they had been held in America against their will. This legal attack against slavery was used in other colonies. Black leaders organized to collect money, hire lawyers, and file suits for freedom. Many individuals sued for their freedom and were successful. Throughout the 1770s, courts and legislatures were being bombarded with freedom petitions signed by larger numbers of black American men and women. In Boston, Prince Hall and others worked to end the system of slavery by using pamphlets and petitions to stress the close connection between freedom from England and freedom from the system of slavery. In 1777, he and seven other Black Bostonians sent a petition to the general court of Massachusetts to abolish slavery and, as he put it, to restore the 'natural rights of all men'.

Thomas Jefferson had written that people form governments to protect the rights of life, liberty, and the pursuit of happiness. People, wrote Jefferson, had a duty and a right to change a government that took away the inalienable rights of its citizens. One woman who believed these words and acted upon them was Elizabeth Freeman. In 1781, she learned that the Bill of Rights of the new Massachusetts State Constitution said: 'All men were born free and equal.' She believed that this applied to her too, and had the courage to take her 'owner' to court. She sued him for her freedom. The success of Elizabeth Freeman's case, along with several others, brought about the legal end of slavery in Massachusetts. Freeman was one of many during this period who helped to change the government by believing in American principles of freedom.

Among African Americans of the eighteenth century, belief in American principles of freedom took many forms. Benjamin Bannaker, scientist, mathematician, inventor, and astronomer, is known for writing almanacs and for surveying the land that would become our nation's capital. He also wrote a carefully stated yet scathing letter to Thomas Jefferson in 1791 pointing out the contradictions of a society founded on principles of freedom that enslaved millions of its inhabitants. Below is a section from that letter:

Here, Sir, was a time [Revolutionary War period] in which your tender feelings for yourselves engaged you thus to declare, you were then impressed with proper ideas of the great valuation of liberty, and the free possession of those blessings to which you were entitled by nature; but Sir how pitiable is it to reflect, that altho you were so fully convinced of the benevolence of the Father of mankind, and of his equal and impartial distribution of those rights and privileges which he had conferred upon them, that you should at the same time counteract his mercies, in detaining by fraud and violence so numerous a part of my brethren under groaning captivity and cruel oppression, that you should at the Same time be found guilty of that most criminal act, which you professedly detested in others, with respect to yourselves.

Crispus Attucks, often portrayed as the first who 'happened' to die in the Boston Massacre, was actually the leader of a group of citizens who marched up King Street to confront British soldiers. Black colonists were part of the Minutemen at Lexington and Concord, and joined the Continental army by the thousands when Washington slowly opened the ranks to free and then enslaved African Americans. The British had offered freedom to all men held in slavery who would fight for them, and thousands of Native Americans were fighting on the side of the British because of their conflicts with colonial settlers. These factors, along with the need to replace deserters and lost soldiers during the bitter winter at Valley Forge, caused black soldiers to be a crucial factor in winning the Revolutionary War.

The above examples demonstrate how the integration of multiple and collective accounts on common themes (experienced in some way by all people of each era) would stimulate a multicultural orientation in education materials and classroom instruction. Those who counter that it all won't fit (in the textbooks and the curriculum), only reveal their lack of imagination and will to conceptualize knowledge as an equitable and interrelated whole, rather than the sum of unequal and separate parts.

The effects on all students of legitimizing a narrow world view are costly. When omissions and distortions occur consistently for any culture or group, the cumulative weight of this truncated version of history (as well as all other disciplines) plays a role in 'confirming' that group's invisibility and lesser value. In this way, the continuous gaps and voids in curricula shape thoughts and feelings about 'self' and about one's own and others' cultures (Swartz, 1989).

For example, past and present suppression of indigenous African, Asian, and American accounts of colonial invasion and exploitation in curriculum and textbooks, causes these vehicles of learning to be gatekeepers of knowledge and perpetrators of cultural amnesia. The proliferation of this hegemonic educational practice is internalized by generations of students whose one-sided view of Europe's 'great colonial adventure' paves the way for a portrayal of cultures, from which many students descend, as voiceless, passive, and 'less developed'. These ancestral cultures, from which Europe's Renaissance and Industrial Revolution were funded and nourished, were, in the process, raped, depopulated, exploited, and often destroyed. As most textbooks tell it, or more often omit it, this all happened in voiceless passivity and anonymity, and was somehow natural and inevitable. Between the lines of most textbooks, students get the message that these cultures 'deserved' such treatment because they couldn't 'cope' with the advances of 'modern civilization'. Do we really need to ask what role, if any, the academic content of 'standard' educational materials plays in building or undermining self and communal esteem?

Critics of multicultural education may ask, 'What then is "standard" according to multicultural education? How do you determine what is to be taught and what students should know?' It is important to clarify that multicultural standards or criteria, such as inclusion with representation and non-hegemonic scholarship, should not be confused with or perceived as a pathway toward establishing a new 'standard' or expanded canon — a multicultural canon if you will. Just as multicultural education disavows the textual dominance of any culture or group, it disavows the need for and inherent dominance implicit in canonized knowledge. In the field of literature, the canon has a definite form and can be identified through the largely monocultural lists of literature in most student anthologies and English courses and curricula. In the study of history, the canon is more amorphous, but no less restrictive and misrepresentational. In this discipline we have no list to purview, but an analysis of textbooks produced for public school consumption (as well as the curricula tailored to them) consistently reveals the monocultural 'master script' at their foundation. The a priori censorship inherent in the 'master script' results in a Eurocentric canon — exclusionary and distorted. The task of multicultural education is not to replace the monocultural canon with a more inclusive multicultural one. The notion of canon itself is hegemonic. If the standards or criteria of a multicultural education are used to select a canon — albeit a more inclusive one — the emancipatory capacity of multicultural education will be delimited. Yes, standards or criteria are needed for the selection of textbooks, the compilation of literature lists, and the development and delivery of curricula. These standards should promote greater accuracy and inclusion, indigeneity, and the recognition of knowledge as hybrid, collective, and steadily evolving. Thus, the real standards of multicultural education are those that continuously disavow dominance and monological thought, not a specific set of materials or information chosen by those standards. In this way, multicultural education conceives of knowledge as fluid and evolving in its diversity and capacity to critically stimulate and engage students in the process of knowledge production. The canonization of any discipline places boundaries on knowledge. Multicultural education proposes that the engagement and ultimately the empowerment of students as seekers of knowledge depends upon the removal of imposed boundaries. Such an education provides the framework for conceptually unlimited content and perspectives. By broadening their base of knowledge, students are encouraged to critically define, analyze, and synthesize the knowledge they need to 'handle' the diverse dynamics present in various disciplines, historical events, and issues. Searching for and selecting knowledge to solve problems, rather than reiterating predetermined sets of information, empowers students to select and delineate their own boundaries for each learning situation.

Increasing global interconnectedness requires that Western students, who collectively represent the cultures of the world, know who they are, where they have come from, and what their ancestral cultures have achieved and experienced. It also requires that students know how to think and solve problems — ultimately to be knowledge producers. The enrichment that comes from this type of engagement with knowledge is the liberative energy of future achievements. Without this energy, the educational engagement of millions of our students will continue to wane. By requiring the non-hierarchal, non-hegemonic representation of diverse cultural repertoires, and by sowing scholarship and the hybrid collectivity of knowledge in the foundational soil of knowledge production, multicultural education can open up the boundaries around knowledge and facilitate the reaping of one of the most fundamental goals of education: to teach and promote the values and the skills of positive cultural evolvement, and thus to encourage its continuance.

Notes

1 Recommendation of Commissioner Thomas Sobol to the New York State Board of Regents, included in a 2 February 1990 memo from Thomas Sobol to New York State Board of Regents. This recommendation, along with specific action steps, was passed by the Regents on 16 February 1990.
2 As used in this article, the word 'groups' in the phrase 'diverse cultures and groups', refers to traditionally omitted and misrepresented racial/ethnic groups, and intra-cultural groups such as women, youth, senior citizens, people of various religions, and those who are physically and mentally challenged.
3 Western culture is not inherently a monolithic construction. For example, the cultures

of European countries are as diverse as the cultures of African countries or the countries of any continent. However, the common goal of European powers to conquer, exploit, and often destroy people and civilizations in Africa, Asia and the Americas during the colonial and neocolonial periods, linked European countries together in an unworthy alliance. This coalescence was accompanied and supported by a deeply rooted psycho-social belief system entrenched in the racial categorizations of nineteenth century anthropologists, and fueled by the schismatic and imperialist literature and unfounded genetic postulations of white superiority during that same period (Said, 1978). The current economic, social, and political disparities, for example, between European countries and African countries are directly a result of these engineered divisions of dominance, and are contextualized in educational materials through the absence or misrepresentation of the values, traditions, achievements, etc., of African, Asian, Latin American, and indigenous peoples. Thus, the censorship explained above maintains the 'hegemony of the familiar' — Western culture remains 'master'.

4   *Nation* (with a capital *N*) refers to a people, usually the indigenous inhabitants of a specific territory, who share common customs, origins, history, and frequently language or related languages. Nation (with a small *n: nation*) refers to an aggregate of people organized under a single government. In the United States today, the term 'nation' primarily signifies a political body — the citizens united under one independent government, without close regards for their origins. Secondarily, 'nation' refers to a physical territory. In order to distinguish between the aggregate of people who live in the United States (nation), whose lands of origin are all over the world, and people who are indigenous to a land, we are capitalizing the N of nation when referring to indigenous peoples. For example, the Cherokee Nation and the Anishinabe Nation are indigenous to the nation in North America today called the United States; the Yoruba Nation and the Igbo Nation are indigenous to the nation today called Nigeria.

References

BADILLO-SUED, J. and CANTOS-LÓPEZ, A. (1986) *Puerto Rico Negro*, Río Piedras, Puerto Rico Editorial Cultural.

BERNAL, M. (1989) 'The roots of ancient Greece', *Newsday*, 29 October, p. 5.

BUNRON, B. (1988) 'The Iroquois had Democracy Before We Did.' *Indian Roots of American Democracy*. Northeast Indian Quarterly, **4**, 4, pp. 44–48 Ithaca, Cornell University.

DIOP, C.A. (1974) *The African Origins of Civilization, Myth or Reality*, Westport, CT, Lawrence Hill and Company.

GAGNON, P.A. (1987) *Democracy's Untold Story*, New York, Education for Democracy/ American Federation of Teachers.

GRINDE, D. (1988) 'It's Time to Take Away the Veil', *Indian Roots of American Democracy*, Northeast Indian Quarterly, **4**, 4, pp. 28–34, Ithaca: Cornell University.

HARDING, V. (1983) *There is a River*, New York, Harcourt, Brace, Jovanovich.

HAWKINS, J. (1984) *Inverse Images: The Meaning of Culture, Ethnicity and Family in Postcolonial Guatemala*, Albuquerque, NM, University of New Mexico Press.

JOHNSON, H.G., SMITH, F. and GEARHART, G. (1989) 'The contributions of African Americans to science, medicine and invention', Rochester, NY, Rochester City School District.

KAPLAN, S. (1973) *The Black Presence in the Era of the American Revolution, 1770–1800*. Greenwich, NY, New York Graphic Society, Ltd., with Smithsonian Institution Press.

KRAUTHAMMER, C. (1990) 'Education: Doing bad and feeling good', *Time Magazine*, 5 February, p. 78.

LAWRENCE, H.G. (1962) 'African explorers of the new world', *Crisis Magazine*, June-July, pp. 321–32.

LAWRENCE, H.G. (1987) 'Mandinka voyages across the Atlantic' in VAN SERTIMA, I. (Ed.) *African Presence in Early America*. New Brunswick, Journal of African Civilizations, Ltd., Inc.

LEO, J. (1989) 'Teaching history the way it happened', *US News and World Report*, 27 November, p. 73.

McCARTHY, C. (1990) 'Multicultural education and the challenge of curriculum reform', presented at 'Winds of Change' Conference, Albany, New York, 9 January.

RAVITCH, D. (1990) 'History and self-esteem', *History Matters*, 2, 7, February.

SAID, E.W. (1978) *Orientalism*, New York, Vintage Books Edition/Random House.

SCHMIDT, P. (1990) 'European upheaval sparks curriculum debate', *Education Week*, IX, 16, 10 January.

SLEETER, C. and GRANT, C. (1990) 'Race, class, gender and disability in current textbooks', in APPLE, M.W. and CHRISTIAN-SMITH, L.K. (Eds) *Politics and the Textbook*, New York, Routledge, Chapman and Hall.

SWARTZ, E. (1989) *Multicultural Curriculum Development, A Practical Approach to Curriculum Development at the School Level*, Rochester, NY, Rochester City School District.

USNER, D. (1988) 'Colonial history: 300 years of cultural encounter', *Indian Roots of American Democracy*, Northeast Indian Quarterly, 4, 4, pp. 26–7.

VAN SERTIMA, I. (1976) *They Came Before Columbus, the African Presence in Ancient America*, New York, Random House.

VAN SERTIMA, I. (Ed.) (1987) *African Presence in Early America*, New Brunswick, Journal of African Civilizations, Ltd., Inc.

VENABLES, R.W. (1989) 'The founding fathers, choosing to be the Romans', *Northeast Indian Quarterly*, VI, 4, Winter. pp. 30–55.

WEINER, L. (1922) *Africa and the Discovery of America*. (3 Vols) Philadelphia, PA, Innes and Sons.

WILL, G. (1989) 'Tampering with history doesn't serve education', *Gannett Rochester Newspapers, Democrat and Chronicle*, 20 December.

Part 2

*Conducting Multicultural Education
Research*

Chapter 4

Reflections on the Researcher in a Multicultural Environment

Lois Weis

Although multicultural education as a field of study has grown somewhat within the past twenty years, studies by Carl Grant and Christine Sleeter (1986) point to a clear absence of serious research in the area. Whether quantitative or qualitative in orientation, in-depth work on the topic is virtually non-existent.

This raises two questions regarding what research on multicultural education entails: (i) what questions should be asked; and (ii) what does it mean to be a researcher in a multicultural setting? In other words, are there any special issues or problems related to conducting research in multicultural environments? I do not intend, in this chapter, to address the first question. Others in this volume will do so. I will, however, begin to explore the second through a set of reflections upon my two ethnographies, both of which were conducted in multicultural settings and both of which were conducted in cultural environments far removed from my own background. The first was an examination of the construction of black student culture in an urban community college which served a high proportion of poor students (Weis, 1985a and 1985b), and the second, a study of the process of white working class male and female youth identity formation in a high school located in a deindustrializing area of the United States (Weis, 1988a, 1988b and 1989). Although data from both studies have been reported extensively elsewhere, this essay will explore some of the issues related to what it means to do work in a multicultural environment and, indeed, an environment often far removed from the researcher's own original cultural location.

Some of the issues raised in this chapter relate to the meaning of being a researcher in any environment, whether multicultural or not. Others relate specifically to what it means to conduct research in an environment which is removed in some sense from one's own background. The points raised here relate specifically to qualitative or ethnographic work. I will raise, in this chapter, several key points: (i) know who you are before going into the field; (ii) respect those with whom you are working; and (iii) conduct yourself with the utmost of integrity at all times. A researcher has to make a number of difficult decisions in the field and if one cannot live by these three points, he or she should not be out there. The data will be useless and we, as researchers, will do immeasurable damage to people's lives.

Lois Weis

Entering the Field and Acknowledging Ourself[1]

It is never easy to gain access to people's lives for the period of time necessary to conduct careful ethnographic work. One is literally asking to be part of people's everyday existence for very often a year. How one approaches the field and its power brokers is critical. Many multicultural settings, especially those located in poorer neighborhoods, have been abused by the press and members of the dominant class to such an extent historically that people are very reluctant to allow access. This is understandable and prospective researchers must recognize this. When, for example, I requested access to the Urban Community College in 1979, I was faced with the fact that the Community College had just won a long drawn out fight for a new campus. This fight has spanned over ten years and the press had been engaged in the struggle from the beginning and had not always been sympathetic to a new campus. Reports of rapes in the neighborhood, thus creating the impression that 'these people' were unworthy, were frequent and were run on the front page. Similar such reports of rapes in the suburbs did not receive these front page headlines. Thus people were understandably wary of my intentions when I raised the possibility of conducting an ethnographic study for a year. I was asking to become a part of people's lives just after they had won an exceptionally difficult fight for a new location. Well into the first semester numerous faculty members thought I might be associated with the press and suspicion ran high among certain faculty. They simply did not trust me. Given a history of abuse, this is to be expected in any institution in this country which serves the poor. While not all multicultural institutions serve the poor, some do, and this is a problem if one is attempting to gain access.

I must say here that, unfortunately, the rampant sexism in this society does have, in this case, some advantages. When I ask for access to such institutions, I am simply not taken as seriously by most as would a white male, for example. Power brokers do not expect quite as much of me as they would a white male who announced that *he* was from the university and wished to conduct a similar study. Faculty and administrators are certainly not aware of this, and would, no doubt, deny that this is the case. In my experience, however, it is true. It does not occur to me that I will not gain access to even the most difficult and most controversial of settings.[2] Part of this is undoubtedly due to personal style but at least part of it is due to unfettered sexism. This, of course, is not to suggest that this attitude characterizes all such people. Many in the field are quite aware of the fact that a woman has to be good to get to where I am today. Others, however, are not conscious of this and it is these people who are more willing to let me be part of their lives when they might very well turn a male down.

Given the difficulty of gaining access to the field, and the fact that one's own self interacts with one's ability to obtain such access in a variety of ways, it is important to understand that the field can be a very lonely place for this reason. People will assign a social location to you, often based upon their own social location and you become that person for them, despite what you may think of yourself. In the white working class high school, for example, numerous white male faculty persisted in thinking that I was a graduate student working on a Masters' degree. Each faculty member at the school received a letter from me indicating that I was an Associate Professor at SUNY and that I intended to write a book based on my year spent in the school. In addition, I had meetings with all faculty units at the beginning of the school year in which I conducted the research and met individually with almost every teacher at one time or another before systematic data collection was begun. Nevertheless, male teachers persisted in asking me, 'How is your masters' going'?; or, 'How is your little project coming'? Occasionally I was asked how my dissertation was going but generally male faculty had placed me in the category of being a first level graduate student. They had simply assigned me to this role. At first, I corrected everyone by reminding them that I was a faculty member who was writing a book — a book for which I already had a publisher (Routledge). After several months of this, however, I simply stopped correcting people. I did decide that there was nothing I could do to convince others that I was other than a graduate student, which is the category that I had been placed in and with which many faculty obviously felt comfortable. Since the vast majority of teachers themselves had a Masters', they then could assume that I was still striving for the position which they had already obtained. These teachers were themselves largely from the Traditional Proletariat (Edwards, 1977), escaping the steel plant and so forth only by virtue of their education. They did not have the most progressive attitude toward women. That they assigned to me the social location of working on a 'little project' obviously made them feel comfortable and I simply stopped contesting the location.

I point this out only to suggest that people will assign a researcher to a certain social location and that one has to know oneself before entering the field. If I did not know who I was, I would have spent my time contesting their definition and being upset by it rather than gathering data which was my purpose there. The field can be a very lonely, albeit fascinating, place. People do not know you there, and it is not your job to have them necessarily get to know you and accept you for who you are. Your job is to get to know them, and this may occur through their assigning you a certain place — one with which you may feel less than comfortable. I did not feel particularly comfortable being relegated to the position of 'little girl', but that is what many male faculty did in the 'Freeway' project. No one in the school really knew who I was, despite what I told them and my own well-established professional style as a faculty member. Others in the world did, however, and this is terribly important. If you spend eight hours a day or more with people who do not really know you, you have to know yourself and be able to go back to a world where you are known. There is one caveat here, however. True community studies in which the researcher by himself/herself or with her or his family actually moves into the community do not seem to take quite the same form. Some of the community studies such as Joseph Howell's *Hard Living on Clay Street* (1973), Bettylou Valentine's *Hustling and Other Hard Work* (1978), and Carol Stack's *All Our Kin* (1972), where researchers actually move into the area and conduct a full community study rather than a study in a school seem to be able to lessen the fracturing of self I am describing here. Alan Peshkin, however, raises the same point I do with respect to his study of both Mansfield (1978) and the fundamentalist Christian school (1986). In both cases he actually lived in the community. In the second case, he was defined as an outsider by virtue of the fact that he was a Jew (Peshkin, 1982, 1986). Thus living in the community does not ensure that one does not meet these imposed definitions of self but it might lessen them a bit.

Lois Weis

Let me restate my point here. As a researcher you will be what people in the field choose to define you as and you have little control over this since you are entering *their* cultural totality — they are not entering yours. You had best have a good self-concept to begin with or the field work is not worth doing. In the white working class high school the male teachers systematically defined me as a little girl since this fit neatly with their own definition of women in a patriarchal community.

In the Community College, I faced a different problem. The students refused to believe that I was who I said I was. In this case, I again entered the field and let everyone know who I was. This is, however, a very poor group of students for the most part, many of whom have few academic skills. There was a great deal of self-redefinition in the College among the student population. For example, students, on a number of occasions, would tell me that, 'I had intended to go to the University of ——, but changed my mind at the last minute and ended up at Urban College'. The 'blank' here could be the University of Pennsylvania, New York University, or whatever. I heard this on numerous occasions. It must be noted that many such students were reading on a ninth grade level at best. Many other such examples of taking on the role of others were more coded. One woman, who I later learned had been a prostitute for many years, informed me that she had been a 'physical therapist' for many years before coming to Urban College. Another woman told me that she had a first husband who died; I later found out that this was not true. This is not to judge these statements in any way. I am simply pointing out that there was quite a bit of shifting identity among the student population and individuals often took on roles in an attempt to be other than what they were. This was known among the population and not simply done for the benefit of an outsider. Students did it to one another and everyone knew it. This is important only insofar as the fact that I was assumed to have a shifting identity also. Thus, when I said I was a faculty member at State University, students expressed interest, and then immediately asked me how I had done on the Business Organization test last period. They honestly thought I was a student for quite some time. Again, this is not universally the case in the College, but I am quite certain that many students did not believe that I was a faculty member until well into the year. Again, the fact that I do not reflect the stereotypically faculty member (white male) appearance definitely contributes to this. It ran deeper, however. In an environment where shifting identities are the norm, it was simply assumed that I had a shifting identity as well. This is not an unrealistic expectation given the reality of the students' lives. One is what others define you to be in these settings and this definition is likely to be more removed from one's 'real' self the further removed from one's original culture when doing fieldwork. These settings were not mine and I was categorized much as white middle class researchers place others in categories in so much of our research.

To this day, I only wear skirts and dresses to the University because when I did the research in the Community College I wore slacks to the College and skirts to the University so that I could keep my identity straight to myself. We become different people in the field as well. The fact that people define us in certain ways does have an effect on us, whether positive or negative. It is, therefore important that researchers know who they are before entering the field because others will define you as they see fit. In suggesting that those who do not know themselves ought not enter the field, I am not suggesting that one should engage in any personal rigidity once one is out there. One of the most fascinating things about field work is what we learn about ourselves as we interact in different cultural milieus. Learning about oneself in such a setting, however, does assume that one has a base from which to depart.

Acknowledging Our Perspectives

It is important that we acknowledge the perspectives from which we operate. This holds true in all research settings, of course, but in dealing with cultures not our own it is critical to be honest about where we are coming from theoretically and personally. When I engaged in the study of the Community College I was involved with the reproduction framework, and my own biography of marginality enabled me to understand what it meant to be marginal in terms of mainstream institutions and culture. I am a Jewish female — a woman who has always felt marginal in a number of ways. Being Jewish and spending most of my youth in a non-Jewish community meant that I understood marginality to its core. I understood in a very real way what it meant to be an outsider. I remember full well introducing my non-Jewish peers in elementary school to Jewish culture through a variety of skits and so forth. I was always different. Although confident personally, I felt the outsider nature of my existence. I had dark hair and dark skin in a mid-western community populated by light skinned, blonde haired and blue eyed Scandinavians and Germans. I felt different and I was. I could not say the Lord's Prayer when others did. I was Jewish. They were not. Ultimately this gave me a great deal of strength but I felt my own marginality as a child. As I matured, I again lived marginality in that I was a Jewish female who was not proceeding along the correct path. I did not wish to marry just out of college, select silver and china, and raise children. I wanted a public life also and did not come from a family or a community where this was either understood or condoned. I was rejected in many ways because of it. My own marginality as a striving Jewish female from Milwaukee therefore was part and parcel of my own biography and enabled me to understand marginality in terms of mainstream culture and institutions of the Urban College students. My politics of the 1960s enabled me to be sympathetic with the determined location and oppression of the underclass. *Between Two Worlds* was a statement of marginality in some ways, and a part of my own personal biography.

Although a feminist and political leftist, I did not truly appreciate or acknowledge the importance of social movements in my life until I wrote *Working Class Without Work*. This second ethnography is a study of social movements — the identity formation process of male and female working class youth in school and the ways in which this identity formation process was infused by social struggles — specifically, the woman's movement, the state of the American labor movement, and the new right. I was personally past the point of seeing my own life and work as the result of personal striving and success. My life was now infused with a spirituality and a sense of collective struggle that I had not fully understood before. This is not to say that I was not political when I wrote *Between Two Worlds*. I was. However, I did not fully appreciate the extent to which I was and am part of a social movement. I understand now the insight that felt marginality in my own biography provides, but it is no longer a driving force for me. My life has been able to take the shape and form it has because of the women's and the civil rights movements. While this was always objectively the case, it did not fuel my creativity in the way it does now. I was older when I wrote *Working Class Without Work* and I have children. I am part of a set of historic struggles involving meaning making. I am part of the struggle to redefine the female subject, in particular, and my daughters are, by virtue of the fact that they are female, part of it as well. My children remind me on a daily basis that there is a future and that the future will involve change in collective identity formation and struggle. Perhaps it is this shift — from a feeling of marginality (not to be read as aloneness in any sense) to one of collective identity that led to some of the differences in my two ethnographies. My second book focuses on identity formation. I now understood that I was, and am, part of the shaping of identity, not in an individual sense but in a collective one as well. My book reflects this shift. I saw working class male and female youth in a struggle for identity formation in a struggle to create a 'self' in a world that was increasingly programmed. I saw competing identity formations in the case of males and females, in particular, rather than the motif of reproduction in the case of *Between Two Worlds*.

All this is not to deny the importance of available paradigms in the literature itself. When I wrote *Between Two Worlds*, I was very much influenced by the notion of cultural reproduction and contestation as a number of scholars were employing these ideas (Willis, 1977; Apple, 1982; Giroux, 1983). When I wrote *Working Class Without Work*, the notion of collective identity formation was being introduced into the debate (Wexler, 1988). It is too simple, however, to suggest that I or any scholar simply makes theoretical shifts as the discourse changes. There is a variety of competing frameworks or ways of seeing available to us and we 'choose' to work within and/or push forward one or another of these at different times in our lives. It is our own biography which intersects with these frameworks in meaningful ways; none of us simply alters our perspectives because the theoretical winds shift.

I do not know what I would see if I did the Community College study now. While I still have great faith in the integrity of the data, I am certain that I would have seen the students engaged more in a struggle for collective identity formation than I did then. I would have interpreted the data more, I suspect, in terms of what it means to be part of a collective movement and the ways in which this movement is fractured. This reflects *my* movement both personally and theoretically. All scholars ought to be aware of the way in which their personal biography intersects with their own work. Alan Peshkin (1983) has been brutally honest about this. He suggests that his own growing up within the Jewish community of Chicago led him to value perceived community when he was in Mansfield. This very same aspect of biography led him to see as indoctrination the teaching within the fundamentalist Christian school. Others, he suggests, may have seen indoctrination in an avowedly racist Mansfield, and community in the Christian school.

While the awareness of one's biography is important in all work, it is perhaps even more important in multicultural settings where the scholar does not know the culture of the people in the field. It is our job as researchers to become an insider in these settings much as we are insiders, in a sense, within our own class cultural locations. In a middle class setting there would be more shared understanding between myself and people in the field initially than there will be at the outset between myself and those in the field in a working class environment. It is our job to get to know the 'other' in the field. If the 'other' is far removed in some sense from our own biography, the way in which our own biography encourages us to 'make sense' of the other is critically important. We must be brutally honest about this. It would be most helpful, for example for middle class researchers to engage in such soul searching when they interpret the actions, words and silences of the poor, blacks, Hispanics and others. What leads one to 'see' certain things about others?

I must add here that I truly do believe that work done from an outsider's perspective once this level of honesty is achieved is possibly better than that which could be done by an insider. It is true that I could study the middle class and have less far to go in terms of 'understanding' them. However, since it is my own original culture, I fear that I would take too much for granted, thereby missing a great deal. I would lose the invaluable perspective of the outsider. The outsider is, in many ways, the best social critic once he/she acknowledges the role of personal biography in one's work.

Exhibit Integrity

It is important always to conduct oneself with the utmost of integrity in the field. In multicultural settings, the researcher will often be extremely distrusted. In the case of the Community College, as I mentioned earlier, I was distrusted by faculty initially because they feared that I was a spy. The students initially distrusted me because I was white. This is not surprising. There is a history of abuse that determines the way in which whites are perceived by blacks and other people of color which is going to determine initial acceptance or lack thereof. After this initial period, however, it has been my experience that people will, in fact, open up and trust those whom they feel deserve to be trusted. The turning point in the Community College came when, as the only white member of the class, I was privy to a class discussion (when the teacher was not present) about how racist (the term used was 'prejudiced') that particular teacher was. I never said anything to anyone. I just sat there listening. When students realized that nothing negative ever came of my overhearing that particular 'insider' discussion and that I continued to interact with everyone in the same way I always did, the road was much clearer for further relations with the students. In the high school, students soon learned that nothing ever came of my hearing their discussions about drinking and using drugs. In the College, it was the same. People will talk to you as a researcher if they trust you. They will not talk to you or, alternatively, hand you a line if they do not. You have to be the judge of that.

In any multicultural setting it is terribly important that one be in the field for an extended period of time. I recommend a year. It is perfectly ludicrous to think that a researcher can enter the field and immediately start interviewing people whom they do not know, whose culture they do not share, who are often perceived as hostile, and yet expect to get anything even remotely resembling accurate information. It simply will not happen. As noted above, there is a history of abuse here which will lead people to offer inaccurate information and the further removed from one's own culture a researcher is in the field, the more likely that is to happen. In both studies, I sat in on classes three full days a week for at least three months before I began formally interviewing anyone. It is important to establish oneself as a trustworthy member of the community before attempting to conduct interviews. By the time I conducted interviews with Community College students and high school students, I was well known and I did not 'rat' on anyone — I did not give away trade secrets. I did not tell what I knew about drug trafficking, drug use, drinking within the institution, cheating in the high school and so forth. Nothing happened as a result of my knowing.

This could, of course, pose some moral dilemmas for the researcher, depending on the nature of what one hears. William Foote Whyte (1955) brings up this same point in *Street Corner Society*. What does the researcher do if he/she hears something patently illegal or, more importantly perhaps, that which is likely to harm other people? Although I heard about many illegalities, I was and am not particularly concerned with these. I do suspect I would engage in many of the same illegalities if I was in the same structural location as the Community College students. Fortunately, I never had to deal with overhearing something that could likely seriously hurt another person. I must say, however, that my role as a researcher is to listen and later analyze, not be a member of the police force. I have heard a great deal and I have never once been tempted to share this information with anyone that could directly impact upon the individual that was doing the sharing. As a researcher, you must conduct yourself with integrity — integrity here relating to the fact that you are on the terrain of others. One is a guest, so to speak, when one is a fieldworker. It is not our job to intervene as if one is a member of the police. That is not to say that on an individual level a researcher should not try to use his/her contacts and skills to help others. In the Community College, in particular, I did quite a bit of this. That, however, is different than intervening in a legal or moral fashion in territory that is not one's own. My job is to conduct myself with the utmost of integrity in the field. I cannot assume that it is my job to see to it that others conduct themselves with what I consider to be integrity as well. That is for them to decide. It has been my experience that if I do that well, most things around me will run that much more smoothly.

Some Caveats

There are people who simply should not do fieldwork. I have taught qualitative methods for years, and I have come to this conclusion. Those who are rigid and who are unable to listen to others ought not be in the field. Fieldwork demands that one be able to suspend judgment and become an insider to the best of one's ability. You must become what others wish you to be and listen to what others say, whether you like what you hear or not. I did not like the racism expressed by the Freeway males as reported in *Working Class Without Work*. I did not care to hear the term 'nigger' slip easily from their lips. I did not like hearing the high school males talk about how they would like to beat their mothers, or how they envisioned their future patriarchal families. I really hate bigotry in any form and I did not like to hear it and have to engage with it seriously in order to obtain a picture of the white working class. I also did not, as I mentioned above, like being treated as a 'little girl'. In fact, I felt it was demeaning. However, I had to do it. I had to flow with what it is that people said to me — overtly or otherwise, in order to do the social analysis which I had deemed important. It is my job to articulate on paper the words, thoughts, actions and silences of others, whether I like what they say or not. This means I have to truly listen and ask questions, not argue with them.

It is also my responsibility in all of this to be what they wish me to be whether I like it or not. I did not like the fact that there were separate male and female teacher lounges (not bathrooms) in Freeway and that men liberally walked in and out of womens' space but women never invaded mens' space. This said something to me that I found personally repulsive, and the women in Freeway never challenged it. It was not my role to do so, however. If one cannot sit and listen to the words of others without engaging in a debate with them about their ideas, then stay out of the field. You will not be able to gain data that are meaningful.

All of us make mistakes. I will never forget when, in the Community College, I referred to the fact that I might work in a bar during the summer, get a 'shit job', when talking with one of the students I knew very well. I really bit my tongue. I could not believe I had said that. These people would, in many cases, give anything for what I had so liberally called a 'shit job'. I was horrified that I had done it but he paid no attention. The point is that we all make mistakes. We are of a particular social location and try as hard as we might, that location intervenes at times in inappropriate ways. We have to set ourselves in motion, however, and yet check ourselves at every turn. If you make a mistake as a fieldworker, do not agonize over it. Nothing is that important. Just keep moving and try very hard not to make the same mistake again. If you do make the same mistake, forgive yourself again, and try not to err in the same direction.

On another occasion in the Community College, in October, Basic Education Opportunity Grant (BEOG) checks were late and students were organizing in the cafeteria over this issue. I was so interested that I literally ran up to the group and started asking questions, thus reinforcing the notion among some teachers that I was a reporter. One of the faculty members (a minority male who was a supporter of mine throughout the year) took me aside and told me that I was simply behaving inappropriately. I was too aggressive. The information would come to me, he said, but I had to wait for it. 'There is a right way and a wrong way of gaining information here, and you just demonstrated the wrong way'. I backed off immediately and thought carefully about what he had said. I relied heavily on a couple of insiders in both settings and they guided me through the minefields. In the Community College, in particular, I relied upon the perspectives and true wisdom of one part-time minority faculty member. Unfortunately, he was part and parcel of the contradictory culture described in the book and I am quite certain that he landed back in jail. A brilliant man — a true social analyst who I had hoped would complete his degree at the University (in which case he would have been made full-time), but he did not. He could not break out of the boundaries of the contradictions he full well knew. He was my strongest informant at the College. Without him I could have never done the study.

The researcher in the multicultural setting needs to rely heavily on key insiders. They must be chosen carefully, however. More than anything, the researcher needs to know where to be, when, how to listen, who to rely upon, and when to back off or get out completely. Before anything else, we are ourselves in the field. It is our true self (not in the sense of social location, but a deeper sense of self) that will show through the institutions in which we are gathering data. People in the field have a keen eye for this and they will deliver nonsense to those whom they deem unacceptable. They will hand you a line, or make it all but impossible to conduct the research.

Many should not be engaged in qualitative work in multicultural settings. Those who are so inclined should proceed cautiously, ever mindful of the fact that people are people, whether from our original cultural location or not, and that they are quite adept at figuring out the degree to which we are truly interested in them and the story which they have to tell.

Notes

1 Metz (1983) has raised the issue of 'self' in ethnographic investigations.
2 Peshkin has suggested that he, too, felt this way until he was denied access to a number of Christian institutions before obtaining access of 'Bethany'. He indicated (personal communication) that he will 'never again' assume he can gain access.

References

APPLE, M. (1982) *Education and Power*, Boston, MA, Routledge and Kegan Paul.
EDWARDS, R. (1977) *Contested Terrain*. New York, Basic Books.
GIROUX, H. (1983) *Theory and Resistance in Education*, South Hadley, MA, Bergin and Garvey.
GRANT, C. and SLEETER, C. (1986) 'Race, class and gender in education research: An argument for integrative analysis', *Review of Educational Research*, 56, pp. 195–211.
HOWELL, J. (1973) *Hard Living on Clay Street*, New York, Anchor Books.
METZ, M. (1983) 'What can be learning from educational ethnography?', *Urban Education*, 17, 4, pp. 391–418.
PESHKIN, A. (1978) *Growing Up American*, Chicago, IL, University of Chicago Press.
PESHKIN, A. (1982), 'The researcher and subjectivity: Reflections on an ethnography of school and community' in SPINDLER, G. (Ed.) *Doing the Ethnography of Schooling*, New York, Holt, Rinehart and Winston, pp. 49–67.
PESHKIN, A. (1983) 'Virtuous subjectivity: In the participant observer's I's' (mimeo).
PESHKIN, A. (1986) *God's Choice: The Total World of a Christian Fundamentalist School*, Chicago, IL, University of Chicago Press.
STACK, C. (1972) *All Our Kin*, New York, Anchor Books.
WEIS, L. (1985a) *Between Two Worlds: Black Students in an Urban Community College*, Boston, MA, Routledge and Kegan Paul.
WEIS, L. (1985b) 'Without dependent on welfare for life: The experience of black women in the Urban Community College', *The Urban Review*, 17, 4, pp. 233–56.
WEIS, L. (1986) 'Thirty years old and I'm allowed to be late', *British Journal of the Sociology of Education*, 7, 3, pp. 241–63.
WEIS, L. (1988a) 'The 1980s: Deindustrialization and change in white working class male and female cultural forms, *Metropolitan Education*, 5, pp. 87–122.

WEIS, L. (1988b) 'High school girls in a deindustrializing economy' in WEIS, L. (Ed.) *Class, Race and Gender in American Education*, Albany, NY, State University of New York Press, pp. 151–72.

WEIS, L. (1989) *Working Class Without Work: High School Students in a Deindustrializing Economy*, New York, Routledge and Kegan Paul.

WEXLER, P. (1988) *Social Analysis of Education*, New York, Routledge and Kegan Paul.

WHYTE, W.F. (1955) *Street Corner Society*, Chicago, IL, University of Chicago Press.

WILLIS, P. (1977) *Learning to Labour: How Working Class Kids Get Working Class Jobs*, Westmead, Saxon House Press.

VALENTINE, B. (1978) *Hustling and Other Hard Work*, New York, Free Press.

Chapter 5

Using Quantitative Methods to Explore Multicultural Education

Gary Glen Price

I've addressed this chapter to researchers whose preconceptions about quantitative research lead them away from it. For this audience, I hope my chapter will break some stereotypes and blur some false distinctions between quantitative and qualitative methods. A secondary audience is researchers who seek methodological ideas that might help to advance understanding in multicultural education. Included in this second audience are persons concerned with the fact that the legitimacy of an emerging field is enhanced by the methodological soundness of studies done in it.

Thoughts on the Hazards, Potentials, and Future of Quantitative Research in Multicultural Education

I have often been struck by a curious asymmetry in dialogues between 'quantitative' researchers and 'qualitative' researchers. Sometimes qualitative attacks on quantitative methods are met with a patronizing yawn. Sometimes quantitative researchers fault qualitative researchers for failing to follow rules of the game (their game) without recognizing that those rules themselves are under attack. 'Rules of the game' as used here is synonymous with Kaplan's (1964) term *reconstructed logic*. Kaplan used this term to describe retrospective (and inevitably incomplete) attempts to isolate, formalize, and canonize processes that appear to have been present in studies perceived to be exemplary. (Kaplan contrasts *reconstructed logic* with *logic-in-use* — the complex, informal, meandering, and metaphoric processes actually followed by researchers.)

At other times, to the ire of qualitative researchers who fancy themselves as scions of a new paradigm[1], a quantitative researcher will claim to assimilate qualitative research as a part of the quantitative enterprise — a part usually filed by the quantitative researcher somewhere in the neighborhood of pilot studies, instrument development, and hypothesis generation.

Red herrings — One goal of this chapter is to separate some overblown criticisms of 'quantitative' research from some fair ones. Overblown criticisms obscure real differences. Therefore, I consider them under the rubric of *red herrings*. Alas, some red herrings come not from passionate rhetoric, but from pure and simple ignorance of the logic and intellectual traditions of quantitative research. (I admit that qualitative zealots' ignorance of their opponent is matched by that of quantitative zealots, but such ignorance of qualitative research is outside the scope of this chapter.)

Real vices — The ignorance that spawns red herrings also shrouds real vices. Under the rubric of *real vices* I offer my own (hopefully informed) criticisms of traditions of quantitative educational research. I make a distinction between 'a vice of quantification' and 'vices of quantifiers'.

Real differences — After defending quantitative research from red herrings and criticizing it for real vices, I attempt to probe beneath surface methodological differences between qualitative and quantitative research. I go beneath methodological differences because, to my eclectic eyes, neither camp seems to have a compelling proprietary claim to any particular research technique. Beneath the methodological surface, there appear to be some seldom-articulated philosophical differences that separate the camps. These are discussed as *real differences*.

Red Herrings

Collected under the rubric of red herrings are misleading criticisms of quantitative research — some overstatements, others altogether unfounded.

Quantification is Reductionistic

One often-heard criticism of quantification is that it is reductionistic. The assertion itself ventures close to being reductionistic. It resembles the quip that 'All generalizations are false ... including this one.' I am never certain which of various meanings of reductionism is intended when I hear the assertion that quantitative research is reductionistic. Possible interpretations of the assertion are:

(i)   The use of quantities to describe phenomena (a) blurs important distinctions; and (b) discards related information.

(ii) Theories that generate quantitative predictions about observables inherently oversimplify more than theories that do not.

(iii) The quest for quantitative specifiability of theories makes sense only if one wishes to subsume social theories under physical theories.

I examine each of these interpretations below.

Quantities blur — Quantitative descriptions *can* blur important distinctions, just as equivocal verbal descriptions do. One interpretation of this criticism centers on the adjective *important* in 'important distinctions'. Quantitative research is branded as reductionistic because it blurs distinctions considered by the critic to be important ones. This criticism suggests an arguable corollary, that it is not reductionistic to blur *unimportant* distinctions. Implicit in a judgment of importance is the purpose of the observer; what is important for one purpose can be unimportant for another. Inasmuch as one's judgment of the importance of a distinction is a reflection of one's purpose, claims that a particular research approach blurs important distinctions run the risk of dismissing as unimportant (hence reductionistic) any observations done for purposes other than one's own. The researcher who takes this philosophical posture places herself on a slippery slope, sliding toward *solipsism* (a self-isolating epistemological position in which one denies the beliefs of others, the evidence of others, and even the existence of others). Viewed socially, solipsism exceeds ethnocentrism in self-centeredness; it therefore seems inconsistent with concerns for multicultural education.

Another interpretation of the criticism centers not on the importance of that which is blurred, but on the blurring itself. Quantitative descriptions do not inevitably blur. Unabridged descriptions can be encoded quantitatively without reduction, although it is analytically complex and costly to do. Just as arguments in ordinary language can be translated into formal symbolic logic, verbal descriptions can be translated into lists of dichotomous attribute markers (1 = the adjective applies, 0 = the adjective does not apply). At this uncondensed extreme, qualitative description and quantitative description converge. Quantification is not usually pushed to this uncondensed extreme, but it can be; and, once done, it permits one later to redefine one's categories of analysis through Boolean expressions (logical combinations of *AND*, *OR*, and *NOT*).

The flexibility of such description can be illustrated by data I gathered for my dissertation (Price, 1977). Each clause from transcripts of mother-child dialogue (29,000 clauses spread over sixty-six mother-child pairs) was indexed on fifteen nominally-scaled dimensions, some dimensions having a choice of as many as eight mutually exclusive descriptors to choose from. Some taxonomic dimensions were based on *a priori* questions; others were formed to capture *clinical impressions* gained by observing mother-child dialogues and by reading transcripts of those dialogues. Through carefully constructed Boolean expressions and the capability of computers to perform logic tests, I have more than once gone back to those 29,000 records to construct newly-oriented descriptions of the dialogue. I have also performed ERIC-like searches to lead me to selected parts of transcripts.

Some readers will recognize that the foregoing example describes keyword-based indexing of a kind used increasingly by ethnographic researchers to annotate their field notes. Some may also wish to claim that such indexing is qualitative description — not quantitative description. Granted, it is not a *metric* description (i.e., one involving measurement). But there is a longstanding logical basis for claiming that it is simultaneously qualitative and quantitative (Cantor, 1890; Quine, 1972).

There is yet another way in which the boundary between 'qualitative' and 'quantitative' research breaks down. There exist numerous statistical techniques applicable to qualitative (non-metric) data (Haberman, 1978–79). Researchers who employ these techniques use *descriptions that are qualitative*, and *analyses that are quantitative*. Curiously, few educational researchers have explored this combination, which is more common in anthropology, biology, geography, history, political science, and sociology.

A sensible researcher does not ignore rich description of qualitative (nominally scalable) phenomena and does not force measurement upon such phenomena. But what about phenomena that *are* metric — whose description *does* involve measurement? A sensible researcher should not ignore ordinal-, interval-, and ratio-scale information when it is present in phenomena.

Quantities discard related information — Critics of quantification often assume that it is applicable only to decontextualized, atomistic, behavioristically unpenetrating aspects of social and psychological phenomena. As implied by that assumption, the quantitative researcher cannot see the forest for the trees — losing sight of the context and losing inter-subjective insight into the meanings and experiences of fellow humans. In effect, the claim is that *low inference* description can be quantified, whereas *high inference* description cannot.[2] In this strongly stated form, the claim could only be made in ignorance of the methodological literatures of social psychology (for example, Webb, Campbell, Schwartz, Sechrest and Grove, 1981) and psychometrics (for example, Loehlin, 1987).

The criticism can be stated in a weaker and more defensible form, which asserts that quantification retains some information and discards other information. This loss of information indeed occurs in quantification. It is not, however, unique to quantification: it is common to all forms of abstraction. Such loss is an implication of the proposition that all perception is selective. The richest ethnographic descriptions suffer the same fate.

Oversimplified theories — Do theories that generate quantitative predictions about observables necessarily oversimplify more than theories that do not? That question can be twisted into a reductionistic paradox:

(i) The following statement is not derived from a theory that makes quantitative predictions.

(ii) All instances of deterministic thinking result from the use of quantitative predictions.

The very suggestion that reductionism is proprietary to quantitative theories is itself reductionistic (and to some extent quantitative).

This criticism of theories that generate quantitative predictions stems from three issues. The first issue is whether theories can ever be complete. Apparently some critics fault theories for their incompleteness. Most thoughtful persons — qualitative, quantitative, and otherwise — would claim that theories can never be complete (Cook and Campbell, 1979, pp. 1–36; Kuhn, 1970b; Lave and March, 1975, pp. 1–7). Even avowed determinists limit themselves to a form of *ontological determinism*. They believe that the universe is in fact deterministic, but they also believe that it is so intractably complex that its full comprehension will forever be impossible.

The second issue is whether incomplete theories (as they all are) are useful. 'Usefulness', of course, can be defined in numerous ways. The *scientific usefulness* of a theory in solving old puzzles and paving the way for new ones is best left to the judgment of history (Kuhn, 1970a and 1971; Popper, 1972). The *technical usefulness* of an empirical-analytic theory depends not only on its empirical fit, but also on its pertinence to the priorities (some would say self-interests) of those who apply the theory (Apple, 1979; Habermas, 1968/ 1971). On either of these definitions, it would seem apparent that incomplete theories have some degree of usefulness.

The third issue concerns gradations of usefulness in theories, and the role of quantitative predictions in permitting persons to ascertain and compare gradations of usefulness. Some critics of quantification probably deny that there are gradations of usefulness. Others probably disagree with value judgments underlying a criterion by which theories are compared, but not with the principle of grading theories.

If some theories that make no quantitative predictions appear less simple, it is because they are less explicit.[3] That lack of explicitness has a cost: inexplicit theories lack persuasiveness because they cannot be tested or compared with other theories. Advocates of a theory that has no *commensurability* with other theories (i.e., points of explicit agreement and explicit disagreement) can do no more than preach to the already-converted. Lacking commensurability with other theories, a theory provides limited ability to change the minds of persons who believe in another theory (Kuhn, 1974).

Quantitative theories are by nature physicalistic — Does the quest for quantitative specifiability lead inexorably to physicalism? Some quantitative researchers have quite pointedly argued against physicalism (for example Cook and Campbell, 1979, pp. 32–6), so they would find a peculiar lack of intersubjective understanding on the part of an observer who tells them they *are* pursuing physicalism. It may be true that all physicalists are quantifiers, but it certainly is not true that all quantifiers are physicalists.

Quantification Imposes A Euclidean Framework

Another type of overstatement is the claim that quantification imposes a Euclidean framework on a world that is not Euclidean, and thereby deludes. In the first place, not all quantification uses a Euclidean framework. Techniques of multidimensional scaling (Young, 1987), tree-fitting, and clustering (Anderberg, 1973; Everitt, 1980) are often non-Euclidean. These techniques have been used to study subjective phenomena such as semantic dimensions of words (one example being the conceptual similarity between species of animals), the perceived similarity of colors (which bears little resemblance to the physical spectrum), and the confusibility of complex, naturalistic patterns like faces. I recommend Shepard's (1980) review of those techniques to mathematically literate qualitative researchers. Another promising technique that defies dismissal as 'Euclidean' is the use of *neural network simulations* to detect and classify patterns in data (Anderson and Rosenfeld, 1988; Wasserman, 1989).

Even in the case of methods that are Euclidean, the criticism is shallow, because it does not explain anything about the purported ills caused by misapplication of a Euclidean framework. The criticism presupposes that the costs of such misapplication outweigh the benefits, but the nature of the costs (and benefits) is not described. Moreover, the criticism makes an unsupported ontological assumption that the things viewed through a Euclidean framework are in fact markedly un-Euclidean. Maybe so, maybe not.

Assuming that one is using a Euclidean framework and assuming that it is a bad choice, what are the consequences? Here are some possibilities:

(i) The researcher is led to have high confidence in a distorted picture (i.e., delusion).
(ii) The researcher is led to have low confidence in a distorted picture.
(iii) The researcher obtains no picture.

Critics of using a Euclidean framework seem to assume that the first possibility is the most likely. Persons who subject their theories to quantitative test, however, have been humbled by empirical evidence often enough to know better (for example, Levin, Pressley, McCormick, Miller and Shriberg, 1979). The second and third possibilities are also undesirable, but both do provide built-in incentive for the researcher to revise her or his theory.

Quantification Discards Idiopathic Information

A common overstatement is that quantitative research focuses on statements generalizable to a population, and in the process discards important idiopathic information. Some quantitative applications do that, and others do not (Cronbach, 1957). Quantification can help to detect and illuminate atypical cases. For instance, I have triangulated regression residuals, interview records, and anecdotal descriptions to illuminate the peculiar (and different) preoccupations of two children (Price, 1977, pp. 80–1). In a study of teachers' expectations, Hwang (1982) used the techniques prospectively, selecting for extra interviewing students whose profiles on certain measures were anomalously situated in Euclidean space (i.e., outliers). In a study probing how some kindergarten teachers create immaturity-tolerant environments (and others, immaturity-penalizing environments), Kehl (1989) used achievement-on-age regressions of several successive kindergarten cohorts as a quantitative means of describing individual teachers.

Quantification Entails Unrealistic Distributional Assumptions

The last red herring is the claim that quantification entails unrealistic distributional assumptions. An extreme form of this claim is that observations are forced in quantitative research to conform to a normal curve. Methods of statistically describing a sample generally do not impose normality. Nor, for that matter, do they require one to assume a normal distribution. The assumption of a distribution comes into play only at the point when the researcher wishes to make a probabilistic statement about the population represented by her or his sample. Even in the case where such assumptions are made, they are often approximately true. Moreover, some forms of statistical inference are known not to go far awry even though the real distribution differs markedly from the assumed distribution.

The foregoing list of red herrings will have had its intended effect if well-founded criticisms of quantitative methods replace frivolous criticisms. There are well-founded criticisms, in my estimation, such those described below.

Gary Glen Price

Real Vices

There are legitimate criticisms that can be made of quantitative research. Most of those criticisms concern unexamined traditions widely followed by quantitative educational researchers. As such, those are vices of quantifiers (not of quantification itself). I do see one real vice of quantification.

A Vice of Quantification

Wrong numbers — There is one *risk* in quantification that is so great that I have chosen to consider it a *vice*. That is the risk of *wrong numbers*. These can result from unwitting errors in numerical data records. They can also result from mistakes in logic. Both kinds of error are easy to make, hard to catch after they are made, and sometimes serious. I am sadly sure that wrong numbers regularly lead useful insights to be lost and artifactually erroneous insights to be found. Errors of this kind occur in many research reports, and they occasionally receive critical reanalysis (for example, Price and Gillingham, 1985; Price, Walsh, and Vilberg, 1984).

The reader may believe that incompetent researchers rather than quantification, per se, should be blamed for this problem of *wrong numbers*. But — as with nuclear plant design and automobile safety — somewhere there is a point where one ceases to blame persons who have difficulty with a fussy tool, and one begins to blame the tool (Norman, 1988).

Vices of Quantifiers

In the section on red herrings, I took exception when practices of some quantitative researchers were used to deny certain possibilities of quantitative research. I argued that sensible uses of quantification are feasible, and I dismissed claims to the contrary. For that purpose, it did not matter whether sensible uses are common or rare. In this section, I judge quantitative research by what is prevalent, not by what is feasible.

Vestiges of positivism — Positivism, also known as *scientific empiricism*, refuses to concede the status of reality to things not directly observable. In educational research, the most blatant expression of this view is behaviorism, which eschews mental and cognitive constructs. Although behaviorism lost its dominant position in American psychology a decade or two ago, some positivist habits linger on in educational research. Inattention to the thoughts, customs, and intentions of subjects is one such habit. This vestige of positivism in the habits of some quantitative researchers is antithetical to research on multicultural education. As argued previously, this is a vice of some quantifiers, not a vice of quantification of itself.

Another vestige of positivism is *definitional operationalism* — the tendency of some quantitative researchers to regard theory as no more than parameterized relations between directly measured variables (Wimsatt, 1981). A noted sociologist (Blalock, 1967) provided a clear example of this positivist tendency when he wrote, 'I would maintain that it is preferable to attempt to state general laws that interrelate variables in terms of hypothetical "if-then" statements. These could be of the form, "If X changes by one unit under conditions A, B, and C, then Y should change by b_{yx} units".'

Self-sufficient studies as the ideal — Another vice prevalent among quantitative educational researchers is the disinclination to rest part of an argument on the findings of another researcher. The costly ideal is to have every study be a definitive one — free standing and self-sufficient. The findings of other researchers are cited abundantly to motivate a study, but seldom as premises in a chain of reasoning. There is a paradox in this tendency:

    (i)   Quantitative researchers make much ado about the generalizability of their findings.

    (ii)   Quantitative researchers seldom treat the findings of other quantitative researchers as though they were generalizable.

Role of a priori prediction — The reconstructed logic of much quantitative research derogates *a posteriori* explanation no matter how resistant the *a posteriori* explanation is to rival explanations. In contrast, *a priori* explanations are often accepted uncritically. I would like to argue that the temporal relationship between data collection and the formulation of a theoretical statement deserves much less importance than it is given. More important than the distinction between *a priori* and *a posteriori* is the question of whether known rival interpretations can be nullified. According to the prevalent mentality, the truth value of a theoretical statement is enhanced by the researcher's having anticipated the shape of the data. It seems to me a peculiar sort of researcher arrogance that so much stock should be placed in the researcher's anticipation of a result. Worse still, there is the temptation to say, 'I predicted it, therefore my theory is right', which commits the logical fallacy of *affirming the consequent.*

Caricature of hypothetico-deductive reasoning — The majority of dissertators include hypotheses in their dissertation proposals. Few can give a good answer to the question, 'Of what consequence will it be if your results do or do not agree with your hypotheses?' For those whose hypotheses are directed to empirical replication, their hypotheses are nothing more than projections from past experience. For them, a failed hypothesis is simply evidence that the world is difficult to predict. For those whose hypotheses are personalized projections, a failed hypothesis is evidence of individual failure, if that; as such, the fate of the hypothesis is of little public interest. When hypotheses are (a) logically implied by one theory; and (b) logically at odds with the implications of a rival theory, there are clear theoretical consequences of failed hypotheses. The purpose of hypothesis-testing is clear in this last case, and there is good reason for public interest in the fate of the hypothesis. In the former cases (empirical replicability and personalized projection), there is questionable value in contorting non-hypothetico-deductive studies into the framework of hypothetico-deductive reasoning.

Fashion in quantitative research methods — Research methods do wax and wane in popularity. Although I would never urge a student or colleague to choose methods on the basis of their popularity, thoughtful consideration of methods ought to include cognizance of their past and current popularity. This chapter offers no appraisals of the popularity of particular methods, but a reader can certainly make such appraisals in a particular journal or in the meetings of a particular professional association. In such surveys, one soon finds that a method popular in one network of scholars will be unpopular in another. This waxing and waning can apply to groups of methods (for example, quantitative, qualitative) and to specific techniques within a group (for example, factor analysis). In the aftermath of Darwin's success in biology, the *sine qua non* of educational science became methodical, copious record-keeping, as exemplified in the Child Study movement (Hall, 1891). In the third quarter of this century, it seems to have been the generalizability of observed patterns. In the last decade, it seems to have been the vividness of descriptive categories that emerged from participant observation. The careful researcher will appreciate the fickle nature of such norms. Two memorable reflections on fashion in research methods are quoted below.

> Any brilliant achievement, on which attention is temporarily focussed, may give a prestige to the method employed, or to some part of it, even in applications to which it has no special appropriateness. (Fisher, 1953, p. 184)

> I call it *law of the instrument*, and it may be formulated as follows: Give a small boy a hammer, and he will find that everything he encounters needs pounding.... What is objectionable is not that some techniques are pushed to the utmost, but that others, in consequence, are denied the name of science. (Kaplan, 1964, pp. 28–9)

Susceptibility to swings in fashion, often without compelling reason, is not limited to quantitative researchers. The susceptibility nevertheless exists in quantitative researchers, and it does deserve to be counted as a vice.

Real Differences

I attempt in this section to probe beneath surface methodological differences between qualitative and quantitative research. Beneath the methodological surface, there appear to be some seldom-articulated philosophical differences that separate the camps. These are enumerated and examined below.

The adjectives 'quantitative' and 'qualitative' do a disservice because they suggest that the main differences are in the methodological trappings with which one does research. I believe those surface differences are ancillary. They may excite the neophyte, but surely the emotional commitment of mature researchers to one camp or another comes from something deeper. Of those deeper differences, two are suggested here.

The first deeper difference is a matter of scholarly orientation. Habermas (1968/1971) aptly labeled two orientations as (i) the empirical-analytic sciences; and (ii) the historical-hermeneutic sciences. Empirical-analytic sciences have a referential and ultimately technical thrust. Their theories are about the empirical world and are testable in it. The historical-hermeneutic sciences seek to elucidate meanings by constructing new understanding from existing meanings, as in mathematics, and by analyzing the intersubjective processes through which meaning is generated, as in history. This distinction between scholarly orientations imperfectly separates the qualitative and quantitative camps in educational research. Some qualitative researchers obviously do have a referential and technical thrust. Some quantitative researchers, like several whose work is reviewed by Shepard (1980), elucidate meanings in their special way.

A second and related difference is a matter of disciplinary affiliation and economic self-interest. Persons who affiliate with different disciplines differ in what social and educational phenomena they find most interesting. Limitations in the funding of educational research create a zero-sum game that fosters sniping at competitors for scarce funds; resulting competition is especially likely to affect emerging fields of inquiry like research in multicultural education. Also, disciplines make different assumptions about which simplifications are the most risky to make. To the extent that funds for research are distributed to differing methodological traditions, the amount of research concerning multicultural education will depend on the methodological diversity of persons doing research on it.

Considerations for Improving the Quality of Quantitative Research

Like the slow reader subjected to instruction that exclusively emphasizes low-level skills and thereby never allows him or her to experience the rewards and subtleties of reading, most researchers and graduate students conclude that all of statistics is as constraining as the topics they encounter in entry-level courses. This is regrettable. A sort of quantitative liberation can be achieved with sufficient grounding; precious few substantively directed educational researchers stay engaged long enough in quantitative courses to reach that take-off speed.

A common complaint of persons concerned with a new field of inquiry is that existing quantitative methods seem badly suited to their purpose. A common response to this problem is simply to avoid using quantitative methods. King (1989, p. 3) discusses the problem with this reaction, which also occurs in his field (political science):

> Since data in political science do not permit a standard set of statistical assumptions, some argue that we should use only very simple quantitative methods. But this is precisely incorrect. Indeed, sophisticated methods are required only when data are problematic; extremely reliable data with sensational relationships require little if any statistical analysis.

A corresponding moral can be drawn for research in education in general and multicultural education in particular: problems that fail to conform with ordinary statistical assumptions call for greater statistical sophistication, not for a retreat from statistics.

A productive response is to get well enough grounded in the underlying logic and mathematics to invent one's own methods. Important innovations have usually come from quantitative knowledge coupled with substantive knowledge and inventiveness. Many have followed this path productively, and those wishing to contribute methodological innovations to research in multicultural education could benefit from studying innovations made in other substantive contexts. Some exemplars worth examining are King (1989) in political science; Wohlwill (1973) in the longitudinal study of psychological development; Webb, Campbell, Schwartz, Sechrest and Grove (1981) in minimizing the reactivity of observations; Wright (1920) in complex causal paths in genetics; Spearman (1904) in ferreting out patterns that underlie individuals' performances on diverse psychological tests; Cronbach (1951) and Cronbach, Gleser, Nanda and Rajaratnam (1972) in the dependability of behavioral measurements; Fisher (1953) in agricultural experiments; and Gosset (1908) and Deming (1975) in quality control.

Notes

1 One may seriously question the pretension that 'qualitative research' is a 'new paradigm' (as popularly derived from Kuhn, 1970b). In Kuhn's sense (1970b, pp. 92–110; 1974), scientific revolution occurs when the contending theory *subsumes* the old one by equalling the old theory on the factual turf of the old theory, and bettering the old theory on the other factual turf. Inasmuch as 'qualitative research' does not explain away (or even heed) the factual turf of old theories, its rise to fashion hardly constitutes a paradigm shift.
2 *High inference description* embraces *indirect observables* and *constructs*, as those terms are used by Kaplan (1964) pp. 34–62.
3 Some theories make explicit qualitative predictions. To the extent that their predictions are explicit, they are thereby made *empirically commensurable* with rival theories. They are also, however, thereby made vulnerable to the charge that they oversimplify.

References

ANDERBERG, M.R. (1973) *Cluster Analysis For Applications*, New York, Academic Press.
ANDERSON, J.A. and ROSENFELD, E. (Eds) (1988) *Neurocomputing: Foundations of Research*, Cambridge, MA, MIT Press.
APPLE, M.W. (1979) *Ideology and Curriculum*, London, Routledge and Kegan Paul.
BLALOCK, H.M., JR. (1967) 'Causal inferences, closed populations, and measures of association', *American Political Science Review*, **61**, pp. 130–6.
CANTOR, G. (1890–91) 'Über eine elementare Frage der Mannigfältigkeitslehre', *Jaresberichte der deutschen Mathematiker-Vereinigungen*, **1**, pp. 75–8.
COOK, T.D. and CAMPBELL, D.T. (1979) *Quasi-experimentation: Design and Analysis Issues for Field Settings*, Chicago, IL, Rand McNally.
CRONBACH, L.J. (1951) 'Coefficient alpha and the internal structure of tests', *Psychometrika*, **16**, pp. 297–334.
CRONBACH, L.J. (1957) 'The two disciplines of scientific psychology', *American Psychologist*, **12**, pp. 671–84.
CRONBACH, L.J. (1988) 'Five perspectives on validity argument' in WAINER, H. and BRAUN, H.I. (Eds) *Test Validity*, Hillsdale, NJ, Lawrence Erlbaum.
CRONBACH, L.J., GLESER, G.C., NANDA, H. and RAJARATNAM, N. (1972) *The Dependability of Behavioral Measurements: Theory of Generalizability for Scores and Profiles*, New York, Wiley.

DEMING, W.E. (1975) 'On probability as a basis for action', *American Statistician*, **29**, 4, pp. 146–52.

EASTERLING, D.V. (1987) 'Political science: Using the generalized Euclidean model to study ideological shifts in the US Senate' in YOUNG, F.W. and HAMER, R.M. (Ed.) *Multidimensional Scaling: History, Theory, and Applications*, Hillsdale, NJ, Lawrence Erlbaum.

EVERITT, B.S. (1980) *Cluster Analysis* (2nd edn), London, Heineman Education Books.

FISHER, R.A. (1953) *The Design of Experiments*, London, Oliver and Boyd.

GOSSET, W.S. (1908) 'The probable error of a mean', *Biometrika*.

HABERMAN, S.J. (1978–79) *Analysis of Qualitative Data* (Vols. 1–2), New York, Academic Press.

HABERMAS, J. (1968/1971) *Knowledge and Human Interests* (translated by J.J. Shapiro). Boston, MA, Beacon Press.

HALL, G.S. (1891) 'The contents of children's minds on entering school', *Pedagogical Seminary*, **1**, pp. 139–73.

HOWSON, C. and URBACH, P. (1989) *Scientific Reasoning: The Bayesian Approach*, La Salle, IL, Open Court.

HWANG, J. (1982) 'The determinants and consistency of teachers' expectations: The evidence from Taiwan', (doctoral dissertation, University of Wisconsin-Madison (1981), *Dissertation Abstracts International*, **42**.

JOHNSON, D.J. (1988) 'Identity formation and racial coping strategies of black children and their parents: A stress and coping paradigm', doctoral dissertation, Northwestern University (1987), *Dissertation Abstracts International*, **48**.

KAPLAN, A. (1964) *The Conduct of Inquiry: Methodology for Behavioral Science*, San Francisco, CA, Chandler Publishing.

KEHL, R.L. (1989) '*Kindergarten entry-age and achievement by specific kindergarten teacher groups*', a thesis submitted in partial fulfillment of the requirements for the degree of MS, Department of Curriculum and Instruction, University of Wisconsin-Madison.

KING, G. (1989) *Unifying Political Methodolgy: The Likelihood Theory of Statistical Inference*, Cambridge, Cambridge University Press.

KUHN, T.S. (1970a) 'Logic of discovery or psychology of research' in LAKATOS, I. and MUSGRAVE, A. (Eds) *Criticism and the Growth of Knowledge*, Cambridge, Cambridge University Press.

KUHN, T.S. (1970b) *The Structure of Scientific Revolutions* (2nd edn) Chicago, IL, University of Chicago Press.

KUHN, T.S. (1971) 'The relations between history and the history of science', *Daedalus*, **100**, pp. 271–304.

KUHN, T.S. (1974) 'Second thoughts on paradigms' in SUPPE, F. (Ed.) *The Structure of Scientific Theories*, Urbana, IL, University of Illinois Press.

LAVE, C.A. and MARCH, J.G. (1975) *An Introduction to Models in the Social Sciences*, New York, Harper and Row.

LEVIN, J.R., PRESSLEY, M., McCORMICK, C.B., MILLER, G.E. and SHRIBERG, L.K. (1979) 'Assessing the classroom potential of the keyword method', *Journal of Educational Psychology*, **71**, pp. 583–94.

LOEHLIN, J.C. (1987) *Latent Variable Models: An Introduction to Factor, Path, and Structural Analysis*, Hillsdale, NJ, Lawrence Erlbaum Associates.

MESSICK, S. (1988) 'The once and future issues of validity: Assessing the meaning and consequences of measurement' in WAINER, H. and BRAUN, H.I. (Eds) *Test Validity*, Hillsdale, NJ, Lawrence Erlbaum.

NORMAN, D.A. (1988) *The Psychology of Everyday Things*, New York, Basic Books.

PAULOS, J.A. (1988) *Innumeracy: Mathematical Illiteracy and its Consequences*, New York, Hill and Wang.

POPPER, K.R. (1972) *Objective Knowledge: An Evolutionary Approach*, Oxford, Oxford University Press.

PRICE, G.G. (1977) 'How cognitive abilities of preschool children are influenced by maternal teaching behavior: A causal model analysis', doctoral dissertation, Stanford University (1976) *Dissertation Abstracts International*, **37**, 6377A (University Microfilms No. 77-7149, 135).

PRICE, G.G. and GILLINGHAM, M.G. (1985) 'Effects of mothers' overestimations and underestimations of their children's intellectual ability: A reanalysis of Hunt and Paraskevopoulos', *Journal of Genetic Psychology*, **146**, pp. 477–81.

PRICE, G.G., WALSH, D.J. and VILBERG, W.R. (1984) 'The confluence model's good predictions of mental age beg the question', *Psychological Bulletin*, **96**, pp. 195–200.

QUINE, W.V. (1972) *Methods of Logic* (3rd edn) New York, Holt, Rinehart and Winston.

SPEARMAN, C. (1904). 'General Intelligence', objectively determined and measured. American Journal of Psychology, **15**, pp. 201–92.

SHEPARD, R.N. (1980) 'Multidimensional scaling, tree-fitting, and clustering', *Science*, **210**, pp. 390–8.

SLEETER, C.E. and GRANT, C.A. (1987) 'An analysis of multicultural education in the United States', *Harvard Educational Review*, **57**, pp. 421–44.

WASSERMAN, P. (1989) *Neural Computing: Theory and Practice*, New York, Van Nostrand Reinhold.

WEBB, E.J., CAMPBELL, D.T., SCHWARTZ, R.D., SECHREST, L. and GROVE, J.B. (1981) *Non-reactive Measures in the Social Sciences* (2nd edn) Boston, MA, Houghton Mifflin.

WIMSATT, W.C. (1981) 'Robustness, reliability, and overdetermination' in BREWER, M.B. and COLLINS, B.E. (Eds) *Scientific Inquiry and the Social Sciences*, San Francisco, CA, Jossey-Bass, pp. 124–63.

WOHLWILL, J.T. (1973) *The Study of Behavioral Development*, New York, Academic Press.

WRIGHT, S. (1920) The relative importance of heredity and environment in determining the prebald pattern of given fig. *Proceedings of the National Academy of Science*, **6**, pp. 320–32.

YOUNG, F.W. (1987) (edited by HAMER, R.M.) *Multidimensional Scaling: History, Theory, and Applications*, Hillsdale, NJ, Lawrence Erlbaum.

Chapter 6

Using Multiple Strategies to Assess Multicultural Education in a School District[1]

Kathryn M. Borman, Patricia Timm, Zakia El-Amin and Markay Winston

Common ground among academicians on the tenets of multicultural education has been difficult to reach since theorizing on the subject began in earnest during the early 1980s. However, advocates of a multiculturalist form of education have increasingly reached consensus on a number of points.

For example, multiculturalists are united in their rejection of the ethnocentrism and denial of differences that characterized the assimilationist beliefs of the 1960s.[2] Further, although less consensus has been reached in the realm of teacher preparation than in the areas of school context (Lynch, 1986) and curriculum, major school policy reforms such as the creation of an egalitarian institutional environment in schools by the elimination of tracking are becoming accepted wisdom (Oakes, 1985). However, despite the growing consensus among scholars, it appears that we may have miles to go before common ground is approached by school board members, school administrators, teaching staff and members of a particular school system's community constituency. This was perhaps the most discouraging lesson we learned in conducting the study we discuss in this chapter.

Although we are rather skeptical about the intent of the district in question to change fundamental approaches to school practices and the curriculum, we believe that our approach in assessing its racial environment uncovered information that could be used by this or any other district to alter structural and organizational features in the areas of administrative practices, home-school relations, race relations and multicultural education. In order to establish a multicultural agenda for school practices, it is necessary to first assess where current practices are falling short of the ideal. This was the assumption guiding the school district assessment that we describe in the remainder of this chapter.

Our major intention is to provide an overview of the research carried out in the district in question, describe the methodologies employed in the study, present a portion of the findings, particularly the set of findings on deep divisions between parents and teachers and between African-American and white parents, and conclude with a partial discussion of recommendations based on our assessment. Our discussion of recommendations is limited to the realm of multicultural education and is juxtaposed to our assessment of the sobering realities we fear may prevent their implementation. The interest in presenting the narrative in the fashion we have just outlined is not to gauge either how effective the method was or how appropriate the recommendations were — it's too soon to tell — but rather, the hope is that our experience might provide a useful commentary for others contemplating similar research in a multiracial school district context.

Background to the Study

The setting for the research was a low income, biracial suburban school district contiguous to a large midwestern city. The 1460 students in grades K-12 come from the small city of South Riverside[3] and the neighboring unincorporated community of West Riverside. South Riverside has a declining population of 11,000 predominantly white residents. This working class community is characterized by a bipolar population of older citizens who have been in the city since birth and young families in starter homes who move out as they grow more affluent. The city's small, tract houses constructed during the building booms which followed both World Wars are well maintained and line quiet, residential streets.

West Riverside, contiguous to South Riverside, was settled by African-Americans at the turn of the century. They purchased parcels of land from a white developer who, for reasons that are unclear, established the sub-division solely for them (Redman-Rengstorf, 1955). Relative followed relative, purchasing the lots with small down payments, leaving the tenements of the city for the security of home ownership. Homes were built room by room as materials and funds were available. Today, West Riverside's population is nearly 1100. Census data reveal that 10 per cent of the residents are college graduates, while 35 per cent have less than an eight grade education. Twenty-five per cent of households in West Riverside have annual incomes above $25,000; 11 per cent have no employed workers. Those who are employed, for the most part, work either as laborers or in technical, sales and clerical occupations. A smaller number are employed in managerial and professional positions while approximately 10 per cent of West Riverside residents receive public assistance.

West Riverside has seven active congregations including the influential First Baptist Church where a succession of pastors has taken up a number of efforts to improve community services. Over the years, mail service, a sewer system, and paved roads have been installed as a result of community activism led by the redoubtable Reverend Edward James, Minister of the First Baptist Church for fifty-five years. It is clear that despite the community's relatively limited political and economic resources, it has throughout its history mobilized to claim its due.

The South Riverside School District maintains two elementary schools and a combined junior-senior high school including grades 7–12. Having suffered a series of financial catastrophes as a result of a number of failed tax levies and the fiscal mismanagement of a recent superintendent, the district was sent reeling in April 1988 when a mid-morning fist fight among several students in the South

Riverside High School building closed the school for the day and surfaced charges from the West Riverside community of pervasive racial inequities. Today, a year after the fight, adolescent residents of both communities are philosophical about the occurrence and discount it as a media event, although African-American students, such as one 17-year-old young woman, assert that her West Riverside peers are pressured to conform to a white standard in their behavior and dress. Further, while there may be little or no overt hostility perceived by adolescents of both races, some adult authority figures in the community such as police and local business people are judged to be prejudiced by the students.

At the time of the event, some, particularly school teaching staff, dismissed the fight or 'the incident' as it was generally termed by the white community as a creation of the media. Indeed, the media's coverage of the story for the press and local television as a racially motivated eruption of hostility was thoroughly unflattering and ill-founded from both the teachers' and the school board's perspectives. However, others, particularly adult residents of West Riverside, were reluctant to dismiss it as a non-event or to put the matter aside. For them, and decisively so for members of the West Riverside Civic Association, the fight, or 'the riot', as they termed it, was a violent manifestation of issues that had been unresolved in the school district for years.

In order to create a 'better school environment' in the district, members of the West Riverside community formed the Student Affairs Committee (SAC) and took as its mission the charge 'to bring about positive changes in the South Riverside School system in relation to practices, policies, programs and personnel'. These changes would result, the SAC organizers declared, in benefits to all students by creating a 'better, more productive educational atmosphere'.[4] Changes would be achieved by a process that was 'logical, peaceful, bi-partisan and harmonious' and that was requisite in a 'troubled school system at least twenty years out of step with progress'. The Student Affairs Committee pushed its demands to the attention of the school district not only in meetings with the outgoing School System Superintendent but also in statements to the press and ultimately to the State Superintendent of Schools.

A letter requesting state intervention was filed 13 May, 1988 citing the insensitivity of the current school administration, the psychological oppression and physical abuse by teachers and aides of African-American students; the lack of an African-American presence in the district in the ranks of the school board and administrative staff; and the fiscal irresponsibility of the current administration which, the petition charged, had led to a 'decrease in teacher morale and increased teacher apathy toward students, especially the black student population'.[5] Copies of the letter were sent to a range of politically prominent individuals including US Senators John Glenn, Stanley Aronoff and Howard Metzenbaum and Secretary of Education William Bennett.

The response from the State was swift. The Assistant Superintendent of Public Instruction for the State of Ohio appeared at an August meeting of the Student Affairs Committee pledging to provide $5000 to be matched by the district to fund a study to evaluate the racial climate of the schools. It was at this point that we were requested by the new South Riverside superintendent, Solomon Williams, to undertake 'a cultural assessment' study of the district.

The Study

Because he had inherited the legacy of a school district plagued not only with charges of racism from a constituent community but also saddled with a $575,000 deficit, Superintendent Williams was reluctant to request funds from his board to support the study, a project he consistently stated had his full support.

At the time that he made his initial request to the University of Cincinnati, the Superintendent's hope was that the Dean's Office in the College of Education would provide services in conducting the study without charge. However, because the effort of graduate students in the College was necessary to carry out the work, a campaign was undertaken to gain supplementary funding from two Cincinnati-based foundations which together matched the State's grant of $5000. This sum partially covered the stipends of three doctoral students (El-Amin, Timm and Winston). The College absorbed costs connected with secretarial support, xeroxing and data analysis, as well as the effort of the Associate Dean of Graduate Studies and Research (Borman). A mission of the University of Cincinnati and of the College of Education is to provide community service in the form of applied research and the project was viewed as consistent with this goal. By any reasonable estimate, the study generated at least $50,000 worth of data analysis. Without question, the district got a bargain.

The next task was to assemble a team that would have credibility with all the constituencies involved: school system administration; school staff and faculty; and both the white and African-American communities, the major racial populations represented in the district. Zakia El-Amin, director of educational programs for the Cincinnati Urban League, Patricia Timm, community activist and founder of Cincinnatians Active to Save Education, an advocacy group organized to rally community support for a crucial tax levy campaign in 1980, and Markay Winston, an African-American whose roots were not in Cincinnati but whose cultural heritage emphasized a strong church-based community activism, comprised the graduate student research team.

Timm, a neighborhood activist trained in Alinsky organizations in Chicago, urged the formation of an Advisory Committee. This interdisciplinary group of scholars and practitioners included a political scientist who lead the fair housing office in the metropolitan area, several specialists in organizational development and change, a corporate trainer, and an officer of the local chapter of NAACP, as well as race relations specialists from the University. The Advisory Committee met with the assessment team three times during the study, initially to guide the formation of the research questions and the procedures, later to look at the questionnaire results, and finally to review the findings. It was in the Advisory Committee proceedings that the plan was made to have constituent groups in the school district explore the meanings of the research findings in focus groups and then to generate recommendations for district action.

With the team in place and funding secured, we were ready in the fall of 1988 to begin our work in the schools and the community. The immediate concern expressed by both school district administrative staff and community members was to understand how the fight that had broken out in April among high school students was or was not a reflection of deeply felt hostilities and alienation. From the outset, school district administrative staff held firm to the belief that the fist fight was an isolated incident rather than one event in an ongoing series of occurrences. The team's conversations with the residents of the West Riverside community prompted us to view the administration's perspective cautiously.

As the team of researchers developed the scope of work for the study, a number of objectives were formulated. These included:

At the district and administrative staff levels:

1 To assess the nature of school/community relations.
2 To describe student educational programs, teaching staff characteristics and the nature of student achievements and aspirations.
3 To determine the rank order of school objectives as assessed by school principals and district objectives as assessed by the Superintendent and Assistant Superintendent.
4 To document district and school level programs that address issues related to cultural diversity, inter-group relations and the like.

At the school level, focused on teachers:

To assess teacher perceptions of school and classroom conditions related to equity issues and intergroup relations in particular.

At the school level, focused on students:

1 To profile 6–12 grade students, including family demographic data, student experiences, values, attitudes and self-esteem.
2 To assess student perceptions of school race relations, including text-books, classroom activities, extra-curricular activities, sports programs, and friendship policies.
3 To identify any differences in the perceptions and experiences of black and white students.

At the community level, focused on parents:

1 To profile parents of students enrolled in grades K-12, including family demographic data, parental perceptions of their child's program placement, participation in extra-curricular activities and other child-related activities.
2 To assess parent perceptions of school and classroom conditions related to equity issues and intergroup relations in particular.

These four sets of objectives were anchored to the four constituencies that we identified both as stake holders in the research and as sources of information: the administration, representing the district, and including the superintendent, his staff, school board members and building principals; the teaching staffs at the district's three schools; the students, especially those in grades 6–12 whose age and experience would enable them to understand and articulate multi-racial issues; and parents who as representatives of the community would have direct experience with the district's stance on matters related to racial equality in the schools.

At the conclusion of the study in June, an initial report was submitted by the researchers to the Superintendent. It was organized to provide information based on the four sources of data. A subsequent report in August provided recommendations based on the findings and on discussions in focus groups held in the community. We will return to a discussion of both findings and recommendations in a later section of this chapter. We turn next to the methodological concerns that influenced our approach to the study.

Determining the Methods of Research

In undertaking a project with a timeline extending from the beginning of the school year in September to the following June, we faced the constraint of a limited timeframe in which to gather information from a number of individuals inhabiting a large variety of organizational niches. Our objectives and initial research plans dictated a research schedule that would not allow an in-depth observational study much less a true ethnography of schooling (Spindler, 1982). As a result, we were confronted immediately by the need to explore an overall research design that would incorporate multiple methodological strategies.

Thus, data sources for the school district and administrative staff profiles included interviews, questionnaires, individual school and district records, and observations in schools.[6] A series of interviews were conducted with central office staff including Superintendent Williams and Assistant Superintendent Collins. Interviews were also carried out with principals and counselors in each of the three district schools: Beacon Elementary, Calumet Elementary and South Riverside Junior/Senior High School. Observations were carried out in classrooms and schools and school board minutes were consulted.

In order to gain an understanding of school administrators' perceptions of various facets of the school system's current administrative practices, a questionnaire including items extracted from a 1974 survey constructed by the Educational Testing Service was administered to the Superintendent, Assistant Superintendent and school principals. Items on the questionnaire addressed school organizational features, school goals, attendance rates, school/community relations, race relations, extracurricular activities and curricular program offerings. School building and district records were also examined in order to document student programs, enrollment patterns, college plans of students and other indicators of student aspirations and accomplishments.

The data for parent profiles were obtained from a telephone survey conducted with 454 parents of students in grades K-12 in the district. Names and telephone numbers of all parents having at least one child in the district were provided by the school district. Telephone interviews were conducted by university students, supervised by the research team, on evenings and weekends. Of 1059 household listings provided by the district, the 454 completed interviews represented approximately 43 per cent of households having at least one child in a district school.

Respondents included 349 women, 77 per cent of all parents interviewed. The respondents also included ninety African-American parents or 20 per cent of all those interviewed. This percentage is equivalent to the percentage (25 per cent) of African-American students enrolled in district schools.

The development of the survey instrument used to collect information on parents' perceptions of students' school experience included a review of several measures used in previous research designed to capture parental and community responses to the academic and racial climate present in the districts that the earlier researchers had studied. The primary source for items used in the survey was an instrument constructed to evaluate the effects of metropolitan-wide segregation in Indianapolis.[7] The final form of the instrument used in the parent survey portion of the study included sixty-two questions overlapping with similar items investigated in the separate but parallel studies of teachers and students carried out during the research. Subsequent analyses allowed the development of several specific points for discussion, namely teachers' knowledge and practice of multicultural curriculum; race relations; home-school relations; and administrative practices, including discipline and student program placement.

The data for student profiles were compiled from questionnaires completed by 528 district students (80 per cent of eligible enrolled students) in grades 6–12 on 9 February 1989. The survey was administered to students by the research team in the school auditorium. Rather than administering the measure in individual classrooms over a period of four to five days as it would have taken us to do, we were able to meet with all of the students over the course of a single morning, eliminating the likelihood that students from the morning's first session would have had the opportunity to talk about the measure with those whose session was scheduled at a later time. This procedure enabled us to virtually eliminate contamination effects. Students were asked to work independently and were assured that response anonymity would be preserved. The student survey instrument was designed in three parts: Part I included demographic information about the student and the family, including information about self-esteem and student values; Part II assessed student inter-racial experiences, attitudes and values; and Part III was a friendship patterns measure. Many items were developed from instruments used in national research projects.[8] Future analysis comparing these district students to student respondents in national data sets could thus be undertaken.

The data for teacher profiles were drawn from surveys administered to sixty-eight teachers in the South Riverside District, approximately 77 per cent of the teaching staff, on 19 and 20 October 1988. Development of the survey instrument included input from administrators and teachers to determine the appropriateness of the proposed questionnaire. Teacher surveys were administered by members of the University of Cincinnati research staff. The purpose was to assess teacher perceptions of school conditions affecting home-school relations and race relations. Teachers from two of the three schools, Beacon Elementary and the Junior/Senior High school, agreed to participate in a group administration of the survey, requiring approximately thirty minutes to complete. Teachers at the third school, Calumet Elementary, decided not to respond to the survey during the allotted time, and instead returned the surveys by mail approximately two weeks after the initial administration. Because teachers in this school apparently completed the questionnaire as a group, responses to most items were uniform.

The final form of the teacher questionnaire contained forty-eight items focusing on the areas of multicultural curriculum and multicultural teaching; home-school relations, rules and discipline; staff and students' internal integration, and program placement of students. These items, in addition to demographic information, provided the foundation for the subsequent discussion of the results of this portion of the study.

As is clear from the previous discussion of the study's objectives and the methods selected to guide the inquiry, our overarching goal was to provide the district with as clear a picture as possible of constituent perceptions and institutional practices which affect race relations. Our initial report to Superintendent Williams was a summary of the data gathered during the study. Our intent was to inspire the district to confront its multiple images, make sense of the contradictions and divisions that presented themselves and to construct appropriate recommendations for making major system-wide reforms. To accomplish this goal, following a presentation of findings to the administration and to the West Riverside Student Affairs Committee, a series of focus groups was scheduled with constituent groups in the community.

Focus group discussions are, in our view, an important vehicle for conducting multicultural research studies. The focus group method allows for group interaction and insight into why group members hold particular opinions.[9] In the case of our study, we used data collected in the parent, student and teacher-focused portions of the study to organize participant discussion. We conducted two sessions: one with leadership from the Student Affairs Committee in West Riverside; the other with parent organization leaders from South Riverside. The construction of these two sessions is atypical of focus groups both because of the relatively small size and racial homogeneity of the groups that were organized. Each group had four parent participants in addition to two school administrators and two research team members (a facilitator and a recorder). The goals for this phase of the project had been to involve at least seven to ten participants in each group and to hold a series of two focus group sessions. The first series was to have included individuals from specific school sectors (one of parents, teachers, administrators); this would have allowed people who had already established trust and common understanding to explore the research findings together. The second series was to have included participants from each of the constituent groups who would benefit from cross-cultural discussion. The Superintendent had announced the focus group sessions in the local newspapers; he had made no special effort to recruit participants. In both instances, the four who attended were active school-parent leaders. Facilitators for discussion in these groups were in all cases members of the research team.

To encourage initial discussion leading to suggestions for ways to improve race relations in the district, findings were arrayed to illustrate points of contrast and comparison in the data. Thus, as an example, African-American and white parents' and students' responses to questions concerning race relations in the district were profiled together. In all cases white respondents had a more sanguine view of race relations in the district. For example, in response to the statement 'my child has opportunities for positive interracial contact within the school', 63 per cent of African-American parents as compared with 87 per cent of white parents agreed that this is usually or always the case. Only 5 per cent of white parents thought that this is seldom or never the case while 20 per cent of African-American parents held this position. This pattern of results held throughout the data.

Particularly provocative, we felt, were contrasting findings from teacher and parent surveys. These data showed that although equal percentages (63 per cent) of African-American parents *and* district teachers believed that communication between the school and African-American parents is usually or always effective, almost a third of African-American parents stated that communication is seldom or never effective, while *not a single teacher in the district* shared this view.

While we felt it was important for participants in focus group discussions to comprehend the deep divisions that existed in the district between African-Americans and whites and between parents and teachers, we were most concerned that the discussions move from defensiveness and blaming toward sharing personal ideas, feelings and observations. Participants genuinely sought to understand the data before them, and the process allowed interaction to occur among participants building on each other's insights. In both cases, the focus group discussions permitted parents to sort through some of the conflicting data, giving voice and legitimization to their opinions. African-American participants concluded that although parental responses to items were frequently negative, the data did not accurately reflect the depth of alienation felt by residents of West Riverside. The white parent school leaders agonized over other parents' unwillingness to join in their school parent organization efforts.

Our evaluation of the outcome of the focus group discussions is mixed. On the one hand, parents who attended the session thought that progress was being made. The media, a factor in district events from the April 1988 fight onward, reported the optimism and hope for the future expressed by the parent participants who were interviewed following the July focus group sessions. On the other hand, only a small number of parents attended each of the two focus group meetings held in the community. Among white parents the discussion often became stuck on such points as interpreting the meaning of the results. For example, in noting the tendency of African-American parents to report that communications between home and school are seldom or never effective, white parents offered the interpretation that this response might simply indicate that parents were out of the home and couldn't be reached by the school or that African-American parents might view communications as poor or ineffective if they were not securing the results they desired. In fact, the overall conclusion reached by white parents in this focus group discussion was that *parents* needed to exert more effort to improve home-school communications.

In their discussion of multicultural education, white parents suggested that supplementary materials should be provided by the district or at least identified by the central administration. In this way teachers could be encouraged to provide multicultural materials throughout the school year rather than during Black History Week alone. We found this recommendation from white parents to be encouraging. However, these same parents persisted in their belief that *parents* should teach children about their heritage since this was not necessarily the teacher's job and that *teachers* should teach 'equality' rather than address cultural difference in their classrooms.

The focus group sessions failed to generate specific recommendations intended to change school practices, but they provided an essential step in the progress of the study. Having had an opportunity to gather, share their frustrations and defend their efforts, focus group participants seem ready at this writing to move forward with the district to solve its problems. The question remains to what extent the district administrative and teaching staffs are prepared to move ahead. We turn to this question in the final section of this chapter.

Conclusion

We have written this chapter at a time when we are still engaged with the South Riverside School District in jointly forming recommendations and at a time when teachers have not as yet met to discuss results and to plan ways they wish to direct their efforts. Although there will be additional discussions and plans have already been made by the district for human relations training for the 1989/90 school year, we are not optimistic about an implementation of a comprehensive district-wide change effort, particularly at the classroom level. However, we are convinced that the West Riverside community has become politically energized through the process of the assessment study. For the first time in school district history an African-American candidate, a resident of West Riverside and parent of three children attending district schools, has come forward as a contestant in the school board election. Moreover, he has mounted a campaign and appears to be gaining ground in the white neighborhoods of South Riverside. We were present at a meeting of the West Riverside Student Affairs Committee when Reverend Birdsell's candidacy was announced and have provided technical support to his campaign.

In addition, we have submitted a second report for the Superintendent's use. This 'Report of Findings and Recommendations' contained very precise recommendations in each of the four areas examined in the study: administrative practices, home-school relations, race relations and multicultural education. Although it will be up to the district to devise the specific committee structures, timelines and evaluation plans to implement our recommended strategies, we have been very specific in our recommendations, have connected them to the data base assembled during the course of our year-long study and have used the existing literature as a knowledge base for our recommendations (see Modgil *et al.*, 1986; Ramsey, Vold and Williams, 1989; Bennett, 1986; and Nixon, 1985).

As we have mentioned, the report made recommendations in the areas of multicultural education, race relations, administrative practices and home-school relations. We will limit discussion here to multicultural education. Our seven recommendations in this area were presented as action steps. We cautioned that they must be taken with full discussion and support from all parts of the school community, an action that would signal a dramatic departure from current practice. Administrative leadership would need to take an active stance, articulating a multicultural educational goal as a part of the district's educational plan, and faculty would need to learn to integrate multicultural studies and competencies into the total curriculum, something our data quite clearly indicated they were not currently doing.

Our recommended action steps included the following:

(i) establish culturally inclusive content, language and graphics as essential criteria in textbook adoption;

(ii) establish a Resource Center for the collection of culturally inclusive teaching materials at each school site;

(iii) design classroom and extracurricular opportunities to foster interaction between African-American and white students;
(iv) expand cooperative learning opportunities and mixed ability grouping;
(v) eliminate cultural bias in ability grouping and establish expectations of each child based on realizing his/her full potential;
(vi) whenever appropriate, structure classroom experiences that provide students with the opportunity to learn about their own and others' cultures, customs, and behaviors;
(vii) structure classroom opportunities to allow students to discuss controversial issues, encouraging them to examine and understand their own and others' beliefs, and values and attitudes.

These action goals and practices for multicultural education run parallel to other sets of goals and strategies for race relations, administrative practices and home-school relations presented in the document. Should the district mobilize its efforts around the agenda we have proposed, it would move, as the West Riverside Student Affairs Committee had hoped during the aftermath of the April fight, to bring about a 'better, more productive educational atmosphere'.

In determining why, at least at this juncture, and despite our strongly articulated goal statements, we nonetheless hold relatively little hope for the constituent groups to work together, we have identified three issues and predispositions that may function to keep change in the district at bay. We present them here because we also believe that these factors are likely to surface in most school districts undertaking an assessment of their multicultural programs, patterns of race relations, and administrative practices such as student program placement.

The three factors that seem to present the greatest obstacles to change are racial tension exacerbated by the historical separation of the white and black residential communities that comprise the district; denial and defensiveness, most vigorously displayed by those associated with the school district as members of the administrative staff, board and teachers; and the motives underlying the study. We discuss each of these in detail below.

Long-Standing Racial Tension

Deep divisions between the South Riverside and West Riverside residential communities comprising the district have existed for 100 years. While housing patterns remain segregated and African-American and white institutions, particularly churches, are enclaved, members of both communities will persist in being isolated from each other. It is this isolation that is the fundamental issue in the district because it undergirds patterns of denial and defensiveness and the expedient course taken by the district in undertaking the assessment study we have described here.

The Superintendent and board members throughout the period of study consistently maintained that problems in race relations did not exist before the April 1988 incident. One board member speculated that the African-American community's perceptions both that the police department was racist and that administrative disciplinary practices were discriminatory had *caused* the increased racial hostility. One principal warned that the current study was bringing undesirable attention to 'race'. Far from being either a recent or an ephemeral issue, racial tension has in fact been a persistent problem in the district. School board minutes consulted during the period of study revealed long-standing patterns of racial tension dating back to the early 1960s when the Cincinnati Chapter of the NAACP threatened the district with legal action for maintaining segregated schools.

Site observations by members of the research team revealed that students chose racially homogeneous groups when interacting socially outside the classroom in the lunchroom, corridors, and informal school groups. Participation on athletic teams was viewed by some faculty and community members as bi-racial; while others found that student interest in specific sports activities resulted in teams dominated by one race or the other.

The district has made some efforts to decrease racial isolation since the April fight. A Student Equality Group was organized and supported by teachers in the high school. It was designed to promote discussion and resolution of problems as perceived by the students. The limited participation by all students, especially white students, has, however, minimized its effectiveness. While the district can point to it as a school-led initiative to address racial problems, its failure to involve significant numbers of students in genuine interaction about their beliefs, values, and differences, makes it a rather superficial and low impact strategy. While the high school principal had identified improvement of race relations as a primary objective, new efforts which reach into both formal and informal school settings must be attempted if progress is to be made. Racial isolation, as Myrdal (1944) observed almost fifty years ago, is a persistent American societal dilemma rooted in such racist practices as 'redlining' residential areas to exclude African-Americans. Many whites persist in advocating 'equality' as a goal while not recognizing the insufficiency of their assimilationist and ethnocentric views.

Denial and Defensiveness

In addition to holding to a doctrine of cultural homogeneity and denial of differences cloaked with the veil of 'equality', district parents, school board members, teachers and administrative staff consistently responded defensively at every phase of the study. Although we previewed instruments with teaching staff whom we realized felt embattled, our inquiry was frequently met with hostility.

As we mentioned earlier in this chapter, during the administration of teacher surveys at Calumet Elementary School, teachers refused to complete the questionnaire at the scheduled time. Not surprisingly, once teachers did complete the questionnaires, their patterns of response threw the validity of these data into question. Elementary school staff at this school indicated in their survey responses that they were uniformly satisfied with what they, to a person, described as open, warm, frequent interactions with both African-American and white parents. In contrast, a sizeable percentage (20 per cent) of all black parents were not even aware that they took part annually in making decisions

about their child's academic program and many indicated their general dissatis-
faction with their interactions with their child's school.

Teachers were not alone in their defensiveness. The school board president
acknowledged that the board *never* involved parents and community members
on ad hoc or sub-committees to assist with educational planning and evaluation
or with any other matter. Assistance from individuals in the community was
sought only during repeated and usually unsuccessful efforts to pass school tax
levies. Yet the board president attributed the alienation of the African-
American community to *their own* preconceived (but, in fact, accurate) views of
unfair school disciplinary practices.

Electronic and print media attention following the April fight was a cause of
great concern to some of the board and staff. They felt that they had been
unreasonably accused and tried in advance of a fair hearing. It was argued that
the coincidence of TV reporters' presence in a neighboring community and
subsequent arrival at the school had brought unfair and undeserved negative
attention to the district. Throughout the course of the study, the neighborhood
press stayed in touch with the Superintendent, the College of Education researchers and the West Riverside leadership, seeking updates and outcomes of
the research activities. The resulting accounts in the press were not managed by
the district in such a way as would benefit South Riverside Schools. At times it
appeared that conflicting goals and values of the district and the research team
were played out in print. Rather than working together to develop a program to
improve race relations in the district, it appeared we were at odds with one
another. This may have been another consequence of a defensive administrative
posture. However, media attention can present an extraordinary opportunity to
involve community members in important school discussions; and if managed
well, can bring needed support when undertaking change in a district. Unfortunately, denial and defensiveness persistently blocked such an outcome in this
case.

Motives Prompting the Study

District administrative staff were always responsive to our requests for meetings
and data. Indeed, district administrative staff assembled information on parents
and students and orchestrated and helped supervise the administration of questionnaires to students. However, throughout the study we felt that they were
primarily interested in a 'report card' that found no wrong doing and would in
the end simply make recommendations for small add-ons to the program rather
than fundamentally restructuring it. It may very well have been that this was the
position in the best alignment with the expectations of their board. The staff
seemed to be defensive when looking at the data rather than intent to find a
better understanding of the alienation underlying the racial tension. They consistently spoke about the research, the final report and the final set of recommendations as a 'cultural assessment', appearing to want to avoid facing faculty,
board, or community with issues of racial tension and community alienation.

Had the decision to do an appraisal of the attitudes and experiences of
African-American and white constituents been made by a representative team of

people concerned in the aftermath of the April incident, we believe that we would have met with more cooperation and interest in the results on the part of all concerned. All stakeholders might then have looked forward to what could be learned in the study and how the district could benefit from it. One of the results of the failure of district administrative leadership to gain real support for the study was that teachers, as we have mentioned, were reluctant to participate and were anxious about carrying the burden of guilt should the inquiry find the accusations of the West Riverside residents to be well founded. South Riverside teachers seemed unready to examine the social and political convictions which shape equality policies. They were not seeking innovative practices or collaborative processes, clinging desperately to classroom autonomy.

Faculty, staff, board, and parent organization leadership appeared to hope that the results of the study would get the West Riverside community and the media 'off their back'. In fact, this sentiment was frequently expressed to us by these groups as the primary purpose for the research. It often seemed that only the small group of people who met at the West Riverside Community Center wanted any real change to result from the inquiry.

Questions We Wish We Had Asked

Based on our experiences in the South Riverside School District, we can offer a set of questions to guide other researchers who undertake similar work in racially volatile school systems. These are the questions that we would certainly raise were we to be called upon again to investigate multicultural educational policies and practices in a school system.

- *Why is the school (or district) undergoing the study? What expectations for change are held by key stake-holders?*

A school or district might seek a race assessment in response to either internal or external pressures. Internal pressures from students, parents, faculty or administration may come from a need to resolve a conflict or they may come from a desire to make general improvements in student and staff relations across cultural differences. Internal pressures generated by one constituent group may not be understood by others with either the same commitment to change or the urgency that is felt by another constituent group. External pressures from community members, the media, or governmental units can be resisted by schools and result in defensive or superficial responses. South Riverside School District Administrators sought the study to improve public relations. It was our impression that this purpose limited their commitment to learning things which might seem harmful to the District's public image. In addition it provided little incentive for systemic change when study findings pointed in that direction.

- *What risks is the district taking when inviting outsiders to examine race attitudes, behaviors, and practices?*

As researchers it was essential for us to understand the school staffs fears about what harm might come to their institutions as a result of our investigation. We were mindful of their concern that disclosure of hostile attitudes, negative incidences, or discriminatory practices would have serious public relations consequences. These fears threatened to undermine the study, because they caused the participants to question the validity of the research methodology and to reject the findings. When initiating such a study, the district takes a chance that placing practices under the spotlight will result in improvements. There can be considerable discomfort if the spotlight intensifies everyone's experience of racial differences and provides no pathways to improvement.

- *What researcher methodologies would empower stake-holders to prepare and plan change in personal and institutional practices?*

It may be that our research team's failure to adequately address this question caused us the most difficulty in pursuing with the District improved practices. In particular, our administrative and teacher surveys seemed designed to lead us into the heart of denial. We would be reluctant to enter another study without first working with an administrative leadership core, helping them to identify the feelings and ideas which surround personal and institutional change, and designing appropriate research methodologies. It might be interesting in a future investigation if the researchers planned such a workshop at the outset of the study and included in the workshop design a report of the West Riverside findings. In a simulation exercise participants could consider how they would respond to similar findings. Such an exercise could prepare them for the kinds of feeling, fears and commitments undertaking such a study involves.

- *Could constituent groups have carried our some of the research activities effectively?*

We think so, and that such participation would have resulted in a better understanding of the findings. Had parents participated as telephone interviewers, had teachers sought information about classroom resources for multicultural education, had administrators explored with parents their aspirations and experiences assisting their children, we might have had less resistance to, and a better understanding of, the data collected. We utilized participants in the interpretation of the survey results, but we were disappointed that so few parents joined us in these activities. Had parents, teachers, administrators, and community members been more actively engaged in the design and execution of the study, they would likely have been eager to sort out the meaning of the findings with us. Anyone could have been trained quickly to use the survey instruments. Consider the level of sophistication that participant interviewers might have achieved if they had been involved in obtaining information from the multiple sources.

- *Why use a team research approach?*

Our research team included two African American and two white members. We came from the fields of psychology, sociology, educational administration, and policy analysis. Without the versatility that these backgrounds provided, we could not have collected, managed, or interpreted the data with the comprehension and depth that was required. This was particularly invaluable when we worked together to find the meaning in data analysis. Just as importantly, though, the team effort assured a supportive presence when faced with defensive, entrenched persons. We could look to one another and find the helpful criticism, the friendly support, and the enduring strength that permitted candor, foresight and valor.

- *How do researcher values drive the study and the recommendations?*

As school participants found that the data failed to support assumptions about the presence of race relations problems, either because they believed the problems to be worse than the analysis indicated, or because the analysis revealed levels of differences that they believed could be tolerated, we became increasingly clear that whatever the levels of tension the data indicated, we would want to help the district to design policy and program improvements. That is, that while the analysis would provide a better understanding of the expectations and experiences of school community participants, our value for multicultural education would drive the recommendations we would make to the district. The analysis would help everyone to see the variation and complexity of race relations experience, but no matter how one would interpret that pattern, the ways to improve it would remain about the same: comprehensive multicultural educational programming would improve every school member's understandings and skills for living in a multicultural society. It was this value, in the end, which would drive our recommendations.

- *What decision points might have been established along the way which could have allowed the emerging findings to guide the study effectively?*

At the recommendation of the Advisory Committee, we had identified the focus group discussions as a decision point where the research inquiry could assume new directions. In this investigation it was at this point that we reviewed the low participation, the propensity of white participants to interpret black participant responses, and the defensive posturing of administrative participants. We came to the conclusion that there was not sufficient commitment to make attitude, behavior and policy changes; and thus we prepared a report of the findings and the recommendations for developing a multicultural education program; then we exited.

It would be useful to reflect on the entire investigation and to determine the decision points that might result in flexible and improved investigatory strategies. If initial leader-core sessions or workshops were held, this would provide a point of choices: what constructs would organize the investigation? who would conduct the interviews? how would the data be sorted and interpreted? Following the leader-core session, similar constituent group sessions could be held, perhaps one with teachers, one with other school staff, one of parent leaders.

A second decision point might occur after initial surveys are conducted. Interviewers could compare experiences in data gathering, establishing a set of field notes for later analysis of the research processes. Decisions could be made about missing or insufficient information, and plans could be made for additional inquiry. Researchers could begin to compare the information from various data sources so that the differences and similarities begin to reveal the meaning.

An ideal study would probably allow for a time period in which findings and improvement initiatives overlap, allowing a recursive process to generate recommendations. At this decision point, researchers would work with constituent leaders to identify early initiatives they feel prepared to undertake. Ground would be laid in constituent groups for creative solutions to commonly identified problems to begin to emerge. Groups would begin to report findings to one another and tentative proposals for improvements. The fields would be cross-fertilized allowing new ideas to be tested without undue fear. The decision points that follow would have to do with when and how new policies and programs can be put into place with support from the multiple constituent groups.

Notes

1   The authors acknowledge the helpful comments by William T. Pink on an earlier draft of this chapter and the support of Dean Lonnie H. Wagstaff throughout the course of this study.
2   See Modgil *et al.* (1986), Cummins (1988), Ramsey, Vold and Williams (1989), Bennett (1986) and Nixon (1985).
3   All names associated with the study have been altered.
4   From an article 'The Chairman Speaks' by Robert L. Jones which appeared in the first edition of the Student Affairs Committee Newsletter published by the neighborhood civic association.
5   Letter to the Superintendent of Public Instruction, State of Ohio, Department of Education, 13 May 1988.
6   All data gathering instruments used in this study are available from the authors on request.
7   The Parent Telephone Survey developed by Dr Mary Quilling, Advanced Technologies Inc.
8   See, for example, Forehand, Ragosta and Roc (1976).
9   For a detailed discussion of focus groups as a research tool see Krueger (1988). See also McMillan (1989).

References

BENNETT, C.I. (1986) *Comprehensive Multicultural Education*, Boston, MA, Allyn and Bacon Inc.

CUMMINS, J. (1988) 'From multicultural to anti-racist education: An analysis of programmes and policies in Ontario' in SKUTNABLE-KANGAS, T. and CUMMINS, J. (Eds) *Minority Education*, Philadelphia, PA, Multilingual Matters Ltd.

FOREHAND, G., RAGOSTA, M. and ROCK, D. (1976) *Conditions and Processes of Effective School Desegregation*, Washington DC, US Department of Education, Office of Educational Research and Improvement (OERI).

KRUEGER, R.A. (1988) *Focus Groups: A Practical Guide for Applied Research*, Newburg Park, Sage Publications.

LYNCH, J. (1986) 'An initial typology of perspectives on staff development for

Kathryn M. Borman, Patricia Timm, Zakia El-Amin and Markay Winston

multicultural teacher education' in MODGIL, S., VERMA, G., MALLICK, K. and MODGIL, C. (Eds) *Multicultural Education: The Interminable Debate*, London, Falmer Press.

MCMILLAN, J.H. (1989) 'Focus group interviews: Implications for educational research', paper presented at the annual meeting of the American Educational Research Association, San Francisco, March.

MODGIL, S., VERMA, G., MALLICK, K. and MODGIL, C. (Eds) (1986) *Multicultural Education: The Interminable Debate*, London, Falmer Press.

MYRDAL, G. (1944) *An American Dilemma*, New York, Macmillan.

NIXON, J. (1985) *A Teacher's Guide to Multicultural Education*, New York, Basil Blackwell.

OAKES, J. (1985) *Keeping Track: How Schools Structure Inequality*, New Haven, CT, Yale University Press.

RAMSEY, P., VOLD, E.B. and WILLIAMS, L. (1989) *Multicultural Education*, New York, Garland Publishing Inc.

REDMAN-RENGSTORF, S. (1985) 'To better the conditions: The annexation attempts of West College Hill', *Queen City Heritage*, **43**, spring, pp. 3–16.

SPINDLER, G. (1982) *Doing the Ethnography of Schooling*, New York, Holt.

Chapter 7

Manifestations of Inequality: Overcoming Resistance in a Multicultural Foundations Course

Roberta Ahlquist

The urban minority community continues to be in crisis. Despite the hardworking efforts to restructure schools, empower teachers, include more technology, involve the larger community, and revitalize the school community, there is a very simple missing piece. The missing piece is the presence of more teachers who are perceived as reflecting and valuing the ethnicity, culture, potential, and relationship needs of minority students — teachers who challenge, enjoy and care for our students — teachers who refuse to accept 'NO' as an answer to education, for every 'NO' is balanced by a 'YES' to something else — teachers, who in turn, are respected, honored, supported and given the resources and authority to teach. Power will follow from these things. (Howard, 1988)

The goals of equal educational opportunity, equal rights, social justice and democratic schooling for millions of students in inner cities, urban and rural areas, and on Native American reservations have not yet been realized. Teacher educators can play a pivotal role in the process of preparing new teachers to bring these goals to fruition. To teach from a multicultural and anti-racist perspective is inherently controversial in a society which to a considerable degree pretends there is no privilege growing up white, middle class and male, nor any oppression growing up poor, or a male or female of color (Brandt, 1986). Whether unconscious or conscious, intentional or unintentional, prospective teachers find it difficult to accept that whites have benefited economically, socially and psychologically from institutional and interactional racism, and males have benefited from sexism. Teaching a multicultural curriculum from an anti-racist perspective can help prospective teachers understand how existing power and economic structures promote inequity and injustice. Hopefully this knowledge will be used in the interests of social justice and equality in their classrooms.

To fulfill some of the goals of addressing the needs of an increasingly diverse student population, teacher educators have created guidelines for multi-cultural curricula. Proposals to recruit minority faculty into the teaching profession also have been developed. Various incentives have been spelled out in an attempt to lure minority candidates into professional education programs. But the status and pay of teachers is still a major obstacle, especially for minority candidates who are often given more attractive incentives in fields which have both higher status, pay, and better working conditions. Additionally, some people of color have experienced the institution of schooling as oppressive and therefore choose to work outside of the educational system for change.

It is evident that we will not be able to provide the number of minority teachers needed to reflect the quickly growing ethnically diverse student population. Minority teachers, who now account for 11 per cent of the US teaching faculty, will increase to about 17 per cent during the same time period in which minority students will increase to 54 per cent of the total school age population, according to the *1988 Survey of the American Teacher*. The reality is that currently, and in the forseeable future, most people entering teacher education programs will be white, middle and lower middle class, and overwhelmingly female. Furthermore, because of the increasing need for teachers at all levels, many teachers will enter schools without adequate professional preparation let alone preparation that is multicultural and anti-racist (Olsen, 1988).

Establishing the Context

In the university in which I teach the overall student population corresponds approximately to the urban community in which it is situated. The minority population of San Jose, California is roughly 40 per cent and is made up of Mexican Americans, Vietnamese, blacks, Portuguese, Latinos and other Asians. However, student enrollment in the School of Education is about 70 per cent white (SJSU Census Data, 1989). Faculty and staff are making efforts to recruit more minority faculty and students into the School of Education. Concurrently, many teacher educators recognize the need to prepare the current predominantly white and female prospective teacher population to teach from a multicultural and (fewer faculty agree on this latter point), an anti-racist perspective. It is assumed that non-minority candidates can develop the skills to be culturally sensitive, equitable teachers. It is also not assumed that minority candidates automatically embrace these qualities (Howard, 1988).

The teacher education division has recently developed a multicultural foundations of education course which is an option for prospective elementary education students. All credential candidates must take a foundations course, but it need not be a course labeled multicultural foundations. During the past year I taught one such course. Using critical and feminist reflective methodology, (Grumet, 1988; Miller, 1983; Ellsworth, 1989), I want to examine and reflect on this course and my teaching, in order to learn from it, recognizing that individual reflective practice has its limitations. We are influenced by our biases such that we can never see the entire picture fully, clearly, and from all angles, (not objectively, for the subjective foreshadows objectivity). Furthermore, using 'research as praxis' as a methodology, (Lather, 1986), I would like to describe forms of resistance from both the students and teacher, in response to my use of an anti-racist and critical approach to multicultural education and how I attempted to address this resistance. I invite reader response to this situated or contextual critique to better understand my pedagogy. Pedagogy here refers to the contextualized interrelationship between teacher, students and the specific conditions which contribute to the production of knowledge.

As a critical theorist and feminist, I am committed to the view that learners construct their own learning, that students and teachers are co-investigators in the process of such construction, and that knowledge is not transmitted from teacher to student but rather invented and reinvented together in a dialogical exchange. I believe that the learner is more important than the content, which is constructed in relation to the backgrounds, needs, and interests of the students. I believe that the best learning occurs when the content speaks to the lived experiences of the learners. Learning should help students and teachers make sense out of the world through a process of dialogue and reflective action in the interests of a more just and equitable society. I believe in the knowability of pedagogy. Past and current practice, intersubjective and group critique, and ongoing reflection guide me to make fairly good predictions.

I use broad guidelines by which I try to fashion my curricula to promote these goals:

1 To raise student consciousness of the ways in which racism and other isms are imbedded in our thinking, values, and beliefs as a result of living in this society. To have those students who exhibit racist, classist and sexist values confront those values, beliefs and behaviors.
2 To make students aware of the rich cultural diversity among people in the world and more specifically in the urban center the university serves.
3 To provide students with ways to take more control over their learning/ thinking/behavior and to promote this in their students.
4 To model an emancipatory, dialogic, and student-centered classroom.
5 To help students define their philosophy of teaching and learning and the concomitant teaching methods which reflect such a philosophy.
6 To make the educational experience a way of developing personal and social meaning to a level of knowing that is deeper than the acquisition of information to create mutual trust, openness, a secure willingness to risk and explore, to develop self-confidence and an understanding of personal and social responsibility. Such things must be experienced in the classroom to be understood.
7 To assist students in the development of curricula which unveils the hidden curriculum (tracking, testing, and rewards for docility and conformity), is multicultural, promotes social justice, and confronts racism/ isms in a constructive way.
8 To create a relationship between teacher and students which gives the support necessary to strengthen the student's integrity.
9 To engage in individual confrontation and communication in order to discover and share personal meaning. This means that we have to spend time together discovering and sharing how we feel about what we know, don't know and need to know.
10 To make teachers aware of the role they will be asked to play in either

perpetuating oppressive structures or in taking an oppositional stance against that oppressive role in the educational system.

The Anatomy of a Classroom: A Case Study

My students reflect common attitudes held by the larger society. Many students see the world in individualistic, personal and apolitical terms. Many are non-confrontational and reluctant to take risks. They most often want to be told what to do, many see teachers and texts as absolute sources of knowledge, they are driven by grades and 'right answers', and many of them have little sense of agency about their own learning. Because many students have seldom examined, questioned or challenged their taken-for-granted acceptance of the world view that they hold, it is difficult for them to peel the layers of such socialization away without assistance and without resistance. The role of the teacher is complex and multifaceted. My primary goal is to intervene or interrupt their world in such a way that they don't unconsciously reproduce what they have experienced in their own schooling. I want students to discover and experience a powerful alternative to past educational experience, which will be a challenge to the status quo. Resistance to these alternative views of reality takes many forms. A persistent difficulty is to translate theory into practice. I will get back to this later.

This was the first class of elementary teacher candidates I had taught. This multicultural course included thirty-one students: twenty-seven white women, one white man, one black man, (who dropped the class after the first week and subsequently dropped out of the program) and two Mexican American women. The average student age was 29. Many of the students were very young (20 or 21) and politically had not yet developed an articulate ideology, yet ten women were in their late thirties or early forties and had children in school. Nearly one-third of the class worked in addition to attending classes. The overwhelming majority of students defined themselves as middle class. Their fathers, mothers, or husbands worked at middle level management jobs.

Several women volunteered that they were fundamentalist in their religious beliefs. The student level of consciousness about what multicultural education, racism, and other inequities was mixed, but the majority of students stated (in questionnaires and verbal interviews) that they didn't really have a good idea of what multicultural education meant. A few students offered definitions which mainly included foods, holidays, and customs. The majority of students said they had little to no contact or ongoing experiences with people of color or with poor people. One white working class single parent said that her daughter's father was black, and that he had no contact with the family. One 45-year-old white woman described herself as a disabled, single parent on disability who had been homeless several times and had ongoing experiences with people of color and with poor people. She said she had met and befriended many interesting people while on the streets. She had a tendency to interrupt the class to share a viewpoint or provide an example from her experience. Because of this behavior several students were impatient with, and a few downright hostile to, her views. Class biases like this were openly expressed at the beginning of the semester. The only male in class was generally very quiet, although he spoke with me in private about his changing awareness of social and cultural issues we addressed in class. Several students volunteered during one conversation that poor people, people on welfare and some minorities were lazy and that was why they were poor. Others stated that they were angry because new immigrants from Southeast Asia and Central America were taking the diminishing number of available jobs away from Americans. Early in the semester, comments which pitted people of color and poor whites against middle class whites were common during class discussions. The level of political consciousness about ways in which workers were divided around the questions of race was very low. Racism seemed to 'make sense' to many students based on the social construction of their consciousness and experiences (Hall, 1980). I felt there was much to do to provide alternative points of view and to increase awareness.

Initially I tried to inventory the beliefs and values of students, based first on a discussion of cultural, then race issues and their experiences with such issues. In response to this approach several students claimed I was idealistic and utopian for advocating cultural diversity. Assimilation, they argued, was the only solution for the future of the world. As I look around at the developing pogroms against the Jews in Eastern Europe, the separatist movements by Armenians, Turks, Lithuanians, and other Baltic republics, the ethnic Hungarians, the Afghanistanis, and Azerbajanis, I realize the complexity of this issue and the need to address those complexities. When I advocated consideration of bilingual education several students responded, 'Well, why do we have an *English only* policy then?' What does *English only* say to students about diversity, I asked myself? We talked about the need to hear a multiplicity of viewpoints, to hear from students with very different experiences and beliefs from our own in order to clarify and articulate our positions in relation to those of others. Some students looked uncomfortable. I reminded myself that these were not students of the 1960s but rather the 1990s. The times and conditions shape consciousness. Several students openly expressed condescending views of people who they felt would not 'make it' in society. We were setting the stage for dialogue. These issues were important to address because they came from their education or experience. Examples of dualistic thinking prevailed. 'That's the way things are and always will be; poverty has been with us forever.' Students had placed some of their thinking on the table for scrutiny.

The Importance of Knowing Teacher Ideologies

Each semester I spend considerable time trying to understand the beliefs or ideologies of prospective teachers about teaching and learning, and the role they see themselves playing in that process. If we are to be successful in offering alternatives to the powerful forces of racism, sexism and other isms in today's society, as well as to challenge the far too prevalent behaviorist, authoritarian and didactic practices of beginning teachers, we need to understand and speak to their preconceptions. A majority of students in the class I taught strongly believed that knowledge emanated from experts, and their own role was to passively absorb content generated by teachers. Many students were unwilling to see knowing as constructed, a process in which students individually weigh their personal beliefs against a critical examination of alternative possibilities. I wanted students to investigate, theorize and act on their new understandings of what role they wanted to play as teachers. I was depending upon 'right' thought to lead to 'right' action. Many disagreed about what was right. Most were unconvinced by my reasoning. Here were dialectical tensions we needed to address.

It has been my experience over the past twenty years, that a critical mass of students who are open to alternative points of view is necessary to challenge taken-for-granted views of teaching and society. I don't assume that all prospective teachers come into programs with racist and sexist values, but I do believe that a great majority do and that this majority tend to either be unconscious of that reality or want to deny it. I have been very successful over the past twenty years raising consciousness about racism. I often volunteered, 'how can we not be racist when it is embedded in and perpetuated by the dominant culture'. The assumption underlying this view is that students aren't willing to accept that reality without powerful evidence to convince them. Some of that evidence needs to come from efforts to put students into the shoes of a victim of racism. I encouraged students to share experiences which illuminated that viewpoint. Some students refused to acknowledge this reality even after given powerful evidence.

Resistances — Theirs and Mine

I am aware that teaching from an anti-racist perspective generates resistance (Brandt, 1986; Banks, 1986). Teaching from an inquiry-based or feminist perspective also creates resistance (Maher, 1987). Teaching from both a critical and anti-racist perspective compounds the resistance (Sleeter and Grant, 1988; Berlak, 1989). In fact, for some, merely the process of interactive student-centered teaching was very painful. At the same time, I tried to provide prospective teachers with a view of teachers as agents of resistance. I urged students to take an active part in the class by being critical, by questioning; I urged them to take risks, to assume responsibility for their learning, to critique their own education, to evaluate themselves and each other. They were often bewildered by such requests. They had had few previous experiences with such approaches to learning. When students felt they couldn't articulate their position, they tended to either strike out in an emotional outburst or to blame and devalue themselves, rather than to see conflict as an opportunity to clarify their positions and to see learning as a process towards that clarification. These are typical early semester responses to such urgings:

* 'But, you're the teacher. I don't know what questions to ask.'
* 'Are we going to learn something today, or are we just going to talk about all the problems in society?'
* 'I'm not a racist. But it seems like racism is everywhere.'
* 'I've never had a class like this. Generally I just go to class, take out my notebook, take notes, occasionally disengage and think about what I have or haven't done for the next class, shut my notebook and go on to the next class. In this class I can't do that.'

* 'I've never before been asked what I think or what I believe is important in any other class.'
* 'It's a little frustrating because you don't give us the answers to the questions you raise.'
* I've never before critiqued or had my papers critiqued by students.'
* I never considered myself racist before. Now I think maybe I am.'

These statements are symptomatic of historical conditions grounded in students' previous experiences of schooling. The passivity and fear of failure that I observed at the beginning of the semester among a majority of students was overwhelming to me. Most students were particularly uncomfortable with the lack of clear structure and direction, compounded by their fear of addressing controversial issues. Most were performance-oriented. Several students complained about ambiguity and uncertainty, and a few students said I was arbitrary and unfair in my evaluations of their work. Many students lacked a sense of agency about their own education and questioned the uncertain direction of their lives in general. They often mistrusted their own experiences as well as me. I have observed many beginning teachers who exhibit this behavior, but never to the degree I experienced with these prospective elementary teachers. Never had I seen a group of students who were so cautious, silent, anxious, so tentative, so unwilling to take risks. Never had they asked so often how they were going to be graded, and what were my specific writing requirements. Yet their general demeanor was light and bubbly, especially after receiving papers with grades that they found acceptable. These students appeared to be excited about the prospects of becoming teachers. Many stated that they entered the credential program because they liked children. When asked what their expectations were for the course (at first they were silent, 'But this is your course, I don't know what to expect') they said they wanted me to 'tell them how to teach multiculturally'. The predominant dualistic view of learning, the lack of familiarity with abstraction, the limited experience with multiple 'ways of knowing' of these students seemed limited to a concern with the transmission of decontextualized factual information by an expert, with little or no experience with higher levels of contextualized discourse (Perry, 1970). But, I asked myself, how often had they encountered (and perhaps rejected) teachers who raised issues of racism and sexism, and had encouraged the kinds of responses I sought from them? Why shouldn't they resist other ways of knowing? Hadn't they encountered some of these ideas before? In response to their requests I gave them clearly defined handouts of all writing and project expectations. I also restated that it was important for them to participate in class discussions. I felt compelled to appease and direct. This wasn't very dialogic. I knew this was going to be a difficult semester.

I resisted their resistance. I argued that emancipatory pedagogy from an anti-racist perspective and reflective teaching are more viable approaches to education. My students perceived the rigor of my argument as an attempt to impose my point of view on them. This was not my intention. I realized that the contradiction between authority and emancipatory pedagogy was more striking for me as a female teacher. Males have authority by virtue of their gender. Females do not. Even though most of their elementary and high school teachers were probably women, and during this time those authorities taught many of them to be docile and to obey, they nonetheless seemed more willing to question female authority. Yet the power imbalance between students and teachers must constantly be contested if we are to empower our students. I reflected on Barbara Christian's caution, 'One must distinguish the desire for power from the need to become empowered (Christian, 1987). I had never before felt that women teachers needed to establish their credibility before they relinquished their authority (Bridges and Hartman, 1975). Power is automatically bestowed on the role of teacher. The question for me was how to relinquish my power and authority such that students could become agents in their own learning. Yet my gender seemed to be a factor in this dynamic. These were contradictions and dialectical tensions over which I agonized.

We began the semester attempting to define terms and to locate the course in a social context. Several students said racism and sexism no longer existed. It had ended with the Civil Rights Movement and the '60s. I encouraged students to speak about their experiences in school, family, communities, or to describe experiences their children were having in school, from the perspective of race, gender and social class. A few students shared stories of unequal treatment. I observed that many students didn't trust their own experience, let alone that of others, and that they showed little empathy and outrage for the plight of those less fortunate than they (Berlak, 1989). They were uncomfortable speaking out; they complained of a lack of structure in the class; they wanted me to be a 'talking head'. I resisted. They resisted. 'This doesn't feel empowering' (Ellsworth, 1989).

Some students gradually responded to requests to speak out by providing examples of the 'illusion of progress' (Sleeter and Grant, 1988). Several students argued that racism no longer was a problem in society. The legal system had made discrimination illegal, thus we need not worry any longer about racism. I described how small, but mostly superficial examples tended to obscure the reality that racism and sexism continue to be major forces in our society which have an impact on the lives of many people. I distributed handouts which documented the political, economic and social subordination of blacks, Hispanics and Native Americans. This was not very dialogic. I needed another way to bring this content before students. I needed to uncover a generative theme which might have brought them to this awareness or might have made them more receptive to this information.

'Poverty will be with us forever', one student replied, when asked what they knew about the homeless. I raised questions about class domination and the way our economic system is structured. I asked them about the impact of social class on race and gender. I realize now that I was asking them to provide information and answers which they had scant likelihood of knowing. I became aware of their limited experience to have thought about such issues; it became an exercise in futility to ask them for thoughtful discussions of these questions. Their understanding needed to grow out of reflective examination of their own experience. I may have let my own agenda and the urgency of the issues I sought to discuss lead me away from the slower, deliberative, and more haphazard process of focusing on their lived experience and allowing generalizations to grow out of that process. The categories of thought associated with race, ethnicity, gender and class operate independently at times as well as interdependently. Students needed to see how they intersect in peoples' lives (Rothenberg, 1988). Although we came to some agreement about the role inequality plays in people's lives, students were reluctant to talk about their experiences using these terms. The terms racism and sexism were as explosive to students as the term communism continues to be. This informs me about how to approach these concepts. These terms (racism and sexism) are abstract and deserve skepticism. They need to be rendered in the form of concrete examples drawn from their own lives. Students nowadays have learned to distrust the use of such terms because all too often they are used as clubs to make them feel guilty. However, we tried to include working definitions developed by the class. Use of the terms racism and sexism elicited student responses of guilt, shame or anger. Students felt they were being held responsible for the inequities in society. We talked about 'blaming the victim', about internalizing oppression, and what these concepts meant in their experience. I urged them to use their own words and to reflect on their experiences and those of people they knew. I realized that the trouble they were having accepting the words indicated a lack of willingness to acknowledge what the words meant. If racist experiences can remain unnamed and then go unrecognized, people can thus claim no responsibility for such experiences (Brandt, 1986). Consciousness comes very slowly.

Purposes of Schooling

What I think to be the entire purpose of education in the first place ... the whole process of education occurs within a social framework and is designed to perpetuate the aims of society. Thus, for example, the boys and girls who were born during the era of the Third Reich, when educated to the purposes of the Third Reich, became barbarians. The paradox of education is precisely this — that as one begins to become conscious, one begins to examine the society in which he is being educated. The purpose of education, finally, is to create in a person the ability to look at the world for himself, to make his own decisions, to say to himself this is black or this is white, to decide for himself whether there is a God in heaven or not. To ask questions of the universe, and then learn to live with those questions, is the way he achieves his own identity. But no society is really anxious to have that kind of person around. What societies really, ideally, want is a citizenry which will simply obey the rules of society. If a society succeeds in this, that society is about to perish. The obligation of anyone who thinks of himself as responsible is to examine society and try to change it and to fight it — at no matter what risk. This is the only hope society has. This is the only way societies change. (Baldwin, 1963)

Although written by James Baldwin in 1963, this statement still rings true to me. I asked students to give consideration to these views. I wanted them to define their own goals and purposes. Student resistance to Baldwin's words made me feel as though the class was taking two steps back, a quarter step forward. I felt I was going too fast, pushing too hard.

Time to reflect and reassess. An ongoing question I addressed was how to challenge thinking without being prescriptive. Students are victims of the current educational system which has socialized them, and teachers too are victims. Most of us haven't had an education that was empowering, anti-racist, problem posing or liberatory. If we know no other way, how can we provide alternatives for our students? To overcome the effects of my own mis-education, I have felt a growing need to examine critically and reflect on my own beliefs and constraints and formative influences which have shaped my practice. I am trying to challenge my own taken-for-granted views of students. I am learning to slow down, reflect, and draw students into the dialogue.

Controversy is not readily embraced by most students. We have socialized our students to believe that argument, conflict, debate, and disagreement is something to be avoided, that it has no place in the classroom. In fact, we need to provide more opportunities for controversial discussions to help students get beyond their mechanistic and dualistic thinking. Students need to understand how the subordination of any group or person is dehumanizing to all of us. If education can't help provide ways for the disenfranchised in our society to critically examine and act on their world in the interests of change, then it merely serves to reproduce the status quo (Bowles and Gintis, 1976; Apple, 1982). When I raised these issues, students framed their responses in terms of either/or, or felt fatalistic and helpless.

As the semester progressed, some students continued to argue that racism doesn't exist anymore. A few others continued to believe that people of color and poor people were lazy, undeserving or drug addicts. Yet after several weeks of class discussion focusing on their personal experiences with discrimination and prejudice, most students wanted to tell each other that racism and other isms were everywhere, but that they weren't responsible for it and they didn't engage in it.

I provided them with readings and with several media presentations which addressed race, gender and social class issues. However, denial is strong and facts aren't enough (Berlak, 1989). In an effort to break through their defenses, I used self-disclosure. I often talked about my own experiences growing up in a home where unconscious and conscious racism was a regular experience. Where did I learn about equity and social justice? Not at home, not at church, but in the streets and at school.

Schooling plays a complex dual function, to mystify and demystify, to shape and mold and yet at the same time to provide space for resistance (Bowles and Gintis, 1976). I told them many personal stories of my experiences with people of color and workers during my childhood. I described incidents of discrimination based on my class background and gender. I shared how my teachers expected less of me because I was working class. I told them I didn't realize what discrimination was until in elementary school I overheard a classmate ask another friend why I had an Indian for my best friend. I described how my geometry teacher had become frustrated with my boardwork in high school and one day had shouted out in class, 'Why are girls in this class, anyway; they weren't meant to do math!' Using my own experiences as a base, I talked about what it meant to be a white female then and now. I told them why I felt racism was the most serious social problem facing us today. I urged them to talk. I kept facing the recurring dilemma of how to provide alternative viewpoints without being impositional (Berlak, 1989; Ellsworth, 1989). We talked about personal fairness and equity, and most agreed that they didn't intentionally discriminate against anyone because of their race, ethnicity, or gender. We talked about institutional racism and the powerful forces of socialization, especially tracking, training for conformity and docility, IQ testing, and unequal access to resources. I tried to assist in demystifying the system's effects on their thinking and to offer a view of possibility. We critiqued the white, middle class, consumer-oriented media, especially the advertising that flashed continously across the television screen. I asked students to look at ways in which the media reinforces the status quo. I asked them to critique Saturday morning cartoons from the point of view of race, gender and social class. We watched several videos, *Racism 101* and *Killing Us Softly: Images of Women in the Media*; students were shocked by the blatant displays of racism and sexism depicted in these presentations. To help facilitate the unveiling of racial stereotypes in the beliefs of the majority of prospective teachers, I encouraged journal writing; keeping notes on class discussions, reaching back and looking at the values, beliefs and behaviors of our parents through family histories, asking students to reflect on how their race, gender and class has influenced or shaped their world view, defining roles they wanted to play as teachers, and defining the purposes of schooling. Some of their journal entries are shared in class, some are read by me, some of the content is reserved for the writer's privacy, but all of this seems to further dialogue and helps clarify points of view, attitudes, and questions which students address in classroom discussions.

As obvious as it might seem, many of these beginning teachers hadn't looked at the effect of point-of-view on their perceptions. Analyzing how being white and middle class in this society results in seeing the world from a predominantly white perspective was a revelation to many students. This new awareness of the power of point-of-view provided a basis for much reflection about their beliefs.

To move away from tunnel vision viewing we tried to look at experiences from different perspectives. White students looked at television programs or discussed issues or conflicts from the perspective of a person of color; if male from a female perspective; if middle class, from a working class view. Many students became both frustrated and resistant when they found their attitudes about the reality they wanted to believe in were in conflict with the attitudes about the reality they experienced in the shoes of others. This activity helped break down stereotypes but also made some students hostile. I tried to address this hostility on an ongoing basis. Nevertheless, several students began to withdraw from discussions. I unsuccessfully fought this trend among several students to disengage from this process of self-examination. For some the growing awareness of their own biases proved more disturbing than they wanted to admit. A student commented on the course the following semester:

> ... the course was an assault of horrors ... every class some new injustice was presented ... students were not sure what these had to do with them. She went overboard in her concerns. Things aren't all that bad. And even if they were, one person couldn't do that much to change them. Some of them just didn't want to deal with this order of

things because they were trying to do what they needed to do for their own life and they had no more energy. And besides they were nice people and not participating in these injustices.

Comments such as these made me ask: What can I learn from these statements? They reflect passivity, fatalism, denial and resistance. Did I provide examples and alternatives for change? How responsible was I for their feelings of powerlessness? I needed to break through the fog which surrounded their thinking. Freire has remarked that there is more fog, more opaqueness in the US than in Brazil. He says that in Brazil things are much more clear-cut between rich and poor.

The Myths of Objectivity

The most heated discussion occurred over whether teachers should take a position on controversial issues, specifically issues of racism and sexism. This debate represented one of several instances in which many students displayed their intolerance of diversity and their strong resistance to alternative points of view. The debate also represented a turning point for my self-critique. The majority of the class took the position that it was wrong for teachers to state their viewpoint to students, even if doing so was in the interests of challenging racial, gender or other forms of discrimination. Deeply embedded in these students' world views was the notion that teachers must always be objective or neutral in expressing their views, especially controversial views. I argued that for change to occur, teachers had a responsibility to take a position in support of change and against racism. They didn't have to agree with my view; I encouraged them to counter it, but I had a right and a responsibility to state it. I stated that I firmly believed that 'teachers should attempt to live part of their dreams within their educational space' (Freire and Macedo, 1987). Teachers could not help but be partisan. I was dismayed by their response. This was provocation at the risk of disengagement. I felt it crucial for students to develop a clear point of view on this issue and be able to articulate and defend that view. This exchange lasted several class meetings. I stood my ground. I tried to engage students in a dialogue around partisanship. Many fell back on the so-called 'experts' in the field, teachers who had told them not to take stands. They were divided. I argued that racism and sexism had to be countered, not with one overall solution, but from multiple fronts. For me to be silent, feign neutrality or claim no perspective would have been dishonest.

Both feminist and critical pedagogy challenge the concept of objectivity (Maher, 1987). However, the manner in which I presented my view intimidated students. I stated that my anti-racist position was based not only on morality, but that to demystify racism also demystifies the inequalities of the economic system. As the argument continued, tensions developed over the issue of teacher authority and power. On the one hand they relied upon teacher or expert authority, on the other hand they resisted it. I felt that the important issues of racism and sexism were being diffused in a clash between teacher/student authority. The debate degenerated into a power struggle. I did not wish to violate, limit or oppress student voice in the name of liberatory teaching, but

I also didn't want students to limit or stifle the discussion of visions of a better world. There is a very fine line between imposing and asserting a world view. I was insistent. I wanted them to see as well as to accept my view. This was not an invitation to a dialogue about an issue. My interest in having them accept my view had become a directive; either accept the view that racism must be eliminated, or else. This was the very dualism I was fighting against. I too was guilty of it.

The question for me becomes: How can the teacher as problem-poser reflect student reality back to the student in a non-threatening problematic way which will induce self-examination and critical questioning, without imposition. The larger question is: How to awaken and bring students out of their limited consciousness without being impositional. In other words, how do I use my power and authority to 'abolish' power and authority? (Bridges and Hartmann, 1975). This is the major contradiction in my teaching from a critical and anti-racist perspective.

Teachers need an essential number of students in a classroom open to alternative points of view. The few students who tended to agree with me often withdrew from the discussion, especially if classmates saw them as taking sides with the teacher. Some students who disagreed also withdrew. It was a double bind situation for me as teacher; if I withdrew from the discussion the support for my position was lost; if I continued I exerted unfair authority and advantage in the role of teacher. I wondered if I should go back to a more fundamental approach to teaching about race, gender and class as separate issues. How could I get students to reconsider their ways of viewing the world? How could I present my view without being impositional? I felt tempted to regress to methods of teaching which I had discarded years ago. Should I distribute additional factual articles showing concrete evidence of both personal and institutional racism, sexism and class bias? Should I change directions and respond to their repeated requests to 'just show us how to teach from a multicultural perspective', 'we can talk about these issues some other time. I'd rather you tell us how to teach a multicultural lesson'. We had conflicting definitions of the term multicultural.

A few students became frustrated when they were unable to articulate their views on the issue of taking a position. They turned this frustration into anger at themselves and at me for not being able to clarify their views. I took a stand, arguing that teachers must take a stand against racism whenever they encountered it. But in so doing, I alienated a portion of the students from hearing more of my views. Several of the most vocal students adamantly opposed partisan stands by teachers. One irate student came back each class session for the next two weeks with arguments in favor of the position that teachers remain neutral. She talked to other teachers, most of whom agreed that teachers should be non-partisan. She talked to parents who supported her view, she spoke of her own experience. Her position was that all sides of an issue need to be expressed and students can then make up their own minds. Objectivity should prevail. Everyone's point of view was as legitimate as another, and teachers should not play a role in taking a position on a issue, especially a controversial issue, because teachers inherently, by the nature of their position, had too much power. I strongly agreed with the latter part of this statement, but disagreed that a teacher couldn't or shouldn't counter or challenge a point of view if it was harmful, discriminatory, or privileged one person over another on the basis of race, gender or social class background. I said there should be a clear distinction between explicit and hidden partisanship. Teachers had a responsibility to let students know where they stood on such issues. The complex and multi-faceted issues of this topic were reduced to the notion that because teachers were powerful forces they should remain non-partisan otherwise students would automatically assume a teacher's position was correct and would not have the opportunity to determine their own position independently.

I felt simultaneously like oppressor and oppressed. Did my students also feel this way? How could I convince students that well-intentioned people were capable of being racist and that it was important for students to hear that everyone had a responsibility — teachers, parents, students, whoever — to take a position against racism as well as to acknowledge how often racism is embedded in their own behavior. Students took sides and lines were drawn. The effect of this exchange had created a chasm between the students and me. My efforts to develop a non-hierarchical, anti-racist, dialogical, student-centered environment had been undermined by this discussion over objectivity. It was them against me.

For the first week after the exchange about explicit versus hidden partisanship had ended, I attempted to ignore or downplay the effects this conflict had had on the class and became determined to get on with the rest of the course. Then I realized that this exchange, and its awkward resolution, had had a significant impact on student views about the class in general. I had invited a discussion which turned into a debate that no one had clearly won; yet my position remained most powerfully stated. I had not truly invited students into a dialogue about an issue, but instead had imposed my viewpoint upon them. Nevertheless, this decision still 'feels right to me' (Lorde, 1984). Teachers have a responsibility to take a stand in the interests of equity and social justice, which may, in fact, alienate students. How best to take this stand is the question. The effect my approach had with a few students was that because there was resistance to my authority on this issue, my other views also became merely alternative points of view to be considered and/or resisted, and thus all my views were suspect. Perhaps this is as it should be. At times teachers must provoke at the risk of disengagement. There is a thin line between assertion and imposition which in this case I had crossed.

Student standardized course evaluations for this class were much lower than usual. It is hard to know how to read this. (Actually, the standardized evaluation questions better serve a didactic teacher than a dialogical teacher). Some peers have suggested that these could be read as positive: I was effective in provoking considerable reflection and thought around some difficult issues. I also ask students to write a narrative evaluation of the class, the teacher, and themselves. These evaluations were much more positive. Students stated they had a more critical perspective on race, class and gender issues. Narrative evaluations were also solicited from students in this class during the past year which also have been much more positive. Students who have commented have stated that over time they have come to see the merit of the class in a way which they could not measure at the time of the course. Time will tell.

My interpretation of some of the reasons for student resistance may inform my teaching and the teaching of others working within the paradigm of critical pedagogy. Imposition and resistance are complex and powerful dynamics in the classroom which have to be addressed. Some students resisted both the content as well as the methodology in this class. My reaction to student resistance led me into some pedagogical pitfalls. Other educators attempting to teach from similar perspectives have experienced similar forms of resistance (Hollins and King, 1989; Quintanar, 1989). In this case, my practice continues to inform and influence how I teach the theory.

Teacher educators need to acknowledge prospective teachers' belief systems, cultural ideologies and experiences and work to assert anti-racist views in the least impositional way possible. Obviously there is no simple formula for non-impositional anti-racist teaching. The following are some of the lessons I learned, the limitations and possibilities which may inform others teaching from a critical and anti-racist perspective:

The term *multicultural* is problematic. It generally does not mean education for social justice, or anti-racist education. We need to clarify the terms and inform students of our perspective.

We need to be more cognizant of the problem of imposition and power relations and ways to address constructively both power and resistance.

We need to be explicit in our partisanship. Hidden ideologies must be exposed and critiqued.

We need to use student experience as a means to make students self-critically aware of their and others' heritage and how it shapes us. If experiences are limited we need to seek them out, if this is not possible, bring in speakers who can share such experiences and educate prospective teachers about the many forms which racism take in this society. New approaches to teaching content need to be reinvented with each class we teach, realizing that sometimes we won't succeed.

We need to be more patient with students unfamiliar with abstract ideas and those who are unconscious of the racism which is embedded in all of us.

We especially need to struggle against blaming the victim and internalized oppression.

Content which is anti-racist must permeate *all* teacher education curricula, not just be relegated to one optional course.

Student teachers should be provided with early field experiences in diverse ethnic settings to overcome misconceptions, fears and anxieties about working with diverse groups of students.

Emancipatory teachers need to work with students to provide clear direction, avenues and possibilities for hope and change, to counter student fatalism and feelings of powerlessness.

We need to foster appreciation for the dialogical process which is a powerful teaching tool to promote values of social justice in the classroom.

We need to support others trying to teach from a critical and anti-racist perspective. We also need good role models of people engaged in fighting against racism in their daily lives.

We need to clearly spell out how our classes will appear different, less structured, with different grading policies, etc. to allay student anxieties about liberatory teaching.

The use of standardized teacher evaluations is problematic. These should either be revised to provide for more accurate assessment of teaching from a dialogical, anti-racist view or other forms of assessment should be used.

The more vigilant we can be about acknowledging and addressing our contradictions, the more informed will be our teaching. Linda Valli's model of reflective teaching allows us to see how easily we can move away from being critical, ethical, and reflective (Valli, 1988). The goal is to be a morally reflective teacher, a critical pedagogue. To reach that goal we must view our teaching as an ongoing process of trial, error, critique, reflection, and action on that reflection. This critique is offered as a contribution to that process.

References

APPLE, M. (1982) *Education and Power*, Boston, MA, Routledge and Kegan Paul.

BALDWIN, J. (1963) 'A talk to teachers' in SIMONSON, R. (Ed.) (1988) *The Graywolf Annual Five: Multicultural Literacy*, Saint Paul, Graywolf.

BANKS, J. (1986) 'Race, ethnicity and schooling in the United States: Past, present and future' in BANKS, J. (Ed.) *Multicultural Education in Western Societies*. London, Holt.

BERLAK, A. (1989) 'Teaching for outrage and empathy in the liberal arts', *Educational Foundations*, 3, 2, pp. 69–93.

BOWLES, S. and GINTIS, S. (1976) *Schooling in Capitalist America*. New York, Basic.

BRANDT, G. (1986) *The Realization of Anti-Racist Teaching*, London, Falmer Press.

BRIDGES, A. and HARTMAN, H. (1975) 'Pedagogy by the oppressed', *Review of Radical Political Economics*, 6, 4, pp. 75–9.

CHRISTIAN, B. (1987) 'The race for theory', *Cultural Critique*, 6, pp. 51–63.

ELLSWORTH, E. (1989) 'Why doesn't this feel empowering? Working through the repressive myths of critical pedagogy', *Harvard Educational Reivew*, 59, 3, pp. 297–324.

FREIRE, P. (1972) *Pedagogy of the Oppressed*, New York, Seabury Press.

FREIRE, P. and MACEDO, D. (1987) *Literacy: Reading the Word and the World*, Boston, MA, Bergin and Garvey.

GRUMET, M. (1988) *Bitter Milk*. Boston, MA, University of Massachusetts Press.

HALL, S. (1980) 'Teaching Race', *Multiracial Education*, 9, 1.

HOLLINS, E. and KING, J. (1989) Personal interview, March, East Palo Alto, CA.

HOWARD, B. (1988) *Symposia Proceedings*, The Teacher Corps Alumni Network. University of South Alabama Press, pp. 7–12.

LATHER, P. (1986) 'Research as praxis', *Harvard Educational Review*, 56, 3, pp. 257–77.

LORDE, A. (1984) *Sister Outsider*. New York, Crossing Press.

MAHER, F. (1987) 'Inquiry teaching and feminist pedagogy', *Social Education*, **51**, 2, pp. 186–91.

MILLER, J.L. (1983) 'The resistance of women academics: An autobiographical account', *Journal of Educational Equity and Leadership*, **3**, 2, pp. 101–9.

OLSEN, L. (1988) *Crossing The Schoolhouse Borders*, California State Department of Education.

PERRY, W. (1970) *Intellectual and Ethical Development in the College Years: A Scheme*, New York, Holt Rinehart and Winston.

QUINTANAR, R. (1989) Personal interview, October 1989, Menlo Park, CA.

ROTHENBERG, P. (1988) 'Integrating the study of race, gender, and class: Some preliminary observations', *Feminist Teacher*, **3**, 3, pp. 37–42.

SAN JOSE STATE UNIVERSITY CENSUS DATA (1989) President Fullerton, Re. AAEES 89–93, Educational Equity Goals, 30 November.

SLEETER, C. and GRANT, C. (1988) *Making Choices for Multicultural Education: Five Approaches to Race, Class and Gender*. Columbus, OH, Merrill.

VALLI, L. (1988) 'Reflective teaching: A critical theory perspective', keynote address notes for U-Maryland Master's Certification Program Spring Research Conference, 22 April.

Chapter 8

Culturally Relevant Teaching: The Key to Making Multicultural Education Work[1]

Gloria Ladson-Billings

Understanding the Problem

If we focus upon the introduction of ethnic studies into the curriculum with only an afterthought to the teachers and teaching strategies used, the future is fairly predictable. My guess is that two decades from now ethnic studies will exist, but they will be a shell with all content sucked dry by pedantic instruction more concerned with form than substance. Perhaps ethnic studies will go the way of Latin and Greek, given time and dull educational leadership. (Cuban, 1973)

Perhaps Larry Cuban did not consider himself a prophet or a seer when he wrote the above mentioned words for a brief article in the National Council of the Social Studies' *43rd Annual Yearbook* entitled, *Ethnic Content and 'White' Instruction* but it appears that his prediction has come to fruition. What his article did not predict was at the same time that ethnic (and multiethnic/multicultural) studies courses and programs were 'drying up', the number of ethnic students would be multiplying and the number of ethnic teachers would be shrinking (Holt, 1989).

Several studies have recognized the need to increase minority teachers (Carnegie, 1986; Graham, 1987; AACTE, 1988; Eubanks, 1988; Merino and Quintanar, 1988). In general, this emphasis on increasing the number of minority teachers is centered on providing role models for students, both minority and majority, with little attention paid to the relationship between minority teachers and minority student achievement. Indeed, Rist (1970) suggests that minority teachers who have taken on the values and worldview of the white middle class have a deterimental effect on lower income, minority students — relegating them to the lowest reading group and the least amount of instruction. Thus, while the sense of democracy, equity, and fair play tell us that we *ought* to have more minority teachers with this increase in minority students, a more urgent sense of what is happening to minority students in the classroom should prompt us to more closely examine the kind of teaching that will be most effective for these students regardless of the ethnicity and cultural background of the teacher.

All of the demographic projections suggest that there are few minority candidates in the teacher preparation pipeline (Haberman, 1989). Thus, the teacher who will be called upon to fill the vacancies in urban public schools is most likely to be 'a white, female whose first choice for a teaching assignment was a suburban school' (Grant, 1989, p. 765). What will this teacher need to know to be an effective teacher of minority students? What do we already know about the kind of teaching that will best meet the educational needs of minority students? What does the research tell us about attempts at developing educational strategies more compatible with the lives and cultures of minority students?

Learning Styles Versus Teaching Styles

The past decade has seen educators exhibit a growing interest in the idea that students differ in a personality trait called learning style (Royer and Feldman, 1984). One of the early pioneers in this area, Klein (1951) proposed a perceptual continuum which extended from *levelers* to *sharpeners*. Levelers are learners who hold tight to the categories of perception and judgment and tend not to change their mental set even when presented with new evidence or changing conditions. Sharpeners are those who are attuned to change and capable of spotting shades of difference. Witkin (1962) along with his associates (1977) distinguished between field dependence and field independence. Field dependent learners rely heavily on environmental support while field independent learners are less bound by the situations in which they find themselves. Kagan (1964) distinguished between *impulsivity* and *reflectivity*; the degree to which a learner reflects on the validity of alternative solutions. Ausubel (1968) differentiated between *satellizers* and *non-satellizers*; satellizers have an intrinsic sense of self-worth independent of what they accomplish while non-satellizers lack an intrinsic feeling of self-worth and feel the need to prove themselves through accomplishment.

Domino (1971) moved this inquiry into learning styles further by examining how a personality trait could be used to select an optimal instructional approach. However, Cronbach and Snow (1977) did not find any consistent pattern indicating that students with certain personality traits respond better when taking courses from teachers having corresponding personality traits.

Not long after the learning style literature began to gain acceptance there emerged a somewhat parallel body of literature that began to apply the learning styles notions to racial, ethnic and cultural groups. Ramirez and Castaneda (1974) translated Witkin's field-dependent/field-independent typology to field-sensitive/field-independent as a way to explain disparities between Latino and Anglo school performance. Cohen (1976) made distinctions between analytical and relational modes of conceptual organization and indicated that while minority students often demonstrate a preference for relational styles, schools, in general, favor and reward the analytical mode. Hale-Benson (1986) and Shade (1982) have applied the concept of learning styles to the particular needs of African-American students.

Social psychologist and historian Asa Hilliard (1989) has questioned the use of the term 'style' to describe (and perhaps justify) the low performance of minority group students. More importantly, Hilliard has questioned the use of the term as an excuse for both low expectations on the part of teachers and substandard delivery of instruction. Hillard further asserts that although style is cultural (or learned) and meaningful in teaching and learning, we do not know enough about how or whether pedagogy should be modified in response to learning styles.

The learning styles research is open to criticism on several levels. First, only a few styles (for example, field-dependence/independence, reflection/impulsivity) have been extensively researched. Second, this research is rarely linked to issues regarding teachers' learning styles and/or teaching styles. And, perhaps most importantly, there is little evidence to suggest that distinguishing students according to their learning styles makes any significant differences in their academic performance. Each of these areas requires further exploration before we can accept or reject the saliency of learning styles as a way of addressing the educational needs of students.

Much of the learning styles research has as its ideological base the primacy of the individual and individual differences. This perspective is consistent with Western world views which elevate and celebrate individual strivings above collective ones. This perspective is so much a part of Western culture and thought that to suggest an alternative borders on heresy. This thinking is akin to the old riddle about whether a fish, so accustomed to the water, realizes that it is wet. However, it may be that this ideological blindspot is the point at which the learning styles research must be more carefully examined. Researchers must begin to more carefully examine cultural and group explanations for behaviors and attitudes toward schooling without encouraging practitioners to deliver substandard content and instruction to different groups.

Currently, Dunn (1989) is examining whether or not students from different cultures have different learning styles. One of the questions her work seems to raise is whether or not there exists a biological basis for learning styles. That kind of thinking takes us back to the genetic inferiority arguments of the early 1900s that tend to persist and reappear in various forms over time. With the question of students' learning styles mired in debate and uncertainty it is perhaps more useful to shift the focus to teaching styles.

Early attempts at improving minority and urban student performance focused on school level factors and spawned the *effective schools* literature (Brookover *et al.*, 1979; Edmonds, 1979). This research suggests that strong instructional leadership, high student expectations, emphasis on basic skills, a safe and orderly environment, frequent, systematic student evaluation and increased time on task (Stedman, 1987) produces substantial achievement gains among urban students. Stedman's critique of the effective schools research asserts that the effective schools movement 'ignores the cultural nature of schooling' (p. 219), embraces a view of school as white and middle class with a language and worldview alien to students from different cultures and classes and ignores the historical record of indifference and deliberate hostility toward non-mainstream students which has contributed to their academic failure.

The second wave of educational reform[2] has directed educators' attention to the importance of pedagogy. Shulman (1987a) suggests that any improvement in teaching will come from a redefinition of teaching as more than mastering generic skills which are displayed in terms of classroom behaviors. Shulman further suggests that because of the relative lack of systematic research done in the field of pedagogy it is important to examine the 'wisdom of practice' of expert pedagogues. This wisdom of practice includes not only what teachers demonstrate in the classroom while they are teaching but also the *thinking* that underlies the pedagogical decisions that teachers make. It also includes the *context* in which teaching occurs (Shulman, 1987b).

This recognition of the importance of the teaching context is not a new one. There is substantial literature, for example, on teaching urban students. This literature dates back almost 100 years to 1898 (Cuban, 1989). However, most of this literature has addressed the problem of poor school performance of urban children by either blaming the children by asserting that they 'lack ability, character or motivation' (*ibid.*, p. 781) or by blaming their parents and cultural backgrounds. Less frequently heard arguments suggest that urban students fail because the schooling experience denigrates them and their culture and/or the very structure of the school is not able to accommodate the diversity of cultures, needs, and abilities (*ibid.*).

Critical theorists assert that schools function to reproduce the systemic inequalities of the society. Consequently, the way to break the cycle is to focus on the kind of education minority students need. The work of Freire (1973), Aronowitz and Giroux (1985), King (1987) and McLaren (1989) suggest some features of what successful teachers of minority students must do to emancipate, empower and transform both themselves and their students. Aspects of this kind of teaching form the basis for what I have identified as 'culturally relevant teaching'.

Is There a Culturally Relevant Teaching?

Anthropologists have long had an interest in applying their research methodology to complex social institutions like schools (Spindler, 1988). In an attempt to examine questions relating to the denial of equal educational opportunity anthropologists have looked at schools as agents of cultural transmission, arenas of cultural conflict, and sites of potential micro and macro level change (Wilcox, 1988). One of the areas of anthropological study which has proven fruitful for examining the experiences of minority students in the classroom is the attempt (or lack thereof) of teachers to find ways to match their teaching styles to the culture and home background of their students.

During the 1980s there emerged in the anthropology of education literature several terms which describe these pedagogical strategies used by teachers in an effort to make the school experience of students more compatible with their everyday lives. Those terms include, cultural congruence (Mohatt and Erickson, 1981), cultural appropriateness (Au and Jordan, 1981), cultural responsiveness (Cazden and Leggett, 1981; Erickson and Mohatt, (1982), cultural compatibility (Jordan, 1985; Vogt, Jordan and Tharp, 1987) and mitigating cultural discontinuity (Macias, 1987).

Osborne (1989) discusses some of the problems associated with the use of the above mentioned terms. He suggests that cultural congruence implies a kind of one-to-one correspondence between what happens in school and what happens in the home. Cultural appropriateness, according to Osborne, connotes being culturally proper or correct. Cultural compatibility asks for 'educational practices [that] match the children's culture in ways which ensure the generation of academically important behaviors' (Jordan, 1985, p. 110). Mitigating cultural discontinuity which is set within a framework of enculturation and cultural discontinuity, has been researched only within the confines of pre-school settings where students of all cultures are experiencing their first interruption of home-community nurturance and enculturation. Although Osborne states a preference for the term culturally responsive, he notes that neither Cazden and Leggett who originally used the term, nor Erickson (1987), have defined it. Erickson does refer to it as 'one kind of special effort by the school that can reduce miscommunication by teachers and students, foster trust, and prevent the genesis of conflict that moves rapidly beyond intercultural misunderstanding to bitter struggle of negative identity exchange between some students and their teachers' (p. 356).

Educators have also researched the impact of pedagogy on minority student performance (Moll, 1988; Cervantes, 1984; Rodriquez, 1983). Cervantes has identified 'ethnocentric pedagogy' as 'preconceived, idealized, and monolithic values and behaviors and characteristics that students should exhibit to succeed in school. These are most frequently exemplified by Anglo-Saxon middle-class values and experiences' (p. 275). He further asserts that 'the closer one reflects the idealized, the higher probability of school success' (p. 276). Boateng (1988) uses the term, 'deculturalization' to explain the 'failure to acknowledge the existence of [a group's] culture and the role it plays in their behavior' (p. 1). Boateng further suggests that teacher behavior plays a significant role in deculturalization.

Into this cauldron of terminology I am introducing an additional term — 'culturally relevant' teaching (King and Wilson, 1987; Ladson-Billings, 1989a; 1989b). Because it operates along a continuum of teaching behaviors and beliefs and can best be described operationally, culturally relevant teaching is elaborated upon here in contrast to what may be termed 'assimilationist' teaching. The major difference between the two approaches is that assimilationist teaching represents and champions the status quo. Its major function is to transmit dominant culture beliefs, values, myths and ideologies and to induct students into the role that society has determined for them with an unquestioning, uncritical view of the way schools miseducate all children, minority and non-minority, females and males, middle-class and working and lower-class, disabled and non-disabled. By contrast, culturally relevant teaching serves to empower students to the point where they will be able to examine critically educational content and process and ask what its role is in creating a truly democratic and multicultural society. It uses the students' culture to help them create meaning and understand the world. Thus, not only academic success, but social and cultural success are emphasized by the culturally relevant teacher. A more elaborate discussion of culturally relevant teaching and related research will be discussed in the subsequent section.

What We Know about Culturally Relevant Teaching

Because we have almost ten years of research which looks at pedagogy designed to be successful in the teaching of minority students it is important to begin to understand what has been demonstrated by this pedagogy. Osborne (1989) has compiled a list of twenty-four ethnographic studies that confirm eleven assertions related to culturally responsive pedagogies. These assertions include the teachers' recognition that:

— socio-political, historic, economic factors beyond the purview of the school constrain what transpires in the classroom. (Wolcott, 1974; Dumont and Wax, 1976; Osborne, 1983; Erickson, 1987; Macias, 1987; McDermott, 1987; Ogbu, 1987);

— the teacher's cultural background is not the determinant of culturally responsive teaching behavior (Osborne, 1983; Erickson and Mohatt, 1982; Vogt, Jordan and Tharp, 1987; Kleinfeld, 1975; Dumont, 1972);

— student agenda during lessons are often different from that of the teacher (Wolcott, 1974; Dumont and Wax, 1976; Dumont, 1972; Philips, 1972; Beyon, 1984; Hammersley and Turner, 1980);

— students need some flexibility in rules of behavior (Erickson and Mohatt, 1982; Van Ness, 1981; Macias, 1987; Vogt, Jordan and Tharp, 1987; Osborne, 1983, Kleinfeld, 1975);

— individual attention, either positive or negative is undesirable (Van Ness, 1981; Osborne, 1983; Vogt, Jordan and Tharp, 1987; Philips, 1972);

— school language and communication structures should contain links to students' home/community language and communication structures (Philips, 1972; Vogt, Jordan and Tharp, 1987; Erickson and Mohatt, 1982; Osborne and Bamford, 1987; Sindell, 1974);

— students favor group work over individual work (Philips, 1972; Osborne and Francis, 1987; Osborne and Bamford, 1987);

— students need to have the cultural assumptions under which the classroom functions elaborated (Kleinfeld, 1975; Philips, 1972; Osborne, 1983);

— teacher effectiveness is tied to both personal warmth and academic rigor (Kleinfeld, 1975; Dumont, 1972; Osborne, 1983);

— students respond to a more relaxed teaching/learning pace (Osborne and Coombs, 1987; Osborne and Sellars, 1987; Dumont, 1972; Wolcott, 1974; Erickson and Mohatt, 1982);

— the curriculum should be relevant to the students' lives (Osborne and Sellars, 1987; Osborne and Coombs, 1987).

The limitation of this scholarship is in its generalizability. With the exception of a few instances (McDermott, 1987; Ogbu, 1987; Beyon, 1984; Hammersley and Turner, 1980) Osborne's assertions and literature review focuses on the small scale Native American and/or Torres Strait Islander communities.

However, studies looking at successful teaching strategies for particular groups of students are emerging (First and Crichlow, 1989; Moll, 1988). Hollins (1989) suggests that there are three categories of response to improving minority student performance. In the first category, there is an *implicit* attempt to resocialize minority students into 'mainstream perception, behaviors and values' (p. 13). Approaches in this first category subscribe to a belief about the universal nature of learning and deny the need for specific pedagogies tailored to specific cultural groups. Hollins identifies the Chicago Mastery Learning

Reading Program as an example of an approach in this category. The second category of response includes *explicit* attempts to resocialize minority students into mainstream perceptions, behaviors and values. Hollins cites *A Social Skills Curriculum for Inner City Children implemented in the New Haven, Connecticut Schools* by James Comer as an example of a Category II approach. In both Category I and II, the emphasis is on teaching students basic skills. However, in Category II there is a recognition of the significance of socio-cultural factors and a belief in the need to eradicate the 'deleterious' effects of the students' home culture. In Category III, Hollins identifies approaches which represent 'conscious avoidance of explicit or implicit attempts at resocialization of the learner or the inculcation of mainstream ways' (p. 17). The widely publicized Westside Preparatory School founded and directed by Marva Collins in Chicago is cited as a Category III approach.

First and Crichlow (1989) contend that teachers' effective involvement with students, involving students in educational decision making, and making strategic decisions about what to eliminate and include in the curriculum are essential to successful teaching of minority students. First and Crichlow further comment that when comparing effective teachers of minority students with ineffective teachers they found that ineffective teachers, while compassionate, often see their students as victims and in inescapable situations. They treat their students as incapable of handling academically rigorous material. Effective teachers, on the other hand, acknowledge the state of oppression in which their students exist but insist that the students must overcome these negative situations and present them with academically challenging tasks on a regular basis.

Moll (1988) has identified several factors important in the successful teaching of Latino students. Teachers in his study all sought to 'make classrooms highly literate environments in which many language experiences can take place and different types of "literacies" can be practiced' (p. 466). Each of his teachers worked under the assumption that each student was intellectually capable of mastering rigorous academic work and rejected the notion of teaching specific skills or a hierarchy of sub-skills. Each teacher emphasized the 'importance of substance and content in teaching' (p. 467). Thus, these teachers rejected the teaching of reading through basal readers, instead opting for trade books rich with literary meaning and interest to the students. The teachers included a diversity of instruction and social arrangements in the classroom and set up their lessons to ensure that students used their personal experiences and cultural backgrounds to understand the classroom content. Finally, these teachers had considerable autonomy in the classroom. Moll's analysis suggests that the teachers attained this autonomy because they were 'theoretically equipped' (p. 470). They could articulate what they did and why they did it. They could also successfully argue about professional issues with principals and other superiors to preserve a style of teaching that they felt was successful with their students. And, these teachers depended on the 'support of colleagues who shared their approach or orientation to teaching' (p. 470).

In looking at teachers who are successful in teaching black students (Ladson-Billings, 1989a and 1989b) the evidence suggests that these teachers, despite their own personal teaching idiosyncrasies, approach teaching in a similar fashion along three important dimensions — their perceptions of themselves and others, the way they structure classroom social interactions, and their perceptions of knowledge. Teaching performance along these three dimensions is important in determining culturally relevant teaching.

Culturally relevant teachers see teaching as an art as opposed to a science with prescriptive steps and techniques to be learned and demonstrated. Thus, for them, teaching is a creative undertaking:

> ... I did a lot of substituting of things, too. You know, we didn't have health books so we did health another way ... There was a period when we didn't have social studies books, so — well, I never got involved in whether we had the book or not but it was, 'What were some of the skills you need to learn to function in social studies?' ... [Sp1–5, notes][3]

These teachers see themselves as a part of the communities in which they teach and see their role as giving something back to the community. They believe that success is possible for each student and a part of that success is helping students make connections between themselves and their community, national, ethnic and global identities. They believe that black students as a cultural group have special strengths that need to be explored and utilized in the classroom:

> ... [Black children] have always complemented my classroom because they're willing to express themselves [yet] the way that they express themselves other people think that they're out of control, rude and disrespectful ... [Sp2–3]

> Black children bring a sense of cooperation [to the classroom]. They're very willing to help. They're very open-minded ... They're very verbal ... [Sp7–2]

> ... they're just full of life ... enthusiasm. And they're not afraid to show their feelings. [Sp3–2]

> ... I think that black children are themselves, more than any other type of child. To compare them [with other children], many other children look to see what you want and then they do it, where a black child, at least the ones I've come in contact with, they [sic] look to see what you want and if they agree with it they'll do it but if they don't, they waste no bones in telling you that they don't agree. [Teachers] have to know that. They're [the children] not being rude — that's the way they are. [Sp4–1]

Culturally relevant teachers understand that the way social interaction takes place in the classroom is important to student success. Cummins' (1986) theoretical framework for empowering minority student recognizes that the pedagogy for producing empowered students must be 'reciprocal interaction-oriented' as opposed to 'transmission-oriented'. Culturally relevant teachers foster classroom social relations that are 'humanely equitable' (Wilson, 1972) and extend beyond the classroom. The teacher demonstrates a connectedness with all of the students and encourages each of them to do the same:

> [In the classroom] there wasn't a lot of competition. Everybody helped everybody to succeed. They were always willing to sit and teach somebody else ... [Sp1–2]

... I start off being being a role model ... I set the stage, expectations ... WE collectively, what WE are going to do ... WE will. [Sp2–6]

... I operate the class on an extended family concept. I try to treat them the way they will be treated at home ... to love them and discipline them ... [Sp5–2]

Culturally relevant teachers believe that knowledge is continuously re-created, recycled and shared. They take a critical view of the knowledge and content and demonstrate a passion about what they teach (Torres-Guzman, 1989). Through the content, which often is related to students' lives, they help students develop the knowledge base or skills, to build a bridge or scaffolding and often accompany the students across to new and more difficult ideas, concepts and skills (Ladson-Billings, 1989a).

... well, I always had the feeling with black children that they were always under ... we always underestimated what they could do ... I found that another avenue for them was sometimes something that didn't necessarily have to do with academics.... We always had projects going ... something that allowed them to have an avenue to be successful ... I've never been sold that academics was THE most important thing in the classroom ... nobody ever measures what the children really are capable of doing. [Sp1–1, 2]

Yesterday, we had a really good lesson on ... I'm introducing adjectives ... and I did it with the Halloween words and I put ten words on the board ... nouns ... we're getting into nouns and adjectives and for some of them this is so far out of their reach right now but I'm the kind of teacher that I just throw it at you and sooner or later you're going to catch on. And so, they were giving me words like 'bad', 'good' and I said, 'Give me a break! I don't want to hear any more bad witch, good witch, red witch, white witch! Let's think. Let's come on and think!' And it was really interesting how all of a sudden they really got wound up and they really came out with some ... I mean they started using words like 'gigantic', 'huge', and giving me a compound type adjective like 'green-faced' but see, you gotta press ... there are some teachers who'll say 'That's good. Red is good for a devil and green is good for a witch'. But that's not what I wanted. I want to keep pushing and pressing because I know they have those kinds of things in them.... The lesson went on for a long time. I find that you just can't put minutes on good lessons, you'll never get the best out of your students. [Sp2–3, 4]

Both the interview and observation data collected thus far support the notion that culturally relevant teaching is important in improving black student academic success, sociocultural success, and parent and student satisfaction (Ladson-Billings, 1989a). Parents of the teachers in the study expressed a strong desire for their students' schooling experiences to equip them academically without alienating them from their homes, families and culture. The interview, observational and anecdotal data suggest that culturally relevant teaching helps meet these needs.

Despite the research on culturally relevant pedagogy there is still a huge need for further explorations in this area. There are a few investigations of how minority independent schools are developing specific pedagogies and curricula for students (CIBS, 1989) but much more must be done. There are fundamental questions concerning teachers' beliefs and interaction styles that must be examined. We must look more closely at the link between what teachers say they do and the actuality of their instruction. Despite the long history of teacher preparation in the United States there is little in the way of follow-up and longitudinal studies that help us understand the ways in which preparation programs influence the kind of pedagogy we see in the classroom. Researchers must be willing to challenge the notion of a culturally relevant pedagogy with theoretically sound, well designed studies. They must also be willing to ask the hard questions like, can you have good pedagogy for some groups which is not good for others or can you have student academic success and emotional and social well-being without a culturally relevant pedagogy? Inquirers in this field must move beyond an intuitive sense of what is the 'right' kind of teaching for minority students to concrete evidence of pedagogy and approaches that work. Minority researchers in this area of study are still grappling with questions about what constitutes success. Can researchers of culturally relevant pedagogy be content to merely use student standardized test performance as the sole arbiter of success without asking at what social and psychic costs that success may come? If we are going to examine teaching, as Shulman suggests (1987b), in terms of conception, cognition and context, we must carefully consider the type of pedagogy that is most effective in the minority and/or urban school context.

Perhaps most helpful for prospective researchers in this area would be ways to begin to conceptualize the processes by which we can more systematically examine and uncover (or perhaps, discount) culturally relevant pedagogy. First, we need much more anecdotal and ethnographic evidence of teachers who are experiencing academic success with urban and minority students. We need the kind of 'thick description' (Geertz, 1973) that is only available through careful observation and documentation over time. Second, we need to be able to unravel important variables that may impact those successes — school level factors such as administrative leadership and school climate as well as district level factors such as funding and academic policies. We must carefully examine aspects of these classrooms — teacher-student interaction, class size, teacher knowledge and beliefs, teacher experience, curriculum, etc. — to determine what specific factor(s) or combinations of factors are important in producing these successes. Third, researchers need to examine which kinds of successful practices are truly replicable and which kinds are idiosyncratic so that theoreticians can begin to construct models of teacher education that better serve the variety of students that more and more teachers are likely to meet in the classroom. Finally, enquiry along these lines represents a special opportunity to open up new forms and ways of conducting research. The recognition that continued 'paradigm wars' (Gage, 1989) will do little to advance the cause of educational research is a starting point. However, more important than striking compromises between quantitative and qualitative lines of enquiry and among competing ideological and political interest, research and scholarship around these issues must provide bold new initiatives that inform policy makers, practitioners, other researchers and the community at large that there exists a multitude of ways to conceive, construct and solve research problems and dilemmas. Researchers must be willing to move from the traditional 'either-or' posture to a more inclusive, diverse, 'both-and' one. The research waters continue to be very murky on these issues, but we need not wait for a storm to clear them.

Linking Up with Multicultural Education

Throughout this chapter I have been making the case for research enquiry into culturally relevant pedagogy to better meet the educational, social and cultural needs of minority students. Perhaps I could argue, in a tongue-in-cheek manner, that the kind of teaching that is currently occuring in public school classrooms IS culturally relevant. However, the culture to which it is relevant — white, male, middle-class — is not the culture of reference for increasing numbers of students. Multicultural education represents an attempt to make the curriculum more responsive to the educational needs of all students. However, the term, itself, lacks clarity. In a review of eighty-nine articles and thirty-eight books on the subject, Sleeter and Grant (1987) detail five prevailing approaches to multicultural education — teaching the culturally different, human relations, single group studies, multicultural education and education that is multicultural and social reconstructionist. It is this last approach, education that is multicultural and social reconstructionist, that is compatible with the notion of culturally relevant pedagogy. This approach is one that 'prepares young people to take social action against social structural inequality' (Sleeter and Grant, pp. 434–5). Suzuki (1984) points out that this approach needs the type of teaching that will give students an opportunity to practice democratic principles in the classroom. Unfortunately, the literature suggests that schools and classrooms are not particularly democratic institutions (Engle, 1988; McLaren, 1989). For minority students (in predominately minority schools) the school and classroom (including activities such as student government) are likely to be more rigid and authoritarian than those experienced by middle-class white students (Ladson, 1984).

In order to make multicultural education work schools will have to move beyond altering the curriculum to understanding the significance among the 'what', 'how' and 'why' of instruction. In the black schools where black children routinely perform at and above grade level there are important aspects of the curriculum AND the pedagogy that should be considered.[4] The curriculum often stresses cultural affirmation while the teaching methods draw from the students' cultural strengths. The 'teachers are committed to the students and the students are committed to the teachers' (Rauber, 1989, p. 106). Even in those instances where what teachers are doing looks, 'old-fashioned' or 'traditional', a deeper sense of commitment to the students and the community is what essentially drives the teachers to discount educational fads and fashions (Delpit, 1986). Indeed, the effective schools/teaching research indicates that there are a variety of methodologies that can be employed in attempting to reach minority, urban, or so-called 'at-risk' children (Cuban, 1989). Those methodologies include direct instruction, building on the strengths that students bring with them by making connections to their real life experiences, and placing students in situations which have mixed ages and mixed abilities (*ibid.*).

While this chapter has been directed at finding ways to better meet the educational needs of minority or urban students, it is important to note that public education is not working particularly well for a broad spectrum of students. The major reports and blue ribbon commissions[5] have all indicated that public education for most students in the United States is failing to live up to the kind of standards and expectations that parents, students, communities and employers need and want. Thus, while there is a critical need to improve minority education, this effort cannot stand apart from efforts to improve education for non-minority, suburban and rural students. The need for research which examines culturally relevant pedagogy is not restricted to minorities. It is also not restricted to meeting the needs of practicing teachers. The need to improve pre-service teacher education is an important aspect of developing sound research related to culturally relevant teaching. Teacher candidates are themselves locked into their own 'monocultural' backgrounds (Grant, 1989; Fuller and Ahler, 1987) and resist enrolling in courses or practicum experiences that are likely to expose them to multicultural perspectives or themes (Mahan and Boyle, 1981). And, according to Santos (1986), 'the majority of prospective teachers do not speak any language but English, do not have numerous relationships with people of other races, cultures or religions, and have rarely been instructed by anything but an Anglo-centric curriculum ...' (p. 20).

The struggle to legitimize alternative and specific pedagogies to meet the needs of minority and urban students must go hand in hand with the struggle to improve the quality and quantity of multicultural education. Teachers must know more about the backgrounds and cultures from which their students come and be prepared to teach them in ways that maximize their chances to succeed in the school, the community, the nation and the world.

Notes

1 Work on this chapter was supported in part by an award from the National Academy of Education's 1988–89 Spencer Post-Doctoral Fellowship Program. The contents of this chapter do not necessarily reflect the views or policies of the National Academy of Education or the Spencer Foundation.

2 The first wave of educational reform was sparked by the Commission on Excellence in Education's *Nation At Risk* report that called for an overhaul of the nation's public school systems. The second wave of reform was ushered in by the Holmes Group and Carnegie reports which focused on reforms in teaching and teacher education.

3 These notations represent codes from interview data from my ongoing Spencer funded study on teachers who are successful in the teaching of black students.

4 Examples such as A. Phillip Randolph Campus High School in New York City, Harriet Tubman Elementary School in Newark, NJ, Oakland Tech's, Paideia Program, in Oakland, CA, and independent black schools such as Westside Preparatory in Chicago, IL, Bethel Christian School in Baltimore, MD, Roots Alternative Learning Center in Washington DC and the Ivy Leaf Schools in Philadelphia, PA, each represent the kind of curriculum and pedagogical excellence referred to here.

5 This includes *A Nation At Risk*, The Holmes Group Report and The Carnegie Report.

References

AMERICAN ASSOCIATION OF COLLEGES FOR TEACHER EDUCATION (1988) *Minority Recruitment and Retention: New AACTE Policy Standard*, Washington DC, AACTE.

ARONOWITZ, S. and GIROUX, H. (1985) *Education Under Siege*, South Hadley, MA, Bergen and Garvey.

AU, K. and JORDAN, C. (1981) 'Teaching reading to Hawaiian children: Finding a culturally appropriate solution' in TRUEBA, H., GUTHRIE, G. and AU, K. (Eds) *Culture and the Bilingual Classroom: Studies in Classroom Ethnography*, Rowley, MA, Newbury House, pp. 139–52.

AUSUBEL, D.P. (1968) *Educational Psychology: A Cognitive View*, New York, Holt, Rinehart and Winston, Inc.

BEYON, J. (1984) '"Sussing out" teachers: Pupils as data gatherers' in HAMMERSLEY, M. and WOODS, P. (Eds) *Life in Schools: The Sociology of Pupil Culture*, London, Open University Press, pp. 121–44.

BOATENG, F. (1988) 'Combatting deculturalization of the black child in the public school system: A multicultural approach', unpublished manuscript, Eastern Washington University, Cheney, WA.

BROOKOVER, W. *et al.* (1979) *School Social Systems and Student Achievement: Schools can make a Difference*, New York, Praeger.

CARNEGIE FORUM ON EDUCATION (1986) *A Nation Prepared: Teachers For The 21st Century*, New York.

CAZDEN, C. and LEGGETT, E. (1981) 'Culturally responsive education: Recommendations for achieving Lau remedies II' in TRUEBA, H., GUTHRIE, G. and AU, K. (Eds) *Culture and the Bilingual Classroom: Studies in Classroom Ethnography*, Rowley, MA, Newbury House, pp. 69–86.

CERVANTES, R.A. (1984) 'Ethnocentric pedagogy and minority student growth: Implications for the common school', *Education and Urban Society*, **16**, 3, pp. 274–3.

CIBS (1989) *Minority Trendsletter: Schooling Ourselves*, Council of Independent Black Schools.

COHEN, R. (1976) 'Conceptual styles, culture conflict, and nonverbal tests of intelligence' in ROBERTS, J. and AKINSANYA, S. (Eds) *Schooling in the Cultural Context*, New York, David McKay Co., pp. 290–322.

CRONBACH, L.J. and SNOW, R. (1977) *Aptitudes and Instructional Methods*, New York, Irvington Publishers.

CUBAN, L. (1973) 'Ethnic content and "white" instruction' in BANKS, J. (Ed.) *Teaching Ethnic Studies*, Washington DC, NCSS 43rd Yearbook, pp. 91–9.

CUBAN, L. (1989) 'The "at-risk" label and the problem of urban school reform', *Phi Delta Kappan*, **70**, 10, pp. 780–4.

CUMMINS, J. (1986) 'Empowering minority students: A framework for intervention', *Harvard Educational Review*, **56**, 1, pp. 18–36.

DELPIT, L. (1986) 'Skills and other dilemmas of a progressive black educator', *Harvard Educational Review*, **56**, 4, pp. 379–85.

DOMINO, G. (1971) 'Interactive effects of achievement orientation and teaching style on academic achievement', *Journal of Educational Psychology*, **62**, pp. 427–1.

DUMONT, R. (1972) 'Learning English and how to be silent: Studies in Sioux and Cherokee classrooms' in CAZDEN, C., JOHN, V. and HYMES, D. (Eds) *Functions of Language in the Classroom*, New York, Teachers College Press, pp. 344–69.

DUMONT, R. and WAX, M. (1976) 'Cherokee school society and the intercultural classroom' in ROBERTS, J. and AKINSANYA, S. (Eds) *Schooling in the Cultural Context: Anthropological Studies of Education*, New York, David McKay, pp. 205–16.

DUNN, R. (1989) 'Do students from different cultures have different learning styles?', *Inter Ed*, **16**, 50, pp. 3–7.

EDMONDS, R. (1979) 'Effective schools for the urban poor', *Educational Leadership*, 37, pp. 15–24.

ENGLE, S. (1988) 'Conformity or independent thought: Why teach the social studies in a democracy?', *Democratic Schools*, 3, 3, pp. 12–3.

ERICKSON, F. (1987) 'Transformation and school success: The politics and culture of educational achievement', *Anthropology and Education Quarterly*, 18, 4, pp. 335–56.

ERICKSON, F. and MOHATT, G. (1982) 'Cultural organization and participation structures in two classrooms of Indian students' in SPINDLER, G. (Ed.) *Doing the Ethnography of Schooling*, New York, Holt, Rinehart and Winston, pp. 131–74.

EUBANKS, E. (1988) *Teacher Education Pipeline*, Washington DC, American Association of Colleges of Teacher Education.

FIRST, D. and CRICHLOW, W. (1989) 'Effective teachers' knowledge and practice in working with "at-risk" students in an urban school district: A collaborative investigation by teachers and researchers', paper presented at the Tenth Annual Ethnography in Education Research Forum, University of Pennsylvania, 24–25 February.

FREIRE, P. (1973) *Pedagogy of the Oppressed*, New York, Seabury Press.

FULLER, M.L. and AHLER, J. (1987) 'Multicultural education and the monocultural student: A case study', *Action in Teacher Education*, 9, pp. 33–40.

GAGE, N.L. (1989) 'The paradigm wars and their aftermath', *Educational Researcher*, 18, 7, pp. 4–10.

GEERTZ, C. (1973) *The Interpretation of Cultures*, New York, Basic Books, Inc.

GRAHAM, P.A. (1987) 'Black teachers: A drastically scarce resource', *Phi Delta Kappan*, 68, 8, pp. 598–605.

GRANT, C. (1989) 'Urban teachers: Their new colleagues and curriculum', *Phi Delta Kappan*, 70, 10, pp. 764–70.

HABERMAN, M. (1989) 'More minority teachers', *Phi Delta Kappan*, 70, 10, pp. 771–6.

HALE-BENSON, J. (1986) *Black Children: Their Roots, Culture and Learning Styles*, Baltimore, MD, Johns Hopkins University Press.

HAMMERSLEY, M. and TURNER, G. (1980) 'Conformist pupils?' in HAMMERSLEY, M. and WOODS, P. (Eds) *Life in Schools: The Sociology of Pupil Culture*, London, Open University Press, pp. 161–75.

HILLIARD, A. (1989) 'Teachers and cultural style in a pluralistic society', *Issues 89: NEA Today*, 7, 6, pp. 65–9.

HOLLINS, E.R. (1989) 'A conceptual framework for selecting instructional approaches and materials for inner city black youngsters', draft document for the California Curriculum Commission Ad Hoc Committee on Special Needs Students, Sacramento, CA, 20 July.

HOLT, R. (1989) 'Who will teach the kids?', *NEA Today*, 7, 10, May/June, pp. 4–5.

JORDAN, C. (1985) 'Translating culture: From ethnographic information to educational program', *Anthropology and Education Quarterly*, 16, 2, pp. 105–23.

KAGAN, J. (1964) 'American longitudinal research on psychological development', *Child Development*, 35, pp. 1–32.

KING, J. (1987) 'Black student alienation and black teachers' emancipatory pedagogy', *Journal of Black Reading and Language Education*, 3, pp. 3–13.

KING, J. and WILSON, T.L. (1987) 'On being African-American: Beyond cultural democracy and racist education', unpublished manuscript, East Palo Alto, CA.

KLEIN, G. (1951) 'The personal world through perception' in BLAKE, R.R. and RAMSEY, G.V. (Eds) *Perception: An Approach to Personality*, New York, Ronald Press, pp. 328–35.

KLEINFELD, J.S. (1975) 'Effective teachers of Eskimo and Indian students', *School Review*, 83, pp. 301–44.

LADSON, G. (1984) 'Citizenship and Values: An ethnographic study of citizenship and values in a predominately black school setting', unpublished doctoral dissertation, Stanford University, Stanford, CA.

LADSON-BILLINGS, G. (1989a) 'Like lightning in a bottle: Attempting to capture the pedagogical excellence of successful teachers of black students', paper presented at the Tenth Annual Ethnography in Education Research Forum, University of Pennsylvania, 24–25 February.

LADSON-BILLINGS, G. (1989b) 'A tale of two teachers: Exemplars of successful pedagogy for black students', paper presented at the Colloquium in conjunction with the Tenth Anniversary Meeting of the College Board's Council on Academic Affairs, New York, 4–5 May.

MACIAS, J. (1987) 'The hidden curriculum of Papago teachers: American Indian strategies for mitigating cultural discontinuity in early schooling' in SPINDLER, G. and SPINDLER, L. (Eds) *Interpretive Ethnography at Home and Abroad*, Hillsdale, NJ, Lawrence Erlbaum Associates, pp. 363–80.

MAHAN, J. and BOYLE, V. (1981) 'Multicultural teacher preparation: An attitudinal survey', *Education Research Quarterly*, **6**, 3, pp. 97–104.

McDERMOTT, R.P. (1987) 'The explanation of minority school failure, again', *Anthropology and Education Quarterly*, **18**, 4, pp. 361–4.

McLAREN, P. (1989) *Life in Schools*, New York, Longman.

MERINO, B. and QUINTANAR, R. (1988) 'The recruitment of minority students into teaching careers: A status report of effective approaches', Boulder, CO, Far West Regional Holmes Group, University of Colorado.

MOHATT, G. and ERICKSON, F. (1981) 'Cultural differences in teaching styles in an Odawa school: A sociolinguistic approach' in TRUEBA, H., GUTHRIE, G. and AU, K. (Eds) *Culture and the Bilingual Classroom: Studies in Classroom Ethnography*, Rowley, MA, Newbury House, pp. 105–19.

MOLL, L. (1988) 'Some key issues in teaching Latino students', *Language Arts*, **65**, 5, pp. 465–72.

OGBU, J. (1987) 'Variability in minority school performance: A problem in search of an explanation', *Anthropology and Education Quarterly*, **18**, 4, pp. 312–34.

OSBORNE, A.B. (1983) 'An ethnographic study of five elementary schools at Zuni: "Are we doing what we think we are?"', Albuquerque, NM, unpublished dissertation, University of New Mexico.

OSBORNE, A.B. (1989) 'Towards an ethnology of culturally responsive pedagogy in small scale communities: Native American and Torres Strait Islanders', paper presented at the Tenth Annual Ethnography in Education Research Forum, University of Pennsylvania, 24–25 February.

OSBORNE, A.B. and BAMFORD, B. (1987) 'Torres Strait Islanders teaching Torres Strait Islanders II '*Torres Strait Working Paper 4*, (OSBORNE, B., Ed.) James Cook University of North Queensland, Townsville.

OSBORNE, A.B. and COOMBS, G.C. (1987) 'Setting up an intercultural encounter: An ethnographic study of "settling down" a Thursday Island high school class,' *Torres Strait Working Papers 6*', (OSBORNE, B., Ed.) James Cook University of North Queensland, Townsville'.

OSBORNE, A.B. and FRANCIS, D. (1987) 'Torres Strait Islanders teaching Torres Strait Islanders III', *Torres Strait Working Papers 5*, (OSBORNE, B., Ed.) James Cook University of North Queensland, Townsville.

OSBORNE, A.B. and SELLARS, N. (1987) 'Torres Strait Islanders teaching Torres Strait Islanders I', *Torres Strait Working Papers 3*, (OSBORNE, B., Ed.) James Cook University of North Queensland, Townsville.

PHILIPS, S.U. (1972) 'Participation structures and communicative, competence: Warm Springs children in community and classroom, in CAZDEN, C.B., JOHN, V.P. and HYMES, D. (Eds) *Functions of Language in the Classroom*, New York, Teachers College Press, pp. 370–94.

RAMIREZ, M. and CASTANEDA, A. (1974) *Cultural Democracy, Bicognitive Development and Education*, New York, Academic Press.

RAUBER, C. (1989) 'Schools that work', *San Francisco Focus*, March, pp. 101–16.

RIST, R. (1970) 'Student social class and teacher expectations: The self-fulfilling prophecy in ghetto schools', *Harvard Educational Review*, **40**, pp. 411–50.

RODRIQUEZ, R. (1983) 'Educational policy and cultural plurality' in POWELL, G. *et al.* (Eds) *The Psychosocial Development of Minority Group Children*, New York, Brimmer-Mazell, pp. 499–512.

ROYER, J. and FELDMAN, R. (1984) *Educational Psychology: Applications and Theory*, New York, Alfred A. Knopf, Inc.

SANTOS, S.L. (1986) 'Promoting intercultural understanding through multicultural teacher training', *Action in Teacher Education*, **8**, 1, pp. 19–25.

SHADE, B.J. (1982) 'Afro-American cognitive style: A variable in school success? *Review of Educational Research*, **52**, 2, pp. 219–44.

SHULMAN, L. (1987a) 'Knowledge and teaching: Foundations of the new reform', *Harvard Educational Review*, **57**, 1, pp. 1–22.

SHULMAN, L. (1987b) 'Assessment for teaching: An initiative for the profession', *Phi Delta Kappan*, **69**, 1, pp. 38–44.

SINDELL, P.S. (1974) 'Some discontinuities in the enculturation of Mistassini Cree children' in SPINDLER, G. (Ed.) *Education and Cultural Process: Toward an Anthropology of Education*, New York, Holt, Rinehart and Winston, pp. 333–41.

SLEETER, C. and GRANT, C. (1987) 'An analysis of multicultural education in the United States', *Harvard Educational Review*, **57**, 4, pp. 421–44.

SPINDLER, G. (1988) *Doing the Ethnography of Schooling*, Prospect Heights, IL, Waveland Press.

STEDMAN, L. (1987) 'It's time we changed the effective schools formula', *Phi Delta Kappan*, **69**, 3, pp. 215–24.

SUZUKI, B.H. (1984) 'Curriculum transformation for multicultural education', *Education and Urban Society*, **16**, pp. 294–322.

TORRES-GUZMAN, M. (1989) 'Stories of hope in the midst of despair: Culturally responsive education for Latino students in an alternative high school in New York City', paper presented at the Colloquium in conjunction with the Tenth Anniversary Meeting of the College Board's Council on Academic Affairs, New York, 4–5 May.

VAN NESS, H. (1981) 'Social control and social organization in an Alaskan Athabaskan classroom: A microethnography of "getting ready" for reading' in TRUEBA, H., GUTHRIE, G. and AU, K. (Eds) *Culture and the Bilingual Classroom: Studies in Classroom Ethnography*, Rowley, MA, Newbury House, pp. 120–38.

VOGT, L., JORDAN, C. and THARP, R. (1987) 'Explaining school failure, producing school success: Two cases', *Anthropology and Education Quarterly*, **18**, 4, pp. 276–86.

WILCOX, K. (1988) 'Ethnography as a methodology and its applications to the study of schooling: A review' in SPINDLER, G. (Ed.) *Doing the Ethnography of Schooling*, Prospect Heights, IL, Waveland Press, pp. 457–88.

WILSON, T.L. (1972) 'Notes toward a process of Afro-American education', *Harvard Educational Review*, **42**, pp. 374–89.

WITKIN, A.H. (1962) 'Origins of cognitive styles' in SCHEERER, C. (Ed.) *Cognition: Theory, Research and Promise*, New York, Harper and Row, pp. 127–205.

WITKIN, A.H. *et al.* (1977) 'Field-dependent and field-independent cognitive styles and the educational implications', *Review of Educational Research*, **47**, 1–64.

WOLCOTT, H. (1974) 'The teacher as enemy' in SPINDLER, G. (Ed.) *Education and Cultural Process: Toward an Anthropology of Education*, New York, Holt, Rinehart Winston, pp. 411–25.

Chapter 9

Riding the Wave: Collaborative Inquiry Linking Teachers at the University and the Urban High School

Martha Montero-Sieburth and Cynthia A. Gray

Charting the Course: Development of Collaborative Inquiry

The concept of collaboration is currently popular in the field of education (Lieberman, 1986; Hord, 1986; Sirotnik and Goodlad, 1988). It has been interpreted in many ways — from the pairing of students with teachers, to studies of classroom interactions, to cooperating on larger school projects. Some of the more notable cooperative ventures have been between and among single teachers, small team projects, curriculum efforts, and major sharing of human and material resources between institutions.[1] Information on the degree to which any of these versions achieve collaboration or describe the specific processes involved are limited, but even more limited are the accounts which acknowledge and describe diversity issues within urban schools.

This chapter presents the reflective interpretations of the coordinators of a university collaborative inquiry team composed of a professor and teaching fellow, six graduate students in education, and seven teachers in a Boston urban high school during the first year of an ongoing school-based inquiry process. The process, which incorporated methodologies from interpretive and collaborative action research, created a working forum for teachers to learn about each other while attempting to understand critical issues within a specific context — a public urban high school.

The evolution of the collaborative process and how it changed existing ways of thinking of the group members and their context is described through the negotiation of entry into this urban high school, building of trust, personal and professional relationships created among team members, re-definition of roles and power of group members, the emergence of an inquiry plan, the obstacles and crises encountered, the understanding of cultural differences among themselves and students, and the potential of the collaborative inquiry process to create change and reproduce itself for continuing school-based inquiry.

What follows is a narration of the humor and pain, as well as of the science of navigation, that we, the supervising faculty member and teaching fellow, experienced during this process of collaboration. It describes how we 'rode the wave', a metaphor that we used for those moments in which a sometimes unwieldy group process and dialogue required us to refrain from controlling the decision-making process.

The Experienced Teachers Program, known as ETP, was designed as a master's level and Certificate of Advanced Study (CAS) degree program at the Graduate School of Education, for incoming students who were experienced, certified teachers with no less than three years' experience, and who were interested in innovative school-based projects, leadership roles, and understanding schools. The goals of this newly-organized program were to bring faculty and students from the academic world and teachers in the 'trenches' of public schools[2] together in order to explore the realities of school life, to determine issues and teacher concerns, to learn about the art and craft of teaching, and, possibly, to apply their ideas to their contexts during an academic year. The intent in developing such collaborative projects was to create innovations which were mutually advantageous for site and experienced teachers alike. It was with those concepts in mind that the faculty member in this particular collaborative project set out to knock on the doors of public schools, searching for our 'co-collaborators'.

Negotiation of Entry[3]

During August of 1988, negotiations for selecting an urban school site were begun by the faculty member. While several sites had been suggested, one of Boston Public School's administrators encouraged her to consider this particular urban school because it had some 'basic and important needs given its diverse student population, its unique history and development'. Meetings were held with other Boston Public School administrators and the Headmaster of the school, who approved of the concept with enthusiasm. Two general school-faculty meetings were held in which we introduced the program to all teachers. Fifteen teachers signed up and were individually interviewed from October to December to assess their expectations and concerns.[4] One of the teachers, upon reflection, characterized her interview as a 'humbling experience' since she couldn't remember the last time she had been interviewed for anything. She was prepared to give the usual fill-in-the-blank answer to formal questions.

> This was my first surprise. We had a conversation. Now, this seems a simple idea, but had become an unusual occurrence to me. I do not have conversations about my philosophy of education or at least any that someone would be attentive to. I have only limited contact with faculty members during the day and, when time does allow a greater amount of interaction, it's pretty standard 'quick' questions — what are you doing, does it work? How are you handling Guinivere? Teachers, as a whole, are exhausted after a day. We are isolated and it has become a lonely profession ... I never had time, never had an audience, never really thought out what I felt about education in general or my place in it. And so, we had a conversation — what my teaching role is, what my gender and background meant in the context of the educational system, what my dreams not my goals — were, and when I was at my best.

A second round of interviews took place by November in order to see if a fit existed between the interests and backgrounds of the team members. At this point several teachers bowed out due to time commitments elsewhere. A total of seven volunteer teachers remained to attend a first general meeting which took place before the Christmas break.

Crew

The teachers' common histories reflected much of the school ethos. Of these seven teachers, five were twenty-year veterans in the school. The exceptions were the new ESL teacher, and the computer science/math teacher who had been at the school for over seven years. Four of the teachers taught through the desegregation of the high school and often spoke compellingly of their experiences during and since that time. Subjects taught by these teachers included English, economic geography, mathematics, English as a second language, and social studies; one of the teachers was a Title I reading specialist. The majority of the teachers were of Irish-American backgrounds. One teacher was of Portuguese descent and one was Afro-American.

Those university students who joined our team had quite varied experiences as well. One of them had just returned from working with Palestinians on the West Bank, and she was seeking 'opportunities to be where the action was'. Another had just returned from Israel after serving in the army there, and wanted to 'professionally reflect with practitioners'. Yet another was interested in the organizational structures and the role of teacher collaboration in urban schools. One English teacher from a preparatory school was interested in 'hearing other visions, other realities'. Two teachers, with over ten and twenty-one years experience, respectively, simply wanted to become better teachers, to work with diverse populations. Like the students, these teachers represented different ethnicities: Franco-American, Jewish, Irish-American, Italian-American, and Anglo. All seemed ready for action.

Our own experiences — as a faculty member at Harvard with experience both in the US and overseas in teaching, research, and community development; and as a teaching fellow, a doctoral candidate and former college professor with a background in special education and teacher training — appeared to blend well into the team.[5]

Testing the Water

'Don't collaborate until you see the whites of their eyes' one of the high school the teachers said in jest. He, along with six fellow urban high school teachers, was reflecting on his response to our initiative to collaborate with our team of six graduate students, a faculty member and a teaching fellow from a graduate school of education. Truth be known, his reflection was an apt description of the awkward encounters that initially took place between the teachers and ourselves as part of the graduate school team, as together we began, what academicians have facilely coined, the 'collaboration process'.

It was evident from the first meetings with the teachers, that they regarded university interventions as intrusions upon their turf, or as additional instances of teacher evaluation practices. When we introduced the ETP program to the teachers, these concerns were probably exacerbated by our use of educational jargon, such as 'collaboration involving inquiry, a process with evolving ideas'. During one of the interviews, such concerns were expressed directly:

> I resent ivory tower concepts of inner-city education. I do not want to be, along with my students, a guinea pig for some 'nouveau' experiment, doomed to be abandoned, after glowing promises, because of lack of funds and support.

As the observers, we on the university team also had to address our own biases and preconceptions of the urban school and classroom practices. Accounts from colleagues and interested outsiders to the community depicted our future site as a 'tough school' in a 'racist town'. Some of our colleagues at the university expressed skepticism at the likelihood of getting the Experienced Teachers' Program off the ground at this school. One of our faculty colleagues, most seasoned in schooling issues, had written about the difficulty in forming working relationships between school and universities:

> Schools are unforgiving places for academics, places that reject foreign bodies as a human body rejects organ transplants. The respect, capacity for reflection, success, and recognition professors may enjoy within the ivory tower seldom accompany them into the schools (Barth, *Commentary*, 1989)

The local media depicted their version of violence and tensions found in this community on a weekly basis with headlines such as: 'X student found to be part of drug gang'; 'Joey finally gets caught after ditching police in X'; or 'Boston's Student Services Offices deal with physical and emotional pain'. In addition, we were told by one of the administrators at the high school who had over twenty-five years of experience: 'In such and such a community, you receive threats and you cringe; in this community, threats are carried out'. A 1988 neighborhood profile described the community during the 1960s as:

> a declining neighborhood ... [Its] population has been reduced by one-half since 1950; its housing stock was old and deteriorated ... inadequate, unsafe, and unattractive. Its narrow streets were congested and in bad repair, the elevated line cast a blighting shadow on Main Street, and a general lack of confidence prevailed. [The only] blighting influence on the surrounding neighborhoods is the public housing [afforded by the projects which surround the high school].[6]

Urban renewal had been proposed as a major solution for these problems, and, in subsequent years, private and public investments in renewal projects and real estate development have transformed this community's physical appearance and 'restored resident confidence in the future of the area' (Neighborhood Profile, 1988). A 1985 report described the community as being 'virtually white

with no minority residents'. Since then, new, young, upwardly mobile professionals have made their way into the community, yet they remain 'outsiders' to
the townspeople.

Our high school is one of twelve Boston public high schools servicing
adjacent communities. It has a complex history of segregation, desegregation,
busing, and a number of media reported racial incidents. During the initial year
of our project, the high school also served the local community after school
hours. Over 80 per cent of the approximately 1000 students enrolled in the high
school are bused in from other parts of Boston as part of a court-ordered desegregation plan. Twenty-five per cent Asian, 20 per cent Latino, 30 per cent black,
20 per cent white and 2 per cent Native Americans dramatize the ethnic diversity
of the school. There are 100 teachers plus an additional administrative and support staff of twenty-five. Some of the teachers have been in the system for over
twenty-five years; others are newcomers. The high school includes departments
in bilingual education for Spanish-speaking and Chinese-speaking students, and
includes general secondary courses plus special education and guidance and
health support services. The school teachers and the university each carried its
own history and preconceptions to the collaboration. We carried with us not
only the legacy of the university's limited experience in exploring and intervening in urban school issues, but an incomplete knowledge of Boston urban
schools and the many issues teachers face.[7] The high school teachers brought
their past images of forced university interventions and 'expertise' to the collaboration. The expectations of 'both sides' of the table were struggling to
reverse that negative history.

As the coordinators we, the faculty member and teaching fellow, therefore
began the first phase of the process with only two major principles in mind for
ourselves and to model for the students: (i) to listen with respect to each other's
perspectives and dilemmas; and (ii) to allow for the creation of dialogue and our
stories to unfold. Although the weekly meetings were the focus of these activities, the dialogue extended into hallways, over school lunches, in the teachers'
lounge, and during teachers' hall guard duties. We came to realize that, because
teachers traditionally have limited opportunities for sharing their experiences
and insights with fellow practitioners, creating a forum within their school site in
which they could talk with each other and with us was one way to begin.[8] We
also learned how to suspend our biases, which we had to admit were probably
idealized as academics, during observations of and interviews with teachers and
students, since we were 'outsiders' who could too easily make inferences and
conclusions without knowing the contexts or reasons that teachers used to take
the actions they took. Collaboration also forced us to become aware of our
actions within this setting and reinforced our need to continually reflect on what
we were doing. Only by reflecting on how our reactions, as outsiders to the new
environment, might be incomplete or biased by our own ideologies and assumptions, were we able to get closer to an 'insider's view'. The dichotomy of
'outsider-insider' began to diminish when we took the time to become like the
'other', only then, were we able to begin to understand and describe the
process.

In preparation for the process, the university team discussed readings from
interpretive research as a point of departure in our bimonthly small-group
meetings. In these meetings, held at the high school and university, we discussed

what we were seeing and what sense we were making of the school. We began to build our knowledge about the school as a cultural site from which the rules of social and cultural organization could be decoded and used to understand the internal mechanisms and constraints which teachers experienced in this school.

Such a process incorporated the methodologies used in interpretive research and what is commonly known as *collaborative action research*.[9] The underlying structure of collaborative action research is a method of research in which teachers become active participants in defining goals, collecting and analyzing data, decision-making, planning, and implementing changes (Sirotnik, 1988).

We 'shadowed' teachers at different intervals, observing them throughout all of the activities of the day; interviewed administrators, teachers, and students; audio-recorded our school meetings and our own observations after each school day; videotaped the school context; and collected an array of field notes, school documents, and quantitative and qualitative data during our two-day-per-week visits over the spring semester. As the data was collected, the school site teachers helped us review the existing data, suggest further sources, aided us with the computerized information, gave us moral support and gained administration clearance when needed.

Our goal was to develop a horizontal rather than vertical knowledge base, avoiding a hierarchical configuration, so that the construction of the expertise of the group was shared by all. We did not want to bypass the expertise of teachers who best knew what was going on in their school. To that end, we developed a collaborative inquiry process based on the teachers' choice of issues for investigation whereby we could serve as additional eyes and ears to hear and see aspects of practice which they could not identify nor assess because of their embeddedness in their own practice. One of the veteran teachers succinctly described their need:

> ... most teachers are just too busy to step back and look at their school, their job, their way of coping with the stresses and responsibilities of teaching, or too busy to systematically address those concerns.

Maintaining Course

During our collaboration, it became evident that straying off course was a unique and necessary part of the process. At all levels, contingent on where teachers found themselves on that given day and on the degree to which they needed to be heard, especially if there had been a crisis in school, teachers and graduate student needed to vent frustrations and to reconstitute themselves (Miller, 1987). Consequently, participation in our weekly after-school meetings was not always smooth. As described by one of the teachers:

> This was not a linear progression. I found we would move two steps forward in deciphering a problem, only to fall three steps behind by digressing on a different issue altogether that needed to be discussed.

At times, we sensed their frustration as well as our own and, at other times, conversation about our anxiety to 'get started' on the project dominated the meeting. In the spirit of shared leadership, we rotated the chair of each meeting so there would be sharing of leadership and individual styles as well. Discussions became alternately heated, humorous, and serious. Every one of us experienced frustration more than once. Yet it was during those meetings that 'fifteen individuals with distinct personalities and histories learned how to share leadership roles, negotiate each plan of action, establish consensus before taking the next step' (p. 13).[10] Throughout these meetings, which progressed in spurts and leaps, the question which remained was 'Can we effect some positive change?'

Building of Trust

Although, during the first semester, the energy of a 'team' was carried by the faculty member, a teaching fellow and ETP students, by the start of the second semester, a single team combining the site teachers and the university members was in place. Trust and the creation of relationships among team members was achieved through several tasks and activities. One of these was the conducting of a community survey which allowed teachers to guide us in the use of their knowledge of the town and its surrounding areas. Data from local historical records and archives, and interviews with the locals allowed us to make sense of the social, economic, and political make-up of this community. In order to test the accuracy of what our students found, site teachers were presented with the community survey to which they added comments during one of the seminar meetings. In addition, mapping and description of the physical environments were made.

Rapport was also developed through the smaller group projects in which students and teachers agreed to work on specific-site teacher issues. These ranged from understanding the administrative leadership of the school to analyzing diverse teaching styles, and multicultural concerns via journal writing. An edited video documentary developed by the teaching fellow complemented our efforts to identify aspects of the school considered to be positive. The projects resulted in introspective learning about one's teaching, adjustment of one's expectations of students, development of non-traditional lesson plans, and creation of cultural exchanges in classrooms.

What was important about the individualized projects was the ETP students' ability to change hats from their previous teaching experiences, and to be placed in the position of observer, learner and reflective practitioner. The single most important principle emerging in this process required that the students' judgments about the site teachers' practice be suspended until we each knew and trusted each other enough to share their knowledge so as to effect change. For the teacher, the need to guide students to gather information on a topic, lesson, or issue they wanted to investigate placed them in the role of experts, a role rarely experienced within schools. In addition, being able to work with other teacher colleagues also elicited different degrees of power and control which, as we learned, they had rarely expressed within the 'system'.

The most compelling development of trust, however, evolved from the teachers' specific need for our ETP students to focus on school-wide attendance issues. Several meetings were dedicated to sorting out what were central issue of the school. Topics included scheduling, discipline, gender, community, motivation, academic standards and attendance. After site teachers met on their own, they decided on 16 March that attendance was the most significant issue since it affected every aspect of every classroom, every school program and their teaching. As one teacher said, 'You can't teach if there aren't bodies in the classroom.' An investigation of attendance patterns could provide useful base-line data for measuring the effects of internal changes in scheduling and course offerings. Whether the findings would confirm or deny teachers' impressions and experiences of their classrooms, or offer some surprises, the teachers felt it would be a valuable beginning *in* and *of itself*.

Shifting of Crew

As described, during the initial phase of entry negotiations, our roles as university members were generally perceived by the site teachers as that of being the 'experts', having available answers to the site teachers' problems (Noffke and Zeichner, 1987). After each observation and interview (whether it was about their teaching or ideas they were exploring), site teachers requested feedback on how they were doing.

What made tensions dissipate and created common ground throughout the course of the year was the high school teachers' sense of humor. They modeled this humor through wonderful quips, gentle teasing and puns, which became our favorite. Even during the 'shadowing' phase when teachers were followed in their daily tasks from the moment they arrived at school, to when they left, they requested that they not be observed for several days simply because the intensity of our shadowing seemed more like 'cohabitation than collaboration'. As one of the teachers reflected:

> The fun — and we did spend at least half of every session laughing — was coupled with the heat of a many-layered discussion. We disagreed; we ate, we laughed; we fought; we sympathized; we blamed.

In a special presentation produced by the high school teachers to the entire ETP program with the other teams of teachers and students for the other two school sites at the University, the site teachers performed song and dance that gave an entertaining yet honest appraisal of their interpretation of the collaboration process up to that point. The Headmaster joined in the celebration donning Irish bowler hats. Aside from all teachers doing a soft shoe strut, one teacher played the piano while they sang and flipped a chart with the following notes:

> 'The History of the Urban School/University collaborative'
> 'Issues Identified by the Urban School Faculty'
> 'Spanish Lady Rises Again'[11]
> 'England Expects Every Man to Collaborate'
> 'Collaborate or Cut Bait'
> 'Do Not Collaborate Thy Neighbor's Wife'
> 'Those Who Can, Do; Those Who Can't, Collaborate'
> 'The Journey of a 1000 Miles Begins with a Single Collaboration'
> 'There is Nothing as Satisfying as a Good Platitude'
> — Oscar Wilde   (ETP Seminar, 15 March 1989)

The team members from the graduate school responded energetically and, we believe, gratefully to these invitation to lighter exchange. On another occasion, one of the site teachers during a serious meeting brought in a poster of a man in a raincoat exposing himself to a group of cows lying in a field. The title read: *Expose Yourself to Ireland*. The realization of our exposure to each other's differences was paralleled by this off-beat gesture.

We feel that, in our collaboration, the humor was the glue which held the bond of the group through storm and unproductive calm. It allowed us to relieve tensions while at the same time permitting members to disagree with each other. We felt that the significance of the role that humor played in our endeavors, although for this group may have been unique, is an interesting characteristic of the process and one that sets the right tone for the challenges and fears that the collaboration process evokes.

Teachers continued to clarify their needs and shared them in earnest. The after school meetings provided a forum in which (a) we began to model the sharing of decision-making by rotating the leadership in the group; and (b) in which the concerns of site teachers, ETP students, and coordinators of the collaborative team could be raised. At this point, we began to realize the full extent of teacher isolation. The collaboration process, i.e., the talking, venting, and laughing, carried its own value and momentum regardless of intended outcomes. It allowed teachers to 'break out of their silence'.[12]

Likewise we noticed gradual changes in the portraits which teachers presented initially. They had painted somewhat of a dreary picture of their school and its problems, filled with generalizations about their students. By March, we saw these teachers appraise a videotape of various activities at the school, produced by the teaching fellow with surprise, reflecting that the context was perhaps not that bad, and that explorations and sharing of the positive aspects of school life would be a worthwhile endeavor. After viewing the video, they wanted to probe issues that the video did not show and, in so doing, attempt to gain a more balanced picture of their school.

As we collected statistical data on attendance and began to analyze it, they began to direct us and suggest other areas for our exploration. Thus, the teachers became guides for our inquiry into their issues. The shift in roles became most evident during the final sessions in which, with their input, we produced a matrix of our preliminary data from observations and interviews. This was a far cry from the feelings we had encountered as stated by one of the teachers during the first meeting:

We can see a lot of negative things because we're bogged down ... and there are so many overwhelming things at the school right now. When I first came ... in 1981, there was a big shake-up of teachers in the city, and four or five of us banded together, not knowing anybody here, to get to know the faculty. We thought this was great, we met some wonderful people ... I thought ... this is wonderful! How am I going to make it even better? I began to see that this could be improved and that could be improved ... Then you'd hear the disgruntled comments of the other teachers who had been here for a long time. It took me at least a year before I knew what they were talking about because I hadn't been 'christened' into the system till then ... No one wants to help you make it better. You start hitting walls ... The students start hitting walls and now, seven years later, I'm a very drained teacher and I'm also a teacher who isn't necessarily going to go over that border any more. I've hit the wall too many times.

As 'facilitators of the collaboration', we were also changing. As we grew to know the teachers and related to them on their issues, we also became less defensive and willingly gave direct feedback to share our own concerns. We came to know the teachers' strengths and weaknesses and how they tried to make sense of the difficult world of urban schooling. For example, at one of the longer university seminar meetings, when one of our site teachers was relating his frustration over the behavior of some urban school students by making negative statements about them while overemphasizing the need for discipline, one of the ETP students from another field site confronted the teacher openly, and chided us for not having put him in his place earlier. Our group discussed our role in this matter in depth. We knew that the whole ETP group, including the other two school sites, did not have the participant-observer advantage that we had gained by our regular presence in the school. They did not see this same teacher hug students as they cried, or lovingly address them in the hallways. We learned that the world which the site teachers had created was complex and beyond simple understanding, and as complex as our own strengths and weaknesses in many given contexts.

During the last two months, we began to talk about the school as though it were 'our' school and to come to the defense of these teachers in relation to criticisms levelled at them from the larger ETP group. They were not in the trenches. We also had to assess some of our frustrations about certain practices in the school that we wanted to see change more quickly, and we searched for the right moments to present our suggestions in a forthright manner. It is this mixture of shift of roles and power relationships, where common vulnerabilities about your position within an institutional framework is shared, which both energized and depleted us so that we often found ourselves 'riding the wave' until the next meeting, or the next encounter. We knew things would change, but how and in what direction was always uncertain.

Retrospect on Journey

It can be argued that while the collaborative identified some important school factors in need of immediate and long-term change, for continued action inquiry to occur, teachers with the support of the administration can effect change; but, left to their own, teachers can only use that knowledge to effect change in their own classrooms or on their practice.

Having gone through both the process of collaboration and inquiry of attendance issues, an assessment of what was gained by such inquiry appears to be the formulation of practical ideas for use in classrooms, the need for further classroom and school inquiry, and identifying ways to think about collaboration for those contemplating it.

Practical Ideas for Use in Classrooms

At this school, the types of changes evident were small but significant — teachers gathered and talked to each other and to university people and other teachers, they created a network of like-minded people willing to discuss issues of relevance in their lives, they joined in inquiry research, attempting to find the causes for absenteeism in their school, and they collaborated.

For one teacher, being aware of the cultural differences of her students enabled her to consider them as she taught; for another, being able to draw upon the skills of her colleagues meant a shared sense of empowerment; for another it meant being engaged in introspection which would not have occurred. For some of the teachers collaboration came to mean different things. For one teacher it meant:

... intelligent people actually asking you important questions and listening to your answers as if they meant something. Could I say that this is the most important first step that any person considering collaboration could take? I can and I do.

Collaboration comes down, at last, to finding the 'something' I had missed. I am not able, even now, to define it. I can only recognize its elements. There was communication in my craft, my art, where someone whom I respected finally asked me what my ideas were and actually listened to my answers as if they mattered. That translates, in my view, into mutual respect. There was real learning, where I joined with other teachers, other professionals, and saw how close and how far apart one can be in a profession.

For another:

Collaboration has meant viewing things differently. The whole issue was a turn-around for me about treating the kids. *When you understand where the kids are coming from in their culture*, I think you get things back from them. I am not having as much frustration and I have kids coming to my door and the discipline is still there. I started out by looking at my class, the frustration level, scheduling problems, teaching, but it ended with a broad brushstroke with things coming together. We've been changed. I can't put a finger on it, but there is something different about the way I teach.

The Need for Further Inquiry

While several of the recommendations drawn by the collaborative team suggest the possibility of change, the fact of the matter is that unless teachers have access to the decision-making processes which affect all of their school, their work becomes relegated to anecdotal evidence of a collaborative. The creation of a 'product' or project becomes limited to the group itself. In order to shift the onus of decision-making at that level, teachers must have a greater voice than that allocated to inquiry projects. Their recommendations need to be validated through administrative support, release time for initiating plans for change, and the opportunities to systematically reflect on their own beliefs as they become involved in decision-making.

In Essence, What Did We Learn from This Process Which Others Who Are Contemplating Collaboration Might Consider?

From the teaching fellow's journal entries, it became obvious that the collaborative inquiry tested her belief that:

academicians should come out of their book-lined offices and step into the reality of schooling to help *make* changes, not solely analyze or predict them.

Collaboration is not a glitzy consultantship for which I powdered my nose and polished my briefcase once a week. It is a commitment that requires you to roll up your sleeves and believe you are no better or wiser than your fellow teachers. The process astounded me with what I yet have to learn about collaboration as action science. I'm not sure that a pure form of shared leadership is possible, yet. I can't wait to do more. I feel that the commitment that this kind of research requires is not for everyone; it's unpredictable, but it will make the difference between success or failure of school reforms. The expert model is dead for me. You can't understand the urban school from a distance. These teachers are dealing with complexities of a student body whose histories are embedded in a socioeconomic environment about which I, as a middle class white educator, have much to learn. The teachers and students in this school are teaching me.

For the faculty member, it became compellingly clear that there needs to be a place for collaborative endeavors in schools, and that collaboration is based on building relationships and trust over time. Collaboration does not occur simply by having people come together, there needs to be a purpose and a vision of what is meaningful to question (Sirotnik and Goodlad, 1988). Collaboration takes place in a context and understanding the roles of those participating is essential. It requires nurturance of all involved. Some collaborators are more in need of attention than others and yet some will gradually allow themselves to be known. Some of the teachers were so frustrated and frazzled during the seven or eight hours we observed daily in their school that, at times, their intended actions and collaborative speech did not mesh with their classroom practice. Authoritarianism and oppressive measures crept up on occasion as some site teachers made students write their mistakes over or redressed them openly, making the desired collaboration an undesirable ritual to the onlooking ETP student. At other times, the smoothness with which we navigated through a day seemed questionable.

Collaboration also engenders mentoring and caring in ways that are often not visible. It is hard to know when as a facilitator you are influencing the decisions of others. Knowing when and just how much to intervene becomes an art in itself. On occasion there were small or unexpected surprises. One of the site teachers holding on to ingrained ideas about the futility of students who he considered to be 'unteachable' continued to come to every meeting because, he said: 'I can still learn at my age'.

There is no linearity to collaboration. It is not a clear-cut controllable process which has a beginning, middle and end. Nor does collaboration always function out of consensus. At times, conflict prevails, collaboration comes in spurts and gushes and without any preconceived timing. At other times collaboration requires some members pulling the oars much harder than others.

Our learning taught us that collaboration is a realization about behavior at a micro-level which allows participants to understand meaning and to think about being tolerant of differences in the way they encounter students, parents, other teachers, administrators, and themselves. It is a means in which school communities can be held responsible for becoming inquiry-prone to produce knowledge which presents liberating alternatives (Argyris *et al.*, 1985). Diversity is not based on the numbers of students or teachers who represent different ethnic groups in urban schools, but rather lies in the kinds of social relationships and interactions that occur. Teachers need to celebrate their own diversity before they can celebrate that of their students. Thus collaboration requires (i) making time and space for expressing one's ideas with the administration's support; (ii) identifying the diversity among participants as resources and models to emulate; (iii) develop awareness and sensitivity toward those you disagree with (iv) moving from understanding general cultural generalizations such as 'Hispanics are like this, or Asians are the model students' to individual characterizations; (v) creating a balance between consensual and conflictual argumentation; (vi) developing tools for facilitators to act on the process; and finally (vii) understanding that the professed notion of collaboration as a common occurrence is challenged by the lived experiences of those involved. Collaborators cannot fool each other about their roles or their assumed stations (the academic world versus life in urban schools), therefore they need to genuinely take those risks that move them beyond their assumed roles to acknowledging their differences. When you least expect collaboration to run smoothly is when you know that your own voice has been thrown into the ring.

There were times when the faculty member and graduate fellow least expected things to work out — the meetings had been too rushed, and there had not been enough time to go around to everyone — yet by the next meeting there was a sense of directionality which prevailed. Then there were those moments when it worked for all concerned — when riding the wave was made altogether possible by our shared passion for learning.

Appendix A
Results from Inquiry into Attendance Patterns

Although understanding attendance patterns became the central focus of our inquiry, and we proceeded to conduct inquiry into its manifestations, it is the actual process and reflection in action that we would like to address. The fact that inquiry research was adapted by the site teachers in such a short time was surprising to us. Several meetings on how we would understand attendance patterns in the school were held by the ETP team in which not only statistical data would be analyzed, but interviews which reflected the perspectives and attitudes of teachers, students and administrators with respect to attendance would be developed. It was thought that the interview data could provide reasons, from the students' perspective, about why they were absent so often. From this method-planning stage, ETP students spent time with individual teachers asking questions about where data could be found. It was decided by both ETP and site teachers that the third quarter, consisting of a ten-week period, would be the appropriate time frame to identify evident patterns. Our process attempted to uncover the criteria used for defining student absenteeism, and coding forms used — for dismissal, suspension, and use of waivers (excused absences). The ETP team realized that the data could be interpreted across ethnic affiliations so that we would be able to identify which groups were or were not coming to school. This information would also be important since the majority of the students are bused to school. Site teachers enabled us to conduct computer searches to obtain the quantitative data sets. These were analyzed on the basis of most likely days of high and low attendance, ethnic representation and bilingual and regular program attendance patterns. However, the ETP students and teachers alike discussed the fact that the numerical information would still not tell them why students weren't coming to schools.

Open-ended interviews from teachers, students, and administrators would round off the survey. Our regular meetings became biweekly meetings during the last two months, as teachers inquired about what else needed to be included in our analysis. Over 100 students (21 per cent black, 20 per cent Latino, 15 per cent white, and 34 per cent Chinese) were interviewed using individual and focus group approaches. All twenty-five administrators and staff and sixteen teachers were interviewed.

Triangulation of Inquiry Data

By using Glaser's (1978) constant comparative method, data from each of the interviews were analyzed and reduced to categories which could be triangulated with other data sources. Each of the ETP students worked on different areas of the inquiry process. Thus the unifying element was our weekly in-school meeting coupled with our bimonthly meetings at the university. We struggled with finding the relationships between all data sets. However, the meetings with the site teachers and their continual questioning of where we were headed with the information made us reflect on the data base itself and the process in general.

The quantitative data revealed that attendance patterns differ markedly for students in the bilingual education programs as compared to students of all ethnic groups in the regular or mainstream program. That the diversity of the student body is an issue in attendance was hinted at by the data, but not confirmed. Yet it is clear, given the propensity of the bilingual program to receive additional funding for activities and resources, that the issue of higher attendance, while attributable to the program, may also have to do with the ethnicity or culture of the students in the program. Qualitative findings from each set of administrator, teacher, and student interviews yielded the following perspectives.

Administrators

For administrators, attendance was to a great extent determined by external factors beyond the control of the school, that is, social conditions on the streets, single-parent families, constant transfers, etc. However, within the school, administrators signalled those programs receiving outside financial and human resource support as being able to retain students — bilingual education, special education, etc., where supervision, special activities, and community outreach had an impact. This was not the case for the regular programs where classes are shrinking and cutbacks in resources are strongly felt. Lack of resources meant reduced programming, which was also deemed a factor affecting attendance.

Administrators recognized inaccuracies in the reporting of figures from the city and state sources, yet felt tied to the forms emanating from the Central Office for reporting dismissals and drop outs. The forms, with a certain number of boxes to be checked, make it difficult to explain each individual case where a student who has simply moved out of the school district may not necessarily be a drop out. Lack of follow-up of students makes this particularly hard to ascertain. Depending on who and how student information is interpreted, it is recorded within the specifications of the form.

In their attempt to address student personal needs individually, the inconsistency in implementation of attendance policies, particularly in the form of waivers (excused absences), was brought out as a concern in the interviews. Some administrators will give the student the benefit of the doubt based on his/her individual appeal, thus making it hard for the teachers to know what is the uniform policy.

Teachers

The analysis of teachers' interviews yielded important information with regard to waivers, which were commonly viewed as arbitrary and useless in requesting make-up work from students. Consistency and regularity of policies on attendance were also cited as creating confusion and frustration. The need for better communication between faculty and the disciplinarians was also highlighted, especially in finding out the status of students who had been referred. More importantly, the findings indicated that the interpersonal nature of student and teacher relationships within classrooms has been replaced/overshadowed by the bureaucracy of the system. Attendance becomes an issue of procedures rather than teacher-student relations when teachers write up students, and the disciplinarian determines the consequences without feedback to the teachers. Teachers' decisions about students are entangled between those who have created school-wide policies and those who have ultimate responsibility for discipline.

Students

Individual and focus-group student interviews revealed similar findings. The variation in perceptions was, however, linked to certain cultural issues for some students. In general, students expressed being pressured by parents to be at school. Having to catch up on daily assignments was reason enough to be present. The school's policy was well understood by all and, in fact, had been mastered by many, to the point that they knew what loopholes existed.

While attendance was viewed positively by all students in the cluster of interviews, Latinos felt family demands and responsibilities placed greater weight on their decision to come to school. Illness was cited as the most accepted reason for student absenteeism. However, other reasons were also important — lack of friends, physical threats, peer pressure, work demands, lack of interest in studying, intra-group differences, immigrant students' adaptation of schooling, value contrasts between country of origin and the US, 'mental health' days, parental pressure, family responsibilities and problems.

Although education was considered an important value, none felt it was of particular importance *in and of itself*. Getting a good job ranked high on their horizon. Being known by their teachers on a one-to-one basis was also highly rated by all students; less by the Chinese students. Students wanted to see teachers as 'real people' sharing their personal lives and stories with them and they also wanted to have teachers view them as unique individuals. The Chinese students interviewed in this cluster perceived their opportunities for their future were made possible by their educational and financial attainment. Latinos, especially immigrants, shared perceptions of surviving day-to-day and gradually adapting to school norms in order 'to make it'. Discrimination, while not explicitly perceived, was brought up by Latino students, who felt teachers who shouted at them, or were authoritarian, made them feel uncomfortable. In addition, they also perceived differences among and between Latinos, as influencing their presence in school, especially with regard to the types of peer linkages and solidarity they developed. For example, Puerto Ricans would most likely side with blacks over other Latinos if there were skirmishes in the hallways. Central Americans would not necessarily side with South Americans but would tend to stay within each other's groups.

In sharp contrast to the understanding held by students for being absent, cutting, was not viewed in the same manner by different students. In fact, consequences for cutting were perceived as inconsequential by all students interviewed, except by the Chinese students, who hardly ever cut classes.

Our observations from the analysis of data became the focus for our after-school weekly meetings, a forum in which teachers and faculty participated actively. The interest of the site teachers was evident, reflected by their high attendance and spirited discussions. In those meetings, they pointed out areas where we could further clarify attendance issues, and in turn these meetings, also allowed us to draw upon their ideas and insights on attendance. We presented a matrix of major themes developed from the qualitative and quantitative analysis, to portray the extent to which attendance was an issue at this school. Of these themes, those in order of importance were the following: the value of the bilingual program versus regular program attendance which was higher in the bilingual program; the sense of community or lack of community meaning within the school; the lack of general support from the administration and from within the ranks of teachers for innovations for change; the reliability of information on attendance; the consistency of attendance policy implementation; the need for greater communication; the diversity of students; perceived discriminatory practices; and interpretations on absenteeism, cutting, and programming.

Concerned with these findings, site teachers sought to address these with recommendations for future inquiry on the usefulness of understanding patterns of attendance for the purpose of revision in policy and procedures. One of the most salient and possible alterable immediate concerns was the use of waivers. These site teachers felt that by brainstorming ways to improve communication levels across the school, the consistency of implementation of school policy with regard to attendance might be reinforced. Their agenda for the fall was to gravitate around the discussion of waivers, and extend the inquiry on attendance to include other areas which had been identified.

Acknowledgments

We would like to acknowledge Maryann Matthews, Gerald Sullivan and Annemarie Ryan, whose voices are heard in this chapter, and the rest of the teachers who welcomed us into their school and classrooms. Without their time, wisdom and willingness to explore the craft of teaching, the creation of this special community of inquiry would not have been possible. Recognition is also warmly extended to John Ameer, our friend, colleague and special editor.

Notes

1 Examples of this are the Teachers Network at the Harvard Graduate School of Education, the Teacher's Forum at the Harvard Graduate School of Education, the North Dakota Study Group, etc.
2 Approximately fifteen students were enrolled in the program from which three teams were formed to work in three different schools. This chapter explores one of the three collaborative processes developed at an urban high school site.
3 The Experienced Teachers' Program students could select from one of three school sites (one suburban and two urban). Each school formed a team composed of a faculty member, a doctoral teaching fellow, and a number of ETP students who would join the school site teachers as another affiliated team. ETP students would benefit from the opportunity to examine important educational issues on-site and develop collaborative skills as educational planners, researchers, and resource people. Cooperating schools would, in turn, receive course vouchers from teachers based on the number of students participating, the opportunity to co-author a team publication and collegial support of fellow educators.
4 The criteria for participation in the ETP program evolved from the interviews with teachers. It became evident that there was a need to have school-wide representation, across diverse subject areas and programs, with gender representation, and a mix of new teachers to the school and experienced teachers willing to participate in meetings and in our observations and interviews.
5 The faculty member's own ethnic background is of Mexican and Costa Rican descent. The teaching fellow is of Scottish/Irish descent.
6 Neighborhood Profile (1988) City of Boston, Boston Redevelopment Authority. Brackets are used by this article's authors.
7 Although the university had successfully developed a Principals' Center to attract city-wide administrators to workshops and lectures, and has a history of arranging

field experiences for individual students' placement, it did not have a program specifically directed at developing school-based inquiry in order to look at issues through the reflection of site teachers.

8   The creation of the ETP program sought to respond to the dearth of opportunities for established teachers to share their knowledge about learning. ETP would not only help the Graduate School of Education students deepen their leadership skills, but also enable cooperating teachers to plan together to implement new programs and give education faculty the opportunity to learn about life in schools (Handout on the Experienced Teachers' Program, Harvard Graduate School of Education, 1988).

9   A distinction is made here about ethnographic methods and action research since within the US context, action research has a direct practical application. It has been applied to organizational understanding (Argyris' model, 1985), teachers' reflection (Schon's model, 1983), group dynamics and adult development (Oja and Smulyan, 1989), to name just a few examples, within the US. In other contexts, such as Latin America, action research entails a clearly political message which deals with issues of oppression and involves not only the commitment of the community but the researcher as well. Such action research is also known as 'investigation comprometida' — research of commitment. European derived action research has either a philosophical or Neo-Marxist orientation. See Habermas (1975 and 1984), Marcuse (1964).

10 Robinson C. (1989) 'Rationale for collaborative inquiry', *Collaborative Inquiry of the CHS/Harvard Experienced Teachers Program*, unpublished report, spring.

11 Referring to the university faculty supervisor.

12 This is a phase which Paulo Freire uses to express the transition for oppressed illiterate peasants from their silence to reflective action and literacy.

References

ARGYRIS, C., PUTNAM, R. and MC LAIN SMITH, D. (1985) *Action Science*, San Francisco, CA, Jossey Bass Inc.

BARTH, R. (1989) 'Commentary', *Education Week*.

COOPER, D. with BATTETT, D., HAYHOE, M., HOBROUGH, R., ROWE, M. and RUMBSBY, A. (19??) *Support for Research-Based Inquiry/Discovery Teaching*, Cambridge Institute of Education, Unit 2 Research Methods.

GLASER, B. (1978) *Theoretical Sensitivity: Advances in the Methodology of Grounded Theory*, Mill Valley, CA, Sociology Press.

GOODLAD, J. and SIROTNIK, K. (1988) 'The future of school-university partnerships' in SIROTNIK, K.A. and GOODLAD, J.I. (Eds) *School-University Partnerships in Action*, New York, NY, Teachers' College Press, Columbia University, pp. 205–26.

HABERMAS, J. (1975) *Legitimation Crises*, Boston, MA, Beacon Press.

HABERMAS, J. (1984) *The Theory of Communicative Action*, Boston, MA, Beacon Press.

HORD, S. (1986) 'A synthesis of research on organizational collaboration', *Educational Leadership*, February, pp. 22–6.

KALLICK, B. (1981) *Do Your Own Classroom Research*, Teachers' Center at Fairfield Inc., Fairfield, CO.

LIEBERMAN, A. (1986) *Collaborative Research: Working with, Not Working On . . . Educational Leadership*, February, pp. 28–32.

MARCUSE, H. (1964) *One Dimensional Man*, London, Routledge and Kegan Paul.

MILLER, J. (1987) 'Researching teachers: Problems and emancipatory potentials in collaborative studies', annual meeting of the American Education Research Association, Washington DC, April.

NOFFKE, S. and ZEICHNER, K. (1987) 'Action research and teacher thinking: The first phase of the Action Research on Action Research Project at the University of Wisconsin-Madison', annual meeting of the American Educational Research Association, Washington, DC, April.

OJA, S.N. and SMULYAN, L. (1989) *Collaborative Action Research: A Developmental Process*, London, Falmer Press.

SCHON, D. (1983) *The Reflective Practitioner: How Professionals Think in Action*, New York, NY, Basic Books Inc.

SIROTNIK, K. (1988) 'The meaning and conduct of inquiry in school-university partnerships in SIROTNIK, K.A. and GOODLAD, J.I. *School-University Partnerships in Action*, New York, NY, Teachers' College Press, Columbia University, pp. 169–90.

SIROTNIK, K.A. and GOODLAD, J.I. (1988) *School-University Partnerships in Action*, New York, NY, Teachers' College Press. Columbia University.

Chapter 10

The Language Minority Student and Multicultural Education

Hilda Hernández

Introduction

Linguistic diversity is an integral part of the broader spectrum of cultural diversity that exists within our society. Demographic trends suggest that language minority students — children whose primary language is not English — comprise an increasingly significant proportion of the student population in classrooms in many communities across the nation. Whether many languages are represented locally or only a few, the issues facing those involved in educating language minority students are complex and challenging.

In this chapter, the focus is on one aspect of education that is multicultural — specifically, research directions and the schooling of language minority students. The chapter begins with an overview of the existing knowledge base. With this as a foundation, a research agenda is presented that describes the major areas to be examined and types of research most critically needed. Special emphasis is given to research that addresses concerns related to the academic achievement of linguistic minority students. Finally, recommendations are offered regarding the ways in which teacher education and university policy may be changed to facilitate implementation of the agenda presented.

The Knowledge Base

There exists a substantial body of knowledge related to the schooling of language minority students. In reviewing basic research on bilingualism, Hakuta (1986) has identified important insights having direct implications for education. With respect to the nature of language proficiency, for example, research indicates that language is a complex configuration of abilities. To develop a full repertoire of linguistic skills, learners need both communicative and academic language. From a linguistic perspective, different demands are placed on the abilities of second language learners in conversational and academic settings. Communicative skills are characterized by social interaction, negotiated meaning, and contextualized language use. Academic language skills, on the other hand, emphasize cognitive, content-related applications of language — the kinds of language use that are most dependent on literacy skills. Communicative and academic language skills develop over time — one preceding the other — and both are essential for students to succeed in school.

Hakuta observes that research also has provided a better understanding of the relationship of the first and second language. Studies on second language acquisition indicate that the process varies greatly among individuals (*ibid*.). How children learn language is affected by a myriad of factors, some cultural, some social, and others personal. The process is slower and less efficient for elementary school children than for second language learners at the secondary level. In addition, for language minority students, the primary language serves as a foundation for the acquisition of English. Research reveals that most of the subject matter knowledge and literacy skills learned in one language transfer readily to another. Contrary to popular belief, bilingualism does not impact negatively on cognitive development, but rather enhances thinking skills if the second language is learned in addition to, and with sustained development of, the native language.

Recent research on second language acquisition also has provided the basis for developing some principles to guide the effective use of English in teaching second language learners. Ervin-Tripp (1985) suggests that teachers should use English in the classroom in ways that adhere to principles encompassing concepts such as the following:

- Second language learners need language which is real, meaningful, and comprehensible.
- Teachers can facilitate comprehension by keeping form and content as simple as possible — modifying language by simplifying sentence structure, repeating vocabulary, etc.
- Classroom activities must provide opportunities for second language learners to use English and participate in language development activities.
- While children are in the initial stages of second language acquisition, use of their primary language should be accepted.
- When two languages are used for instructional purposes, they should be used separately — differentiated by time or subject matter — rather than concurrently.
- Teaching *about* language is less effective than teaching *through* language when opportunities for interaction are provided and affective considerations are taken into account.

The existence of a substantive knowledge base and the principles that are emerging from research into second language learning are very significant (Mehan, Trueba and Underwood, 1985). First, they provide evidence of a well-established interdisciplinary research tradition in this field. Clearly, the factors and conditions that influence the academic achievement of language minority students have been the focus of significant and systematic inquiry across disciplines. Second, this knowledge base provides the solid foundation necessary to define new research agendas and to explore emerging avenues of enquiry. As researchers in the University of California have recognized, it represents the basis for developing better research methodologies and more comprehensive theories concerning cognition, culture and society.

Choosing the Right Words

Who are language minority students? As a group, how homogeneous are they? How should diverse ethnolinguistic populations be treated? As these questions posed at a UC Linguistic Minority Project Conference suggest, adequately defining the terms to be used in identifying the population to be studied and making explicit their underlying assumptions is critical (Underwood, 1986).

As commonly used, the term 'linguistic minorities' includes all populations with a different language or English dialect heritage (Mehan and Trueba, cited in Ervin-Tripp, 1985). Central issues to be resolved involve identification of the groups that are to be considered language minorities and a determination of the extent to which language should be considered a defining characteristic. With respect to the first issue, important distinctions need to be made between students of different backgrounds. For example, students who are non-English dominant must be distinguished from those who are members of ethnic minority groups but English dominant. These students experience different problems in school, and need to be approached differently in terms of policy and research (Underwood, 1986).

In terms of the second issue, there is a real danger that problems in academic performance be thought of as either primarily attributable to the linguistic identity of students or as an outcome of the interaction of other factors within the broader sociopolitical and cultural context (Hakuta, 1986). Simply stated, language is central to some cognitive, social and cultural processes, and of lesser importance to others. Differences in the sociocultural history of diverse groups have resulted in distinctive patterns of achievement and underachievement in school. Consequently, problems differ from one group to another, creating a need for research directed toward the development of specific educational approaches sensitive to the uniqueness of each group within a given situation.

Mehan (Mehan *et al.*, 1985) and others (Underwood, 1986) have called for the use of a new, non-pejorative terminology — most especially a redefinition of such widely used terms as 'linguistic minority' and 'underachievement' — that would enable researchers to focus on basic issues more clearly. What is the ultimate goal of education for language minority students? What are the precise language needs of students and what levels of English language proficiency are appropriate? At present, 'no clear image yet exists concerning the specific direction linguistic minority education should take' (Underwood, 1986, p. 116). Defining the terms used — perhaps opting for 'second language learners' as some have suggested — may help move researchers toward consensus in setting the goals and research directions that are so sorely needed.

A Research Agenda

The primary goal of researchers in this field is to develop a substantial body of knowledge describing how to educate language minority students. First and foremost, achieving this goal requires a research approach that is *multidisciplinary*, *collaborative* and *action-based*. Specifically, research on the schooling of linguistic minorities must draw from diverse interdisciplinary perspectives including education, linguistics, psychology, history, anthropology, and sociology (Mehan *et al.*, 1985). The research endeavor should be practice-oriented and action-based, with researchers and practitioners working together to develop and conduct research. Only through collaboration, can researchers and practitioners effectively modify and improve educational practice: practitioners helping to define the most salient problems to be addressed; researchers providing the methods for investigating them. Only through cooperation can they can engage in the kind of problem-solving and positive action necessary to improve educational policies (*ibid.*; Samaniego, 1986). Second, from a methodological perspective, the research approach must be, by definition, *holistic*. The nature of the problems to be addressed requires the integration of insights provided by both quantitative and qualitative methodologies (Chavez, 1985; Underwood, 1986). Although they address different concerns, they are complementary and compatible.

Researchers and practitioners have yet to confront many significant questions concerning the schooling of language minority children. Given the discussion thus far, it is increasingly obvious that the issues involved are complex and interrelated. It is also apparent that if educational changes related to the schooling of linguistic minorities are to be implemented effectively, research efforts will need to encompass three essential dimensions of teaching and learning. Specifically, these are the multiple contexts in which education takes place; the dynamic processes that are the realities of classroom life as experienced through the interaction of teachers and students; and the content which provides the academic focus for instruction. Thus, for purposes of discussion, *context*, *process* and *content* will provide the unifying themes for presentation of this research agenda.

Context

Issues in the schooling of linguistic minority children are so complex that they cannot be effectively addressed unless they are viewed within the broader societal context: 'We can only understand students and classroom practices in the context of the school, the school in the context of the community, and the community in the context of the culture and political economy of the United States and its relation to its neighbors' (Underwood, 1986, p. 49). Clearly, the focus of research endeavors must extend beyond the individual child, beyond the classroom in isolation. Teachers need to know how classroom realities are influenced by conditions and events outside the school, and researchers can provide, at least, some of the answers.

There are several primary research areas related to what Valdes has referred to as 'non-instructive features' of linguistic minority groups (1986). Cultural background, particularly as it relates to home and family life, is one of the most important: 'As children begin to identify with the social world around them — their family, peers and community — their experience becomes embedded in an intricate web of cultural meanings and historical conditions' (Matute-Bianchi, 1985, p. 36).

There is a particular need for basic research to examine the influence of family socialization patterns on attitudes, learning styles and academic achievement (Underwood, 1986). One area of considerable interest involves the relationship between socialization patterns and the development of literacy skills. One illustration is Heath's work describing how the educational achievement of language minority children is influenced by literacy practices in the home. Heath (1985) contends that in some ways, *how* students use language appears to be more critical than *what* language they speak. The development of certain academic language and literacy skills must begin prior to schooling if children are to participate fully in classroom activities. Another example is provided by Moll, Yelez-Ibañez, and Greenberg (1989). In their research project, community knowledge and classroom practice are combined to achieve educational change. After describing how knowledge and skills are shared among households in an Hispanic community, they relate community information to literacy instruction in an after-school educational program, and then apply what is learned to change literacy instruction in the classroom. Both of these studies reaffirm the notion that research efforts related to literacy skills development should (a) involve parents, teachers and researchers; and (b) focus on establishing links between children's experiences in home and community contexts with classroom instruction.

Cultural background factors related to the family environment affect the schooling of language minority students in other ways too. Parents are central figures in the schooling of language minority students. Although educators realize that parental involvement is almost synonymous with 'empowerment', there are significant gaps in our knowledge of how to bring parents into the educational process most effectively (Underwood, 1986). Foremost among the unanswered questions are the extent to which parental involvement affects academic achievement and the nature of the process through which this takes place. How does parental involvement actually empower children to succeed in new learning environments? How does involvement give parents a sense of efficacy as participants in their children's education and as members of their communities? How do parents in different language groups work to secure educational opportunities for their children?

Closely related to the issue of involvement is that of parental awareness and expectations. Of considerable concern is the nature of parents' knowledge regarding their children's schooling (Valdes, 1986). Better understanding what the parents of language minority students know about school and how much they know is essential if teachers are to work more effectively with these parents and share strategies that can enhance their children's academic performance. In many respects, surprisingly little is known about parents' awareness of and attitudes toward the school system (Underwood, 1986). What meanings do they attach to 'education' and 'school'? How do the parents define success and failure? What expectations do they have regarding their children's education? How do they see their role in helping their children achieve academically?

In summary, socialization patterns and parental involvement represent but two of many 'non-instructive features' of context critical in the schooling of language minority students. Clearly, researchers must also direct their attention to other important elements of the societal context, such as the impact of popular media and ethnic segregation on teachers and students, and the interaction of conditions outside the school with student factors and classroom performance (Cortes, 1985; Hansen, 1985). As noted earlier, these issues are complex, and — if they are ever to be fully understood — must be viewed as embedded within the broader context of community, culture and society.

Process

The creation of optimal learning environments must be approached through investigation of classroom processes. Classrooms are highly organized, social and cultural learning environments. Within each classroom, there are processes — social, interactional and organizational — that provide the channels through which sociocultural factors influence students' academic performance and personal development. To influence the quality of schooling for language minority students, researchers must cooperate with practitioners to explore the dynamic processes that are central to classroom life.

One of the most important dimensions of the classroom learning environment is in the interaction of teachers and learners. Describing schools and classrooms as pervasive language environments, Stubbs (1976) asserts that 'classroom dialogue ... *is* the educational process, or, at least, the major part of it for most children' (p. 68). Recent research looks to the many manifestations of language in the classroom as a key to understanding social and cultural dimensions of teaching and learning. For example, Hawkins (1987) looks at classroom interaction for insights into linguistic and cognitive development. In her observation of patterns of family interaction, Valdes (1986) finds that some behaviors appropriate to the immigrant home context are misinterpreted or perceived negatively in a classroom setting. These studies raise the kinds of questions that need to be addressed by researchers. What is the relationship between language acquisition, cognition and content-area instruction? Why do some teachers appear to be more sensitive to cultural differences than others? What kinds of experiences enable teachers to better appreciate children's real potential for academic success?

Social context encompasses the dynamics of interpersonal relationships between teachers and students. Teacher attitudes, for example, particularly as they influence the differential treatment of children, can be difficult to modify. As Valdes (1986) has observed, 'It is not that we are mean people, way down deep, but that in fact the society has done such a good job of socializing us that we just brutally expect certain kinds of things and are thoroughly mystified by other kinds of things' (p. 54). To bring about change, teachers must evaluate exactly how they interact with particular children in different situations. Projects such as TESA (Teacher Expectations and Student Achievement) can be helpful in addressing indifferent or negative attitudes. However, as Valdes has asserted, collaborative research efforts are crucial in focusing attention on teachers' actual experiences with students and on the factors — within and beyond the classroom — that influence these experiences.

We are just beginning to comprehend how important classroom learning environments are to the academic performance of linguistic minority students (Mehan *et al.*, 1985). With this heightened awareness has come the realization that the key to creating a climate conducive to high levels of performance is through interaction, social context and organization. In the final analysis, teachers must be empowered to change the character of the classroom environment, for 'it is in the classroom itself that the climate must be created to provide for the academic achievement of language minority students' (Chavez, 1985, p. 34).

Content

If significant changes in the schooling of language minority students are to result from research, then attention must be directed toward content. As defined by Shulman (1986), content encompasses subject matter, formal curriculum, instructional methods and materials, and the particular set of skills, processes, and understandings transmitted. From a teacher's perspective, 'the content and purposes for which it is taught are the very heart of the teaching-learning process' (*ibid.*, p. 8). The issues involved in dealing with content could not be more basic. In considering this segment of the research agenda, three areas of concern stand out most prominently. These include subject matter content and curriculum design, multilingual methodology, and testing and assessment.

First and foremost, attention must be given to subject matter and curriculum-related issues. Given the relatively large dropout rate in certain language minority populations, researchers and practitioners must join forces to look critically at one of the most basic aspects of the educational enterprise: the transmission of mastery over the contents of a curriculum that comprises many subjects, skills and attitudes (*ibid.*). Growing numbers of educators (Lopez, 1986), voice their concern that greater numbers of students with diverse linguistic and cultural backgrounds be prepared to enter and perform successfully in higher education. Educators face an equally troublesome situation in meeting the needs of students who will not continue their formal education beyond high school. The dilemma is like a double-edged sword: to offer students job-oriented skills without channeling them into strictly vocational tracks. Further complicating matters is the unknown impact that the implementation of new model curriculum content and standards will have on linguistic minority students in states like California.

To confront this challenge, Mesa (1986) calls for collaboration between universities and districts in the design of a curriculum that 'allows full access to all children' (p. 65). The curriculum he envisions is coordinated and coherent. By providing breadth and depth in the treatment of subject matter, it enables students to master content at a given level while preparing them to work beyond to the next level. Using math as an example, Mesa criticizes designs that fail to prepare students in basic math for higher levels of the subject. Ideally, taking a basic math course should present students with multiple options, not channel them in limited directions. To accomplish this, math curricula will need to incorporate greater linkages between levels, for example, basic math and algebra (and higher math). Providing a curriculum that is relevant, stimulating and practical while providing depth of knowledge within domains is crucial to the academic achievement of language minority students (Berliner, 1990; Underwood, 1986).

Research issues in curriculum and subject-matter content are closely related to concerns involving multilingual methodology. 'We have a number of languages being spoken in a single classroom in many schools. The question is: what is the best way to approach the instruction of these students?' (Underwood, 1986, pp. 26–7). As many contemporary classrooms become more multilingual, it is becoming increasingly apparent that approaches developed with the special needs of 'prototypical' student populations in mind often fail to address the actual needs of large segments of learners (Underwood, 1986). Hence, there is also a significant need to establish what instructional methods and approaches work most effectively with students from diverse linguistic and cultural backgrounds and in different situations. Chuong (cited in Hakuta, 1986) and Hakuta (1986), for example, have criticized the scarcity of research examining the educational situation of recent immigrants from Southeast Asia. Relatively little is known about the learning skills involved in the acquisition of non-alphabetic languages and how they compare with those used in learning alphabetic languages. Important questions exist regarding the extent to which communicative strategies used with other language minority groups are appropriate for pre-literate students of English.

Other researchers — like Ervin-Tripp (1985) — have focused attention on the programmatic implications of the issues involved by posing research questions such as the following: When bilingual education is not an option, what is the best educational approach for language minority students? For what groups of children and in what circumstances is bilingual education not appropriate? What is the experience of monolingual English-speaking students in bilingual classrooms? It is clear that although researchers and practitioners alike accept the notion that 'no single approach represents the best solution for all situations' (Ervin-Tripp, 1985, p. 45), collaborative research efforts are needed to provide direction as to exactly what methods teachers should use with learners from different backgrounds in various settings.

Finally, there is a critical need for more effective ways of assessing language proficiency (including literacy skills) and academic ability in culturally and linguistically diverse student populations (Hernández, cited in Underwood, 1986). In many schools the assessment of language proficiency is not addressed in a broad curricular fashion but rather narrowly in relation to placement and reclassification. As a result, specific information as to what language minority students are able to do with the language they know is often limited and of little instructional value. Those working closely with language minority students realize that there are significant gaps in our knowledge of exactly what students' language needs really are. Generally speaking, we need to know with greater precision what constitutes the mastery of English required for academic success, and how long it actually takes for different learners to perform in various areas of an English-only environment (Fillmore and Martinez, cited in Underwood, 1986).

In addition, if we are to understand the relationship between language, learning processes, and content-area instruction, we also need new and better ways to evaluate both language proficiency and subject matter competency. This includes development of instruments that are sensitive to different functions of language use. Teachers need tests that can provide instructionally-relevant information regarding relative strengths and weaknesses in students' command of different language functions. Along parallel lines, they also need the kind of diagnostic instruments described by Samaniego (1986) as geared to the 'anatomy' of subject matter skills. These are measures identifying individual student's strengths and weaknesses in different content areas so that teachers can make strengths of the latter and monitor the ability of language minority students to deal with subject matter in the second language.

Research and Teacher Education

Given the important role teacher education plays in determining the quality of schooling for language minority students, researchers must join efforts with teachers, teacher educators, and administrators to develop more effective teacher preparation programs. According to Ervin-Tripp (1985) research on language learning and linguistic minorities has had relatively little impact on teacher education in general. Although considerable research has been done in the field, much has been of limited practical use to most classroom teachers; applicability to teacher preparation has not been a primary consideration in research design.

New teachers in the 1990s will need specialized preparation that emphasizes the creation of optimal learning environments and the use of teaching methods appropriate for specific groups and situations. As Trueba (1987) has observed, traditional concepts of teacher 'training' prove to be inadequate as we 'encounter a student population with a language, culture, and outlook on life that are profoundly different from that of the teachers' (p. 71). Although institutions of higher education cannot realistically prepare teachers for the full range of diverse settings and student populations they may encounter, they must make a commitment to the idea that 'the essence of effective teaching lies in the individual teacher's ability to communicate with each and every group of students she/he encounters' (*ibid.*, p. 71).

How, then, can researchers help revise existing assumptions about teacher education? There is a need for researchers to closely examine the process and substance of teacher preparation programs. Ervin-Tripp (1985) asks why sound principles of second language learning are not presently being applied in the classrooms of language minority children? It's a valid question.

Research involving bilingual teacher training programs, for example, has identified a number of effective practices that appear to contribute significantly to the transfer of content from training to classroom (Calderon, 1985). These include knowledge of theories related to communicative competence; familiarity with current approaches to literacy instruction; emphasis on classroom discourse; and use of empirically-tested teaching models. The Eastman Plan (Dolson and Rubio, 1987) provides a case study of how a theoretical framework for the schooling of language minority students can be effectively implemented schoolwide.

Taking what we already know and putting it into practice is a major task facing everyone involved with teacher education, but research has already demonstrated that it can be done. Our task now is to do it on a broader scale. As many parts of the nation become increasingly multilingual, work needs to be done to determine what the essential features of teacher preparation are for regular classroom teachers likely to find themselves working in multilingual settings (Underwood, 1986). What should comprise the content — the particular knowledge, attitudes and skills — most important for these teachers of linguistic minority students? How can this content be taught most effectively to teachers who are not specialists in the field?

The Research Agenda and University Policy

Enacting the research agenda described in this chapter will require a strong institutional commitment from universities across the nation. Changes are needed to facilitate research directed toward the goal of enhancing the quality of education for language minority students. For many researchers, those issues related to the process of faculty evaluation are central. It is no secret that there is a lack of prestige associated with research in applied areas. To quote Hakuta (1986), 'education-related research is a second class citizen within the halls of academia' (pp. 19–20). However, given the nature of the issues involved in bilingualism and the education of language minority students, Hakuta is on target in describing this situation as paradoxical. Universities must recognize the inherent importance within this field of classic issues such as the relationship of language and thought; the relationship of cognition, language and culture; the nature of language acquisition processes; the social psychology of group relations. Likewise, if the type of research agenda described here is to become a reality, then attitudes toward less traditional types of scholarly activities — specifically, applied collaborative research in a school setting — will also have to be changed. Simply stated, they cannot continue to be given less consideration than theoretical research and publications in decisions related to retention, tenure, and promotion (Nieto, cited in Underwood, 1986). Given the commitment of time and effort involved, alternative means of faculty assessment are needed. Faculty must not be penalized for engaging in the types of inquiry and professional activity most likely to have a profound influence on the schooling of language minority students.

Conclusion

As we approach the year 2000, many complex issues challenge those involved in educating language minority students. The research agenda just presented recognizes the importance of employing a research approach that is multidisciplinary, collaborative and action-based. Furthermore, it supports the integration of insights gained via quantitative and qualitative methodologies. For research efforts to make a difference in learner outcomes, researchers and practitioners must work together to explore the dynamics of context, process and content. Outside the classroom, they must examine the 'non-instructive features' of linguistic minority groups. Inside the classroom, they must focus on the creation of optimal learning environments and examine crucial aspects of curriculum and instruction. They must also work in conjunction with teacher educators to ensure the application of current knowledge and insights in teacher preparation. In the final analysis, the issues to be confronted are classic; their potential impact on second language learners far reaching. Within the broader spectrum of research directions to be encompassed within multicultural education, research related to language minority students has a significant place and a great deal to contribute.

References

BERLINER, D. (1990) 'Research on teaching: Insight and promising direction', Lecture, California State University, Chico.

CALDERON, M. (1985) 'Classroom learning environments' session in MEHAN, H., TRUEBA, H.T. and UNDERWOOD, C. (Eds) *Schooling Language Minority Youth*, Proceedings of the Linguistic Minority Project Conference, Lake Tahoe, CA, Vol. I, University of California Linguistic Minority Project, pp. 33–5.

CHAVEZ, R. (1985) 'Classroom learning environments' session in MEHAN, H., TRUEBA, H.T. and UNDERWOOD, C. (Eds) *Schooling Language Minority Youth*, Proceedings of the Linguistic Minority Project Conference, Lake Tahoe, CA, Vol. I, University of California Linguistic Minority Project, pp. 33–5.

CORTES, C. (1985) 'Cultural membership and school achievement' session in MEHAN, H., TRUEBA, H.T. and UNDERWOOD, C. (Eds). *Schooling Language Minority Youth*, Proceedings of the Linguistic Minority Project Conference, Lake Tahoe, CA, Vol. I, University of California Linguistic Minority Project, pp. 36–8.

DOLSON, D.P. and RUBIO, B. (1987) 'The Eastman plan: An approach to educating language minority children for academic success' session in MEHAN, H., TRUEBA, H.T. and UNDERWOOD, C. (Eds) *Schooling Language Minority Youth*, Proceedings of the Linguistic Minority Project Conference, Los Angeles, CA, Vol. III, University of California Linguistic Minority Research Project, pp. 39–44.

ERVIN-TRIPP, S. (1985) 'The structure of our knowledge' plenary address in MEHAN, H., TRUEBA, H.T. and UNDERWOOD, C. (Eds) *Schooling Language Minority Youth*, Proceedings of the Linguistic Minority Project Conference, Lake Tahoe, CA, Vol. I, University of California Linguistic Minority Project, pp. 42–6.

HAKUTA, K. (1986) 'Societal and policy contexts of research with language minority students' speech in MEHAN, H., TRUEBA, H.T. and UNDERWOOD, C. (Ed.), *Schooling Language Minority Youth*. Proceedings of the Linguistic Minority Project Conference, Berkeley, CA, Vol. II, University of California Linguistic Minority Project, pp. 7–20.

HANSEN, D. (1985) 'Linguistic issues' session in MEHAN, H., TRUEBA, H.T. and UNDERWOOD, C. (Eds) *Schooling Language Minority Youth*, Proceedings of the Linguistic Minority Project Conference, Lake Tahoe, CA, Vol. I, University of California Linguistic Minority Project, pp. 28–30.

HAWKINS, B.A. (1987) 'Scaffolded classroom interaction in a language minority setting' session in MEHAN, H., TRUEBA, H.T. and UNDERWOOD, C. (Eds) *Schooling Language Minority Youth*, Proceedings of the Linguistic Minority Project Conference, Los Angeles, CA, Vol. III, University of California Linguistic Minority Research Project, pp. 169–82.

HEATH, S.B. (1985) 'Learning and literacy' session in MEHAN, H., TRUEBA, H.T. and UNDERWOOD, C. (Eds) *Schooling Language Minority Youth*, Proceedings of the Linguistic Minority Project Conference, Lake Tahoe, CA, Vol. I, University of California Linguistic Minority Project, pp. 19–21.

Hilda Hernández

Lopez, G. (1986) Opening remarks in Mehan, H., Trueba, H.T. and Underwood, C. (Ed.) *Schooling Language Minority Youth*, Proceedings of the Linguistic Minority Project Conference, Berkeley, CA, Vol. II, University of California Linguisitc Minority Project, pp. 1–6.

Matute-Bianche, E. (1985) 'Cultural membership and school achievement session', in Mehan, H., Trueba, H. and Underwood, C. (Eds) *Schooling Language Minority Youth*, Proceedings of the Linguistic Minority Project Conference, Lake Tahoe, CA, Volume 1, University of California Linguistic Minority Project, pp. 36–38.

Mehan, H., Trueba, H.T. and Underwood, C. (Eds) (1985) *Schooling Language Minority Youth*, Proceedings of the Linguistic Minority Project Conference, Lake Tahoe, CA, Vol. I, University of California Linguistic Minority Project.

Mesa, R.P. (1986) 'Barriers to academic success for language minority students', session in Mehan, H., Trueba, H.T. and Underwood, C. (Ed.) *Schooling Language Minority Youth*, Proceedings of the Linguistic Minority Project Conference, Berkeley, CA, Vol. II, University of California Linguistic Minority Project, pp. 60–5.

Moll, L.C., Yelez-Ibañez, C. and Greenberg, J. (1989) *Community Knowledge and Classroom Practice: Combining Resources for Literacy Instruction* (Year one progress report) University of Arizona; authors.

Samaniego, F. (1986) Opening remarks in Mehan, H., Trueba, H.T. and Underwood, C. (Ed.) *Schooling Language Minority Youth*, Proceedings of the Linguistic Minority Project Conference, Berkeley, CA, Vol. II, University of California Linguistic Minority Project, pp. 1–6.

Shulman, L. (1986) 'Paradigms and research programs in the study of teaching: A contemporary perspective' in Wittrock, M.C. (Ed.) *Handbook of research on teaching*, 3rd edn, New York, Macmillan, pp. 3–36.

Stubbs, M. (1976) *Language, Schools and Classrooms*, London, Methuen.

Trueba, H. (1987) 'Cultural differences or learning handicaps? Towards an understanding of adjustment processes', session in Mehan, M., Trueba, H.T. and Underwood, C. (Eds) *Schooling Language Minority Youth*, Proceedings of the Linguistic Minority Project Conference, Los Angeles, CA, Vol. III, University of California Linguistic Minority Research Project, pp. 45–85.

Underwood, C. (Ed.) (1986) *Schooling Language Minority Youth*, Proceedings of the Linguistic Minority Project Conference, Berkeley, CA, Vol. II, University of California Linguistic Minority Project, pp. 102–8.

Valdes, G. (1986) 'Individual background factors related to the schooling of language minority students', session in Mehan, H., Trueba, H.T. and Underwood, C. (Ed.) *Schooling Language Minority Youth*, Proceedings of the Linguistic Minority Project Conference, Berkeley, CA, Vol. II, University of California Linguistic Minority Project, pp. 34–49.

Chapter 11

Success Stories

Lourdes Diaz Soto

Introduction

The educational research viewing ethnically and linguistically diverse learners has continued to perpetuate a philosophy which 'blames the victim' (Neisser, 1986; Cummins, 1984). Such a philosophy has emanated from the well intentioned compensatory education movement or the sociopolitical climate of the era. Much of the educational research viewing diverse learners is driven by a need to draw comparisons among races and classes, especially with regard to school achievement. The need to place the blame on the learner, the family, or the accompanying socioeconomic status is prevalent. Rarely have the existing research paradigms or the ongoing interpretations of previous educational research models been blamed. With the notable exception of two researchers (Erickson, 1987; Ogbu, 1986) who have noted weaknesses within the educational and social system; the search continues to uncover what is inherently 'wrong' with diverse learners. The purpose of this chapter is to introduce the origins of deficit research and to relate a personal account of a researcher's search for reflective insights within the multicultural education research arena. The need to view diverse learners in a more positive light and for researchers to gain in-depth reflective experiences prior to formulating hypotheses or research questions is related.

Deficit Philosophies

Much of the research investigating culturally and linguistically diverse learners has tended to originate from a perspective employing a deficit philosophy. A biased perspective pointing to inherent deficiencies and pathologies has permeated educational research to such an extent that the successful aspects of growing up as enriched individuals capable of speaking a variety of languages or familiar with a variety of cultures and customs is completely overlooked. Examples of glaring deficiencies, problems, difficulties, and mental health issues were especially prominent in the 'compensatory education era' of the 1960s.

A book entitled, *Compensatory Education for Cultural Deprivation* by Bloom, Davis and Hess (1965) relayed a state of the art research conference on education and cultural deprivation and serves as one example in a myriad of research typologies of the era. This volume was well-intentioned but assumes a clearly deficit philosophy when it states that the root of the problem for students who do not make 'normal' progress in their school learning can be traced to the following:

(a) *homes* — which do not transmit cultural patterns necessary for learning in school and larger society, nor provide a stimulating environment, and do not have the same intellectual and material resources as middle class families;

(b) *socioeconomic status variables* — assumes that middle class status should serve as the yardstick and relays descriptions such as the lack of a stimulating home, deficient speech patterns, lower expectations, lack of motivation, lower educational 'development', absence of a father, and lack of family interactions;

(c) the need to learn *communication patterns* — since existing language patterns are less elaborate, inadequate, lack abstract words, lack auditory and visual discrimination. A comparison is made among lower class and middle class families regarding the elaboration of language. The latter finding favoring middle class families is frequently cited in the literature as originating from research conducted by Hess and Shipman (1965) and Deutsch (1967);

(d) *races* — are compared with reference made to the fact that membership in an ethnic group should not be equated with cultural deprivation 'yet a large number of Negro children are likely to be culturally deprived' (p. 5). The cultural deprivation in this case was notable because of a different dialect, lack of drive for achievement, lack of stimulus, lack of parental interest, and lack of parental encouragement when compared to middle class parents. The stereotypical notions portrayed, clearly reflected a society where whole groups of people are viewed as more desirable, while others as less so;

(e) motivation is also depicted as deficient since the authors pointed out a lack of ability to defer gratification, as well as lower aspirations.

This type of research not only assumed a clearly deficit philosophy but also confused issues of race, class, and gender; and continually portrays the middle class family typology of the era, as the norm and the example to be emulated. Additional compensatory education research included stereotypical portrayals of black, Hispanic, American Indians, and European immigrants (Bereiter and Engelmann, 1966; Beck and Saxe, 1965; Deutsch and Brown, 1964). Beck and Saxe, for example, state that the socially disadvantaged (defined in Brottman's chapter as Negroes, Appalachian whites, Puerto Ricans, Mexican American farm workers, reservation Indians) have been denied the same social experiences as 'normal' children, and cite the *home* as the key to modification of behavior. Racial comparisons among black and white learners included achievement, aspirations, families, intelligence, language, personality, and social class (Ausubel and Ausubel, 1963; Battle and Rotter, 1963; Bernstein, 1962; Bloom, Whiteman, and Deutsch, 1963; Osborne, 1960; Pettigrew, 1964; Thomas, 1963).

The problem with the latter comparisons is that one group will naturally out-score the other, reflecting inherently biased research designs and instrumentation.

A volume by H. Miller (1967) entitled *Education for the Disadvantaged* attacked the compensatory research notion by noting that such studies were too broad, misleading, inconclusive, dehumanizing and mythological (Mackler and Giddings, 1967). The authors cite the civil rights movement as indicative of parental interests and state 'until the white professional gives up his seat as omnipotence and looks at Negroes as fellow human beings, eye-to-eye, we shall not have true equality' (p. 34). Miller's work, as well as Ginzberg's (1972) *Myth of the Deprived Child*, were largely ignored. The stage had been set for research viewing whole groups of people as deficient.

A more recent work entitled *The Puerto Rican Child in New York City: Stress and Mental Health* by Canino, Earley, and Rogler (1980) is also well intentioned but upon close scrutiny leads the reader to conclude that it is a more sophisticated version of the compensatory era research typology. The main hypothesis postulated by the authors is that Puerto Rican children are at a higher risk of mental health problems when compared to other groups yet include impressionistic statements throughout their work, rather than clear data for example, 'it is reasonable to suggest, we have not been able to identify sources of information . . . but we can only assume . . . it may also be that the mental health of Puerto Rican children is similarly poor'. Mention is also made to 'bilingual confusion', an issue which clearly needs to be treated separately and has been documented as erroneous (Cummins, 1984; Sato, 1991).

Sociopolitical issues have affected multicultural research endeavors to such an extent that even the original research questions are often biased. The origin of the myth of the 'bilingual handicap' serves as an example. Research viewing linguistically diverse learners have been guided by a need to prove the effects of bilingualism on intelligence. The comparisons have been drawn among biling-uals and monolinguals with tests earmarked to measure the 'intelligence' con-struct. According to Hakuta (1986) the first half of this century has been guided by a search for whether or not there are negative effects of bilingualism on intelligence, while recent research has attempted to uncover positive effects. The fact that measures relied heavily on verbal intelligence, did not deter researchers from concluding that bilinguals were genetically inferior or plagued by a kind of mental confusion.

Even the most objective researchers are products of a culture and a system influencing their initial research design. For example, Smith (1939) conducted a quantitatively rigorous study with 1000 children and concluded that bilingualism caused retardation in language development. The latter conclusion was based on a comparison on the number of errors made by monolingual children residing in Iowa and bilingual young learners residing in Hawaii. Errors were defined as deviations from standard usage. The fact that the initial research question was based on the number of 'errors' is indicative of a deficit philosophy in search of what is wrong with bilinguals regardless of additional capabilities and abilities. Madorah Smith continued to vigorously oppose early childhood bilingualism with additional research.

The negative consequences of bilingualism continued to be documented through the compensatory education era. Jensen (1962) for example, when summarizing over 200 studies, found that the consequences of childhood biling-ualism (according to the studies) included handicaps in speech language, intellectual and educational progress as well as emotional instability. Bilingual learners were said to be only capable of learning by rote, suffered from mental fatigue, were handicapped on intelligence tests, were handicapped in reading and studying, and could become schizophrenic. Similar negative consequences were cited by Darcey, (1953), Diebold (1968), Macnamara (1966) and Vildomec (1963). The negative findings leading to the bilingual handicap myth have little credibility in light of severe methodological problems (see Cummins, 1976; Peal and Lambert, 1962). There was no opportunity for learners to communicate previous knowledge or strengths in these studies, nor language proficiency, information processing, cultural strengths, learning potential, or affective capa-bilities. With the notable exception of case study research (Leopold, 1939), it was not until Peal and Lambert's (1962) Canadian research that a differing view of bilingualism began to evolve.

The language and terms used in the current literature continue to exemplify a pervasive deficit model. For example, frequently used terms include disadvan-taged, at risk, and limited English proficient. Slavin (1989) draws a distinction among the terms disadvantaged and at risk. Disadvantaged is a term used to describe children from poor families, while 'at-risk' originated as a medical term and is now being applied to education. The term at risk denotes children who are not performing well in school; while disadvantaged refers to socioeconomic differences.

Pallas, Natriello and McDill (1989) relate the 'five key indicators associ-ated with the educationally disadvantaged: minority racial/ethnic group identity, living in a poverty household, living in a single-parent family, having a poorly educated mother, and having a non-English language back-ground' (p. 17). According to Pallas, *et al.* minority racial/ethnic group status is the single best known factor associated with being educationally disadvan-taged. The latter has implications for both researchers and practitioners.

The term limited English proficient, implies that there is an inherent limitation in the second language learner, as opposed to an enriching attri-bute. Language minority classifications by researchers often denote home language use other than English as well as ethnic group membership (Gring-as and Careaga, 1989). It is obvious, however, that neither home language use nor ethnic group membership can assess language proficiency skills. Gringas, and Careaga, underscore the fact that proficiency in English is a continuum ranging from 'no English' to 'native-like proficiency in English' and is not related to sociological attributes.

We rarely read about fluent Spanish speakers; fluent Hmong speakers; fully proficient speakers; multilingual speakers. Children continue to be viewed as deficient language receptacles instead of enriched individuals; the 'half empty glass syndrome' as opposed to a 'half full' philosophy continues to prevail. Cuban (1989) points out that popular explanations for low academic achievement of at risk children place the blame on the children and their accompanying families; while Pallas *et al.* (1989) point out that educators need to learn to draw upon the strengths of families and com-munities in order to enhance current educational experiences.

Needed Directions

In order to view the inherent possibilities and contributions of culturally and linguistically diverse people, an alternative stance needs to be incorporated into our current research agenda. A positive approach would be to view successful ethnically diverse learners and their accompanying learning environments, intrinsic components, and interactions. A whole world of research needs to address important assessment issues when one group continues to be used as a yardstick for other groups to measure up to. For example, why are bilingual learners constantly compared to monolingual learners? Why are instruments translated into one language for whole groups of learners without viewing the difference between cultural and linguistic equivalence? What individual differences and within group differences are important to pursue and relate, for example, Hispanics are comprised of immigrant groups, colonized groups, a variety of language dialects, and unique customs and traditions.

Highlighting success stories, successful ethnically diverse learners, the salient features of successful educational programs, teaching and parenting practices enhancing success, and attitudes contributing to success would help in alleviating the deficit philosophy so prevalent on the mainland. The hidden message to families and children has continued to be: 'You cannot make it, you are not good enough, so why try?' More positive approaches and philosophies could force innovative policy directions, alternative program implementation, introduce societal role models, and alleviate stereotypes. The need for policy makers, for example, to support multicultural educational research should be highlighted. Funding issues need to be addressed in order to enhance the field. Multicultural research can no longer be seen as a stepchild of educational research when so many important issues are at stake for learners.

Personal Insights

As researchers we need to begin to explore the hidden implications of our own initial research questions and theoretical frameworks. The fact that families, children, schools and communities do not exist in a vacuum with interactions and overlapping among intermediary systems, appears to be common sense, yet needs to be adequately addressed in the theoretical framework chosen by researchers. Issues of race, class, and gender need to be integrated within educational research (Grant and Sleeter, 1986). The complexity of the systems affecting ethnically diverse learners needs to be explored, described, untangled in order to eliminate stereotypes and begin to examine individual differences and contributions to processes. We also need to examine our own personal frameworks, biases, and world views in order to discover and experiment with alternate avenues and approaches.

As a female Hispanic American, this researcher grew up in a mainland society where the majority of role models and leaders were unlike her. Growing up in such an environment allows you to note certain discrepancies and to question the evidence present in the immediate environment. For Puerto Rican children a comparison among island and mainland culture can be easily observed as they travel back and forth from the island to the mainland. Personal child-hood observations helped to initiate questions, focus on needed research, draw comparisons, and to examine sociopolitical agendas. For example, why are Puerto Rican islanders able to achieve successful professional goals more readily than mainlanders? Why are mainland Puerto Rican citizens continuing to live in poverty and are referred to as deficient, lacking in educational skills, limited in English proficiency, or 'at risk?' Why are mainland Puerto Rican children experiencing apparent school failure at such alarming rates (Valdivieso, 1986)? Why are mainland Puerto Rican parents expressing high educational expecta-tions for their children which are incongruent with their child's attainment (Soto, 1986)?

These initial experiences led to the research quest for the rationale behind the documented and differential school achievement by mainland Puerto Rican students. The initial question focused on a comparison among lower achieving and higher achieving children experiencing and living in similar environments: 'Why are some children rated as lower achievers while others appear to succeed even in very similar conditions?' The population for the study consisted of mainlanders, because this is where the overriding deficit philosophy is most apparent. Just as prior experiences, observations, and cultural knowledge can affect an individual's behavior, so a researcher's initial investigative interest may have been so affected. Previous research interested in cross cultural and anthro-pological concerns have noted the need for investigators to gain appropriate strategies when examining relationships among culture and individual behavior (Segal, 1979; Lonner and Berry, 1986; Spindler and Spindler, 1981). In addition, it needs to be emphasized that it is just as important for researchers to gain insights and awareness of past (and present) events and experiences influencing their *own* research avenues and agendas.

Adjusting the Informational Lens

My intent was to gather objective data from families and children regarding the home environment process variables and the motivational orientation (of the children) with regard to school achievement. I could not have anticipated that I would be so personally affected by the families and their respective children. Just as individuals in the medical profession must remain objective (while having a bedside manner), so must researchers. My mission as of late has been to relate the stories that these lives reflect, and I find myself passionately and obsessively relating the valor, resiliency, and individualized portrayals of success in environ-ments that are not earmarked for apparent human enhancement. Questions posed by colleagues appear irrelevant in the face of personal and difficult human elements. It appears that the larger context and framework where these families survive is not being understood.

As a researcher I found myself having to overcome initial emotional reac-tions to poverty, human needs, and inequity in order to view elements which contribute to children's success. What I am suggesting is that part of our role as researchers is to educate individuals not cognizant of the issues faced by diverse families which on the surface appear to overshadow enriching and positive contributions. There were successful children, according to school definitions of achievement, who were among the top achievers in their respective grades. What this means is that we need to pursue beyond the structural variables such as socioeconomic background to view the processes contributing to success.

The socioeconomic issue can easily overshadow positive parental behaviors and child attributes. Sifting beyond the initial reactions to poverty and need, for example, is vital in order to view the cohesive family elements, the caring attitudes of parents, the high educational expectations both parents and children relate, the value placed on family life and immediate responses to human needs (beyond the usual neighborly responses), the value placed on childhood, the giving attitudes, the neat, orderly, colorful environments in the midst of chaotic neighborhoods, the higher order values placed on religious life, hospitality, respect for educational personnel, are among intangibles and issues not generally observed nor related in the literature viewing ethnic families. Some may feel that it is a miracle that these families survive at all, let alone their children. The families visited have indicated tremendous resiliency and have helped to guide additional research questions by sharing their daily life experiences.

The initial first step was to examine previous research. The literature viewing school achievement has noted that the role parents play in the education of their children is of paramount importance. The study conducted by Diana Baumrind (1975), viewing parent child interactions and relating parenting styles is helpful in establishing behavioral links between parents' and children's behaviors. Four family types were defined based on parent behavior rating clusters, authoritarian, authoritative, permissive, and the non-conforming parent. The authoritative parent who engages in rational communication yet enforces parental will had children who were the most competent (friendly, cooperative, and achievement oriented). Baumrind's research emphasizes the role parental behaviors play in the development of instrumental competence of their children.

The home environment literature which speaks to the process variables occurring in the home and how these affect school achievement, has examples of carefully conducted research with convincing evidence. Bloom's (1964) work pointing to the important contribution of the educational role of the family is particularly important and has influenced much of the home environment research. The research conducted by Marjoribanks (1972) in Australia with ethnically diverse families has been the most influential in guiding the initial data collection and choice of interview format for this researcher's work because it is culturally sensitive and allows for additional observations/information gathering.

Researching 'in the trenches', if you will, and viewing the very personal daily lives was a truly unforgettable experience. In order to view the process variables present in the homes of the higher and lower achieving children, personal and individualized home visits were conducted. Since during data collection, the achievement categorizations were unknown, it was surprising to view the resulting data analyses and accompanying home process variables. For example: several children who had been categorized as higher achieving were living with disrupted families and facing insurmountable experiences, such as a mentally ill parent, and an abused parent living in a shelter. These children were successful academically and resilient enough to overcome the odds. The successful elements of these children's learning environment would have been missed if only quantitative data had been gathered. This experience also led me to conclude that there may be smaller within group differences and that the initial grouping of higher and lower achieving is too simplistic.

The child's personal contribution to school achievement is obviously important. Bell's (1968) work points to reciprocal interactions occurring between parent and child, while White (1959) relates theoretical issues related to effectance motivational orientation defined as the inner drive to experience success. While it is intuitively apparent that the child's inner world has to contribute to school efforts and behaviors, it is more difficult to decide which behaviors, which abilities, aside from innate/behavioral genetic contributions. As an example the motivational orientation construct may be differentially defined in a variety of settings, for example, ascriptive and achievement oriented societies. Children living, working, and studying on the mainland are expected to exhibit certain school related behaviors by teachers and educators in order to succeed in the school setting. Researchers viewing motivational orientation may need to clarify the differing orientations and perceptions by culturally diverse peoples. For example, some families train their children to respect adult authority and to think in terms of group efforts; while other families applaud individual efforts and assertive stances by their youth. Puerto Rican children in particular when asked to respond to a measure viewing motivational orientation (Soto, 1988a) tended to consistently choose adult orientations over independent, self differentiated items, reflecting culturally embedded issues of respect ('respeto').

Successful aspects of the mainland Puerto Rican families were found in three data sets (Study no. 1 N–59; Study no. 2 N–20; Study no. 3 N=20). Children considered higher achievers in Study no. 1 by school standards (Soto, 1988b) were sometimes overcoming tremendous odds, for example, disrupted family situations. The younger children in Study no. 2 were children of migrant workers whose lives were often disrupted by the migratory process so vital for their everyday existence. Children in Study no. 3 were often living in federally assisted housing yet experienced a stable and active Hispanic community. All of the families lived within the lower socioeconomic strata yet there were a variety of common and enriching experiences available for children. There were commonly shared cultural and linguistic experiences. The family unit was highly valued as were close interpersonal relations. The families respected and were pleased with the school's role in the education of their children. The role of the mother as a homemaker was emphasized to such an extent that mothers often stayed at home to care for their children (in spite of economic needs), or became part of the informal economy (baking cakes, caring for neighbor children).

It became evident that unique and individualized contributions among families are important to pursue as are the child's contribution to their own educational enhancement. Why were the very top achievers in Study no. 1 living in family situations which most of us would regard as disruptive? What contributions were some children making to cause parents to feel that the child was their only hope? Viewing the child's contribution to the learning home environment may help to uncover clues for parents and teachers. The resilient children in Study no. 1 were affecting the parents instead of vice versa yet little empirical research is available viewing the child's contribution to the environment.

According to Wolman (1985), it has not been until recently that research viewing genotype X environment is beginning to be taken seriously.

How to measure success is a question that needs to be pursued. How can predictions regarding talented and gifted children who are currently portrayed as deficient and limited in their language proficiency be enhanced? Gardner's (1983) conception of multiple intelligences is important and is currently helping to guide measurement research. The idea that individuals can contribute to a society in a multitude of ways with a multiple of talents needs to be emphasized. Gardner's theory of multiple intelligences indicates seven independent forms of information processing with individuals exhibiting differing profiles. The intelligences include: logical-mathematical, linguistic, musical, spatial, kinesthetic, interpersonal and intrapersonal. Cross-cultural research has noted the role of familiarity and experience with regard to assessment (Scribner, 1986). Gardner and Hatch (1989) relate an assessment approach that is linked to the ongoing school curriculum leading to successful experience for learners.

Maslow (1970) studied the lives of highly successful individuals who contributed extensively to our society such as Einstein, Beethoven and Lincoln. Maslow shared a list of fifteen traits for individuals who had obtained high levels of self actualizaton. Among the traits uncovered are: (i) living close to reality and judging life in an accurate manner; (ii) willingness to accept self and others; (iii) display spontaneity and originality yet avoid antisocial behavior; (iv) life is perceived as a mission; (v) occasionally contemplate problems in solitude; (vi) non-conformist; (vii) love life and admire its beauty; (viii) can reach beyond observable facts; (ix) display sympathy and compassion for humanity; (x) develop close personal relationships with a small number of friends; (xi) respect for individuals; (xii) would never choose inappropriate means for reaching goals; (xiii) usually have a good sense of humor; (xiv) are creative and have aesthetic inclinations; and (xv) retain intellectual independence and an independent outlook on life. Maslow's work highlights the attributes of talented and highly regarded individuals in our society. The point is that measuring success needs to be viewed within a broader framework and not just standardized achievement tests. The areas viewing personality, social factors, and multiple intelligences can prove valuable for both educators and learners. In addition, there is a need for researchers to pursue redeeming features within situations as well as the need to redefine achievement orientations for educators and others.

Researchers intent on pursuing multicultural research in our society are faced with a tremendous challenge. We are currently faced with issues such as: how to educate consumers of our research and a society that views whole groups of people as deficient; how to reflect upon our own past experiences and how these affect our research; how to measure processes so that one group is not seen as a yardstick for a whole society; how to interpret research and measurement in an equitable manner; how to emphasize successful and resilient stories in our research; how to develop measures capable of highlighting the talents and gifts of ethnically diverse peoples. The research viewing multicultural issues is in its infancy and viewed as non-traditional by many, yet potentially capable of impacting research trends and societal views. The successful aspects of culturally and linguistically diverse learners will help to guide culturally appropriate research by providing a clear line away from deficiencies and deficits. It may be that *all* families will be seen as worthy and measured in their own unique individual terms, released from the 'comparison burden' so prevalent during the compensatory era.

Conclusion

Research endeavors which continually portray ethnically and linguistically diverse learners as pathological are no longer acceptable. Stereotyping whole groups of people as undesirable and deficient is embedded in a discriminatory socio-political system. As researchers we need to reflect upon our own understanding prior to formulating research questions and theoretical frameworks. Unless we design alternate research avenues we will continue to perpetuate the myth of deficient learners and encourage oppression.

We need to be able to reflect and describe the successful aspects and redeeming features of cultures and socioeconomic situations which have been misunderstood. Culturally and linguistically equivalent measurement issues need to be addressed so that the concept of multiple intelligences and the contribution of learners to the learning environment can be explored. Richer, more complete explanations/clarifications may begin to empower learners who will be seen in a differing light and provide explanations for practitioners and parents. Only when researchers are willing to reflect honestly and openly with hidden personal or social agendas will new alternate stances and avenues begin to unfold.

References

AUSUBEL, D. and AUSUBEL, P. (1963) 'Ego development among segregated Negro children' in PASSON, A.H. (Ed.) *Education in Depressed Areas*, New York, Teachers College.

BATTLE, E. and ROTTER, J. (1963) 'Children's feeling of personal control as related to social class and ethnic group', *Journal of Personality*, **31**, pp. 382–90.

BAUMRIND, D. (1975) 'The contribution of the family to the development of competence in children', *Schizophrenia Bulletin*, **14**, pp. 12–37.

BECK, J. and SAXE, R. (1965) *Teaching the Culturally Disadvantaged Pupil*. Springfield, IL, Charles Thomas Publisher.

BELL, R.Q. (1968) 'A reinterpretation of the direction of the effects in studies of socialization' *Psychological Review*, **75**, pp. 81–95.

BEREITER, C. and ENGELMAN, S. (1966) *Teaching Disadvantaged Children in the Preschool*, Englewood Cliffs, NJ, Prentice Hall.

BERNSTEIN, B. (1962) 'Linguistic codes, hesitation phenomena and intelligence', *Language and Speech*, **5**, 1, pp. 31–46.

BLOOM, B. (1964) *Stability and Change in Human Characteristics*, New York, Wiley.

BLOOM, B., DAVIS, A. and HESS, R. (1965) *Compensatory Education for Cultural Deprivation*, New York, Holt, Rinehart and Winston.

BLOOM, R., WHITEMAN, M. and DEUTSCH, M. (1963) 'Race and social class as separate factors related to social environment', paper presented at the American Psychological Association, Philadelphia.

CANINO, I., EARLEY, B. and ROGLER, L. (1980) 'The Puerto Rican child in New York city: Stress and mental health', Monograph No. 4, Hispanic Research Center, Fordham University.

CUBAN, L. (1989) 'The at-risk label and the problem of urban school reform', *Phi Delta Kappan*, **70**, 10, pp. 780–801.

CUMMINS, J. (1976) 'The influence of bilingualism on cognitive growth: A synthesis of research findings and explanatory hypotheses', *Working Papers on Bilingualism*, 9, pp. 1–4.

CUMMINS, J. (1984) *Bilingualism and Special Education: Issues in Assessment and Pedagogy*, Clevedon, Multilingual Matters Ltd.

DARCEY, N.T. (1953) 'A review of the literature on the effects of bilingualism on the measurement of intelligence', *Journal of Genetic Psychology*, **82**, pp. 21–54.

DEUTSCH, M. (1967) *The Disadvantaged Child*, New York, Basic Books.

DEUTSCH, M. and BROWN, B. (1964) 'Social influences in negro-white intelligence differences', *Journal of Social Issues*, **20**, 2, pp. 24–35.

DIEBOLD, A. (1968) 'The consequences of early bilingualism in cognitive development and personality formation' in NORBECK, E., PRICE-WILLIAMS, D., McCORD, E.W. (Eds) *The Study of Personality*, New York, Holt, Rinehart and Winston.

ERICKSON, F. (1987) 'Transformation and school success: The politics and culture of educational achievement', *Anthropology and Education Quarterly*, **18**, pp. 335–82.

GARDNER, H. (1983) *Frames of Mind: A Theory of Multiple Intelligences*, New York, Basic Books, Inc., Publishers.

GARDNER, H. and HATCH, T. (1989) 'Multiple Intelligences go to school', *Educational Researcher*, **18**, 8, pp. 4–10.

GINZBERG, H. (1972) *The Myth of the Deprived Child: Poor Children's Intellect and Education*, Englewood Cliffs, NJ, Prentice-Hall.

GINZBERG, H. (1986) 'The myth of the deprived child: New thoughts on poor children' in NEISSER, U. (Ed.) *The School Achievement of Minority Children*, Hillsdale, NJ, Lawrence Erlbaum Associates Publishers.

GRANT, C. and SECADA, W. (1988) 'Preparing teachers for diversity' Working draft to appear in HOUSTON, R., HABERMAN, M. and SIKULA, J. (Eds) *Handbook of Research on Teacher Education*, New York, Macmillan.

GRANT, C. and SLEETER, C. (1986) 'Race, class and gender in education research: An argument for integrative analysis', *Review of Educational Research*, **56**, 2, pp. 195–211.

GRINGAS, R. and CAREAGA, R. (1989) *Limited English Proficient Students at Risk: Issues and Prevention Strategies*, Silver Spring, MD, National Clearinghouse for Bilingual Education.

HAKUTA, K. (1986) *Mirror of Language*, New York, Basic Books.

HESS, R. and SHIPMAN, V. (1965) 'Early experience and the socialization of cognitive modes in children', *Child Development*, **36**, pp. 867–86.

HODGKINSON, H. (1985) *All One System: Demographics of Education — Kindergarten through Graduate School*, Washington, DC, Institute for Educational Leadership.

JENSEN, A.R. (1969) 'How much can we boost IQ and scholastic achievement?' *Harvard Educational Review*, **39**, pp. 1–123.

JENSEN, J.V. (1962) 'Effects of childhood bilingualism', *Elementary English*, **39**, pp. 358–64.

KELLER, S. (1963) 'The social world of the urban slum child: Some early findings', *American Journal of Orthopsychiatry*, **33**, pp. 823–31.

LEOPOLD, W.F. (1939) *Speech Development of a Bilingual Child: A Linguistic's Record*, Vol. l, Evanston, IL, Northwestern University Press.

LONNER, W. and BERRY, J. (1986) *Field Methods in Cross Cultural Research*, Volume 8. Beverly Hills, CA, Sage Publications.

LOTT, A. and LOTT, B. (1963) *Negro and White Youths*, New York, Holt, Rinehart and Winston, Inc.

MACKLER, B. and GIDDINGS, M. (1967) 'Cultural deprivation: A study in *mythology*' in MILLER, H. (Ed.) *Education for the Disadvantaged*, New York, The Free Press.

MACNAMARA, J. (1966) *Bilingualism and Primary Education*, Edinburgh, Edinburgh University Press.

MARJORIBANKS, K. (1972) 'Ethnic and environmental influences on mental abilities', *American Journal of Sociology*, **78**, pp. 323–7.

MASLOW, A. (1970) *Motivation and Personality*, New York, Harper and Row.

MILLER, H. (1967) *Education for the Disadvantaged*, New York, The Free Press.

NEISSER, U. (Ed.) (1986) *The School Achievement of Minority Children*, New Jersey, Lawrence Erlbaum Associates, Publishers.

OGBU, J. (1986) 'The consequences of the American Caste System, in NEISSER, U. (Ed.) *The School Achievement of Minority Children*, NJ., Lawrence Erlbaum Associates, Publishers.

OGBU, J. (1987) 'Variability in minority school performance: A problem in search of an explanation', *Anthropology and Education Quarterly*, **18**, pp. 312–34.

OSBORNE, R.T. (1960) 'Racial differences in mental growth and school achievement: A longitudinal study', *Psychological Reports*, **7**, pp. 233–9.

PALLAS, A., NATRIELLO, G. and MCDILL, E. (1989) 'The changing nature of the disadvantaged population: Current dimensions and future trends', *Educational Researcher*, **18**, 5, pp. 16–22.

PEAL, E. and LAMBERT, W. (1962) 'The relation of bilingualism to intelligence', *Psychological Monographs*, **76**, 546.

PETTIGREW, T. (1964) 'Negro American intelligence: A new look at an old controversy', *Journal of Negro Education*, **33**, pp. 6–25.

SCRIBNER, C. (1986) 'Thinking action: Some characteristics of practical thought' in STERNBERG, R. and WAGNER, R.K. (Ed.) *Practical Intelligence: Origins of Competence in the Everyday World*, New York, Cambridge University Press.

SEGAL, M. (1979) *Cross-cultural Psychology*, Monterey, CA, Brooks/Cole Publishing Company.

SLAVIN, R. (1989) 'Disadvantaged vs. at-risk: Does the difference matter in practice?', paper presented at the annual meeting of the American Research Association, San Francisco.

SMITH, M. (1939) 'Some light on the problem of bilingualism as found from a study of the progress in mastery of English among preschool children', *Genetic Psychology Monographs*, **21**, pp. 119–289.

SOTO, L.D. (1986) 'The relationship among the home environment and motivational orientation of Puerto Rican fifth and sixth graders', doctoral dissertation, Pennsylvania State University.

SOTO, L.D. (1988a) 'The motivational orientation of higher and lower achieving Puerto Rican children', *Journal of Psychoeducational Assessment*, **6**, pp. 199–206.

SOTO, L.D. (1988b) 'The home environment of higher and lower achieving Puerto Rican children', *Hispanic Journal of Behavioral Sciences*, **10**, 2, pp. 161–7.

SOTO, L.D. (1991) 'Understanding bilingual bicultural young children', *Young Children*, **46**, 2, pp. 30–6.

SPINDLER, G. and SPINDLER, L. (1987) *Interpretive Ethnography of Education: At Home and Abroad*, New Jersey, Lawrence Erlbaum Associates Publishers.

THOMAS, D. (1963) 'Oral language sentence structure and vocabulary of kindergarten children living in low socioeconomic urban areas', unpublished doctoral dissertation, Wayne University.

VALDIVIESO, R. (1986) 'Must they wait another generation?, *Hispanic Policy Development Project*, Eric Clearinghouse on Urban Education, 93, pp. 1–53.

VILDOMEC, V. (1963) *Multilingualism*, Leyden, A.W. Sythoff.

WHITE, R. (1959) 'Motivation reconsidered: The concept of competence', *Psychological Review*, **66**, 5, pp. 297–333.

WOLMAN, B. (Ed.) (1985) *Handbook of Intelligence: Theories, Measurements and Applications*, New York, John Wiley and Sons.

Chapter 12

Relationships Between Home, Community and School: Multicultural Considerations and Research Issues in Early Childhood

Marianne Bloch and Beth Blue Swadener

Writing this chapter is timely for both of us; we are actively engaged in research and community activities focusing on young children in homes and schools. Both of us are struggling, in our research and praxis, to help children from diverse cultural and socioeconomic backgrounds have a better chance to be successful in and out of school.[1] Further, in our research and collaboration with teachers, we encourage the recognition of the potential and competencies of all children. In our experiences with a variety of projects, we have encountered numerous issues related to research focused on equity issues and on creating 'education that is multicultural'.[2]

In this chapter, we focus our attention on issues related to research on children's experiences in home, community, and school contexts and the ways in which culture, class, gender, language, and ability affect children's experiences in these different contexts. We explore several theoretical frameworks that concern themselves with differences in these experiences, including the theory of 'cultural compatibility' (for example, Delgado-Gaitan, 1990; Tharp, 1989; Tharp and Gallimore, 1989; Vogt, Jordan and Tharp, 1987; Trueba, Jacobs and Kirton, 1990), critical theory (for example, Apple and Weis, 1983; McCarthy and Apple, 1988; Weis, 1988) and feminist theory (Fine, 1988; Lather, 1986 and 1991). Most importantly, we examine dilemmas and resolutions some of this work, especially some of our own, has raised about how, on what, and with whom we do research and report research that concerns children and families of color.

This chapter is focused on research issues related to studying children within home, community and school settings in an effort to learn ways in which culture and other related factors (for example, race, class, gender, language, ability) affect children's success in these different settings. We begin with the problem statement that children from non-majority culture groups in the United States too often have difficulties making transitions between home, community, and school. We suggest that these difficulties are, in part, due to a variety of educationally and socially significant differences in the patterns of behavior, language, cognition, and values that are part of home and school cultures. We examine several research projects that focus on children's experiences in multicultural contexts, and also focus on research that has tried to define issues in these areas with collaborative and empowering strategies. We draw on a variety of studies of young children in different contexts in order to raise different theoretical and methodological dilemmas and issues studies have encountered.

The focus of this chapter is on research issues rather than 'research results'. As we are most familiar with our own research problems and debates, and also find it easier and fairer to be critical with our work, many of the issues and problems we describe in detail are our own. We do not pretend, therefore, to represent all issues encountered by other researchers, but we do intend to present issues that have some generalizability to other researchers' concerns.

Organization of the Chapter

In the first section of the chapter, we illustrate the importance of 'theory' in doing research in multicultural contexts. We describe the theory of cultural compatibility — which is the framework for a current study by the first author — describe some concerns with the theoretical framework, and provide a brief description of one project that uses this framework. In the second section of the chapter, we use the case study description as well as other examples of research in multicultural contexts to raise a variety of issues related to methodology and dissemination of research results; these include: questions of the subject(s) of research (for example, who is the researcher and who is researched; is research 'collaborative'), definition of research question (for example, how do race, class, and gender, and power influence the definition of what is studied?), and definition of research interpretation and dissemination.

Theoretical Debates

A variety of recent studies have focused attention on the concept of 'cultural compatibility' as one explanation for minority and majority culture children's differential success in school. Tharp (1989) suggests that the 'cultural compatibility' hypothesis in a basic form suggests that 'when instruction is compatible with natal-culture patterns, improvements in learning including basic skills, can be expected' (p. 350). Tharp (*ibid.*) also suggests there are three forms of this hypothesis: (i) the strong form or culturally specific form, best exemplified by the definition described above, suggests that effective classrooms must be different and specific to each cultural group; (ii) a weaker form of the hypothesis states that while some non-majority cultural groups are successful in mainstream classrooms, others, who have a broader history of oppression and involuntary immigration find mainstream classroom culture and expectations less conducive to success (for example, Ogbu, 1987). According to this perspective, classrooms required for school success would be different from the dominant culture classroom, but similar for these non-dominant groups (for example, classrooms for Hawaiian and Navajo children would be similar) (Tharp, 1989, p. 350).

The third hypothesis is that of universality — or that effective teaching will improve minority children and other children's chances for success. This stance argues that no changes in environment need to be made except to improve teaching for all children.

The Kamehameha Early Education Project (KEEP) identified significant differences between Hawaiian-American children's home and school culture values and expected patterns of behavior (for example, see Jordan, 1985; Tharp, 1989; Tharp and Gallimore, 1989; Vogt, Jordan and Tharp, 1987; Weisner, Gallimore and Jordan, 1988); when KEEP experimental classrooms were changed to incorporate 'story talk', an oral story-telling method similar to that used by Hawaiian-Americans at home, recognition of children's ability to take care of the classroom as they did at home, and peer helping, numerous reports documented increases in Hawaiian children's school achievement. Similarly, in Vogt, Jordan and Tharp (1987), techniques used in the Hawaiian KEEP classrooms were generalized to a Navajo reservation school at Rough Rock; KEEP teacher-researcher Lynn Vogt found that the patterns that had been successful with Hawaiian children were not successful with Navajo children who were used to greater independence and segregated gender grouping, for example. The Vogt *et al.* (1987) report was used to bolster the cultural specificity hypothesis (hypothesis 1) in the theory of cultural compatability referred to by Tharp (1989).

While few studies have directly tested the notion of cultural compatibility as described in Vogt *et al.* (1987), many other researchers have used variations on the cultural compatibility theory to test whether differences between natal culture patterns and classroom practices affect children deleteriously (for example, Cummins, 1986; Deyle, 1987; Delgado-Gaitan, 1987 and 1989; Erickson and Mohatt, 1977; Florio and Schultz, 1979; Heath, 1982 and 1983; Diaz, Moll and Mehan, 1986; Phillips, 1983; Taylor and Dorsey-Gaines, 1988; Trueba, Jacobs and Kirton, 1990). In Shirley Brice Heath's research (1983), differences in European-American middle-class teachers' style of questioning African-American children resulted in the children's failure to respond as expected to the teachers; when Heath helped teachers to ask questions in culturally and linguistically compatible ways, the children were more successful. In Diaz and Moll's research (for example, see Diaz, Moll and Mehan, 1986), simple restructuring of a reading comprehension task so that children were read to and asked questions in their primary language of Spanish led to markedly better performance.

While many are familiar with the concept of cultural compatibility, and some of the research briefly described above, this theory is a specific representation of a more general strand of research known by a number of different names; these include 'cultural compatibility-incompatibility', 'cultural differences', 'cultural congruency-incongruency', and 'cultural continuity-discontinuity' (Ladson-Billings, 1990). It is also only one recent explanation of why many nondominant culture children fail to achieve well in school. Indeed, there are many alternative perspectives on this issue, and there are numerous critiques of the theory of cultural compatibility. These are described in the next section as a way to illustrate the importance of theoretical framework to the formation of research questions and the interpretation of research findings.

Critiques of the Theory of Cultural Compatibility

The first critique might be termed a *utility-of-the-theory critique*. It does not question the importance of the theory, but rather how easily this theoretical framework can be extended to help children of color in various classroom contexts. Two primary concerns relate to (i) the difficulty of identifying educationally and culturally significant differences between classrooms and homes; and (ii) the difficulty of affecting significant enduring change within classrooms and schools. A variety of studies have shown patterns can be identified and long-term effective change can be made in controlled situations (for example, Heath, 1983; Jordan, 1985). While the debate continues (for example, see Tharp, 1989), the continuing arguments relate to: (i) how easily important natal-school culturally discontinuous patterns can be determined; (ii) how well or poorly patterns fit all members of a given cultural group (for example, Trueba, 1988); (iii) whether changes that can be made in experimental classrooms can be generalized in enduring ways to other classrooms (for example, recent questions of the KEEP project's generalizability to other Hawaiian classrooms); and (iv) whether and under what conditions the theory extends to multicultural classrooms, the most common classroom situation in the United States (Tharp, 1989, p. 357).

The second type of critique leveled at the theory of home-school or natal culture-school culture compatibility as a method for decreasing failure for children of color is one of *defining the role of the school and the source of the problem*. This theoretical debate has been articulated by educational anthropologists (for example, Erickson, 1987 and 1989; Ogbu, 1987), linguists (for example, Delpit, 1988), multicultural education theorists (see Grant and Secada, 1990; Sleeter, 1991; Sleeter and Grant, 1987) and neo-Marxist theoreticians (for example, see McCarthy, 1988).

Ogbu's (1987) critique of the theory relates to his own theory of school failure which suggests that some involuntary immigrant minority groups (for example, African-American, Latino) more frequently fail in school due to a history of oppression and racism in the broader society. To the extent that African-American youth, for example, fail to perceive or believe that school will help them achieve success in the broader society, school success is unlikely, regardless of the degree to which classrooms are culturally compatible. For neo-Marxists, schools are part of the problem, and, depending upon the theorist's perspective, may serve to reproduce or partially determine the class and racial divisions that are part of American society (for example, see McCarthy, 1988, pp. 268–9).

For Grant and his colleagues (for example, Grant and Secada, 1990; Sleeter and Grant, 1987; Sleeter, 1991; Swadener, 1989), changing schools to minimize cultural differences is also insufficient; education that is multicultural and reconstructionist extends other approaches such as a cultural compatibility approach or a cultural difference approach by 'teaching students to analyze inequality and oppression in society and by helping them develop skills for social action' (Grant and Secada, 1990, p. 408).

Delpit (1988) suggests that the voice of minority culture families is insufficiently heard by those who propose cultural continuity as a method for helping minority culture children succeed in school. She claims that this might be a solution proposed by those dominant culture researchers and teachers for non-dominant members. Delpit argues that many African-American parents and teachers, for example, find that cultural compatibility of home and school alone is not sufficient and that they desire a more explicit education in the 'culture of power'.

Grant and Secada (1990) add to Delpit's point. They suggest that, for example, correcting the discontinuity between the cultural and linguistic background of the teaching force and the school population, on the theory that cultural-linguistic compatibility would help, may result, in the extreme case, in segregation of minority students and teachers or an excuse for why European-American teachers would not need to learn effective ways to teach all children (p. 406).

In order to illustrate these points better, we will describe one case study in some detail and, later, will also use shorter examples from other research in order to discuss theoretical and methodological issues encountered in our work in multicultural contexts in homes and schools. The case study, which draws directly on the theory of cultural compatibility, is discussed in most detail in order to give the readers a common example from which research issues can be more clearly presented. Examples from other projects will be included in the subsequent discussion to amplify methodological issues addressed in the chapter.

A Case Study of Three Schools

The following case study describes a study that examines ways in which multicultural classrooms for young children might be changed to better reflect and honor the cultural and linguistic backgrounds of children from three different minority culture backgrounds.[3] The primary goal of the study, which is co-directed by the first author and Robert Tabachnick, is to examine ways in which teachers, administrators, parents, and university researchers can collaborate in determining ways in which largely majority culture (European-American and middle-class) schools and classrooms can be altered to better recognize and empower the skills and values children of color bring to the schools. A secondary, but important, goal is to facilitate better relationships and communication between parents from each of the minority culture backgrounds and teachers, and to empower collaboration.

After the next discussion of specific research, theoretical and methodological issues that have greater generalizability[4] will be discussed.

Setting and Background of the Case Study

In 1984, a federal court determined that there was *de facto* segregation in three elementary (K-5) schools in a large mid-western city, and ordered that the schools be integrated. The school district responded by 'pairing' the three segregated schools, which had minority populations of over 70 per cent each, with three other elementary schools that had largely white, middle class students; students were to be moved from one school to another between second and third grade, and moved from their neighborhoods for the early grades or for the later grades by busing. Two of the six paired schools were transformed into primary schools for kindergarten through second graders, while their 'paired' schools were upper elementary third through fifth grade schools; the other pair of schools both remained K-5 schools with busing used to balance the minority student population in those two schools.

By the time integration had occurred, all schools had reduced their proportion of minority culture students to below 50 per cent of each school's total population, which on the average was 300. The two paired schools with K-2 student populations were included in the study; a third K-5 school with 30 per cent of its student body made up of children of color was also included after the first year of the study (Year 1: 1988/89; Year 2: 1989/90). All schools were multicultural. Each had over 50 per cent of their population made up by European-American children, primarily from middle-class families. In Manhattan School, one-third of the 44 per cent minority culture children were of African-American heritage, while the remaining 11 per cent of the children were children of Hmong (Indochinese) immigrants to the United States. Lakeview School had approximately 45 per cent minority culture population with more Hmong children (25 per cent) than African-American. Longfellow School, the one school that had not participated in the court-ordered integration plan, had the majority of the Latino (Spanish-speaking) children in the district (10 per cent) as well as children from African-American (15 per cent) and Hmong backgrounds (15 per cent).

In each school, the vast majority of the children of color came from what would be classified as low-income family backgrounds. Many, but not all, children lived in subsidized housing complexes; many, but not all, were from single-parent households; many, but not all received AFDC.[5]

In contrast to the student population, and as in many other schools across the nation (see Grant and Secada, 1990), the school administrators and teachers were predominantly of European-American cultural background, and many had had few personal or professional experiences with people of color. While the principals in Lakeview and Longfellow Schools were men and had been principals in their schools for at least six years, the principal in Manhattan was a female of about the same age and experience as the other principals (average age 50 years; average experience as principal twenty years), but who had just been appointed principal of Manhattan School for the fall of 1988. The vast majority of teachers in all three schools were female.

Research Context

In April of 1988, a school district financed evaluation of the integration and paired school effort that included Lakeview and Manhattan Schools was presented to the School Board and reported in the local city media. While some positive things had happened as a result of the integration of the schools, standardized test results showed that children of color in all of the integrated schools were still performing as poorly as they had before integration (based on data from the previous years at the same schools).

In addition, there was a climate of tension and suspicion in the relationships between each of the minority culture groups (African-American and Hmong), school staff in Manhattan and Lakeview Schools, and with the European-American parents whose children attended the school. This climate was represented in parent involvement data (for example, low percentages of parents attending conferences, going to PTO meetings, attending school events, and volunteering in the school) and in verbal and written reports given to the evaluators. The same climate of tension and suspicion was later observed in Longfellow School with Latino, African-American, and Hmong families whose children attended that school. Staff from a neighboring district's university, including Bloch and Tabachnick, were invited by the Chancellor of the University and the School District Superintendent to collaborate with the integrated schools to try to help reduce tension in the schools, and to help increase the achievement levels of children of color in the schools. The project was developed as a collaboration between the university and schools, although the notion of collaboration was instigated as a top-down Chancellor-Superintendent decision; in other words, targeted schools and some strategies were determined by others.

The first spring (May 1988), the university team met with Manhattan School staff members to determine ways in which the university could help the school. Lakeview and Longfellow Schools were added to the research project after this initial collaborative meeting took place, and after funding for research was approved. As described earlier, the project goals (Bloch and Tabachnick, 1988), were to improve the achievement of children of color in multicultural school settings by: (i) increasing home-school cultural compatibility; and (ii) improving low-income, minority culture parents' 'involvement' with the schools.

The university staff coordinated a number of intervention and research projects in the schools with whom they were 'collaborating'. The project described in this case study was defined by the first author and Tabachnick during the course of a June 1988 period when they were pursuing funding to support the research and intervention effort targeted, in part, by the university-school staff joint meeting of May 1988. Bloch and Tabachnick had already discussed a project focusing on home-school compatibilities of children in the newly integrated Lakeview and Manhattan schools, and had had preliminary discussions with one foundation about financing such a project before any meeting with school staff members. The project was funded in November, 1988 and the collaborative research project was begun initially with Manhattan School in January of 1989; Lakeview and Longfellow Schools were included in the fall of 1989 when formal observations of kindergarten age children in their home and school contexts were initiated.

Research Procedures

While both of the principal investigators were from majority culture backgrounds, each had had extensive prior experience working in culturally diverse settings. However, while we were outsiders with considerable experience in diverse cultures, we felt that families would respond to those of similar cultural and linguistic backgrounds and that 'insider' knowledge and interpretation of cultural exchanges was critical (for example, see Delpit, 1988). Indeed, language compatibility was an absolute necessity for interviewing and observing children in many contexts. Thus, a critical first step in the research project was to hire a multicultural, multilingual staff who would be able to work in culturally and linguistically diverse settings including children's homes and schools. African-American, Peruvian Spanish-speaking, and Korean research assistants were hired; it was difficult to locate a Hmong or Hmong-speaking research assistant at first and a Hmong interpreter was added to the project staff. All project assistants needed to be able to work comfortably with children, teachers and administrators in school settings, and with children and families in homes and communities. Finally, research assistants needed to be competent in qualitative research methodology.

One methodological goal of the study was to obtain comparable data on Hmong, African-American, and Latino children in homes and schools; gradually, after a significant period of observation, the research team decided on types of observation that we could obtain in each of the classrooms (teacher-led periods, 'center time' child work time, and 'free choice peer interaction time'), and homes (adult-child and peer play and work times).

Entry into homes and school classrooms was a long and complicated task, which had to be done with sensitivity and integrity, as it was no one's intent to be overly intrusive in classroom or family life. The research strategies, incorporating longitudinal methods over two to three years of children's life (K-2nd grade) and participant observation/ethnographic techniques were chosen specifically to minimize intrusion. Field notes were shared with parents and teachers in order to validate observations and to incorporate cultural meanings and interpretations. After three years of the project, including two year of data collection in kindergartens and children's homes, numerous methodological and ideological issues have been resolved, some remain, and others are still emerging. The following section describes some of these.

Methodological and Theoretical Issues

As the preceding case study highlights suggest, an array of theoretical, ideological, methodological, and practical dilemmas are typically faced by researchers focussing on questions of home-school compatibility and home-school-community relations, particularly in multicultural contexts. To the extent possible, such issues should be confronted and considered before data collection begins; they should be made as explicit as possible to provide the context for the research as it evolves. However, in collaborative and case study research in homes and schools, research choices continue to occur during, not always before, data collection.[6] The dilemmas faced prior to research and the way they color research as well as those faced, frequently, during the course of research as it evolves will be discussed in the sections below.

In the following sections, we will discuss: ideology and paradigm, theory and the selection of research topics and questions, relevant methodological approaches and research designs, research funding, who does research and who is 'researched', notions of collaboration and voice, determination of settings for data collection. Design and paradigm questions include the issue of whether to take a more *emic* or *etic* (insider vs. outsider) perspective in formulating the research project, what it may mean to 'give a voice' to frequently marginalized or oppressed individuals or groups (for example, Delpit, 1988; Fine, 1990), and the notion of 'intervention' and how the notion of change is envisioned. These issues take a variety of forms, depending on the field of the researcher, stage in her or his career, work environment and role models, and personal ideology.

Ideology, Personal History and Formulation of Appropriate Questions and Methods

As other chapters in this volume have noted, formulating research questions is far from an apolitical, unbiased, or uncompromised endeavor. Lather (1986) quotes Hesse (1980) to make these points:

> The attempt to produce value-neutral social science is increasingly being abandoned as at best unrealizable, and at worst self-deceptive, and is being replaced by social sciences based on explicit ideologies. (Hesse, 1980, p. 247, cited in Lather, 1986)

Researchers' autobiographies, choices in foregrounding or privileging of certain issues, perspectives, or paradigms, multiple group memberships and sources of identification (for example, gender, race, language, class, religion) have an undeniable role in shaping research agendas. Examples of the role of personal history in selection of research issues include researchers returning to their region or country of origin to conduct ethnographic research, researchers adapting existing assessment instruments to better reflect African-American children's cultural experience (Green, 1991), or the role of family and cultural background in the research agenda of many bilingual researchers (Trueba, 1990; Soto, chapter 11 in this book).

In an article titled 'Racism in academia: The old wolf revisited', Reyes and Halcon (1988) state,

> As Hispanic academics, our research interests often stem from a recognition that we have endured racial discrimination and from a compelling need to lend a dimension of authenticity to the prevailing theories about our communities. Said another way, we want to provide our own perspectives regarding prevailing negative assumptions about our values, culture, and language. (p. 76)

In the case study described earlier, research team members have represented their own experiences in interpreting ways in which teachers and family members would respond to the research or issues related to the conduct of the research and intervention efforts. Team members suggested, undoubtedly correctly, that parents and teachers would respond differently to researchers depending upon their gender, language, class, and cultural backgrounds (see chapter 4 by Weis in this volume for a further discussion of this point); with some difficulty, the European-American principal investigators did not conduct many of the critical interviews and observations themselves.

The role of teachers' life histories has also been discussed in the teacher development and early childhood literature as a significant influence on classroom praxis (for example, Ayers, 1988; Holly, 1989). Additionally, the failure of many dominant culture and economically privileged researchers to consider the perspectives and experience of individuals from non-dominant cultural and linguistic backgrounds are further examples of the role of autobiography in the formation of research agendas and methodology.

How free one feels, however, to select research issues and questions of obvious ideological and political import is all too often complicated by academic survival issues such as promotion and tenure (for example, Blum, 1988), or personal choices about not being over-identified with research topics of obvious importance to one's personal history (Reyes and Halcon, 1988). Fears of conducting 'soap box research' or raising issues which the prevailing literature has avoided, can be all-too-powerful forces in silencing voices not only in the field (for example, Delpit, 1988; Fine, 1990), but in the Academe.

For example, some Hispanic researchers have avoided doing potentially controversial research on bilingual education, until after obtaining tenure. Such researchers often feel pressure to 'prove themselves' within more mainstream and less culturally identified fields of inquiry. Reyes and Halcon (1988) describe the 'brown-on-brown research taboo', in which the general perception is that minority-related topics do not constitute academic scholarship. The assumption is that minority researchers cannot be objective in their analyses of those problems which are so close to their life experiences, (p. 76).

This pervasive devaluing of 'brown-on-brown' research is further described by Reyes and Halcon as a 'paternal attitude from a white, male-dominated profession' which perpetuates a double standard which 'lends full credibility to whites' conducting research on white populations, but discredits minority academics' research on minority issues' (p. 77). Reyes and Halcon conclude that the major objection to 'brown-on-brown' research is not the credibility of such research, but an 'unspoken objection to a potential undermining of white expertise on minority issues' (p. 77).

Similarly, some feminist scholarship, particularly that which focuses on differential power relations including those in university settings, has been marginalized. Simeone (1987), Lather (1991) and others have described ways in which women in academia had similar experiences to ethnic minorities, including a devaluing of their research and confounding of political, social and perceived congeniality factors with merit review by dominant culture, predominantly male colleagues.

Yet another example concerns African-American researchers who may risk having their work viewed as more politically and culturally motivated than methodologically or theoretically rigorous by dominant culture colleagues. Additionally, many such individuals frequently become overextended in mentorship and other service activities, at the cost of time for scholarship necessary for tenure.

Funding, Ideology, and Power

When applying such often subtle issues to research agendas in early childhood education, child development, or family studies, as in other areas of scholarship, likelihood of funding, eventual publication, and relationship to current 'hot topics' are often influential factors. This can, all too often, be at the cost of taking a more critical or more emic perspective in formulating the problem and research questions.

One example of these issues is represented by several points in the case study described above. While a collaborative effort was initiated by the university and staff members from a school district, issues of financing projects became paramount early in the collaboration. The deadlines and priorities of funding agencies and the grant writers, in this case university faculty, came to influence how the grant proposal was written, what was prioritized, and the nature of collaborative discussion about the process of the work in its earliest stages. Thus, the ideology of collaboration became secondary to funding requirements. A second example of this phenomenon can be found in the current pervasiveness of the construct 'children-at-risk'. In an ERIC search, for example, 1047 recent citations were listed, using the descriptor 'high risk students' and the program of the American Educational Research Association's 1990 meeting listed thirty-five papers on the 'at risk' topic (Swadener, 1990). Calls for papers, federal, state and local funding opportunities, and local initiatives appear to be rapidly increasing. A limited number of researchers, however, are voicing strong concerns about this construct and its personal and collective problematics to children and families overrepresented in this category (for example, Cuban, 1989; Lubeck and Garrett, 1990; Secada, 1989; Swadener, 1990; Soto, chapter 11 in this volume).

Paradigm, Theory and Methods in Early Childhood Research

This last issue is related to the issue that prevailing theories of early childhood education emphasize positivist and individualistic cognitive psychology and child development. These theoretical and methodological frames look at cultural factors as they relate to individual and psychological development, and distract attention from broader structural relations in society that have colored interactions between schools and families. They also ignore or deemphasize other, more holistic ways of looking at the relationships between culture, class, and gender and their influence on children and families.

The early childhood scholars who identify with a non-psychological, critical, and/or feminist perspective are few (see recent discussions in Bloch, 1991; Kessler, 1990; and Swadener, 1991). One reason for this lack of recognition and acceptance of critical theoretical perspectives in early childhood education is the historical prevalence of dominant culture and frequently gender-biased emphases on psychology in the early childhood field (Bloch, 1991; Kessler, 1991). These perspectives have narrowed the parameters of inquiry within early childhood education which has functionally served to silence other possible perspectives within which to view children, the curriculum and home-school relationships. For example, alternative paradigms including early education as caring, cultural and social contexts of early learning (for example, the role of peer culture), or even in-depth discussion of curriculum content have not been part of much of the dominant research literature in early childhood education. A small but growing body of early childhood literature and curricula (for example, Derman-Sparks, 1989; Lubeck, 1985; Ramsey, 1987; and Saracho Spodek, 1983; Whaley and Swadener, 1990), addresses issues of cultural responsiveness and compatibility, linguistic diversity and the strengths or promise, versus risk, such diversity adds to children and schools.

What to Research and Who is Researched

Along with dilemmas associated with formulating relevant and even potentially emancipatory research agendas and questions, is the parallel issue of where to focus — particularly in conducting qualitative and descriptive research, including case studies of classrooms, early childhood programs, schools, and homes. One such example is related to whether researchers should focus on teachers, caregivers, and parents who are struggling to create culturally responsive, reflective and empowering programs and home environments, and working closely with diverse groups in the community, in order to document what is possible, what can be done or is being tried?

The second author has conducted two ethnographic studies focusing, for the most part, on promising practice in early childhood and primary settings. Although neither of these studies could be said to document the most typical practices, curricula or teaching approaches in early childhood education and care, it was considered important to document the struggles, successes and day-to-day social and curricular practices of teachers and parents attempting to implement a culturally inclusive, anti-bias approach in their work with children. The first study documented two mainstreamed, culturally diverse, child care centers' attempts to implement education that is multicultural and documented the successful mainstreaming efforts and pervasive anti-sexist practices of the staff.

The second case study was a teacher-researcher collaborative project which documented teaching toward peace and social responsibility in a Friends Elementary School, including conflict mediation, social problem-solving, consensus decision-making, and co-constructing curricula and experiences with children. The latter collaboration has led to production of a videotape on 'Teaching Peace', which teacher collaborators in the research had requested for use in their workshops with other teachers and parents. Does such research merely have a 'halo effect', instead of representing the hard realities of schooling and day care issues, or does it also have a role in raising possibilities for more culturally sensitive and potentially empowering early education practices?

Intervention and Change as Educational 'Quick Fixes' Versus Transformational Change

The term 'intervention' draws heavily (and historically) from a clinical emphasizing the diagnosis, by professionals, of certain problems and the prescription of potential remedies. As such, there has been little emphasis on genuine collaboration with those for whom the intervention is targeted, nor on non-dominant culture voices or empowerment, as discussed above. Much of this diagnostic and prescriptive approach to educational intervention has also been critiqued as perpetuating a deficit model (for example, the revising of the 'culturally disadvantaged' label to 'at risk' or many of the compensatory parent intervention/training programs, particularly for families with differently abled children). Of particular concern in the abundance of intervention programs discussed in the home-school-community arena is the implicit assumption that parents, home environment, access to material resources, or class, language or dialect, and level or rate of development and functioning are responsible for identified problems, including non-successful academic achievement and lack of positive home-school relations. A related concern is the construct of 'readiness', and whether children must be ready for school, including whatever intervention may be needed (for example, Head Start), versus the belief that schools should be ready for children. The notion of cultural compatibility that emphasizes the differences between school and home culture rather than the deficiencies of, typically, the home culture, is another example. How one views the problem affects the notion of how, by whom, when, and where intervention and change can occur.

In contrast to the short-term intervention approaches prevalent in much of the early childhood and education literature or the 'quick fix' intervention designed by a professional as a top-down strategy, and alternative construct of 'transformative change' has been called for increasingly by researchers and change agents concerned with home, school, and community relations within a broader set of power relations (see, for example, Bloch and Tabachnick, 1990a). The potential for such transformative change is enhanced when there is relative parity (or more equalized power roles) and authentic, *versus* only superficial, collaboration between members hoping to affect change (also see Cummins, 1986; Delgado-Gaitan, 1989).

Transformative change between teachers and parents of color, who have generally had little power vis-a-vis schools, requires a shift of power from schools to homes, from teachers and administrators to parents and community members. While several recent examples of transformational change have been started and documented (for example, see Comer, 1980; and the case of the Chicago Public Schools), the Bloch-Tabachnick research has not found that it is easy to facilitate such change simply through collaborative discussions between teachers, parents, and university staff (for example, see Bloch and Tabachnick, 1990a). What is clear is that the process of enduring and important change or even the possibility for transformation is rocky, and not always desired by all parties. When change is not desired by all, whose voices should be privileged? How should change take place? How long does it take to begin to share a collective voice?

Collaborative Research and the Dissemination of Findings

Interpretation of data and the dissemination process are issues of importance, as illustrated by Borman *et al.* in this volume (chapter 6). Power and political issues once again are critical, and in collaborative research — defined to be part of the research project — these issues become paramount.

One issue is illustrated by the case study research where collaboration began between the school district and university administrators and schools were asked to collaborate with university researchers. In this top-down example, it took many teachers, for example, a full year to feel that there were good reasons to collaborate with university staff although such collaboration had begun to occur. In addition, community and parent representatives were not originally built into the collaborative relationship; in this case, while university staff have built collaborative relationships with community leaders and parents, there have been fewer initiatives, thus far, by the school toward collaborative decision-making with the community/parent groups. Thus decisions made at the outset of a research project often have long-lasting effects, not all of which are desirable.

On a more positive note, university-school and university-home collaboration has occurred frequently, and, given the length of time it takes for trust in relationships to occur, the growth in all relationships, especially university, school and home, signals progress. As many have also been suspicious of the university staff's need to do 'research' and 'publication', our continual sharing of data, and invitations to develop ideas and projects together appears to enhance collaboration.

Once the home-school university collaboration project was funded, school administrators, teachers and parents were invited to share in the construction of many of the research procedures, the interpretation of findings, and in publication. When requests for privacy (for example, 'do not share with the teacher'), or off-the-record comments to a research assistant have been made, they have been honored.

Genuine collaboration is also enhanced when teachers and researchers, for example, have compatible and even shared agendas and goals, and devise research projects together. For example, in a collaborative video ethnography completed by the second author, teacher-researcher collaboration began with both shared and individual interests and needs and has grown into a three-year collaboration of benefit to both.

More specifically, at least two teachers at the Friends School, which was the site of this latter case study, expressed an interest in better documentation of the social problem-solving, conflict mediation and consensus decision-making processes used daily in their classrooms. They frequently had questions from parents and other teachers, and also did a number of workshops which they felt would be enhanced by videotape examples of their practice and the children's interactions.

The university researcher was also interested in videotaping, along with participant-observation and interviews with children and staff, and project goals were developed together with individual teachers and at a preliminary meeting with the full staff of this small school. Teachers were relatively enthusiastic about the project — if not initially about the frequent videotaping of themselves and the children — and even offered to videotape activities which were related to the project, in the absence of the researcher or her assistant. In other words, a video camera was kept at the school throughout most of the two years of research and teachers would occasionally ask the school's secretary, principal or each other to tape an activity or discussion of particular relevance to the project.

Since production of a videotape for use in workshops with parents, teachers, and child caregivers was a major goal for the teachers, a script for this tape was co-written by one of the teachers and the researcher, both of whom remained directly involved through the stages of actual completion of the tape.

This involved, essentially, a form of collaborative data analysis of over thirty-six hours of classroom and playground videotaped observations, a prioritization of examples to be used, and taping a discussion among the teachers, to serve as the narration of the video.

Another way in which teachers were directly involved was in the dissemination of preliminary findings from the case study research, including co-authoring and presenting papers at national meetings of the American Educational Research Association and the American Educational Studies Association, and co-facilitating workshops with teachers and parents. At present, collaboration for dissemination of the project includes co-authoring articles (e.g. Swadener and Piekielek, in press) and considering further collaborative projects.

At the dissemination stage, qualitative researchers employing methods such as ethnography, life history, discourse analysis, and other approaches generating large amounts of data, may experience pressure to 'parcel out findings into different referent groups', social and educational issues, or otherwise potentially undermine the original contextual or parallelist (see McCarthy and Apple, 1988) intent of the overall project. This relates directly to the theoretical framework within which the researcher is operating, and whether a parallelist or more inclusive approach to the topic could be taken. Alternatives to parceling out data in decontextualized ways in order to fit the standard journal length format include writing a book, monograph, or a researcher journal. Recent approaches that include videotapes, readers' theatre, or more 'dramatic' renderings of data from research are being experimented with currently (for example, Ellsworth and Orner, 1989).

Conclusion

In this chapter we have attempted to discuss a number of critical issues facing researchers interested in studying children within home, school, and community contexts, as well as raise structural issues through our stories, as researchers in culturally diverse settings. We have emphasized the importance of theory, research ideology and methods, as well as the external realities facing many researchers and collaborators.

Through a discussion of one research project focusing on home-school compatibilities across three non-dominant cultural groups, issues of theoretical framework, research design, collaboration and inclusion, and possibilities for as well as limitations of change were raised. We further argue that the political and ideological realities of researchers — particularly researchers of color — must be considered, with greater encouragement of so-called 'brown-on-brown' research and less tendency to focus on potentially reductionistic single issues or variables. A parallelist position, in which issues of culture, race, language, class, gender and individual differences are equally included was recommended, as was the struggle for more balanced researcher-teacher-parent collaborations.

The possibilities for viewing culturally diverse families as 'at promise', versus 'at risk', may be enhanced by a diversification of research perspectives, paradigms, methodologies, and — importantly — researchers addressing issues of home-school-community relations, realities and recommendations for change.

Notes

1   This statement is not to give the simplistic impression that we are unaware of issues related to the concept of equality and equity in education; see recent discussions in Secada (1989), for example, for a complex perspective on these seemingly simple terms and concepts.
2   For distinctions between multicultural education and education that is multicultural, see Grant and Millar, chapters in this volume; Sleeter and Grant (1987) and Swadener (1989 and 1990).
3   The university research team consisted of the two principal investigators, Bloch and Tabachnick, and four research assistants, Jay Hammond Cradle, Miryam Espinosa-Dulanto, Seehwa Cho, and Carolyn Dean. It was funded by the Spencer Foundation.
4   The issues will relate to the case study, and to issues that have been mentioned by a variety of other authors or that have affected other, already published, studies.
5   The initial expectation was that some of the children of color would be from 'middle-class' backgrounds; traditional definitions of this phrase led us to the conclusion that there were almost no children of color from white collar worker families in any of the three schools. However, there was enormous variability on other characteristics: Hmong children typically were in extended family households where both the father, mother and other elder relatives resided; while the mothers were usually at home, some fathers were employed and schooled while others were unemployed and the families were on AFDC. Families generally came from Laos, Cambodia, or Thailand, African-American children came from a variety of families, some with both parents residing at home, and both employed and educated at least at the high school level, while others were in single female-headed households and on AFDC. Latino families, were from Mexican-American, Peruvian, and Nicaraguan backgrounds; some were on AFDC and unemployed, while others families had both parents at home and at least one parent employed. As others have noted (for example, Trueba, 1989), the English competence of the kindergarten-age Hmong and Latino children varied in significant ways; most, however, were in ESL programs and were classified as limited English proficient speakers.
6   Qualitative, case study, and ethnographic research methodology incorporates the idea that questions and methods can change or evolve during the course of the study; collaborative research that incorporates the notion of change and evolution of ideas and needs, also assumes change in methods can occur. Some other types of research paradigms and methods assume that questions and methods can all be determined in advance of the research project, and will not be changed during the course of research; even when this assumption is valid, dilemmas discussed in this chapter have relevance for the way a project is designed, how it is conducted during the course of research and intervention, and disseminated.

References

ANDERSON, G. (1989) 'Critical ethnography in education: origins, current status, and new directions', *Review of Education Research*, **59**, 3, pp. 249–70.
APPLE, M. and WEIS, L. (1983) *Ideology and Practice in Schooling*, Philadelphia, PA, Temple University Press.
AYERS, W. (1988) *The Good Preschool Teacher*, New York, Teachers' College Press.
BLOCH, M.N. and TABACHNICK, B.R. (1988) '*Increasing the school achievement of minority children through improved home-school-university collaboration*', unpublished research proposal, Madison, Wisconsin, Wisconsin Center for Educational Research.

BLOCH, M.N. (1991) 'Critical science and history of development's influence on early education research', *Early Education and Development*, **2**, 2, pp. 95–108.

BLOCH, M.N. and TABACHNICK, B.R. (1990a, and in preparation) 'Parent involvement: Rhetoric or Reform?' in GREENMAN, N. and BORMAN, K. (Eds) *Restructuring America's Schools: Educational Quick Fixes*, Norwood, NJ, Ablex Publishing Co.

BLUM, D.E. (1988) 'To get ahead in research, some minority scholars choose to "play the game"', *The Chronicle of Higher Education*, 22 June, p. A17.

COMER, J. (1980) *School Power*, New Haven, CT, Yale University Press.

CUBAN, L. (1989) 'Who's at risk?', *Phi Delta Kappan*, June.

CUMMINS, J. (1986) 'Empowering minority students: A framework for intervention', *Harvard Education Review*, **56**, 1, pp. 18–35.

DELGADO-GAITAN, C. (1987) 'Traditions and transitions in the learning process of Mexican children: An ethnographic view' in SPINDLER, G. and L. (Eds) *Interpretive Ethnography of Education: At Home and Abroad*, Hillsdale, NJ, Lawrence Erlbaum Associates, pp. 333–59.

DELGADO-GAITAN, C. (1990) *Literacy for Empowerment*, London, Falmer Press.

DELPIT, L. (1988) 'The silenced dialogue: Power and pedagogy in educating other people's children', *Harvard Education Review* **58**, 3, pp. 280–98.

DERMAN-SPARKS, L. (1989) *Anti-Bias Curriculum: Tools for Empowering Young Children*. Washington DC, National Association for the Education of Young Children.

DEYLE, D. (1987) 'Learning Failure: Tests as gatekeepers and the culturally different child' in TRUEBA, H. (Ed.) *Success or Failure: Learning and the Language Minority Student*, New York, Newbury Publishers, pp. 85–108.

DIAZ, S., MOLL, L. and MEHAN, H. (1986) 'Sociocultural resources in instruction: A context-specific approach' in TRUEBA, H. (1986) *Beyond Language: Social and Cultural Factors in Schooling Language Minority Students*, Sacramento, CA, Bilingual Education Office, California State Department of Education, pp. 187–230.

ELLSWORTH, E. and ORNER, M. (1989) *Wish We Were Here*, videotape presentation at the Bergamo Curriculum Theorizing and Classroom Practices Conference, Dayton, Ohio, October.

ERICKSON, F. (1987) 'Transformation and school success: The politics and culture of educational achievement', *Anthropology and Education Quarterly*, **18**, 4, pp. 335–56.

ERICKSON, F. (1989) 'Cultural diversity and the schooling of American children', unpublished videotaped presentation at the Twenty-Fifth Anniversary Celebration of the Wisconsin Center for Educational Research, University of Wisconsin-Madison. Madison, WI, Wisconsin Center for Educational Research, University of Wisconsin-Madison.

ERICKSON, F. and MOHATT, G. (1977) *The Social Organization of Participation Structures in Two Classrooms of Indian Students*, report to the Department of Indian Affairs and Northern Development, Ottawa (Ontario) (ERIC # ED 192 935).

FINE, M. (1988) 'Of kitsch and caring: The illusion of students at risk', *School Administrator*, **45**, 8, pp. 16–18.

FLORIO, S. and SCHULTZ, J. (1979) 'Social competence at home and at school', *Theory into Practice*, **18**, 4, pp. 234–43.

FORDHAM, S. and OGBU, J. (1986) 'Black students' school success: Coping with the 'Burden of "Acting White"'', *Urban Review*, **18**, 3, pp. 176–205.

GRANT, C. and SECADA, W. (1990) 'Preparing teachers for diversity' in HOUSTON, R.W., HABERMAN, M. and SIKULA, J.P. (Eds) *Handbook of Research on Teacher Education*, New York, Macmillan.

GREEN, G.M. (1990) '*Cultural self expression and African-American children's self esteem: Reflections on a field study of a Southern Head Start program*'. Paper presented at the annual Ethnography in Education Research Forum, Philadelphia, PA., February.

HEATH, S.B. (1982) 'Questioning at home and school' in SPINDLER, G. and SPINDLER, L. (Eds) *Doing the Ethnography of Schooling*, New York, Holt.

HEATH, S.B. (1983) *Ways with Words*, Cambridge, Cambridge University Press.

HESSE, M. (1980). *Revolution and Reconstruction in the Philosophy of Science*. Bloomington, Indiana University Press.

HILLIARD, A. (1989) *On Being Black: An In-Group Analyses*. (2nd Edition). Bristol, IN, Wyndam Hill Press.

HOLLY, M.L. (1989) *Writing to Grow*, Portsmouth, NH, Heinemann Publishers.

HORNBURGER, N. (1989) 'Creating successful learning contexts for biliteracy', paper presented at the annual meeting of the American Anthropological Association, Washington DC, November.

KESSLER, S.A. (1991) 'Alternative perspectives on early childhood education', *Early childhood Research Quarterly*, **6**, pp. 183–97.

JORDAN, C. (1985) 'Translating culture: From ethnographic information to educational program', *Anthropology and Education Quarterly*, **16**, pp. 105–23.

LADSON-BILLINGS, G. (1990) Paper presented as part of the Minority Lecture Series, sponsored by the School of Education and the Wisconsin Center for Educational Research, the University of Wisconsin-Madison.

LATHER, P. (1986) 'Research as praxis', *Harvard Education Review*, **56**, 3, pp. 257–77.

LATHER, P. (1991) *Getting Smart: Feminist Research and Pedagogy within the Postmodern*, New York, Routledge.

LUBECK, S. (1985) *Sandbox Society: Early Schooling in Black and White America*, London, Falmer Press.

LUBECK, S. and GARRETT, P. (1990) 'The social construction of the "at risk" child', *British Journal of Sociology of Education*, **11**, 3, pp. 327–40.

MCCARTHY, C. (1988) 'Rethinking liberal and radical perspectives on racial inequality in schooling: Making the case for nonsynchrony', *Harvard Education Review*, **58**, 3, pp. 265–79.

MCCARTHY, C. and APPLE, M.W. (1988) 'Race, class, and gender in American educational research: Toward a nonsynchronous parallelist position' in WEISS, L. (Ed.) *Class, Race, and Gender in American Education*. Albany, NY, State University of New York Press.

O'BRIEN, L. (1990) *'Cultural influences on classroom practices of teachers in an Appalachian Head Start program'*, paper presented at Bergamo Curriculum Theorizing and Classroom Practices Conference, Dayton, OH, October.

OGBU, J.U. (1981) 'Origins of human competence: A cultural-ecological perspective' *Child Development*, **52**, pp. 413–29.

OGBU, J.U. (1982) 'Cultural discontinuities and schooling', *Anthropology and Education Quarterly*, **12**, 4, pp. 290–307.

OGBU, J.U. (1987) 'Variability in minority school performance: A problem in search of an explanation', *Anthropology and Education Quarterly* **18**, 4, pp. 312–34.

PHILIPS, S. (1983) *The Invisible Culture: Communities in Classroom and Community on the Warm Springs Indian Reservation*, New York, Longman.

RAMSEY, P.C., (1987) *Teaching and Learning in a Diverse World: Multicultural Education and Young Children*, NY, Teacher's College Press.

REYES, M.L. and HALCON, J.J. (1988) 'Racism in academia: The old wolf revisited', *Harvard Educational Review*, **58**, 3, pp. 299–314.

SARACHO, O.N. and SPODEK, B. (1983) *Understanding the Multicultural Experience in Early Childhood*, Washington DC, National Association for the Education of Young Children.

SCHUTZ, J., FLORIO, S. and ERICKSON, F. (1982) 'Where's the floor? Aspects of the cultural organization of social relationships in communication at home and in school' in GILMORE, P. and GLATTHORN, A.A. (Eds) *Children In and Out of School: Ethnography and Education*. Washington DC, Center for Applied Linguistics.

SECADA, W. (1989) *Equity in Education*, London, Falmer Press.

SIMEONE, A. (1987) *Academic Women Working Towards Equality*, South Hadley, MA, Bergin and Garvey.

SLEETER, C. (Ed.) (1991) *Empowerment Through Multicultural Education* Albany, NY, State University of New York Press.

SLEETER, C. and GRANT, C. (1987) 'An analysis of multicultural education in the United States', *Harvard Education Review*, **57**, 4, pp. 421–44.

SPINDLER, G. and SPINDLER, L. (1987) *The Interpretive Ethnography of Education: At Home and Abroad*, Hillsdale, NJ, Lawrence Erlbaum Associates.

SUAREZ-AROZCO, M.M. (1988) *In Pursuit of a Dream: New Hispanic Immigrants in American Schools*, Stanford, CA, Stanford University Press.

SWADENER, E.B. (1988) 'Education that is multicultural in early childhood settings: A case study of two mainstreamed child care programs', *The Urban Review*, **20**, 1, pp. 8–27.

SWADENER, E.B. (1989) 'Race, gender, and exceptionality: Peer interactions in two child care centers', *Educational Policy*, **3**, 4, pp. 371–88.

SWADENER, E.B. (1990) 'Children and families "At-Risk": Etiology, critique and alternative paradigms', *Educational Foundations*, **4**, 4, pp. 17–39.

SWADENER, B.B. and PIEKIELEK, D. (in press) 'Beyond democracy to consensus: Reflections on a Friends School collaborative ethnography', in KESSLER, S.A. and SWADENER, B.B. (Eds) *Reconceptualizing the Early Childhood Curriculum*, NY, Teachers College Press.

TAYLOR, D. and DORSEY-GAINES, C. (1988) *Growing Up Literate: Learning from Inner-city Families*, New York, Heinneman Press.

THARP, R. (1989) 'Psychocultural variables and constants: Effects on teaching and learning in schools', *American Psychologist*, **48**, 2, pp. 349–59.

THARP, R. and GALLIMORE, R. (1989) *Rousing Minds to Life: Teaching, Learning and Schooling in Social Context*, Cambridge, Cambridge University Press.

TRUEBA, H.T. (1988) 'Culturally-based explanations of minority students' academic achievement', *Anthropology and Education Quarterly*, **19**, 3, pp. 270–87.

TRUEBA, W. (1989) *Raising Silent Voices*, New York, Newbury House Publishers.

TRUEBA, H.T. (1990) Plenary session remarks at the 11th Annual Ethnography in Educational Research conference, Philadelphia, March.

TRUEBA, H.T., JACOBS, L. and KIRTON, J.E. (1990) *Cultural Conflict and Adaptation: The Case of Hmong Children in American Society*, London, Falmer Press.

VOGT, L.A., JORDAN, C. and THARP, R.A. (1987) 'Explaining school failure: producing success: Two cases', *Anthropology and Education Quarterly.* **18**, pp. 276–86.

WEIS, L. (Ed.) (1988) *Class, Race, and Gender in American Education.* Albany, NY, State University of New York Press.

WEISNER, T.S., GALLIMORE, R. and JORDAN, C. (1988), 'Unpackaging cultural effects on classroom learning: Native Hawaiian peer assistance and child-generated activity', *Anthropology and Education Quarterly*, **19**, pp. 327–53.

WHALEY, K. and SWADENER, E.B. (1990) 'Multicultural education in infant and toddler settings', *Childhood Education*, **66**, pp. 238–40, spring/summer, April.

Chapter 13

Teacher Education Programs and Increasing Minority School Populations: An Educational Mismatch?

Mary Lou Fuller

This study was a collaborative effort on the part of the members of the Equity and Excellence Committee, Midwest Holmes Group. In particular: Carl Grant, University of Wisconsin-Madison; Toni Griego-Jones, University of Wisconsin-Milwaukee; Janice A. Seitz, University of Illinois-Urbana; Richard Elardo, University of Iowa; and Michael Scott, Ohio State University.

Introduction

Three Students

Kenneth is a 9-year-old third grader who lives with his mother and two sisters in an apartment on the south side of Chicago. He knows his mother is concerned about supporting him and his sisters on her minimum wage salary. Kenneth also knows that, being a person of color, he is a member of a minority group — although this is not the case in his neighborhood and at school where he is unquestionably a member of the majority population. In contrast to the students, though, the faculty in his school is primarily white and middle class. And almost all of the teachers are women.

The faculty is also white, middle class, and female at the school attended by Anita, a 12-year-old Mexican-American sixth grader living in Fargo, North Dakota. Anita's family — her parents, three brothers, and a sister — recently rented a small apartment and are hoping to find a place with more room. For many years, members of her family were migrant workers who made the long trip from Brownsville, Texas, to North Dakota to work in the sugar beet fields during the summer months. Recently, though, they and many other Mexican-American migrant families settled in the upper Midwest. Although the number of Hispanics is growing in her community, Anita is still very much in the minority both in her school and in Fargo.

Bonnie is a 22-year-old pre-service teacher who attends a large midwestern university. Her parents and her two brothers live in their four-bedroom home on a quiet street in a suburb of Indianapolis. Her parents own a small insurance agency, and their concern at dinner last evening was arranging coverage for the business so they could take the family skiing when Bonnie came home during semester break.

Though Kenneth, Anita and Bonnie do not know each other, they exemplify a phenomenon in contemporary education which is also the focus of this chapter: diversity among the populations in the nation's schools and colleges of education. This chapter has two goals, the first is to explore that diversity using findings of a survey of teacher education programs at Midwest Holmes Group (MHG) teacher education programs to consider the educational implications of that diversity now and in the future. The second goal is to take a critical look at the research, when it is completed, to speculate about ways in which it — and other studies addressing diversity — might be more sensitive to the issues at hand.

Minority Students

The faces of the nation generally, and those of school children in particular, are changing. Traditional European features such as Bonnie's are no longer the embodiment of the American citizen because, as children of color increase in numbers, darker eyes, darker skin and darker hair — like those of Kenneth and Anita — are more commonly seen. This is not new to either our society or the schools; what is new is the rate at which these changes are occurring.

One reflection of these changes is the decline in the percentage of Americans of European ancestry from 87.7 per cent of the population in 1900 to 79.1 per cent in 1980. And these figures are an inflation of the mainstream white population since the 1980 census included in this group about 8.1 million Hispanics who differ culturally and linguistically from other US whites (Moneni, 1985).

What do these changes mean to educators? They mean that by the year 2000 between 33 per cent (Commission on Minority Participation in Education, 1988) and 40 per cent (Hodgkinson, 1985) of all school children will be members of minority groups. This is already the case in several states and in most urban areas where there is a majority of minorities. The National Center for Educational Statistics (1987a) estimates that 60–70 per cent of the students in twenty of the nation's largest districts are children of color (p. 64). And because of the relatively higher minority birth rates and increased immigration, the share of minority children in the United States is increasing while white non-Hispanic birthrates are declining (Griffith, Frase and Ralph, 1989).

Because education is presently designed for (and best meets the needs of) middle class children, economic resources (a defining feature of social class) must also be considered in understanding diversity in American schools. While the schools use their resources to improve the quality of education for the students they have traditionally served (such as Bonnie), the number of children who are 'fiscally at risk' (such as Kenneth and Anita) is both large (a quarter of all children in the United States live in poverty) and growing (the number of children in poverty will swell to one-third of all children by the year 2000

[Haberman, 1989]). This is important because disadvantaged children of color are more apt to be at risk for educational failure (Ralph, 1989).

Not only do children coming from families with limited financial resources lack the opportunities and benefits enjoyed by other children, they also attend less well-financed schools. This is due to property taxes being the primary source of funding for public education, and there being tremendous variation in local property revenues (National Coalition of Advocates for Students, 1985). The result is that students most in need of financial resources are least likely to have those needs met.

Further, the impact of poverty is felt most strongly by children aged 5 and younger — the most developmentally sensitive years — because their numbers are disproportionately larger than other age groups (Children's Defense Fund, 1989). Furthermore, because the age group figures are even higher for Hispanics and children of color (Moneni, 1985) the impact of poverty is even greater on these minority populations.

In short, ethnic/racial demographics are changing in society (with their economic ramifications), and these changes are reflected in the schools. This means children of color — such as Kenneth and Anita — will continue to appear in the schools in increasing numbers. It also means the educational needs of these students must be addressed if they are to avoid being mis- and under-educated. This is another way of saying there is increasing diversity in the schools, and teachers must value and be able to educate highly varied populations of children.

Pre-service Teachers

Being able to value and educate diverse student groups means either or both of the following: drawing pre-service teachers from populations familiar with the needs of minorities, and/or training pre-service teachers to be sensitive to those needs.

The former approach is problematic. Currently, approximately 90 per cent of teachers are white, non-Hispanic, while the remaining 10 per cent are minority (National Education Research and Improvement, 1987). In fact, the proportion of white teachers has actually increased from 1971 to 1986 (Griffith, Frase and Ralph, 1989). And, while the number of minority college students shows an encouraging increase nationally, there is a discouraging decrease in teacher education. Kenneth and Anita's chances of having a teacher of their own ethnic/racial background are growing slimmer.

Significance of Disparity

Minority teachers are needed for several reasons, the most important being they are role models for children of color. According to Bandura and Walters (1963), role models are vitally important in influencing children's values and norms. They argue that people reproduce the attitudes, emotional responses and actions exhibited by real life or symbolized models, and children need to see these role models. Similarly, this point is underscored by Mary Hatwood Futrell (former

National Education Association President) who argues,

> Our schools must help every student understand what the American heritage is all about — "strength through diversity". Today in far too many of our schools, there is no living evidence that drives that lesson home. That's one of the real tragedies of minority teacher shortage.... We're cheating the children of color students of the positive role models who can bolster their pride and self esteem (Holt, 1989).

Not only is it important for Anita and Kenneth to have minority role models, but it is also important for students like Bonnie. Gloria Grant (1978) argues for this saying the teacher as a role model in a culturally diverse society serves two important purposes — providing minority students with real life, everyday persons they can identify with, and allowing children of the majority populations and opportunity to interact with teacher role models from different races and cultures. In others words, all children benefit from minority role models.

In addition to role models, the presence of minority teachers communicates to children,

> something about power and authority in contemporary America. These messages influence children's attitudes about school, their academic accomplishments, and their views of their own and others intrinsic worth. The views they form in school about justice and fairness also influence their future citizenship. (Task Force on Teaching as a Profession, 1986, p. 79)

In the absence of appropriate role models, Kenneth and Anita are reminded daily that their prospects — and their chances of improving those prospects — are indeed limited.

Teacher Education Program

What are colleges of education doing to prepare teachers — like Bonnie — to work with culturally diverse and economically disadvantaged children — like Anita and Kenneth? This question was addressed by the Equity and Excellence Committee of the Midwest Holmes Group (MHG).

Midwest Holmes Group

The Equity and Excellence Committee recognized the importance of creating a profession that is not only representative of society but also knowledgeable about, and appreciative of, its parts. Creating greater student-teacher equity as well as the preparation of non-minority pre-service teachers to meet the needs of a diverse student population are primary concerns for this committee.

In order to examine the similarities among, and differences between, pre-service teachers and their prospective students, the committee reviewed the demographic characteristics of pre-service teachers at the nineteen Midwest

Holmes Group member institutions, as well as looked at the teacher education programs themselves for evidence of major culture preservice teachers' exposure to diversity, appropriate curriculum, and equity.

Background for the Study

The Holmes Group is a consortium of teacher education programs from major research institutions in each of the fifty states. Although the member institutions are innovators in education (as will be shown shortly), these institutions are comparable to other colleges of education nationally. Demographically the pre-service teachers enrolled in the Midwest Holmes Group institutions are generally comparable to the teacher population nationally (Griffith, Frase and Ralph, 1989; Gwaltney, 1990), and a comparison of Holmes Group and non-Holmes Group institutions nationally found these two groups of schools to be more similar than different in terms of both demographics and curriculum (Kniker, 1989) — a conclusion supporting the generalizability of findings from this study to other teacher education programs.

Midwest Holmes Group Institutions

The home communities of the MHG schools (table 13.1) are highly variable: seven institutions are found in metropolitan areas (Chicago, Detroit, Milwaukee, Cincinnati, Lincoln, Minneapolis) while the others are located in suburban settings and small cities in rural areas. MHG institutions have large teacher education programs (the median number of pre-service teachers is 975 with the middle 50 per cent enrolling 604 to 1827 students).

Materials and Methods

Survey Methodology

Since this study was a census, all nineteen eligible schools were asked to participate and survey instruments were sent to each institution.

The questionnaire used both forced-choice and open-ended questions to collect information about the Teacher Education Programs (for example, size, mission), the pre-service teachers served (for example, ethnic/racial background), and the faculty (for example, tenure status, gender, ethnic/racial background). This information was requested from each school's dean while a second part of the questionnaire went to the elementary education department seeking descriptions of pre-service programs.

Analytic Strategy

Completed instruments were returned and the data they contained were entered into the computer for analysis. Forced-choice and short open-ended responses

Table 13.1   Members of the Midwest Holmes Group

State	Holmes Group School
Illinois	University of Illinois at Chicago University of Illinois at Urbana-Champaign University of Chicago
Indiana	Purdue University
Iowa	University of Iowa Iowa State University
Michigan	University of Michigan Michigan State University Wayne State University
Minnesota	University of Minnesota
Nebraska	University of Nebraska at Lincoln
North Dakota	University of North Dakota
Ohio	Kent State University Ohio University University of Ohio University of Cincinnati
South Dakota	University of South Dakota
Wisconsin	University of Wisconsin at Milwaukee University of Wisconsin at Madison

were entered directly in anticipation of their analysis, and extended answers were coded (as described below) prior to being examined.

This study was exploratory in nature and the data analysis was designed accordingly. This meant frequency counts of responses to forced choice questions and computing medians and interquartile ranges for quantitative data. It should be noted that graphic displays (for example, box-and-whisker plots) were prepared for these data as well.

A content analysis was performed on responses to open-ended questions. This meant first identifying themes in the responses and then tabulating the frequency with which each theme appeared.

An important feature of the overall analysis was the absence of statistical hypothesis testing. First, the exploratory nature of the study argued against it, and, second, because the study was a census instead of a survey, the finite population correction (Schaeffer, Mendenhall and Ott, 1986) meant the standard errors were small enough to force rejection of all null hypotheses regardless of whether the observed differences were large enough to be of educational importance.

Final Methodological Note

Since the goals of the study evolved over time, we were concerned that our initial inclinations on how to proceed with the study might be less than optimal.

And so we agreed to reconsider our efforts at the project's end, that reconsideration being a search for ways in which we might have been more sensitive to the issues involved. We hoped that such an examination would be helpful to people reading the report of our study, and to anyone who might wish to replicate our study with a new population of teacher education programs.

Response Rates

All nineteen deans' offices returned completed questionnaires as did sixteen of nineteen elementary education departments. These response rates were sufficient to protect the study's validity.

The World of Teacher Education

Colleges of education at MHG schools varied in size from twenty-eight to 187 faculty with a median of eighty-nine (see table 13.2). Typically, 94 per cent of the professorate was white, a value describing well the faculties generally (the range was 82 per cent to 100 per cent white). Similarly, the faculties were predominantly male with percentages ranging from a low of 56 per cent to a high of 82 per cent with the typical (median) school being 66 per cent male, 34 per cent female. Faculties were commonly tenured: the low was 57 per cent and the high 97 per cent with the median faculty having a little over three-fourths of its members tenured.

These findings suggest tenured Anglo males would make up the largest single segment of the faculty, and this is indeed the case: the largest percentage was 70 per cent of the faculty at one school while the lowest observed value was 36 per cent. The typical value was 56 per cent.

The student body (table 13.2) was like the faculty in some ways (for example, predominantly Anglo) and unlike it in others (for example, predominantly female). For the sixteen schools reporting a racial breakdown for the student body, the percentage of Anglos ranged from a low of 78 per cent to a high of 97 per cent (two schools) with the median value being 94 per cent. The schools reported that the female percentage ranged from a low of 58 per cent to a high of 90 per cent with the middle 50 per cent of the schools reporting women comprising between 69 per cent and 81 per cent of the student population. Not surprisingly, Anglo females made up the largest single segment of the pre-service teacher population: The lowest percentage was 56 per cent with the median being 71 per cent and the high being 82 per cent.

These students were also most likely to come from middle class communities with relatively small percentages coming from lower middle class and upper middle class homes. They most often lived in suburban communities, small cities, or rural areas, and were less likely to come from urban areas.

In short, both the faculty and pre-service teachers were similar in two important ways — being middle class and white, though they differed markedly in a third — gender. Bonnie, in other words, is typical of education undergraduates at Midwest Holmes Group institutions.

Table 13.2   Characteristics of faculty and students in Teacher Education Programs

Attribute	Min	Q₁	Middle 50% Median	Q₃	Max	Notes
Faculty						
Faculty size	28	46	89	154	187	in persons
Student body	303	550	1200	1808	2129	in persons
Anglo faculty	82	91	94	95	100	in percentages
Male faculty	56	61	66	74	82	
Tenured faculty	57	64	76	85	97	
Tenured Anglo male	36	43	56	63	70	
Student body						
Anglo students	78	92	94	96	97	n = 16
Female students	58	75	78	81	90	
Anglo female	56	67	71	75	82	n = 16

Unless otherwise specified, N = 19.

Table 13.3   Characteristics of elementary education teacher preparation programs

Attribute	Min	Q₁	Middle 50% Median	Q₃	Max
Hours within COE	31	36	51	64	94
Hours outside COE	23	49	64	70	94

The Elementary Education Program

The course of study followed by students at the various MHG schools was also strikingly consistent in important ways (table 13.3). Eighty-eight per cent of the programs, for example, required an introduction to education, 94 per cent required a course in educational psychology, and all required methods courses and student teaching (as well as other field experiences). After converting quarter hours to semester hours, it was apparent that a minimum of thirty-one credits was required of students within the college of education while the maximum was ninety-four hours with the median being fifty-one. Similarly, the minimum out-of-college requirement was twenty-three credits and the maximum again ninety-four, and with the median being sixty-four hours.

Indeed, the most striking difference among programs concerned multicultural/ethnic studies courses. While only one school offered no such courses, only about half required courses in this area (56 per cent reported required courses within elementary education while 51 per cent reported these courses might also be available outside the department). Contreas (1987) speculates on reasons colleges of education do not universally offer multicultural education courses:

Teacher educators assume that teacher education students will pick up the necessary knowledge, skills, and attitudes that will help them teach classes of socioculturally diverse students without any direct instruction and planned experiences. Moreover, teacher educators assume that most schools will continue to be 'monocultural' and 'monosocial'; therefore, there is no obligation to commit time and resources to preparing teachers to teach children who are at risk of being miseducated or undereducated.

The error in this logic was spelled out by Larke, Wiseman and Bradley (1990) who describe the value of multicultural education in the classroom:

The more knowledgeable teachers are about the culture of their students and the more positive interactions between teachers and students of different racial/ethnic groups, the less threatened and acceptable teachers and students become of each others' cultural differences. (p. 72)

This implies a role for multicultural education in preparing students for diversity in the classroom. To be effective, though, multicultural education must be offered in conjunction with other instructional activities. Thus, it is important to look at student teaching and field experience in detail because the multicultural/ethnic studies theme can also appear there — student teaching and field experience are where pre-service teachers should have the opportunity to meet and work with the diversity of children they will teach when they graduate. The question, then, is 'What is the reality?'

More specifically, most schools (57 per cent) reported that pre-service teachers received student teaching and field experiences in communities which were 'varied' in terms of their social economic status (SES). Most often these communities were suburban or in small cities where students are primarily white, reflecting the pre-service teachers' backgrounds. However, almost two-thirds (64 per cent) reported sometimes sending student teachers to urban areas — an important activity because, for many students, these schools were different from those they experienced when they were children. Nevertheless, pre-service teachers were generally placed in educational environments reminiscent of their childhoods.

The racial/ethnic mix at the schools in which student teaching took place was either 'varied' (67 per cent) or exclusively Anglo; no college of education reported sending the majority of their student teachers or field experience students to exclusively black or Hispanic schools. In contrast to the racial/ethnic mix of the students at these schools, the cooperating teachers were Anglo about twice as often (69 per cent vs 31 per cent) as they were of varied racial and ethnic backgrounds, and even in the varied settings there was generally a predominance of Anglo teachers.

In short, it appears that the racial/ethnic backgrounds of pre-service teachers differ from those of the diverse school communities in which they will teach upon graduation. In other words, Bonnie is most likely to meet students like Kenneth and Anita only after her graduation.

Bonnie has, however, more in common with the teachers at those schools since they are like those with whom she student taught and those who taught her when she was in school.

Discussion

Implications of the Findings

We now consider the implications of the differences among children in the schools, pre-service teachers and teacher education faculty. First, the gender, racial/ethnic, and economic differences among these groups short-change the pre-service teachers. Pre-service teachers, coming from largely white, middle class backgrounds, appear in the teacher education programs where they realize limited broadening of their racial and ethnic experiences. As a result, those teacher education programs underscore for them the expectations for schools and the values they have previously learned: Bonnie sees, for example, that people who teach in the schools tend to be white, middle class and female while people who teach in teacher education programs tend to be white, middle class and male.

Further, the shortage of women among the teacher education program faculty means pre-service teachers' search for role models requires them to rely on recollections of teachers they have had in grade school and high school. These recollections, accurate or inaccurate, are based on their perspectives as children rather than their observations as young professionals learning to be teachers. In other words, Bonnie brings with her a memory of schools as being white, middle class and female, and her university field experience reinforces this picture.

The second implication concerns pre-service teachers' limited exposure to racial/ethnic and economic diversity, exposure generally unexpanded by either course work in multicultural education or field experiences and student teaching in schools serving diverse populations. The implication of this reduced exposure to diversity is the increased likelihood that pre-service teachers will have difficulty understanding and appreciating students whose cultural and SES backgrounds are different from their own. Stated simply, Bonnie may not have the personal and professional background to be an effective teacher for children like Kenneth and Anita.

When this mismatch of teacher preparation and the diversity of student backgrounds occurs — and when teachers are inadequately prepared to respond appropriately — what follows is frustration on the part of both teachers and students. Anita and Kenneth, for example, may come to feel schools are both inattentive to their needs and places where they are made to feel inadequate by persons who do not understand them.

The third implication involves the absence of minority role models for both pre-service teachers (discussed earlier) and children of color. This is serious as it gives non-white, non-middle class children a demeaning message: power in contemporary society rests with white, middle class people like their teachers and is generally unavailable to persons from their backgrounds. Among other things, this means Kenneth and Anita learn there is no place for them at school when their careers as students are over.

Recommendations Bearing on Minority Pre-service Teachers

These three implications can lead to a large number of recommendations including, but not limited to, the three described below. The most important point, though, does not lie with the recommendations, but rather with the commitment on the part of those implementing them to ensure an education that values diversity. In the absence of this commitment, recommendations lead to short-lived exercises in futility: they raise the expectation of change while underscoring the *status quo*.

Further, plans to change teacher education that do not address diversity are flawed. Diversity must be addressed by the courses of study offered, the attitudes and behaviors of white faculty members and students, and the content of the courses. Both the Holmes Group and other curriculum reformers need to encourage teacher education to examine their complete teacher preparation programs in light of diversity issues. Given this predisposition and the findings of this study, the Equity and Excellence Committee proposes the following recommendations. The recommendations address the three implications just described and center on two areas of concern: (i) the recruitment and retention of minority preservice teachers: and (ii) the better preparation of traditional preservice teachers — like Bonnie — to teach children of color — like Kenneth and Anita. Attention to these two areas should go a long way toward addressing two of the implications just cited; recruitment and retention of minorities in education addresses the role model and gender issues, and improvement of teacher education programs approaches major culture pre-service teachers' lack of experience with diverse populations. Though gender difference between pre-service teachers and teacher education faculty is a problem, its further consideration is beyond the scope of this discussion.

Recruitment

The Equity and Excellence Committee believes that efforts to recruit more minority teachers will produce teacher education programs more reflective of diversity in the American population. How can this be done? Haberman (1989), reviewing research on minority recruitment, identified a number of practices as particularly effective; start early, use peer contact, involve parents, use minority and mass media, access computer data bases for student records, provide generous financial assistance, offer experimental programs, provide academic and psychological support, discuss obstacles and how to cope with them, provide training in how to take tests, provide flexible scheduling, involve minority faculty in the process of admissions and recruitment, survey minority students, provide training on how to teach diverse populations, use enthusiastic mentors, and create consortia to reduce the cost of contacting students and developing materials (p. 771).

These methods address the recruitment of students into teacher education.

Haberman also has things to say about mounting the programs to do this recruitment. What are they? He suggests: provide a career ladder for members of minority groups who have college degrees and now serve as paraprofessionals in urban schools; use support from athletics as a model for supporting minorities in teacher education programs; form working partnerships with two year colleges; redefine the length and nature of the daily, monthly, and annual employment of teachers to more accurately reflect reality; and require university teacher education programs to do more minority recruitment.

Retention

Suggestions already exist concerning the ways in which minorities can be brought into teacher education programs. Once recruited, however, steps must be taken to increase their retention in these programs. The Equity and Excellence Committee agrees with Grant and Gillette (1987) who suggest that in order to address these issues in teacher education we must:

> Endorse loan forgiveness programs for minority students ... and assure that evaluation of professional competence minimizes the influence of handicapping conditions of poverty, race, ethnicity on entry into the profession. (p. 518)

These suggestions all bear on support — fiscal and otherwise. Unfortunately, support in this arena is often half-hearted. For example, the stated desire of former Secretary of Education Lauro Caravazos to decrease by half the difference in degree completion rates between minority and majority culture students (DeLoughry, 1990) is admirable, but since the Department of Education is still unwilling to provide supporting funds, his concerns lack commitment. Because concerns without commitment raise expectations without addressing issues, they aggravate the very problems they are designed to solve. Put another way, children of color need to know that in addition to being welcome, they are also accepted — as evidenced by the varieties of support they receive.

Recommendations Bearing on White Pre-service Teachers

The Committee's last recommendations address better preparation of white pre-service teachers to recognize and value diversity. To do this, teacher education programs must enrich and expand the curriculum designed to prepare those who will teach all children. Not only are experiences with diversity currently inadequate in number (as evidenced by this study's findings), but leading voices in multicultural education question their effectiveness in preparing teachers (Bennett, 1988; Grant and Koskela, 1986). Clearly, multicultural education should be more extensively and vigorously incorporated into teacher education programs. Specifically:

(i) Multicultural concerns must be a required, integral part of the total teacher education curriculum, and faculty members must demonstrate (for example, as part of NCATE reviews) they have considered multi-cultural issues in all their courses,

(ii) There must be required classes helping pre-service teachers better understand and appreciate diversity.

(iii) Field experiences and student teaching sites must provide the pre-service teacher with exposure to children from diverse populations.

These recommendations all bear on experiences which will both sensitize pre-service teachers to problems they can expect to encounter and provide them with the knowledge, skills, and attitudes they must have to meet the needs of children of color. If the campus locale does not offer educational experiences in diverse settings, then appropriate settings must be found.

(iv) Finally, state departments of education need to become involved. States need to make training in multicultural education and super-vised experiences with diverse populations requirements for teacher certification. This would result in immediate and broad changes in teacher educations curricula. The ultimate result, however, would be the presence in the classroom of teachers better trained to understand and appreciate diversity.

As We Watched, Our Research World Changed

Critically examining one's research is a necessary — if frustrating — activity. It is necessary as it allows us to know the research forest and the trees more intimately, and frustrating because, had we a better knowledge of the forest, we'd have paid more attention to some trees, less to others.

One aspect of our research forest was the fact that this project was a group activity. This is a critical factor because, in addition to addressing purely empirical issues, the group was also influenced by the perspectives and predispositions of each person contributing to the project. And to complicate things further, the group's composition changed from meeting to meeting. This research was the effort of an evolving group with the continuous addition of new views, new ideas, and new frustrations.

The original goal of our research was quite simple — to examine the equity makeup (demographics of faculty, students, nature of curriculum, etc.) of the nineteen Midwest Holmes Group (MHG) institutions. But we added a second goal early in our planning — to report back to the MHG an equity profile of member institutions. We did not consider at this time how the MHG would use this information, but once the data had been collected, analyzed, and inter-preted, we realized that the accomplishment of this goal still did not meet the committee's objectives. A third goal became more explicit — to effect changes in the MHG equity agenda and simultaneously to have a corresponding impact on the national Holmes agenda.

Much has happened since we began our study. The point of this discussion is to take a *post hoc* look at our efforts in terms of both equity issues in group research and the ways equity research can effect institutional agendas.

Our group, the Equity and Excellence (E&E) Committee, began by spending a lot of time reflecting on the nature of our task and discussing the equity shortcomings of both our respective institutions and the Holmes Group more generally. Our conversations were enjoyable (since we shared similar views) but, apart from carrying us through the orientation stage of task group development,[1] these conversations were not substantively useful; they didn't move us any closer to productivity. In retrospect, we see we should have (i) defined our task sooner; (ii) identified earlier the audience(s) we wanted to affect; and (iii) spelled out at an earlier date the information and activities we would need to provide to the larger group so that they could make informed equity decisions. However, presenting our study, its findings, and the recommendations growing from them required one last thing of the Committee; (iv) we needed to insist on being heard.

We were slow in acting on the first two items though we were much more responsive and responsible in accomplishing the latter two. We decided to use the research data we had collected as the basis for the information we'd provide to the larger group in addressing goal (iii), information they could use to make informed decisions in regards to equity issues. We presented and distributed our findings at a MHG conference and followed these activities by continually reminding the regional and national organizations of just how the findings should impact on their respective agendas.

After The Fact: Operational Insights

In retrospect, we see that a researcher's gender, race/ethnicity, and class (income level) will affect the direction, interpretation, and recommendations based on empirical inquiry. This is so because researchers bring who they are and the sum of their experiences to their activities. This does not necessarily imply a 'hidden agenda' (since 'hidden' suggests a purposeful deception) but rather — and perhaps more dangerous — the influence of an 'unrecognized agenda': more dangerous because there is the chance of an unidentified bias affecting the research. In group research, the possibility of this bias increases with the number of people involved. This may have been the case in our study. This situation was complicated by the fact that the working group changed as some members left and new ones were added. (Some MHG institutions rotated attendance at these meetings making the membership unpredictable.) Generally speaking, though, the group's largest faction was males of color followed by white females, women of color and white males, all of whom were interested in equity issues. Thus it is not surprising that the study's concerns were first with race/ethnicity, second with gender, and lastly with class. Looking back, this ranking reflects the professional interests and personal experiences of the E&E committee members. Indeed, our interests in race/ethnicity — professional and personal — were certainly related to the fact that most of the educational implications drawn from our study dealt with this specific area and why gender and class received less attention. Had the committee been made up of single mothers living in poverty the implications of the findings and the recommendations growing from them might have looked very different.

Conclusions

Critical examination of one's efforts is a necessary part of the research process. What made the review particularly interesting in this case was a search for ways the study could have been even more sensitive to multicultural and equity issues. Needless to say, sensitivity in this area was of paramount importance to the Equity and Excellence Committee. And, in spite of the fact that we brought to this study — collectively and individually — a great deal of research and related experience in this area, re-examination of our efforts revealed ways we could have made this study more equity/multiculturally sensitive.

What did we conclude from this review? We have two sets of findings, one describing the way the group functioned in addressing research goals, and the other dealing with the recommendations based on the outcomes of the research.

Group Coalition and Action

(i)   While members of the group established working relationships easily (i.e., the orientation stage of group development) we should have identified our tasks and started addressing them much earlier.

(ii) There should have been a greater effort to control the transitory nature of the group. Early on, we should have identified E&E members who anticipated a continuing relationship with the Committee. These people could then have assumed more responsibility for planning and carrying out the research.

(iii) We should have been more sensitive to the biases that each of the group members brought with them to this project.

(iv) As part of our planning we should have considered just how we would have liked those we chose to affect to use our findings.

(v)   We could have enhanced the effect of our study by sending copies of it to teacher education programs elsewhere with the intent of establishing a dialogue. (Do our findings describe you? What additions would you make to our recommendations?)

(vi) Lastly, other regional Equity and Excellence Committees should have been contacted for the purpose of establishing national dialogue.

Reconsidering the Research Recommendations

In retrospect, we should have been much more forceful in making our recommendations: They sounded more like suggestions than proposals for serious action. In order to affect the agendas of the Midwest Holmes Group and the National Holmes Group, we should have made specific recommendations directly to each group, recommendations going beyond those in the body of the paper:

(i)   More field experiences, including internships, should be established in diverse (race/ethnicity, gender, class) settings.

(ii)   More minority teachers (public schools and teacher education faculty) should be recruited into the Holmes Group.

(iii) The Holmes Group should promote the recruitment of membership from inner city schools.

(iv)   All Holmes Professional Development Schools should include teachers of color.

(v)   Professional Development Schools should be as demographically representative of society as possible.

Finally, those of us wishing to affect group and institutional equity/ multicultural agendas must remember our responsibility doesn't end with the completion of our research. Rather, the end is the beginning: we need to use our research experience to improve our next effort and to inform and reform our audience.

Note

1   This period of time is often used as a way of solidifying a group. Group process is important when considering group research although this chapter will not include this as part of the discussion. For an excellent coverage of small group process read Lacoursiere (1980).

References

BANDURA, A. and WALTERS, R.N. (1963) *Social Learning and Personality Development*, New York, Holt, Rinehart and Winston.

BENNETT, C.T. (with OKINAKA, A. and XIAO-YANG, W.) (1988) 'The effects of a multicultural education course on pre-service teacher's attitudes, knowledge and behavior', paper presented at the annual meeting of the American Educational Research Association, New Orleans.

CHILDREN'S DEFENSE FUND (1989) *A Vision for America's Future*, Washington DC, Children's Defense Fund, p. 40.

COMMISSION ON MINORITY PARTICIPATION IN EDUCATION AND AMERICAN LIFE (1988) *One Third of a Nation* Denver, CO, American Council on Education and Education Commission of the States.

CONTREAS, A.R. (1987) 'Multicultural attitudes and knowledge of education students at Indiana University', paper presented at the annual meeting of the American Educational Research Association, New Orleans.

DELOUGHRY, T.J. (1990) 'Secretary Cavazos offers colleges six objectives to improves student education in the 90s', *The Chronicle of Higher Education*, **36**, 20.

GRANT, C.A. (1990) 'Barriers and facilitators to equity in the Holmes group', *Theory Into Practice*, **29**, 1, pp. 50–3.

GRANT, C.A. and GILLETTE, M. (1987) 'The Holmes report and minorities in education', *Social Education*, **51**, pp. 517–25.

GRANT, C.A. and KOSKELA, R.A. (1986) 'Education that is multicultural and the relationship between pre-service campus learning and field experiences', *Journal of Educational Research*, **79**, 4, pp. 197–303.

GRANT, G.W. (1978) 'Values and diversity in education: A progress report', *Educational Leadership*, **35**, 6.

GRIFFITH, J.E., FRASE, M.J. and RALPH, J.H. (1989) 'American Education: the challenge of change. Washington DC', *Population Bulletin*, **44**, 4, p. 16.

GWALTNEY, C. (1990) 'Annual Almanac: Facts about higher education in the nation, the states, and DC', *The Chronicle of Higher Education*.

HABERMAN, M. (1989) 'More minority teachers', *Phi Delta Kappan*, **71**, 10, pp. 771–6.

HOLT, R. (1989) 'Who will teach the kids?', *NEA Journal*, **7**, 10, pp. 5–6.

HODGKINSON, H.L. (1985) *All One System: Demographics of Education — Kindergarten Through Graduate School*, Washington DC, Institute for Educational Statistics.

KNIKER, C.R. (1989) 'Preliminary results of a survey of Holmes and non-Holmes group teacher education programs', presented at a Midwest Holmes Group Meeting, Chicago.

LACOURSIERE, R.B. (1980) *The Life Cycle of Groups: Group Developmental Stage Theory*, New York, Human Science Press.

LARKE, P., WISEMAN, D. and BRADLEY, C. (1990) 'The minority mentorships program: Educating teachers for diverse classrooms', *Multicultural Teacher Education Research in the 1990s Conference Proceedings*, College Station, TX, pp. 70–80.

MONENI, J.A. (1985) *Demography of Racial and Ethnic Minorities in the United States: An Annotated Bibliography with a Review Essay*, Westport, CT, Greenwood Press.

NATIONAL CENTER FOR EDUCATIONAL STATISTICS (1987a) Washington DC, US Printing Office, p. 64 and p. 15.

NATIONAL CENTER FOR EDUCATIONAL STATISTICS (1987b) Washington DC, US Printing Office, p. 60.

NATIONAL COALITION OF ADVOCATES FOR STUDENTS (1985) *Barriers to Excellence: Our Children at Risk*, Boston, MA, National Coalition of Advocates for Students.

National Education Association (1987) *Status of the American Public School Teacher 1985–86*, Washington, DC, National Education Association.

RALPH, J. (1989) 'Improving education for the disadvantaged: Do we know whom to help?', *Phi Delta Kappan*, **70**, 54, pp. 395–401.

SCHAEFFER, R., MENDENHALL, W. and OTT, L. (1986) *Elementary Survey Sampling* (3rd edn) Boston, MA, Duxbury Press.

TASK FORCE ON TEACHING AS A PROFESSION (1986) *A Nation Prepared: Teachers for the 21st Century*, New York, Carnegie Forum on Education and the Economy, p. 79.

US BUREAU OF CENSUS (1989) *Money Income and Poverty Status in the United States*, Washington DC, 1988 Current Population Reports, Series p–60 (166) table 19.

Part 3

The Social Impacts of Multiculturalism in Education

Chapter 14

Schools and Opportunities for Multicultural Contact

Cora Bagley Marrett, Yuko Mizuno and Gena Collins

The Rise of Intergroup Relations as a Field of Study

The systematic study of racial and ethnic relationships began to take root in institutions of higher education within the United States during the 1930s. Although social scientists had paid attention before that time to groups defined as races and ethnic groups, the earlier emphases differed from what later would predominate. Scholars who founded programs in sociology during the late nineteenth and early twentieth century — figures such as William Grahan Sumner and Franklin Giddings — accepted the view from social Darwinism that biology favored some groups over others. W.I. Thomas attributed racial prejudice to an instinct of hate. He wrote in 1904: 'In the North ... there exists a sort of skin-prejudice — a horror of the external aspect of the negro — and many northerners report that they have a feeling against eating from a dish handled by a negro' (p. 610). Edward A. Ross, a central figure in the creation of sociological study at the University of Wisconsin, prepared a treatise in 1904 that ranked groups within American society. His ranking placed at the top those of Anglo-Saxon heritage, and particularly persons who had a Scotch-Irish ancestry.[1]

In the years that followed, analysts moved gradually but steadily towards a social rather than a biological outlook on race and ethnicity. That outlook had marked the writings of W.E.B. DuBois even while Sumner, Giddings and Ross focused on biology. But scholars at the University of Chicago, and not DuBois, generally are credited with redirecting the field. William I. Thomas, Robert Park, and Louis Wirth had access to the students and channels the University of Chicago could provide; DuBois struggled to conduct his research from predominantly black colleges, colleges whose resources compared most unfavorably with those available at Chicago.[2]

By the mid–1940s, a distinctive subarea had arisen within the broader field of race and ethnic relations. The field, intergroup relations, sought to do more than study contacts; it aimed to improve the connections that groups had with one another. The budding group of specialists contended that knowledge should be used to eliminate the tensions that built between groups, tensions that threatened the foundations of the society.

Students of intergroup relations began to look for general principles on which improvements might rest. Cornell University stood at the center of that search. By the 1950s Robin Williams and his associates at Cornell deemed the research to be extensive and solid enough to support a detailed description of the principles it yielded. They assembled these ideas into a manual 'for the many practitioners who are struggling every day to deal with intergroup relations in the communities where they are now working' (Dean and Rosen, 1955, p. xix). The principles in the manual revolved around an idea that remains current: interaction matters. It is this idea on which we center our discussion. We are concerned with the question of contact between groups, on the consequences that seemingly flow from such contact, and on the forces that promote or impede contact — especially contact within the school setting.

Intergroup Relations and Multicultural Education

The field of intergroup relations is relevant to the topic of multicultural education. We consider multicultural education to be an approach that emphasizes the multiple experiences and perspectives one finds in a heterogeneous society, such as the United States constitutes. As Sleeter and Grant (1988) have observed, multicultural education calls upon learners to respect difference; it does not advocate inequality.

Intergroup relations and multicultural education share a common concern with eliminating the misunderstandings and the inequalities that occur in societies where stratification prevails. Indeed, both approaches contend that the inequities — in wealth, status, and power — that characterize systems of social stratification result in no small way from the limited opportunities groups from the different strata have to learn about one another. Members of a group draw distinctions among themselves but see members of other groups as rather undifferentiated. Both multicultural education and the study of intergroup relations attempt to produce a better sense of the diversity that prevails in groups other than one's own. Even more importantly, they seek to promote appreciation for the differences extant in the total society.

From within the broader literature on intergroup relations, we highlight the research on interethnic contact. Consistent with the literature on multicultural education, the reviews on interethnic contact are concerned primarily with the groups we find on the margins or in the lower social and economic strata. Because the material on contact not only describes inequities but suggests a means for reducing them, it deserves the attention of those who wish to promote multicultural education.

After examining the thesis that interethnic contact improves understanding, we turn to forces that might limit such contact in American schools. Specifically, we contend that patterns of racial and ethnic segregation — among and within schools — reduce possibilities for intergroup contact. If contact serves as a route to intergroup understanding, then segregation constitutes a roadblock on that route.

The Drive Towards Multiculturalism

The systematic study of interethnic or intergroup contact predates that on multicultural education. The push for multicultural education accelerated in the late 1960s and 1970s, a period of intense activity among various ethnic groups in American society. Prior to that period, policies for education and other sectors emphasized assimilation.[3] Groups were to be incorporated into the prevailing way of life, a way grounded in the values and beliefs of Anglo-Saxon culture. By the middle of the 1970s, African-Americans, Puerto Ricans, Chicanos, and Native Americans had made manifest their opposition to assimilation.

The protests that these ethnic groups launched championed their own cultures and set in motion the drive towards multicultural education. That drive came to have two phases: one centered on cultural identity, the other on multiculturalism. In the first phase, groups turned inward, looking to their pasts and their values for those forces that made them distinctive. In the second, they worked to bring those distinctions to the consciousness of others. What underlay this second phase was the view that the advancement of minority groups and thus of the society as a whole depended on the extent to which knowledge about cultural differences and contributions spread widely.[4]

The Meaning of Culture and Ethnicity

Studies on race and ethnicity once routinely defined an ethnic group as a category of persons, united by distinctive patterns of family life, language, religion, or other customs. The definitions emphasized the traits of group members: their artifacts and arts, their rituals and routines.

But contemporary accounts emphasize just how fluid is ethnicity. They dismiss the notion that ethnicity is an ascribed attribute that is evident in the practices or traditions of a group. The definitions make identification with a heritage and not the products of that group the core of ethnicity. A definition of ethnic group which Edward Spicer developed with American Indians in mind serves to illustrate:

> By ethnic group is meant a number of people who share a particular Indian group name and other symbols of a common historical experience unique to those who use the group name. Such an identity unit often makes use of a common Indian language and customs or beliefs of Indian origin ... it may be that the language is replaced and only the historical experience, as symbolized, and the group name remain of the Indian heritage. (Spicer, 1982, p. 16)

The contemporary discussions describe ethnicity as 'socially constructed', meaning that people shape and reshape their cultures according to the conditions they experience. Italian immigrants to the United States did not at first label themselves as Italians. Instead, they adopted the appellations of their region or village: Sicilian, Catanian, Sardinian, for example. Ethnicity crystallizes under conditions that promote kinship and friendship networks. The development of ethnicity or a cultural identity requires frequent associations among those who see their origins as common.

The declining emphasis on the content of culture has its parallels in the analyses on race. In the late nineteenth and early twentieth centuries biologists and ethnologists measured and described the features of the peoples they encountered in their attempts to classify human beings. Osborne has written of these efforts:

> There was something of an aura of theological dogmatism hanging over these kinds of classifications, a dogmatism which perhaps has been perpetuated to some extent to the present in the way many people regard 'race' as not only somewhat rigid in nature but also somehow preordained to exist in a 'pure' or original state. Nothing could be farther from the facts. There has never been such a thing as a 'pure' race. Race formation and breakdown is a dynamic process, subject to constant change. (Osborne, 1964)

Since the early twentieth century, sociologists have striven to 'exorcise the biological ghost' from analyses on racial relations (Stone, 1986). In like fashion, these scholars have criticized those views that treat cultures as static and rigid.

The Quest for Cultural Identity

Banks has termed the developments of the late 1960s as 'ethnic revitalization movements'. Those ethnic groups that stood on the economic and political fringes of the society strove to develop a common identity and sense of community. They emphasized their distinctiveness and taught their children to celebrate and not denigrate it. They gathered together to remember the past and envision the future; they gathered to strengthen themselves, not necessarily to win the support of others. These concerns prompted the development of ethnic education: the interest in providing the members of a group with knowledge about their group.

The task of constructing culture and developing ethnic education proved challenging indeed, in part because an emphasis on cultural difference ran counter to the notion of citizenship in the United States. The anthropologist, Renato Rosaldo, has observed that in this nation 'cultural' means different, and to pursue a culture is thus to seek out difference. As a result, 'full citizenship and cultural visibility appear to be inversely related. When one increases, the other decreases. Full citizens lack culture, and those most culturally endowed lack full citizenship.' (Rosaldo, 1989, p. 198).

Despite the obstacles, programs to promote cultural pride proceeded apace. Parents, organizations, and other critics reviewed educational materials to determine their appropriateness to the task of ethnic education.

The Development of Multiethnic Education

All too often, traces of the old order remained. As a consequence, minority groups began to expand their ideas about culture and education. They demanded greater diversity in the standard curriculum. Multicultural education became the watchword: all people, not just those within given communities, would be prodded to learn about cultures other than those the Angles and Saxons had known.

The drive for multicultural education gained momentum in the 1970s. The attempt to redefine the canon, to enlarge the cultures of interest, took varied forms. It prompted publishers to revise their textbooks so that these sources would include a broader spectrum of groups and experiences. It stimulated school districts to establish curricula on the African, Hispanic, and Native American roots of American culture. Whatever the approach, the strategies all intended to bring the contributions and nature of non-Western societies to the attention of students from every background.

These reforms — of materials and curricula — were built on the notion that social conditions block the chance for different groups to get to know one another. Understanding, the usual goal of multicultural education, can take place through contact, but if contact is blocked understanding might be impeded.

Intergroup Contact and Interethnic Attitudes

The interest among researchers in intergroup contact traces to the 1940s, a period of intense interest in views about race. Essentially, the researchers of the period wanted to know the reasons for the racial tensions they saw. Their search led them to the study of *racial prejudice*, an ungrounded and unfavorable set of attitudes held toward a group that society defines as a race. Unfounded views, and particularly those of whites, appeared to undergird racial subordination and conflict.

Gunnar Myrdal helped advance the emphasis on prejudice in his monumental work on race relations in the United States: *An American Dilemma*. Myrdal undertook the study on 'the Negro problem' at the request of the Carnegie Corporation. Believing that an outsider could be more objective than a citizen of the United States, the Corporation called upon a Swede — Myrdal. Myrdal oversaw an army of survey researchers, experimentalists, archivists who compiled mountains of facts, figures and opinions. He mined these materials and his own observations to reach the conclusion that racial intolerance among whites thwarted the progress of blacks. He wrote:

> All our attempts to reach scientific explanations of why the Negroes are what they are and why they live as they do have regularly led to determinants on the white side of the race line. In the practical and political struggles of effecting changes, the views and attitudes of white Americans are likewise strategic. (Myrdal, 1964)

Analysts probed not just for the sources of racial intolerance but also its cure. Interracial contact increasingly seemed to be the antidote. Particularly in the 1950s, one study after another made the telling discovery that interaction across racial lines tended to increase racial tolerance.

That was the conclusion Deutsch and Collins (1956) reached after they studied black and white residents of two public housing projects. Tenants were assigned to apartments in two of the projects without regard to their race. For the other two, race had determined the assignment. Deutsch and Collins determined that the white residents of the integregated projects treated their black counterparts in a more neighborly fashion than did the whites in the segregated projects. Moreover, the residents of the integrated projects became more tolerant on racial issues than did the dwellers in the segregated setting. Finally, the total number of favorable changes was much greater within the integrated than within the segregated projects (*ibid.*, pp. 42–3).

Research with military personnel as subjects produced results consistent with those of Deutsch and Collins. (Stouffer, *et al.*, 1949; Mandelbaum, 1955). Military personnel who belonged to desegregated units expressed less racial prejudice than did members of segregated corps. The findings led to the 'contact hypothesis', the assertion that contact outside of one's usual sphere changes attitudes about that sphere.

Scholars offer at least three explanations for the effects of contact on reductions in prejudice. First, a change in attitude might represent a psychological defense. This line of reasoning follows from the theory of *cognitive dissonance*. Cognitive dissonance occurs when one's behavior or experience clashes with one's views — or cognitions. The individual in such a situation tries to bring behavior and attitude together, for presumably human beings want to avoid the misalignment of attitude and experience. Thus, the white soldier who thought the black soldier irresponsible or lazy could not sustain such a negative evaluation in a desegregated fighting force. To have maintained the prejudiced views would have been to call oneself into question. How could a responsible, energetic person dare to share living quarters with or depend on protection from someone inclined by nature to avoid responsibility and danger? The white soldier who confronted this dilemma could solve it psychologically: he could revise his opinions about blacks and thereby preserve his own ego.

The second explanation has roots in the theory of interpersonal attraction. According to the theory, people are attracted to those whose beliefs and values they share. Contact provides such persons with the opportunity to learn about others whom they resemble psychologically and ideologically. The information will eventually 'neutralize the negative relationship that formally existed ...' (Hewstone and Brown, 1986, p. 5).

Third, contact might have an educational benefit. If prejudice indicates unfounded notions, then interaction with others could provide more knowledge and show the errors of those notions. Possibly, contact works to reduce prejudice by enlarging the experience and knowledge of individuals.

Equal Status Contact

Gordon Allport, whose formulation of the hypothesis remains central, contended that attitudes changed most often when the actors were of equal status, shared common goals, and had support for their interaction from others. Allport made the point that would become pivotal: contact would not always reduce prejudice. Contact among people of similar status — educational or occupational status, for example — would have more positive effects on attitudes than would contact among people of disparate positions. Interaction between master and slave, employer and employee, officer and soldier could promote intolerance and resentment, for it presents in bold relief differences in rank and resources. The contact hypotheses found its reincarnation as the equal status contact hypothesis (Allport, 1954).

Equal Status Contact and Schools

The work on which we have focused thus far centers on settings other than schools. But research on schools lends support to the hypothesis as well. Hallinan and Williams discovered from their study of friendship patterns that students chose friends from among their peers whose classes and subjects matched their own. Concretely, friendships formed among students on the same academic track. The authors reasoned that the students on the same track had increased opportunities to interact with one another, and interaction made similarities in interest evident.

St John conducted a review of studies on contact and schools undertaken over a period of thirty-five years. She looked for the effects of racial desegregation on racial attitudes and found no consistent patterns. She cautioned readers against generalizing from the review, for the designs and procedures of the studies had varied substantially. In addition, few of the situations had in fact represented ideal settings for contact (St John, 1975).

Segregation: Barrier to Contact

When the Supreme Court declared the segregation of schools unconstitutional, it lent support indirectly to the Allport thesis that contact makes a difference. The Court concluded that segregation threatened to generate in African American children a feeling of inferiority that could 'affect their status in their hearts and minds in a way unlikely ever to be undone'. The principle of separate but unequal could not be upheld, the Court contended, for it blocked both the educational and psychological development of minority children.

In the years that followed the decision in *Brown v. Board of Education of Topeka*, the arguments for desegregation broadened. Advocates cited the advantages of desegregated education, not only for minority students but for those of majority group background as well. The chance for students from varying backgrounds to interact with one another seemed to be the path towards lessened racial tension and an open society.

If desegregation creates possibilities for interracial and interethnic contact, then the persistence of segregation deserves our attention. We review recent trends in segregation in public schools, using data from the Office for Civil Rights (OCR). The Office was organized to administer the programs for educational equality that the Civil Rights Act of 1964 created. To fulfil its responsibilities for that Act and for subsequent legislation in 1968 OCR began a regular survey of elementary and secondary schools. Although the survey has counted the number of students in special education and the number expelled or suspended, the information most widely used — and most reliable — is that on the

Table 14.1   School segregation, selected cities, 1980 and 1986

City	Black/Hispanic 1980	Black/White 1980	Black/White 1986	Black/White Change
Compton, CA	41.94	39.88	34.90	−4.98
Fresno, CA	45.75	50.63	48.00	−2.63
Los Angeles	71.28	68.52	69.80	1.28
Oakland	52.70	63.60	66.50	2.90
San Jose	39.87	38.21	23.40	−14.81
Denver	69.50	38.90	43.60	4.70
Corpus Christi	37.67	50.20	51.10	.90
Dallas	64.76	62.89	64.90	2.01
El Paso	55.81	39.13	39.40	.27
San Antonio	68.95	66.57	67.00	.43
New York City	46.59	71.19	73.30	2.11

The numbers indicate the index of dissimilarity, a measure of the fraction of students in a district who would have to change schools for the racial/ethnic composition in each school to match that of the district as a whole. The index can range between 0 and 100; the lower the index, the closer the distribution in schools conforms with the distribution for the district as a whole.

racial and ethnic makeup of school districts and the schools within them. This is the information we discuss.

Studies on the racial composition of schools and districts use the OCR data and similar information to arrive at two measures: an index of dissimilarity, and an index of exposure. The index of dissimilarity considers the proportion of students in the district that a category — blacks or Hispanics, for example — comprises, and then examines the degree to which the individual schools match the district proportion. Essentially, the figures show what proportion of students would have to be moved around in order for the distribution across the schools to fit that of the district as a whole. Scores for a district can range between 0 and 100; the lower the score, the closer the distribution across the schools approximates the distribution for the district as a whole. As we shall interpret them, the lower the score, the lower the level of segregation in the district.

The index of exposure considers the ratio of black or Hispanic students in a school to the total enrollment in that school. The index can range from zero to the percent that minority students represent in the district. Because the index of exposure is affected by the composition of a district and not by the level of segregation, we limit our discussion to the index of dissimilarity.[5]

Racial and Ethnic Segregation in Public Education

Racial and ethnic segregation prevails in the public schools systems of the United States. The large school systems of the nation contain significant fractions of African American and Hispanic students, but in one district after another these students are separated from one another and from white students. Table 14.1 reports the patterns for a selected set of schools systems. These are systems with large concentrations of Hispanic and African American students. If 100 represents complete segregation — individual schools contain only one ethnic group — what is noteworthy are the high indexes for all of the eleven districts. For the segregation of Hispanic from black students certain cities and their indexes stand out: Los Angeles (71), Denver (69), San Antonio (69), Dallas (65), El Paso (56), and Oakland (53).

Generally, those districts in which high levels of black and Hispanic segregation dominated tended as well to have relatively high levels of segregation of blacks from whites. Note the high black/white dissimilarity indexes for 1986 for Los Angeles (70), San Antonio (67), and Dallas (65). A few anomalies stand out. In Denver, the segregation of blacks from Hispanics exceeded that of blacks from whites; the same applies for El Paso. In New York, black/white segregation surpassed the segregation of blacks from Hispanics. It should be noted that for the systems in California and Texas, children of Mexican descent outnumber other Hispanics; for the New York population, Puerto Ricans are the largest Hispanic population.

Separation and Contact: The Forecast

The decision in the *Brown* case outlawed the legal segregation of students in public education. Racial and ethnic separation remain features of public schools systems, nonetheless, usually as the consequence of segregated housing patterns. With a few exceptions, there appears to be no noticeable trend towards greater racial and ethnic admixture within schools. The indexes for 1986 generally matched those of 1980. Moreover, when we compared the 1986 figures with those of 1976 we found remarkably little change.[6]

If interaction with people from other cultures cultivates an individual and deepens that person's judgments, then racial and ethnic isolation hampers learning. There is no guarantee that students who attend the same institution will come into contact with one another within that institution, an issue to which we turn shortly. But such attendance offers more of a potential for contact than does enrolment in different schools.

Course-Taking and Contact

The Supreme Court thought that integration would enhance the self-esteem of black students, for it would give lie to stereotypes about racial inferiority. The Court centered its discussion on the school, not on the distribution of students within it. The same facility can offer very different experiences for students, however. The desegregation of a facility does not require the desegregation of classrooms within it. Research on tracking and on course-taking reinforces this theme.

Enrollment in Mathematics

Commonly, school districts establish requirements that apply to all students. These include requirements about the numbers of credits to be earned for graduation. It is common, too, for districts to offer options to students. From

Table 14.2 Enrollment in advanced mathematics courses in proportion to representation in school population, by race/sex category and school

School	Black females	Black males	White females	White males
		Race/Sex Category		
1	23.0	69.2	135.6	190.0
2	95.6	38.7	118.5	112.3
3	30.0	10.0	109.4	152.5
4	155.0	106.4	51.5	78.7
5	75.1	61.3	127.7	123.4
6	114.4	68.5	112.6	107.4
7	81.9	65.7	117.7	94.9
8	60.6	79.3	120.0	173.8
9	91.9	72.8	115.5	115.5
10	48.3	24.2	127.1	112.9
11	90.0	86.5	146.8	92.6
12	32.9	20.6	136.4	139.1
13	51.3	25.2	87.8	148.8
14	126.1	75.4	83.0	116.8
15	74.3	117.9	63.3	191.7
16	40.0	10.0	199.6	176.1
17	28.8	22.4	118.9	133.3
18	53.3	35.4	178.2	250.0
19	114.9	69.1	64.8	194.3
20	159.2	52.3	71.7	115.0
Mean	77.3	55.3	114.0	140.9
Std. Dev.	37.9	30.0	35.5	42.2

Advanced courses are those for which students had to have had algebra I and one course beyond it. The table reports the proportion of all advanced enrollees that each race/sex category represented in comparison with its proportion in the school. The formula is as follows:

$$\frac{\text{proportion in advanced courses}}{\text{proportion in school}} \times 100$$

several indications, minority and majority students exercise these options differently.

Consider the evidence we have compiled on enrolment in elective mathematics courses among secondary school students. We surveyed the mathematics and science teachers in twenty secondary schools across the country and asked them to indicate (i) the courses they were teaching; (ii) the prerequisites for the courses; and (iii) the racial and gender make-up in each class and course. Although a few teachers reported on Hispanic and Native American students, black and white students dominated in the classes surveyed. Thus, the analysis centers on these two groups.

Black students were less likely than white students to be enrolled in advanced level courses. Advanced courses in mathematics were defined as those having algebra I and at least one other course as their prerequisite. We compared the distribution of students in the advanced courses with their distribution in the school (see table 14.2) and found a tendency for blacks to be underrepresented in the courses. The tendency was slightly more evident for black males than for black females; in five of the twenty schools black female representation

Table 14.3   Enrollment in the most selective courses as proportion of total mathematics enrollment, by race/sex category and school

School	Black females	Black males	White females	White males	Total	
		Race/Sex Category				
1	5.0	10.7	7.7	12.1	9.3	(171)[1]
2	16.1	15.0	18.0	14.3	16.0	(200)
3	7.9	4.5	19.0	24.2	19.3	(368)
4	16.2	10.5	19.2	37.8	17.4	(275)
5	14.8	15.5	36.2	39.4	27.4	(448)
6	3.6	2.8	2.3	10.8	5.0	(181)
7	11.2	11.9	6.3	7.3	7.6	(772)
8	3.7	5.6	6.4	12.9	6.6	(665)
9	10.0	10.6	22.0	24.4	17.6	(131)
10	10.5	7.4	19.7	23.2	19.3	(398)
11	8.7	12.8	13.9	17.1	12.4	(217)
12	8.5	5.7	21.2	20.0	17.9	(1048)
13	4.6	2.6	15.5	22.3	14.0	(485)
14	16.1	10.7	11.3	14.7	13.1	(464)
15	5.5	9.5	3.1	22.7	8.1	(308)
16	20.0	9.1	22.1	23.1	21.4	(173)
17	6.9	4.5	16.0	16.8	15.0	(748)
18	4.2	3.7	7.6	13.5	6.3	(271)
19	8.4	10.0	14.3	3.8	8.6	(151)
20	7.5	3.7	3.6	5.8	5.3	(543)
Mean	9.5	8.3	14.3*	18.3**	13.4	
Std. Dev.	4.7	3.9	8.2	9.1	6.0	

The most selective courses are those in which students had to have had algebra I and two courses beyond it. The calculations for each category are based on:

$$\frac{\text{number in the most selective courses}}{\text{number in all courses, algebra I and above}}$$

* Significantly different from black female mean at .01 level
** Significantly different from black female mean at .001 level

[1] Numbers in parentheses represent number of students on which the total is based.

surpassed what one might have expected; that was true of only two of the twenty in the case of black males.

The data discussed above refer to courses defined as advanced: those having algebra I and one other course as the requirements. We determined, too, the distribution of students, again by gender and race, in the 'most selective' courses. These are courses that required algebra I and two other courses beyond that level. We compared the distribution of students in these highly selective courses with their distribution in all other secondary mathematics courses. Black females were no more likely than black males to be enrolled in the selected courses; both were far less likely than white students of either gender to be in the highest level mathematics courses (see table 14.3).

Tables 14.2 and 14.3 describe the results for individual schools; table 14.4 aggregates the findings across the schools. That table summarizes the patterns in science course taking and reports the trends in two ways. First, it shows for each science area the per cent of the area that each race-gender group comprised.

Table 14.4   Enrollment in science by race and sex

Course	Black		White	
	Male	Female	Male	Female
General Science				
Per cent of course	33.5	34.5	18.1	13.9
Per cent of group	10.9	11.0	4.0	3.2
Physical Science				
Per cent of course	27.7	23.0	25.2	24.1
Per cent of group	24.0	20.2	15.2	15.6
Biology				
Per cent of course	21.4	21.1	28.6	28.9
Per cent of group	53.2	53.0	49.6	53.5
Earth Science				
Per cent of course	15.4	20.2	31.4	33.0
Per cent of group	2.9	3.9	4.1	4.7
Chemistry				
Per cent of course	10.2	12.8	39.4	37.4
Per cent of group	6.9	8.8	18.5	18.8
Physics				
Per cent of course	10.6	12.9	52.3	24.2
Per cent of group	2.5	3.1	8.5	4.2
TOTAL				
Per cent of students	21.0	20.7	30.1	28.2

Black males were 33.5 per cent of all students taking general science, for ex-ample. Second, it looks at each race-gender group and shows the distribution across the subject areas. Of all black males enrolled in science, 11 per cent were in general science and 7 per cent in chemistry.

Black students were overrepresented in general science courses. They com-prised about 21 per cent of the total sample but 34 per cent of the general science enrollees. They were underrepresented in chemistry. Whereas about 19 per cent of white males and females who were taking science were in a chemistry course, that was the case for only 7 per cent of the black students (see table 14.4). The segregated course taking patterns suggest that the classrooms of these schools offered students limited chances for them to interact as equals with persons unlike themselves.

Beyond Mathematics and Science

We have used our data to explore opportunities for contact in mathematics and science. The theme — segregation within schools blocks opportunities for con-tact — finds support in more than our data. Others have found few African American, Hispanic American, and Native American in advanced placement and honors courses in various subjects. There is, too, a higher concentration of these students than of white students in special education courses.

In summary, if multicultural education broadens understanding, and contact serves as a route towards that education, segregation among and within schools warrants attention. Assessing multicultural education demands the study of more than the kinds of images or curriculum presented to students.

Equal Status Contact Reconsidered

We have offered thus far an uncritical look at the contact hypothesis and support for it. In fact, we have proceeded as if contact enhances understanding, and that barriers to contact reduce the likelihood of that outcome. There are limits to this view, however, as several critics have pointed out. What bothers some observers is the inconsistency with which the sources treat the notion of equal status. In some instances, equal status means that the participants in the interaction share similar positions in the larger society. In other instances, the participants are equal if they interact as equals. If equal status contact requires that the participants are on the same level in the society at large, there is little hope that black and white students can interact as equals. The difference in resources suggests that students come to school with varied and unequal economic means. But if equal status means that, within a given situation one group does not outrank another, its realization is possible within the school. So long as some students participate in the more selective courses while others are concentrated in the general ones, ranking will typify the world of the school as well as that outside of it.

Finally, we have proceeded as if opportunities for contact result in actual contact. Several studies show the limits of that assumption. In one, a study of suburban neighborhoods, Hamilton and his associates (1984) discovered that white residents were more likely to know their white than their black neighbors. Opportunity cannot be expected to produce positive attitudes if that opportunity is not acted on. Nonetheless, it seems important for advocates of multicultural education to pay attention to opportunity. Actual contact seems more likely when the opportunity exists than when it is blocked.

Notes

1 For more information on Edward Alsworth Ross see Weinberg (1972).
2 See Matthews (1977) and Persons (1987). In 1908 a sociologist from the southern US published an article in the *American Journal of Sociology* on the inevitability of friction between blacks and whites. As John Stone has observed, only one respondent — DuBois — challenged the thesis of the article that racial antipathy undergirded race relations: 'All the other white sociologists writing in the journal continued to discuss these issues in terms of mental limitations of blacks and the "natural" repugnance felt between members of the white and "dark" races' (Stone, 1986, p. 25).
3 Not all sources emphasized assimilation, however, Francis Brown and Joseph Roucek (1937) edited one of the first textbooks on ethnicity. They expressed their commitment to cultural diversity: 'To overlook the contributions of [minority] groups of American life, both in its historical development and in the present, is to ignore the most obvious facts. Sympathetic understanding and candid appreciation must supplant the formerly much overemphasized idea of the "melting pot"' (p. v).

4 This overview draws heavily on the chronology Banks (1986) provides. For a more detailed chronology see Sleeter and Grant (1988).
5 For discussions on the index of dissimilarity see Taeuber and Taeuber (1965), Wilson, (1985) and Welch, Light, Dong and Ross (1987). Welch and his associates discuss the limits of the index of exposure.
6 The information for 1976 does not appear here. For the supporting information see Marrett and Collins (1990).

References

ALLPORT, G. (1954) *The Nature of Prejudice*, Cambridge/Reading, MA, Addison-Wesley.

BANKS, J. (1986) 'Multicultural education: Development, paradigms and goals' in BANKS, J. and LYNCH, J. (Eds) *Multicultural Education in Western Societies*, New York, Praeger.

BROWN, F. and ROUCEK, J. (Eds) (1937) *Our America: The History, Contributions, and Present Problems of Our Racial and National Minorities*, New York, Prentice-Hall.

DEAN, J.P. and ROSEN, A. (1955) *A Manual of Intergroup Relations*, Chicago, IL, University of Chicago Press.

DEUTSCH, M. and COLLINS, M. (1956) 'Interracial housing' in PETERSEN, W. (Ed.) *American Social Patterns*, Garden City, NY, Doubleday and Co.

HAMILTON, D.L.S., CARPENTER, S. and BISHOP, G.D. (1984) 'Desegregation of suburban neighborhoods' in MILLER, N. and BREWER, M.B. (Eds) *Groups in Contact: The Psychology of Desegregation*, New York, Academic Press.

HEWSTONE, M. and BROWN, R. (1986) 'Contact is not enough: An intergroup perspective on the "contract" hypothesis' in HEWSTONE, M. and BROWN, R. (Eds) *Conflict and Conflict in Intergroup Encounters*, New York, Basil Blackwell.

MANDELBAUM, D.G. (1952) *Soldier Groups and Negro Soldiers*, Berkeley, CA, University of California Press.

MARRETT, C.B. and COLLINS, G. (1990) 'Race and education policy', paper prepared for the Conference on Race and Mid-Sized Cities, University of Wisconsin-Madison.

MATTHEWS, F. (1977) *Quest for an American Sociology: Robert E Park and the Chicago School*, Montreal, McGill-Queen's University Press.

MYRDAL, G. (1964) *An American Dilemma* (rev edn), New York, McGraw Hill.

OSBORNE, R. (Ed.) (1964) *The Biological and Social Meaning of Race*, San Francisco, CA, WH Freeman and Company.

PERSONS, S. (1987) *Ethnic Studies at Chicago 1905–45*, Urbana, IL, University of Illinois Press.

ROSALDO, R. (1989) *Culture and Truth*. Boston, Beacon Press.

ROSS, E.A. (1904) 'The value rank of the American people', *Independent*, **57**, pp. 1061–4.

SLEETER, C. and GRANT, C.A. (1988) *Making Choice for Multicultural Education*, Columbus, Ohio, Merrill Publishing Co.

SPICER, E. (1982) *The American Indians*, Cambridge, MA, Harvard University Press.

ST JOHN, N. (1975) *School Desegregation Outcomes for Children*, New York, John Wiley and Sons.

STONE, J. (1986) *Racial Conflict in Contemporary Society*, Cambridge, MA, Harvard University Press.

STOUFFER, S.A., SUCHMAN, E.A., DE VINCEY, L.C. and WILLIAMS, R.N. (1949) *The American Soldier Vol I: Adjustment During Army Life*, Princeton, Princeton University Press.

TAEUBER, K. and TAEUBER, A. (1965) *Negroes in Cities*, Chicago, IL, Aldine.

THOMAS, W.I. (1904) 'The psychology of race prejudice', *American Journal of Sociology*, **9**, March.

WEINBERG, J. (1972) *Edward Alsworth Ross and the Sociology Progressivism*, Madison, WI, The State Historical Society.

WELCH, F., LIGHT, A., DONG, F. and ROSS, M. (1987) *New Evidence on School Desegregation*, Los Angeles, CA, Unicon Research Corporation.

WILSON, F. (1985) 'The impact of school desegregation on white public school enrollment 1968–76', *Sociology of Education*, **58**, pp. 137–53.

Chapter 15

Multicultural Education: Policies and Practices in Teacher Education

Donna M. Gollnick

In 1964 the Civil Rights Act passed by Congress declared that discrimination based on race, color, national origin, or sex was prohibited. As a result, schools across the nation were forced to desegregate. Within the following decade federal education legislation established race desegregation centers to help schools in this process and provided support for compensatory education for poor students. Congress soon extended its concern with civil rights in education to include students whose first language was not English with the passage of the Bilingual Education Act. Legislation to support sex equity in schools further extended the application of civil rights to another oppressed group. The Ethnic Heritage Act, passed in 1972, supported the development of curriculum materials on different ethnic groups. By the end of the seventies, separate desegregation centers had been established for race, sex, and language groups. However, by 1990 much of the federal support for the extension of civil rights in education had been eroded. Support for ethnic heritage studies was withdrawn in the early 1980s and legislation related to race, sex, and language equity has been revised so that it is no longer as proactive.

What has happened in schools to reflect the recognition of cultural pluralism and the provision of equality across cultural groups? Even prior to the Civil Rights Act, educational movements periodically promoted the rights of ethnic groups to maintain their own identities or developed programs to reduce prejudice and discrimination. In the 1920s some educators promoted intercultural education. The focus was on international education with roots in the pacifist movement. Others believed that intercultural education would help develop more tolerant and accepting attitudes toward recent immigrants. In 1933 the Service Bureau for Intercultural Education began to develop ethnic studies materials, conduct in-service programs for teachers, and offer school assemblies to raise the consciousness about ethnic group differences (Montalto, 1978). However, these efforts never reached national prominence and were usually abandoned by school districts after a few years.

Support for intercultural education did not completely disappear. By 1947 its advocates emphasized overcoming prejudice and discrimination against racial and ethnic groups. During this period, several national organizations supported intercultural and intergroup education (Cole and Cole, 1954). Especially active in convening investigative groups, preparing materials, and training educators were the American Council on Education (ACE), American Jewish Committee, the Anti-Defamation League, the National Conference of Christians and Jews, and the National Education Association. During the following decade, organizational support for intercultural education and intergroup relations again waned. Although some individual teachers and professors probably continued to incorporate these concepts into their own courses and programs, they were not institutionalized.

During the civil rights movements of the 1960s, African-Americans began to demand that courses and programs on their history be added to college and high school curricula. The effects of racism were clearly documented in the differences between whites and people of color in types of jobs, income, resources for education, dropout rates, scores on standardized tests, college attendance, professional credentials, and imprisonment rates. Ethnic studies courses and programs were established, although with reluctance in many cases. Schools again renewed their interest in intergroup relations, primarily to maintain control of volatile environments in which oppressed groups demanded changes.

By the mid-1970s women's studies programs also were being established. Participants in the ethnic and women's studies programs were primarily members of the groups being studied. Although advocates for ethnic studies also promoted the revision of the total curriculum to reflect accurately the multiethnic composition of society and the history and contributions of numerous ethnic groups, changes in curriculum and textbooks were slow. The impact on members of the dominant group was minimal at best.

By the mid-1970s multicultural education became the educational strategy for addressing cultural pluralism and equality in schools and classrooms. At first the focus of multicultural education was on ethnic groups. Advocates encouraged the study of the history of ethnic groups and their contributions to society. Cultural pluralism, rather than assimilation into the dominant culture, was to be the societal goal. The curriculum was to help students confront issues of racism, discrimination, and prejudice. During this period, many educators viewed multicultural education as synonymous with minority studies, especially of African-Americans, Native Americans, and Hispanics. However, its advocates also promoted the recognition and study of white ethnic groups and the importance of all students understanding their own ethnic roots.

As advocates became more aware of institutional discrimination against women, the poor, and the handicapped, the concept expanded to include those groups as well. Today multicultural education encourages the study of the ignored histories and contributions of oppressed groups. Textbooks and curricula are to be examined and revised to reflect the realities of our multicultural society. Racism, sexism, and discrimination against other groups in classrooms and society are to be confronted. Eliminating the differences in academic success between groups is a goal. Key to the implementation of multicultural education are the recognition and acceptance of the right of different cultural groups to exist and share equally in the differential rewards of our institutions.

Donna M. Gollnick

Preparing Educators to Deliver Education that is Multicultural

In the delivery of multicultural education educators must constantly monitor their own interactions with students and communities to overcome biases and low expectations. In working with students from culturally diverse groups, they need to use strategies to promote positive interactions of students. They must work with individuals, not groups or stereotypes (Good, 1987).

Educators must be able to recognize biases in textbooks and other instructional materials and use the opportunity to discuss those biases. They also must know how to use instructional materials and to develop strategies that will expose students to cultural groups other than their own.

The curriculum is an area in which most teachers have some control even when it is mandated by some higher authority. Gollnick and Chinn (1990) propose the following principles to guide educators in providing multicultural education:

1 'Multicultural education must help students increase their academic achievement levels in all areas, including basic skills, through the use of teaching approaches and materials that are sensitive and relevant to the students' sociocultural backgrounds and experiences' (Suzuki, 1980, p. 34).

2 Attention to *voice* must be a part of multicultural instruction. Voice refers to the dialogue between teachers and students that starts from the student's descriptions of their daily life experiences, not the experiences of the teacher nor those that are expected to fit into the dominant school culture (Shor and Freire, 1987).

3 Oral and non-verbal communication patterns between students and teachers must be analyzed to increase the involvement of students in the learning process.

4 The learning styles of students and teaching style of the teacher must be understood and used to develop effective instructional strategies.

5 Multicultural education must permeate the formal curriculum.

6 Multicultural education must impact the hidden curriculum at all levels, including the organizational structures of the classroom and school as well as the interactions of students and teachers.

7 Multicultural education must teach students to think critically by allowing them 'the freedom to ask questions and [helping them develop] the tools to reason, liberating [one's] mind from unthinking prejudice, and promoting an appreciation for pluralistic democracy' (Starr, 1989, p. 107).

8 Multicultural education requires an understanding of the lived cultures of families in the community. The effectiveness of educators can be greatly enhanced if they can learn to teach biculturally or multiculturally rather than stay encapsulated in their own cultural milieu.

9 Multicultural education must use the community as a resource.

To deliver multicultural education educators also need to monitor their evaluations of students to ensure that instruments and practice are not biased against students from oppressed groups. Tracking, or ability grouping, of students is another practice that requires monitoring to ensure instruction that is equitable across groups. A number of researchers (for example, Oakes, 1985; and Good, 1987) have found that the quality of instruction provided to high-ability versus low-ability groups differs significantly. The lack of stimulating activities and expectations for success in low-ability classes is a deplorable condition in most schools.

Educators learn to understand and deliver multicultural education through individual study, in-service education, and initial and continuing preparation programs in colleges and universities. However, this study is limited to an examination of policies that impact on higher education programs and the actual practices at that level.

If we expect educators to respond to the recommendations above, college and university faculty in professional education must be able to teach these skills to prospective teachers, administrators, and support personnel. They should require teacher candidates to show effective teaching of students who are culturally different from themselves. These programs should introduce professional educators to the philosophies and ideologies that undergird multicultural education, provide them a knowledge base, and allow them to develop necessary skills for providing multicultural education. In addition, faculty should model multicultural instruction in their own college classrooms. Finally, policies and practices in higher education, especially in the professional education unit, should reflect a commitment to multicultural education.

Paradigms for Examining Policies and Practices

Two paradigms are used in this chapter to examine systematically the major policies for multicultural education in preparation programs for professional educators and the implementation in higher education: Lynch's (1986) typology of policy options and Grant and Sleeter's (1989) approaches for multicultural teaching.

After studying cultural pluralism and multicultural policies in several nations, Lynch (1986) identified 'three major ideological orientations underlying current perceptions of cultural pluralism and the educational strategies for which they provide the theoretical moorings' (p. 7). These ideologies legitimize the national and state policies that have evolved. They are associated with (i) economic efficiency; (ii) democracy and equality of educational opportunity; and (iii) interdependence and partnership with an emphasis on negotiation and social discourse.

Lynch developed the following typology of policy options for responses to cultural pluralism from the three ideologies and their influence on values and philosophies, the structures of knowledge, human social structures, and social controls:

Ideologies

	Economic	Democratic	Interdependent
Values	elitist technocratic instrumental purposive-rational hierarchical production- oriented	egalitarian subjective sponsorship traditional individual-oriented	community dialectic intersubjective partnership emancipatory- oriented
Knowledge	dominant culture economic literacy traditional subjects compartmentalized unilingual	learner-centered multidisciplinary additive change mother-tongue 'false' demo- cratization	new paradigms interdisciplinary community- centered global bilingual human rights
Structures	economic solidarity social class stratification traditional roles given hierarchical	social cohesion systematic homogeneity equality traditional- evolutionary roles earned	cultural diversity organic equity evolutionary- revolutionary roles changed
Social Controls	economic exigency materialistic coercive administrative multinationalism	formal participatory individual/self control representative democracy national	community norms negotiatory decentralized social discourse international

(Lynch, 1986, p. 9)

The author argues that these relationships are neither static nor discrete. Further, the values of different ideologies could co-exist within the same society.

The Grant and Sleeter (1989) approaches to multicultural teaching provide another way of examining policies and practices that focuses more on the curriculum. They 'provide a framework for examining five different teaching approaches that address human diversity — race, ethnicity, gender, social class, and disability' (p. 7). The authors argue that all five approaches are important in multicultural instruction, but the ultimate goal should be the provision of education that is multicultural and reconstructionist. The approaches are summarized below:

1 'Teaching the exceptional and culturally different' addresses how to help students who do not succeed in the existing classroom or societal

mainstream ... [It] builds bridges between the capabilities of the student and the demands of the school and wider society, so that the student can learn to function successfully in these contexts.

2   'Human relations' is concerned with helping students to get along with one another better by appreciating each other and themselves. This approach concentrates on building positive feelings among people.

3   'Single-group studies' focus on groups that tend to be left out of the existing curricula. This approach teaches students about such groups as women, blacks, Asian-Americans, and the disabled.

4   'Multicultural education' combines much of the first three approaches. It suggests changes to most existing school practices for all students so that the school and classroom may become more concerned with human diversity, choice, and equal opportunity. It is hoped that such changes will bring about greater cultural pluralism and equal opportunity in society at large as today's students become tomorrow's citizens.

5   'Education that is multicultural and social reconstructionist' addresses social inequalities among groups in society at large as well as in students' own experiences. The primary goals of this approach are to prepare students to work actively in groups and individually, to deal constructively with social problems, and to take charge of their own futures. (p. 7)

These five approaches can be classified as goals under the ideologies identified by Lynch. The first two, teaching the exceptional and culturally different and human relations, are democratic goals based on egalitarian values and learner-centered knowledge. The human relations approach is usually designed to maintain social cohesion while allowing cultural groups to maintain their own unique identities within the society.

The focus on recognizing the differences between the school, which is based on the values of dominant society, and the culturally diverse students who attend schools is primarily the provision of equal educational opportunity. An expected outcome is that graduates of this system will be able to function effectively within the dominant society. Ideally this approach uses the cultural background of students to develop effective instructional strategies. Too often the strategy has been compensatory education in which extra resources are made available to schools to help overcome the educational deficiencies. Many compensatory programs support the economic ideology identified by Lynch. They are often remedial in nature and focus on individual responsibility expected in a meritocratic system.

The other three approaches to multicultural teaching fit more appropriately under the interdependent/partnership ideology. All three generally promote cultural diversity and equity. All should be emancipatory-oriented, community-centered, and interdisciplinary. All should be somewhat evolutionary; the focus on reconstructionism in the fifth approach is much more revolutionary. Support for global awareness, bilingualism, and human rights is central to the last two approaches.

One step toward multicultural teaching is the initial preparation of teachers and other school personnel. The remainder of this chapter will focus on policies and practices at the level. National policies supportive of multicultural education in higher education programs for the preparation of professional educators are examined in the next section. In addition, what selected institutions describe as multicultural education will be analyzed against the two paradigms described above.

National Policies: An Impetus for Change

At this time a number of federal policies support aspects of multicultural education for pre-college education. Although not as potent as in the 1960s and 1970s, educational legislation for desegregation, sex equity, bilingual education, and mainstreaming of exceptional students still exists. However, none of these provides a comprehensive policy requiring or supporting multicultural education in the schools at any level. The impact of the legislation on preparation programs for professional educators has been nil unless an institution voluntarily sought funds to develop special programs in one or more areas.

The preparation of professional school personnel is influenced primarily by the regulations of state education agencies and the policies of two national organizations: American Association of Colleges for Teacher Education (AACTE) and National Council for Accreditation of Teacher Education (NCATE). In all fifty states either the state education agency or an independent commission has responsibility for licensing teachers and other school personnel to work in the state. They also evaluate and approve the preparation programs in colleges and universities that prepare those educators. In many states both the licensure requirements, which are usually in the form of course content or competencies, and program approval standards include references to one or more aspects of multicultural education. Because the focus of this chapter is on national policies rather than state regulations and policies, these will not be analyzed here.

Many of the issues that should be addressed in multicultural education were first presented by AACTE in its 1968 publication of *Teachers for the Real World*. In the early 1970s the Association's Board established a Commission on Multicultural Education that continues to work as a task force today. In its 1972 statement, 'No One Model American', the Commission defined multicultural education as:

> Education which values cultural pluralism. Multicultural education rejects the view that schools should seek to melt away cultural differences or the view that schools should merely tolerate cultural pluralism. Instead, multicultural education affirms that schools should be oriented toward the cultural enrichment of all children and youth through programs rooted to the preservation and extension of cultural alternatives. Multicultural education recognizes cultural diversity as a fact of life in American society, and it affirms that this cultural diversity is a valuable resource that should be preserved and extended. It affirms that major education institutions should strive to preserve and enhance cultural pluralism.
>
> Multicultural education programs for teachers are more than special courses or special learning experiences grafted onto the standard

program. The commitment to cultural pluralism must permeate all areas of the educational experience provided for prospective teachers.

In the decade that followed, seven publications on multicultural teacher education were written and distributed to its nearly 800 institutional members. Numerous conferences on the topic were conducted with support from the federal government's Ethnic Heritage Act and the National Institute of Education. At the same time, AACTE received support from the federal government's Office of Special Education to assist institutions in incorporating knowledge and skills for mainstreaming exceptional students into their preparation programs. The emphasis in the past five years has been on tracking the number of minority students who enter teacher education and encouraging the development of strategies to attract more minority teachers into the profession. AACTE currently has six resolutions that provide support in the areas of human rights, educational equity, and multicultural and global education.

National Accreditation

The major impetus for the incorporation of multicultural education in teacher education has been the standards for national accreditation. In the mid-1970s AACTE's Commission decided that more than policy statements were needed to force institutions to address multicultural education in their preparation programs. With support from the National Institute of Education, the Commission appointed a Committee to make recommendations on how to impact the national standards of NCATE. As a result, NCATE added multicultural education to its standards in 1979. All institutions that seek national accreditation must provide evidence that multicultural education is an integral part of their programs.

In the United States accreditation is voluntary and non-governmental. Two types of accreditation for colleges and universities are recognized by the Council on Postsecondary Accreditation (COPA): institutional and specialized. The institutional accrediting agencies periodically review the total institution and its ability to maintain quality programs and services. Specialized accrediting agencies are responsible for periodically reviewing specific programs (for example, medicine, engineering, or architecture) or units (for example, School of Education or School of Library Science) within the institution.

NCATE is the only agency that has been recognized by both COPA and the US Department of Education to accredit professional education units that are responsible for preparing professional school personnel to work in pre-school through secondary settings. These units are responsible for the initial and continuing preparation of teachers, counselors, school psychologists, school librarians, principals, superintendents, etc. There are approximately 1200 colleges and universities that prepare teachers in the United States; 514 of these institutions are currently accredited by NCATE. The agency's standards and policies are determined by the twenty-six national education associations that are its constituent members.[1]

One of NCATE's responsibilities is the setting of standards against which professional education units are evaluated during an on-site review every five years. These reviews are conducted by selected members of the agency's Board of Examiners to determine whether NCATE's standards are met at the basic and/or advanced levels. The examiners' report and the institution's response are reviewed by NCATE to determine whether the professional education unit is accreditable.

Beginning in January 1979, colleges and universities applying for accreditation of their professional education programs by NCATE were required to show evidence of planning for multicultural education in their curricula. In 1981 these institutions were required to provide multicultural education. The major reference to multicultural education in those standards occurred in the section on curricula. Standard 2.1.1, subsumed under 'Design of curricula', was entitled 'Multicultural education'. The preamble provided the rationale for the standard, defined multicultural education, and indicated how multicultural education might be addressed in teacher education programs:

2.1.1 Multicultural education

Multicultural education is preparation for the social, political, and economic realities that individuals experience in culturally diverse and complex human encounters. These realities have both national and international dimensions. This preparation provides a process by which an individual develops competencies for perceiving, believing, evaluating, and behaving in differential cultural settings. Thus, multicultural education is viewed as an intervention and an on-going assessment process to help institutions and individuals become more responsive to the human condition, individual cultural integrity, and cultural pluralism in society.

Provision should be made for instruction in multicultural education in teacher education programs. Multicultural education should receive attention in courses, seminars, directed readings, laboratory and clinical experiences, practicum, and other types of field experiences.

Multicultural education could include but not be limited to experiences which: (i) promote analytical and evaluative abilities to confront issues such as participatory democracy, racism and sexism, and the parity of power; (ii) develop skills for values clarification, including the study of the manifest and latent transmission of values; (iii) examine the dynamics of diverse cultures and the implications for developing teaching strategies; and (iv) examine linguistic variations and diverse learning styles as a basis for the development of appropriate teaching strategies.

Standard: The institution provides for multicultural education in its teacher education curricula including both the general and professional studies components. (NCATE, 1982, p. 14)

In the revision of standards that occurred as a result of the overall redesign of NCATE in the mid-1980s, the number of standards was reduced from twenty-nine to eighteen. A separate standard on multicultural education was dropped. The concepts were integrated instead in four different standards and seven criteria for compliance.

In the standard on professional studies the following three criteria for compliance are examined to determine compliance with the standard:

(21) The professional studies component(s) for the preparation of teachers provides knowledge about and appropriate skills in learning theory, educational goals and objectives, **cultural influences on learning**, curriculum planning and design, instructional techniques, planning and management of instruction, design and use of evaluation and measurement methods, classroom and behavior management, **instructional strategies for exceptionalities**, classrooms and schools as social systems, school law, instructional technology, and collaborative and consultative skills. Courses and experiences ensure the development of classroom and time management, effective communication, **knowledge of different learning styles,** teaching strategies, and assessment techniques.

(22) The unit provides for study and experiences that help education students understand and apply appropriate strategies for individual learning needs, especially for culturally diverse and exceptional populations.

(23) The curriculum for professional studies component(s) incorporates multicultural and global perspectives. (NCATE, 1990, p. 48)

The standard on field-based and clinical experiences requires that 'education students participate in field-based and/or clinical experiences with culturally diverse and exceptional populations' (*ibid.*, p. 49).

Both the student and faculty standards require cultural diversity. The standard on student admission into professional education states that 'the unit's admission procedures encourage the recruitment of quality candidates and those quality candidates represent a culturally diverse population' (*ibid.*, p. 52). Criteria for compliance require that 'applicants from diverse economic, racial, and cultural backgrounds are recruited' (*ibid.*) and 'policies allow for alternatives to the established admission procedure to encourage the participation of individuals from under-represented groups and other students as determined by the unit' (*ibid.*, p. 53).

Finally, the standard on faculty qualifications and assignments requires that 'the unit ensures that faculty in professional education are qualified to perform their assignments and also reflect cultural diversity' (*ibid.*, p. 55). The criterion for compliance states that 'the composition of the faculty represents cultural diversity'.

To assist institutions in knowing what is expected as they respond to these standards, the terms *multicultural perspective* and *cultural diversity* have been defined in the glossary as follows:

A multicultural perspective is a recognition of (i) the social, political, and economic realities that individuals experience in culturally diverse and complex human encounters; and, (ii) the importance of culture,

227

race, sex and gender, ethnicity, religion, class, and exceptionalities in the education process.

Cultural diversity refers to the cultural backgrounds of all students and school personnel with particular emphasis on their ethnicity, race, religion, class, and sex.

Any institution seeking accreditation of its professional education unit (i.e., the administrative structure responsible for the preparation of educators like a School of Education) must provide evidence of complying with all components of the NCATE standards. There often are excuses for non-compliance: This community is not culturally diverse. We can't attract faculty of color to this area. Teacher candidates cannot have direct experiences with students who are culturally different from themselves because there are almost no students of color in schools in our geographic area. We have no faculty with background in multicultural education. The state prevents us from expanding our offerings in professional education.

However, NCATE's policies do not allow excuses for not adequately meeting its standards. Contextual factors that prevent a standard or component from being addressed cannot be taken into account in their application.

Professional and Learned Societies

The standards are not the only part of the accreditation process in which multicultural education components are expected. As part of the preconditions that must be met before a review team is sent to the campus, institutions must show evidence of responding to the curriculum guidelines for program areas that have been approved by NCATE. As of September 1989, guidelines had been approved for the following fifteen specialty areas:

- early childhood education (basic and advanced programs) by the National Association for the Education of Young Children (NAEYC);
- elementary education (basic programs) by a task force of NCATE's constituent members;
- English/language arts education (basic programs) by the National Council of Teachers of English (NCTE);
- educational communications and information technology (basic and advanced programs) by the Association for Educational Communication and Technology (AECT);
- health education (basic programs) by the American Association for Health Education of the American Alliance for Health, Physical Education, Recreation, and Dance (AAHPERD);
- mathematics education (basic programs) by the National Council of Teachers of Mathematics (NCTM);
- middle school education (basic programs) by the National Middle Schools Association (NMSA);
- physical education (basic and advanced programs) by the National Association for Sport and Physical Education of the American Alliance for Health, Physical Education, Recreation, and Dance (AAHPERD);

- reading education (advanced programs) by the International Reading Association (IRA);
- school library media specialist (initial preparation programs) by the American Association of School Librarians of the American Library Association (ALA);
- school psychology (advanced programs) by the National Association of School Psychologist (NASP);
- science education (basic programs) by the National Science Teachers Association (NSTA);
- social studies education (basic programs) by the National Council for Social Studies (NCSS);
- special education (basic and advanced programs) by the Council for Exceptional Children (CEC); and
- technology education (basic programs) by the International Technology Education Association.

The guidelines or objectives for thirteen of these program areas include some attention to aspects of multicultural education. The guidelines for middle school education and physical education programs do not include any references to multicultural education.

The specific elements expected by these organizations are different, in part, because of the nature of the subject matter. Some are very general and others very specific. Three of the thirteen require multicultural studies; three require that the programs have a multicultural and global perspective. One requires that candidates be prepared to work in a culturally diverse society; another that students be prepared to work with students from a range of socioeconomic and ethnic backgrounds. An understanding of students' learning styles is expected in two of the programs. Four expect that candidates be provided the opportunity to interact with students from diverse cultural and socioeconomic backgrounds as part of their preparation program. Five of the guidelines include references to exceptional learners; three refer to women or gender studies; two refer to linguistic differences.

Two require the study of cultures as it relates to their disciplines of social studies and mathematics. Cultural diversity and its implications for schooling is a requirement for early childhood and school psychology. Knowledge of the environment and culture is expected in health and technology. Technology education requires the study of the sociocultural impact of the field. The use of ethnographic research is recommended for reading education programs.

The guidelines for social studies, English/language arts, and elementary education have the most requirements for multicultural components in the program. The social studies guidelines require the study of non-Western history, cultures, multicultural aspects of social studies teaching, gender studies, multicultural and global perspectives, and strategies and materials appropriate for diverse cultural groups. They also require experiences with culturally diverse students. The English/language arts guidelines require the study of dialects, literature by female and minority authors, and strategies and materials appropriate for diverse cultural groups. They also expect that programs will help teacher candidates develop attitudes that acknowledge the worth of all learners diverse in cultures and abilities.

The elementary education guidelines include at least ten requirements for components of multicultural education. A program is expected to include the study and application of research findings about culturally and linguistically diverse populations and students with exceptionalities. Teacher candidates are expected to learn to select and use materials appropriate to cultural and linguistic backgrounds and the exceptionalities of students. They are to be provided experiences in identifying stereotypes in curriculum materials and adapting instruction appropriately. They are to learn to identify and develop appropriate responses to differences among language learners. The program is required to provide multicultural and global perspectives and opportunities for developing strategies for teaching about democratic institutions and processes within the context of a multicultural society. The program should include the study of cultural mathematical developments and applications and the styles and modes of visual and performing arts across cultures. Finally, candidates are required to have experiences with culturally diverse students and students with exceptionalities.

Although there is great variation in the expectations of these different organizations, there is clearly a recognition by thirteen of them that attention to multicultural issues and strategies is necessary. Because the accreditation process requires that these programs be compared to their national guidelines, faculty need to initiate discussions of how and where these multicultural components should be addressed. Still the critiques of programs by these national associations find many programs lacking in the implementation of these components.

Summary

Policies for the inclusion of multicultural education in programs for preparing professional educators are found in the standards for national accreditation and the guidelines of professional and learned societies. These are the only national policies to which colleges and universities may be held accountable, and then it is a voluntary process.

The NCATE standards appear to be based on Lynch's democratic and interdependent/partnership ideologies. They were developed as an outgrowth of the work of AACTE's Commission on Multicultural Education whose membership was, and continues to be, culturally diverse. The AACTE publications on multicultural education promote cultural pluralism within a democratic context in which social cohesion must also be maintained. Issues of equality are also important themes in these publications and current AACTE policies.

The NCATE requirement that professional education programs incorporate multicultural and global perspectives is supportive of the interdependent/partnership ideology in that it moves beyond the individual-oriented values that have been so prevalent in the past. It is a more evolutionary than traditional knowledge base. It suggests that educators should learn to think critically about the inequities that exist in society. A definite shortcoming of the standards in the lack of clarity about the meaning of multicultural and global perspectives and expected outcomes. The definition in the glossary is not very forthright in this regard.

The call for culturally diverse student bodies and faculty pushes institutions to face issues of past inequities in college attendance and granting of professional credentials. The NCATE requirements in these areas go beyond equal educational opportunity. The expectation is equality of results.

When classified within the five approaches to multicultural teaching identified by Grant and Sleeter, both the NCATE standards and national program guidelines fall short of their ideal, 'education that is multicultural and social reconstructionist'. The NCATE standards strongly support the multicultural education approach and encourage the development of strategies for effectively teaching culturally diverse and exceptional populations. The standards include no direct references to human relations or single-group studies although those could be included as part of the multicultural education approach.

The national program guidelines also appear to support primarily the multicultural education approach. Since multicultural education is not defined in any of the guidelines, it is not clear what groups or types of issues are to be covered under that rubric. NCATE's definitions of *cultural diversity* and *multicultural perspective* refer to cultural membership based on ethnicity, race, religion, class, gender, and exceptionality. Since some of the guidelines refer separately to exceptionalities and gender, the organizations' definitions of multicultural education may not be as comprehensive as NCATE's.

Neither the standards nor guidelines include any references to issues of inequities between cultural groups, discrimination, racism, sexism, prejudice, or other social conditions which affect schooling. Nor are there any recommendations that candidates become actively involved in changing these conditions in schools. Although multicultural education as described earlier in this chapter includes these topics, it is not clear that NCATE and the national organizations have the same expectation.

Practices in the Education of Educators

What actually occurs when institutions try to incorporate multicultural education in their programs for the preparation of educators? Just before the requirements for multicultural education in the NCATE standards became effective, the AACTE Commission on Multicultural Education collected data concerning the extent to which multicultural education was being addressed by teacher education institutions. This baseline data indicated the gap that existed between what institutions were doing and what the NCATE standards suggested they ought to be doing. The survey solicited information about the teacher education curricula, faculty, students, research and development, and management of multicultural/bilingual education programs. The instrument was returned by 440 of the 786 institutions surveyed, permitting the development of a descriptive profile of multicultural education in the responding institutions (Gollnick, 1979).

Provisions for multicultural and/or bilingual education were indicated by 81.2 per cent of the institutions. Most often these provisions were found as a component in foundations or methods courses. Less than 25 per cent had specific courses on these topics. Either a major or minor in multicultural education was offered in almost 10 per cent of the institutions while 16 per cent offered a bilingual education major. Although multicultural education was most often addressed as a component of established courses at the undergraduate level, 25 per cent of the institutions also offered courses at the graduate level.

Courses that included multicultural education were found in four general areas; (a) general studies, including anthropology, sociology, etc.; (b) international programs; (c) ethnic/cultural studies of US ethnic groups; and (d) general education courses. Over half of the responding institutions required at least one of these courses for completion of the education program (*ibid.*).

Now that NCATE has been requiring multicultural education for twelve years, what are institutions doing in this area? As of this writing, fifty-nine institutions had been reviewed under the standards that were adopted in 1987. Another forty-five institutions hosted on-site reviews in the fall of 1989, but final action on their accreditation had not yet occurred. To determine how institutions are now addressing multicultural education, the institutional reports of selected institutions were examined. The selected institutions represented small and large private and public institutions in both rural and urban areas. Secondly, the final action reports of the first fifty-nine institutions to seek accreditation under the current standards were reviewed to determine whether NCATE's board thought that multicultural education was being addressed adequately.

The Professional Studies Curriculum

In response to the professional studies standard, most units indicated that multicultural education is integrated throughout the curriculum and cited the unit's objectives, expected competencies, or mission statements as proof of their commitment to it. The following are examples of supporting statements:

- Beginning teachers will be prepared to honor the dignity and rights of every individual learner in agreement with the values of our democratic and pluralistic society.
- Beginning teachers are prepared to implement the concept of providing open and equal educational opportunity for all.
- The teacher organized instruction to take into account individual and cultural differences among learners by (a) organizing instruction to take into account differences among learners in their capabilities, (b) organizing instruction to take into account differences among learners in their learning styles and rates of learning, (c) organizing instruction to take into account cultural differences, and (d) structuring the classroom and assignments in order to provide opportunities which will reflect a multiethnic society and a varying family structure.
- Teacher candidates will learn to examine cultural biases, prejudices, and stereotypes arising from cultural differences.
- Teacher candidates will study students with varying learning styles, achievement levels, and special physical, emotional, and learning needs.
- Teacher candidates will interact with and observe students of varying cultural backgrounds.
- We are committed to the preparation of professionals for service in multicultural communities. We believe it is essential to the professions

for which we train and the communities they serve that representatives from diverse cultures be actively recruited so that models of excellence are available to all.

- The candidate will learn to appreciate differences and/or conflicting values of racial, ethnic, and cultural groups and be able to apply this appreciation in the direct practice of school counseling with children and their families and, when consulting with other personnel employed in educational settings.

Sometimes specific courses are required for specific programs. Course titles include the following: 'Instructional practices and Native Americans', 'Racism and discrimination', 'The at-risk child in the school environment', 'Socialization and education in multicultural societies', 'International and multicultural education', and 'Multicultural education'. It is usually asserted that multicultural content, including that on exceptionalities, is integrated across the professional education curriculum. In one case the syllabuses were actually reviewed by the unit to ensure that appropriate multicultural content is included in each course.

There is great variation in what is included as a multicultural perspective. One institution reported that teacher candidates learn to analyze their own prejudices and make plans to reduce them. At another institution, nonsexist education and communication and learning styles are addressed. Social class, race, school achievement, compensatory education, multicultural education, and bilingual education are included in another program that also addresses the effect of ethnocentricity on curriculum and how to analyze and critique texts for biases.

Only one of the institutions indicated that it has programs in multicultural education, bilingual education, and English as a second language. This institution also co-sponsors an annual multicultural education institute with local school districts.

Attention to global perspectives is limited. Again it is asserted that these are integrated throughout the curriculum, but few examples are provided. One institution does require its teacher candidates to complete an anthropology course, 'People and cultures of the world'. In other cases, similar courses are electives. Several institutions encourage cross-cultural experiences during a winter term or through student teaching abroad opportunities, but they are not required experiences.

Opportunities to participate in field-based and/or clinical experiences with culturally diverse and exceptional populations remain limited. In the urban area candidates are almost always able to take advantage of culturally diverse settings. Outside of urban areas, institutions blame the low proportion of minorities in their service area for the lack of opportunities. Several of these institutions do offer student teaching experiences on Indian reservations or in the southwest. However, few students seem to take advantage of those opportunities.

In a few cases rural institutions have taken some affirmative steps to assist candidates in this area. These vary from case studies and simulations to field trips to at least one field experience in a culturally diverse setting with 30 per cent or more minority population to six weeks of required field experiences in an urban school district.

Donna M. Gollnick

Cultural Diversity in Preparation Programs

Although the incorporation of multicultural education into the curriculum and field experiences is still inadequate, institutions are having even greater problems at ensuring cultural diversity in their student bodies and faculties. Recruiting efforts at most institutions are the responsibility of an Office of Admissions or Graduate School. The professional education unit's recruitment activities appear to focus on freshmen and sophomores who have already been admitted to the college or university.

The nature of recruitment activities varies greatly. The most frequently used strategy is to send recruiters to high schools with large minority populations. These high schools may not be located in the region served by the institution, but usually include those in urban areas in the state or surrounding states. Participation in college/career fairs in urban areas is another strategy. Community college recruitment is being developed as a resource for minority recruitment by some institutions.

Only a few institutions indicate that a recruiting plan to increase the number of minority students has actually been developed. In two of the first fifty-nine institutions reviewed, these plans are institutional and include goals for increasing minority representation annually for the next five years. Two professional education units are developing their own minority recruitment plans as a result of the NCATE self-study. Task forces in two other units have been established by the dean to develop more effective recruitment strategies (Gollnick, 1989).

Affirmative recruitment for advanced programs is sometimes an extension of activities for basic programs, but overall efforts appear to be very sparse. Only three of the thirty-six institutions with advanced programs even describe separate recruiting efforts.

Accreditation Findings

In its review of the first fifty-nine institutions seeking accreditation under the current NCATE standards, NCATE found only eight (13.6 per cent) of the institutions in full compliance with multicultural education requirements. The other fifty-one institutions were cited with one or more weaknesses in this area. The following chart summarizes the number of institutions that did not adequately address the multicultural components of standards:

Standard		Standard not met	Weakness only	Combined per cent of total
I.E	Professional Studies	5	21	44.1
II.A	Clinical and Field-Based Experiences	2	17	32.2
III.A	Student Admission	8	24	54.2
IV.A	Faculty Qualifications and Assignments	10	24	57.6

An institution must now indicate annually what progress it is making in overcoming each weakness identified by NCATE. At the time of the next on-site review, the Board of Examiners team will focus on what the institution has done to remove all standards initially identified as not met and weaknesses. Thus, the responses to these concerns become very important in the continuing accreditation of an institution.

What are the Board's findings regarding multicultural education? In the professional studies curriculum the Board cited the following concerns:

- There is a lack of emphasis on studies or experiences related to culturally diverse or exceptional populations; multicultural experiences are limited. (14 citations)
- The curriculum lacks adequate content and experiences in global and/or multicultural perspectives. (13 citations)
- Preparation to work with exceptional students receives little attention. (2 citations)
- Clinical experiences do not adequately help candidates understand and apply appropriate strategies for culturally diverse and exceptional populations. (2 citations)
- Cultural sensitivity receives little attention. (1 citation)
- Candidates demonstrate little evidence of recognizing differences within culturally diverse populations. (1 citation)
- Little, if any, evidence exists that candidates receive and understand appropriate strategies for individualized learning needs, especially for culturally diverse and exceptional populations. (1 citation)
- Courses with strong multicultural components are electives. (1 citation)

The Board found in fourteen cases that field experiences with culturally diverse students are limited. At seven institutions field experiences with exceptional students are not provided. Three institutions were cited for not having a defined plan to ensure experience with either culturally diverse or exceptional students.

Although many institutions have acceptable recruitment plans to attract a culturally diverse student body, the plan is not changing the student body composition. Seventeen institutions were cited for not successfully recruiting applicants from diverse economic, racial, and cultural backgrounds. Another twelve institutions do not provide incentives nor develop affirmative procedures to attract members of underrepresented groups. Other concerns are that there are no provisions for alternative policies to increase the number of candidates from underrepresented groups (four citations) and there are no incentives for retaining minorities in the programs (two citations).

The problem with the standard on faculty qualifications and assignments is that nearly 60 per cent of the institutions reviewed simply do not have culturally diverse faculties. In one case, there is not even a systematic plan for attracting minority faculty.

Donna M. Gollnick

Summary

The 1978 survey of how multicultural education was being incorporated in teacher education programs found more happening than NCATE is finding in its on-site reviews. In 1978 over 80 per cent of the institutions said that they had provisions for multicultural education. In recent reviews by NCATE only 56 per cent were found to address adequately cultural diversity and/or exceptionalities in the professional education curriculum.

In 1978 over 75 per cent of the institutions reported that teacher candidates did their student teaching in schools with culturally diverse students. NCATE is finding that only 68 per cent even provide adequate field experiences with culturally diverse and exceptional students. Perhaps the first fifty-nine institutions reviewed by NCATE are not a representative sample. Perhaps the 1978 survey was returned primarily by the institutions that were indeed incorporating multicultural concepts throughout their curriculum. Watching future NCATE findings should help determine whether institutions are committed to the serious task of multiculturalizing their curriculum.

The objectives, competencies, and mission statements of most institutions suggest that they are building their multicultural emphasis in support of Lynch's democratic ideology. They recognize the multiethnic and pluralistic nature of society and call for the provision of equal educational opportunity.

Although most institutions included references to multicultural education in the unit's objectives or mission statement, NCATE evaluators were often unable to detect where these were implemented in the curriculum. In the institutional reports reviewed the content of multicultural education usually was not systematically delineated by the institutions. When it was described, the content varied by institution. In some cases the focus was on cultural biases, prejudices, and stereotypes. Knowledge about learning styles was sometimes included. Study of racial, ethnic, and cultural groups was required at some institutions. The primary focus of most programs was on developing strategies for teaching culturally diverse and exceptional students.

Thus, professional education programs focus primarily on preparing educators to teach the exceptional and culturally different — the first approach in the Grant and Sleeter typology. The emphasis in some programs is on the development of the second approach — human relations. A comprehensive approach to multicultural education was reflected in few of the institutional reports. The professional education programs that promote critical and reflective thinking could become multicultural if the concepts of cultural pluralism and equality undergird the program. At this time it is not clear that these concepts are central to the development of the professional education component.

Over half of the institutions reviewed by NCATE under the current standards do not have culturally diverse student bodies or faculties. Overall minority recruitment efforts at many of these institutions, especially the small ones, are just beginning. The professional education unit, for the most part, leaves recruitment to other institutional offices and participates only informally. The lack of recruitment for advanced programs is appalling. Since the professoriate of the future will be drawn from today's graduate students, that population must become more culturally diverse. The recruitment of a culturally diverse student body and faculty is an area that continues to be inadequately addressed by institutions seeking national accreditation.

Conclusion

Why is it that after twelve years of requiring multicultural education, institutions still have not taken seriously its incorporation into its programs and practices? Multicultural education has developed from a democratic ideology and should be evolving toward Lynch's interdependent/partnership ideology. However, colleges and universities are traditional institutions designed to help maintain the status quo. In general they promote the meritocratic system that evolves from an economic ideology; equality and cultural diversity are not central to their missions.

As a part of the larger system, professional education units respond in a similar fashion; the changes implemented may reflect democratic and interdependent ideologies. Even though the national accrediting agency, NCATE, has required that multicultural education be incorporated into the professional education program for the past twelve years, nearly half of the institutions have not responded. Responses are similar: Our candidates will not teach in culturally diverse or minority schools. Those issues are taught in the sociology and anthropology courses for general education. I don't have time to add another topic to my course. The faculty has academic freedom; we can't ask them to teach this stuff unless they want to. How can the faculty learn about multicultural education on top of everything else we ask them to do? We hired someone to take care of that.

Many faculty and administrators have not accepted the underlying ideology and assumptions for multicultural education. They are not convinced of its contribution to the major goals of schools, or they are afraid that it actually might change the traditional goals of schooling.

To make a difference in the professional studies curriculum, faculty need to determine how to deliver multicultural education across required courses. The literature suggests that at a minimum, candidates should learn about culture, ethnicity, cultural pluralism, educational approaches, language differences, power relationships between dominant and oppressed groups, social class, equality, discrimination, racism, sexism, classism, cross cultural interactions, values, gender differences, religious differences, dialectal differences, and bilingualism. Strategies for delivering multicultural education should be included in foundations, psychology and methodology courses as well as the general education requirements. The actual application of these strategies in the classroom should be practiced and evaluated in field experiences and student teaching. Candidates should be provided the opportunity to discuss the philosophical, historical, and sociological underpinnings of multicultural education as well as the development of skills that are important in its delivery. Courses also should foster critical thinking skills as candidates explore multicultural issues.

In addition, universities must begin to attract more students of color into doctoral programs. The future professoriate will be drawn from these students and it should be representative of the culturally diverse groups in society. At the time that greater diversity is being demanded by accrediting agencies, the pool is dwindling. Incentives to encourage a more culturally diverse student body at all levels must be sought. Financial commitments to recruitment and the provision of scholarships and graduate assistantships must be made. A commitment to multicultural education requires strategies to ensure a culturally diverse teaching force at all levels. Serious efforts have hardly begun.

Both qualitative and quantitative research could help in reaching the goals of multicultural education. In the past there has been valuable research that has recorded the existence of race, sex, and class biases in textbooks, curricula, and teacher expectancies. We have discovered the cultural biases in testing and state policies that have contributed to the reduction of teachers of color in the nation's schools. We now must focus on the action that is needed in schools and colleges and universities to overcome the results of institutional discrimination against groups of people.

Schools, colleges, and departments of education should join urban school districts as partners in the challenge of providing quality education for urban youth. Researchers should explore educational and community strategies for making a difference in the neglected schools of our urban, suburban, and rural areas. Research is needed on how to prepare whites, who make up over 90 per cent of the teacher candidates in colleges and universities, to work effectively in communities that are culturally different than their own. Can we teach candidates to recognize and overcome their own biases? We need to develop and test the use of simulations that will help prepare candidates to work in culturally diverse settings. These and many other issues must be explored.

The agenda is demanding and challenging, but can we afford to neglect it any longer?

Note

1   The following organizations are constituent members of NCATE: American Alliance for Health, Physical Education, Recreation, and Dance; American Association of Colleges for Teacher Education; American Association of School Administrators; American Federation of Teachers; American Library Association; Association for Childhood Education International; Association for Educational Communications and Technology; Association for Supervision and Curriculum Development; Association of School Business Officials International; Association of Teacher Educators; Council for Exceptional Children; Council of Chief State School Officers; Council of Learned Societies in Education; International Reading Association; International Society for Technology in Education; International Technology Education Association; National Association for the Education of Young Children; National Association of Elementary School Principals; National Association of School Psychologists; National Education Association; National Council for the Social Studies; National Council of Teachers of English; National Council of Teachers of Mathematics; National Middle Schools Association; National School Boards Association; National Science Teachers Association.

References

AACTE (1990) *AACTE Directory*, Washington DC, American Association of Colleges for Teacher Education.

COLE, S.G. and COLE, M.W. (1954) *Minorities and the American Promise: The Conflict of Principle and Practice*, New York, Harper.

GOLLNICK, D.M. (1979) 'Comparative study of multicultural teacher education in teacher corps and other institutions', unpublished manuscript Washington DC, American Association of Colleges for Teacher Education.

GOLLNICK, D.M. (1989) 'An assessment of national policies and practices aimed at the recruitment and admission of minority teachers in teacher education', paper presented for the symposium, Teacher Education in a Multiethnic Society: Developing an Agenda for Research and Practice at the annual meeting of the American Educational Research Association, San Francisco, March.

GOLLNICK, D.M. and CHINN, P.C. (1990) *Multicultural Education in a Pluralistic Society*, Columbus, OH, Merrill.

GOOD, T.L. (1987) 'Teacher expectations', in BERLINER, D.C. and ROSENSHINE, B.V. (Eds) *Talk to Teachers*, New York, Random House.

GRANT, C.A. and SLEETER, C.E. (1989) *Turning on Learning: Plans for Race, Class, Gender, and Disability*, Columbus, OH, Merrill.

LYNCH, J. (1986) *Multicultural Education: Principles and Practice*, London, Routledge and Kegan Paul.

MONTALTO, N.V. (1978) 'The forgotten dream: A history of the intercultural education movement, 1924–1941', *Dissertation Abstracts International, 39AA, 1061*, University Microfilms No. 78-113436.

NCATE (1982) *NCATE Standards for the Accreditation of Teacher Education*, Washington DC, National Council for Accreditation of Teacher Education.

NCATE (1990) *NCATE Standards, Procedures, and Policies for the Accreditation of Professional Education Units*, Washington DC, National Council for Accreditation of Teacher Education.

OAKES, J. (1985) *Keeping Track: How Schools Structure Inequality*, New Haven, CT, Yale University Press.

SHOR, I. and FREIRE, P. (1987) *A Pedagogy for Liberation: Dialogues on Transforming Education*, South Hadley, MA, Bergin and Garvey.

STARR, J. (1989) 'The great textbook war', in HOLTZ, H., MARCUS, I., DOUGHERTY, J., MICHAELS, J., PEDUZZI, R. (Eds) *Education and the American Dream: Conservatives, Liberals and Radicals Debate the Future of Education*, Granby, MA, Bergin and Garvey, pp. 96–113.

SUZUKI, B.H. (1980) 'An Asian-American perspective on multicultural education: Implications for practice and policy', paper presented at the Second Annual Conference of the National Association for Asian and Pacific American Education, Washington DC, April.

Chapter 16

Policy Analysis of State Multicultural Education Programs

Robert Crumpton

You can only write so many national reports and pass so many acts by the legislature. Eventually you have to go back and ask what is happening in individual schools. (Ernest Boyer, President of the Carnegie Foundation for the Advancement of Teaching)

Introduction

Policy analysis is a research area that seeks to address the kinds of concerns expressed by Boyer (1987). Concerned with 'the nature, causes, and effects of alternative public policies, policy analysis aims to empower educators to more effective collective actions to solve or reduce significant policy problems' (Nagel, 1980, p. 391). Toward this end, policy analysis places special emphasis on 'the use of reason and evidence to choose the best policy among a number of alternatives with explicit recognition of the realities involved in implementing policies' (MacRae and Wilde, 1979, p. 3).

The purpose of this chapter is to discuss problems and issues related to characteristics of policy analysis and its impact on theory and practice in the educational policy-making process and multicultural education. The discussion is organized around the following questions: (i) What is policy analysis?; (ii) What are the characteristics of policy analysis?; (iii) What is the nature of state policy studies in multicultural education?; (iv) What should be the future direction of state policy studies in multicultural education?

Since the early 1960s, educators have increasingly employed policy analysis as a key measure to improving government policies and programs and to solving, or at least reducing social problems (Boyer, 1987; Coleman, 1984). Because the schools generally have been viewed as one of the United States' primary means of solving social problems, policy analysis has been heavily applied in the public education arena. Since the early 1980s, there have been a number of major education studies which have employed policy analytic techniques; for example, *A Nation At Risk: The Imperative for Education Reform, A Report of the National Commission on Excellence in Education* (1983); *Educating Americans for the 21st Century: A Report to the American People and the National*

Science Board (1983); *A Nation Prepared: Teachers for the 21st Century* (1986); and *Tomorrow's Teachers: a Report of the Holmes Group* (1986). However, the results of the application of policy analysis to educational issues have been as Boyd (1978) warned us, something less than an unqualified success. Rather than clearing away confusion and ambiguity, policy studies often have added new layers of perplexity to an already murky scene (Cohen and Garet, 1975), and rather than providing data to depoliticize the sensitive and sometime explosive issues of education, policy studies sometimes have heightened political tensions and even created new political issues (Warwick and Pettigrew, 1983). For example, examination of the report, *One Third of a Nation* clearly indicates that the American Council on Education and the Commission of the States in 1983 intended to challenge the status quo of educational leaders regarding full equality of education for all American citizens. The Commission argued that acceptance of the following challenges would be a positive step toward putting America back on the track to full equality of opportunity for all its citizens.

1 We challenge America's institutions of higher learning to renew and strengthen their efforts to increase minority recruitment, retention, and graduation.
2 We challenge national leaders to identify and implement policies to stimulate economic growth and restore national solvency.
3 We challenge the nation's elected officials to lead efforts to assure minority advancement.
4 We challenge private and voluntary organizations to initiate new and expand existing programs designed to increase minority participation and achievement.
5 We challenge each major sector of our society to contribute to a new vision of affirmative action around which a broad national consensus can be found.
6 We challenge minority public officials, institutions, and voluntary organizations to expand their leadership roles.
7 We challenge education leaders to improve coordination and cooperation among all levels and systems.

Policy analysis has also produced powerful and undeniable benefits for the matching of additional educational policy and the management of educational groups. Many decisons are now made with greater information. For example, since the enactment of Mississippi's Education Reform Act in 1982, that desegregated the public schools and established the development of more stringent standards for both school accreditation and teacher certification, virtually every state in the United states has substantially increased funding for education and, at the same time, enacted new policies, programs and regulations to raise performance standards for students, teachers and schools (Cohen, 1987).

There often is a richness and variety of purposes and approaches involved in policy studies. Therefore, it is not surprising that sometimes there is ambiguity about what constitutes policy analysis. Most policy studies examine new programs. It is usually the program where new money is being invested that raises the immediate questions about viability and continuation. Today most comprehensive federal and state policy studies are in response to a request-for-proposal by a government funded agency or a heavily funded private foundation such as the Carnegie or Ford Foundation.

During the past ten years, state policy has had a particularly dominant effect on educational issues, especially in the area of school reform. State education reform initiatives in the early part of the 1980s focused on raising performance standards and providing the resources to achieve higher levels of performance. Albeit, there was very little attention in these reform efforts toward policy that would seriously deal with multicultural education. However in November 1987, Thomas Sobol, the Commissioner of Education of the State of New York, convened a Task Force on Minorities: Equity and Excellence. One of the Task Force's major tasks was to review the State Education Department's curriculum and instruction materials to see if they adequately reflect the pluralistic nature of our society, and to identify areas where changes and additions may be needed. The Task Force report entitled *A Curriculum of Inclusion*, was submitted to the Commissioner and the Board in July 1989. The report raised a number of useful questions about how effectively the Regents' long-standing policies to increase students' understanding of cultural diversity were being implemented. Accordingly, the Task Force studied the matter extensively: drawing on its own considerable experience gained from implementing past policy statements, reviewing the literature, consulting nationally known experts, and examining other states' and localities' implementation of curricula reflecting cultural diversity. The Report reviewed the curriculum materials published by the New York State Department of Education and made nine recommendations for reform, ranging from a revision of many curricular materials to the revision of teacher education and school administrator programs. The nine recommendations which follow are comprehensive and reflect the nature of the questions raised by the Task force.

1 We recommend that the Commissioner of Education give continuing vitality to the initiative for multicultural education by creating the position of Special Assistant to the Commissioner for Cultural Equity. This should be a staff position reporting directly to the Commissioner.

2 We recommend that the Commissioner direct appropriate staff to undertake without delay the revision of all curricula and curricular materials so as to ensure that they are compatible with the goals of equity and excellence for all cultures within our society.

3 We recommend that all groups involved in the development, dissemination and evaluation of curricular materials reflect in their own composition the multicultural diversity found in New York State Schools.

4 We recommend that the State Education Department staff be led to a better understanding that adequate presentation of multicultural diversity within curricular materials requires that the history, achievements, aspirations and concerns of people of all cultures be equitably and accurately infused into and made an integral part of all curricula.

5 We recommend that the State Education Department begin intensive discussions with textbook publishers to encourage them to publish texts that are multicultural in substance.

6 We recommend that the Regents mandate new conditions of teacher

and school administrator certification in the State of New York, to include appropriate education and competence in multicultural education.

7　We recommend that the State Education Department find ways to encourage school districts to provide immediate, effective opportunities for current staff members to gain competence in multicultural education.

8　We recommend that the State Education Department work with all school districts and colleges and universities to develop and implement effective recruitment programs to increase the number of cultures represented in their faculties and staffs.

9　We recommend that the Commissioner of Education give this curriculum report the greatest possible attention and widest possible circulation to key individuals in the State of New York.

Indeed, the recommendations of the Task Force might be useful to any state or local education agency considering revising their curriculum to more accurately reflect the cultural diversity of our society.

While it is important for educators to elevate school achievement of students from all backgrounds, states must develop policies which help students and staff gain an understanding and appreciation of the cultural diversity of the United States as well as the historical and contemporary contributions to society by women, men, and handicapped persons. There is a growing recognition that accomplishing these goals will require changes in our education systems which are as profound and radical as those occurring in the broader society. This viewpoint is consistent with the recommendations by the National Council on Science and Technology Education reported in the *Science for all Americans* report in 1989. In that Report, the Council argued that schools need to pay more attention to the education of minority students, especially in the science and technology area. The report further argued that: (i) curricula must be changed to eliminate rigid subject matter, to pay more attention to the connections among science, mathematics, and technology; and to present the scientific endeavor as a social enterprise; (ii) the effective teaching of science, mathematics, and technology must be based on learning principles that derive from systematic research; (iii) educational reform must be comprehensive, focusing on the learning needs of all children, covering all grades and subjects, and dealing with all components and aspects of the educational system; and (iv) reform must be collaborative. Additionally, the report pointed out the need to involve administrators, university faculty members, and community, business, labor, and political leaders as well as teachers, parents, and students themselves in the curriculum development process. Although this report can be applauded for the attention it focused on the education of minority students, like many other reports, it failed to address teaching and learning from a multicultural perspective (see, for example, Grant and Sleeter, 1985). Grant and Sleeter (1985) reviewed nine major reports on school reform, including: The College Board, *Academic Preparation for College*; National Science Board Commission on Precollege Education in Mathematics, Science, and Technology, *Educating Americans for the 21st Century*; and National Commission on Excellence in Education, *A Nation at Risk*. They concluded that these reports did not stress multicultural education issues, nor did they pave the way for such issues to be addressed. They further argued that as these reports stand, they were inadequate at best and in some cases seriously flawed as blueprints for school reform.

Characteristics of Policy Analysis

Policy analysis assesses the extent to which goals are realized and looks at factors associated with success or unsuccessful outcomes. By objective and systematic methods, policy analysis examines the effects of policies and programs on their targets (for example, individuals, groups, institutions, communities) in relationship to the goals to be achieved.

Nagel (1980, p. 391) points out that policy analysis is concerned with the nature, causes, and effects of alternative public policies, with special emphasis on 'the use of reason and evidence to choose the best policy among a number of alternatives'. As this definition suggests, policy analysis involves a methodology emphasizing evaluation, a systematic comparison of alternative policies, and assessing the costs trade-offs involved in making informed decisions.

White (1983) similarly suggests that policy analysis may be viewed as a rational means of problem-solving or of providing data for informed decision-making. He describes the subtle functions of policy analysis as follows:

> Policy analysis is a complex social process of creating and applying knowledge to public policy. Few policy choices are final, unambiguous, or fully articulated: and few policies are independent, self-contained, unquestioned, or consensually understood. Policy analysis, as a result, is turbulent and open-ended rather than neat and easy. Decisive studies are very much the exception rather than the rule. Problems throw at analysts more variables for consideration and interest for accommodation than single studies can encompass. The task of policy analysis is to produce that decisive recommendation, but, instead, to contribute toward consensual understanding of actualities, possibilities, and desirabilities. Properly understood, policy analysis does produce new patterns of social interaction. Equally important, policy analysis produces new 'psychosocial' forms, new collective understandings relevant to the specific functions of government. (p. 11)

Peterson (1983), however, argues that 'policy studies typically do not address the most difficult conceptual and political issues'. Instead, they reassert what is well known, make exaggerated claims on flimsy evidence, pontificate on matters about which there could scarcely be disagreement, and make recommendations that either cost too much, cannot be implemented, or are too general to have any meaning (p. 3).

In his review of the educational policy analysis studies, Mitchell (1984) observed that there is little agreement on the methods or goals of educational policy research, and few 'classic' or exemplary studies for defining the area's thrust or overall theoretical perspective. Nevertheless, policy analysis is a rational enterprise that takes place in a political context. Political considerations intrude in three major ways, and the policy analyst who fails to recognize these considerations is in for a series of shocks and frustrations. First, the policies and programs with which policy analyses are aimed are creatures of political decisions. They were proposed, defined, debated, enacted, and funded through some form of a political process; and in implementation they remain subject to pressures, both supportive and hostile, which arise out of politics. Second, because policy analysis is undertaken in order to provide direction for the decision-making, the analysis is placed in the political arena, where evaluative evidence of program outcomes compete with other political factors. Third, and perhaps least recognized, policy analysis itself takes a political stance. It makes implicit political statements about such issues as the problematic nature of some programs and the unassailableness of others, the legitimacy of program goals, the legitimacy of program strategies, the utility of strategies of incremental reform, and even the appropriate role of the policy analyst. Only when the analyst has insight into the interests and motivations of the actors in the system, understands the role he/she is consciously or inadvertently playing, realizes the obstacles and opportunities that impinge upon the analysis, and the limitations and possibilities for putting the results of the analysis to work, can the analyst be as creative and strategically useful as he or she should be.

What is the Nature of State Policy Studies in Multicultural Education?

A review of policy analysis records in the Eric System by this author revealed that only fifty-one records used the term multicultural; and thirty-nine of these records specifically used the term multicultural education. However, on reading the abstracts of these thirty-nine records, it was found that only three of these specifically dealt with state-level multicultural education policy studies. Mitchell (1985), using a questionnaire, surveyed forty-eight of the fifty states, regarding the existence of a state-level program; a responsible person; multicultural certification requirements; and screening of textbooks and curricula for racism or sexism. Two important findings of the Mitchell (1985) survey were that: Educators didn't understand that racism takes many forms; and that the subtle forms of racism are denied. It was also found that multicultural education is inadequately funded. Freedman (1983) solicited information from twenty-two states and territories which showed that: (i) America's secondary schools offer relatively little that theoreticians would consider to be true multicultural education; and (ii) state departments of education exercise little inluence in that area. Most existing multicultural education attempts to redress racial injustices and prejudice. The American Association of Colleges for Teacher Education (1978), through two questionnaires, elicited information on state provisions and policies related to multicultural education and on multicultural activities in state departments of education. Among the findings were that thirty-four states address multicultural education through legislation, regulation, guidelines, or policies. Most states indicated that activities related to multicultural education are undertaken by units that are usually federally supported in the State Education Agency, such as those responsible for equal education opportunity, teacher certification and education, and bilingual education. It was also found that the approach to multicultural education taken by state departments of education often excludes people who are not members of specific categories of eligibility while the state provisions focus on teaching about cultural diversity to all students.

In summary, the three policy analysis records found in the Eric System contained information on state regulations and policies related to multicultural education and a bibliography of multicultural education resources from state departments of education. Although, no empirical studies were found, these reports might be helpful to educators in determining what policy analysis materials are available in the area of multicultural education. Clearly, there is a paucity of research in this area. In short, the major education policy studies reviewed for this study were not complete in their analysis, giving multicultural education issues inadequate or no attention at all. This was the case with the major national studies as well as with the state policy studies. Gollnick *et al.* (1976) and Mitchell (1984) studies are notable exceptions, they present a comprehensive picture of the vastness of the problem. Both studies, although completed eight years apart from one another, concluded that there are very few policy studies in the area of multicultural education; and a limited amount of money to support multicultural education initiatives.

Four year later, Mitchell (1988) conducted a follow-up study and revealed that twenty-seven states had initiated a multicultural education program, as compared with twenty-six states which responded affirmatively four years earlier. Twenty-eight states reported that they had a person responsible for multicultural education. This number did not change from the earlier study. Twenty states presented multicultural certification requirements, compared to just nine in the 1984 study. Twenty-five states now require textbook screening for racist/sexist content compared to thirty-one in the earlier study. Finally, twenty-one states now have specific laws or policies pertaining to multicultural education.

The 'open-ended' responses on the questionnaire were the following: (i) the most commonly-mentioned multicultural education topics were ESL, bilingual education, ethnic studies, race awareness, and multicultural education, respectively; (ii) the biggest problem in multicultural education was that educators didn't understand that racism takes many forms and that many of the subtle forms of racism are denied. The second largest concern was inadequate funding. The national budget line-item for multicultural education increased from $44,171,812 in 1984 to $87,707,751 in 1988. A large percentage of these funds were designed for certain programs which seemed to only address a limited area of multicultural education. For example, New Jersey reported $30 million for expenditures on bilingual/ESL programs, and Texas spent $35,715,302 for LEP (limited English proficiency) student services. The third was a preoccupation with 'basic skills'. These three studies (Gollnick *et al.*, 1976; Mitchell, 1984; Mitchell, 1988) show major deficits in the multicultural education knowledge base; for example:

1 The number of multicultural education studies is infinitesimally small.
2 No standard textbook definition (or agreement) of multicultural education exists.
3 There are few empirical research studies on multicultural education.

What Should be the Future Direction of Policy Studies in Multicultural Education?

In order to address the critical issues concerning the dearth of policy studies in multicultural education identified by Gollnick *et al.* (1976) and Mitchell (1988), state departments of education will need to assume larger responsibilities for setting educational goals and defining outcome standards; stimulating local inventiveness; and establishing assessment and evaluation systems linked specifically to multicultural education goals.

Currently, a majority of the country's state departments of education have formal multicultural education programs (Mitchell, 1988). However, few states have established specific long-range multicultural education goals. If state departments of education are to develop policies to elevate school achievement and help students and staff gain an understanding and appreciation for cultural diversity, they will have to institute long-range planning in the area of multicultural education. It is especially important that these plans reflect the cultural diversity of the United States, the historical and contemporary contributions of women, men, and disabled persons in our society.

State departments of education will need to develop policies that stimulate local creativity and inventiveness. The development and implementation of effective multicultural education programs will require new school structures that allow more instructional arrangements, collegial interaction among students, teachers and parents, and teacher involvement in curriculum development. How schools could be restructured to best meet the objectives of multicultural education are not yet well defined or developed. New multicultural education concepts must, therefore, come through carefully supported local efforts, from which new ideas can emerge, and be empirically tested against, the realities of schools and classrooms. In conclusion, the results of the studies by Gollnick *et al.* (1976), Mitchell (1988), and this author indicate that state departments of education should give the highest priority to providing leadership in at least the following five areas to establish a significant multicultural education research base.

1 Articulating a vision of multicultural education. That is, there should be greater efforts to define and identify some standard tenets of multicultural education.
2 Encouraging local experimentation with different approaches to multicultural education. State departments of education should encourage local school districts and other education agencies to pilot different approaches to multicultural education to determine its effectiveness in increasing school achievement.
3 Providing an ongoing implementation support and teachnical assistance as well as financial assistance to schools and districts trying new approaches to multicultural education. State departments of education should increase their own level of expertise so that they can more effectively provide technical assistance to schools and local districts trying out new approaches to multicultural education.

4   Researching and disseminating results of effective multicultural education programs to other schools and districts. State departments of education should join in collaborative efforts with colleges and universities designing relevant policy studies and teacher education programs.

5   Providing an appropriate set of sanctions and incentives attached to accountability mechanisms so that together they can stimulate increased participation in the development of effective multicultural education programs. This also calls for increased collaboration between colleges, universities, and state departments of education, especially in the area of licensing.

Of course, these five areas do not exhaust the critical policy issues regarding multicultural education that need to be addressed. Indeed, the suggestions herein are presented as a beginning approach to three major deficits in the area of multicultural education: (i) knowledge base, that is, too few policy studies in multicultural education; (ii) the lack of a standard definition for multicultural education; and (iii) too few empirical research studies in multicultural education. Indeed, much remains to be learned about the most effective methods of teaching a multicultural education curriculum. Research efforts should be increasingly oriented in this direction. Additionally, state and federal support should be provided to evaluate experimental programs designed to incorporate multicultural approaches into the school curriculum.

References

AMERICAN ASSOCIATION FOR THE ADVANCEMENT OF SCIENCE (1989) *Science for all Americans, A Project 2061 Report of Literacy Goals in Science, Mathematics and Technology*, Washington DC, AAAS.

AMERICAN ASSOCIATION OF COLLEGES FOR TEACHER EDUCATION (1978) *State Legislation, Provisions and Practices Related to Multicultural Education*, Washington DC.

BOYD, W.L. (1978) 'The study of educational policy and politic: Much ado about nothing?', *Teachers College Record*, **80**, 2, pp. 249–71.

BOYER, E.L. (1987) 'A Blueprint for Action II', paper presented at the National Conference on Educating Black Children, sponsored by the Washington Urban League, Washington DC.

CARNEGIE FORUM ON EDUCATION AND THE ECONOMY (1986) *A Nation Prepared: Teachers for the 21st Century*, New York, Carnegie Forum.

COHEN, M. (1987) *Restructuring the Education System: Agenda for the '90s*, Washington DC, National Governors Association.

COHEN, D.K. and GARET, M.S. (1975) 'Reforming educational policy with applied social science research', *Harvard Educational Review*, **45**, 1, pp. 17–43.

COLEMAN, J.S. (1984) 'How might policy research in education be better carried out?', *Improving Education: Perspectives on Educational Research*, Pittsburgh, National Academy of Education, University of Pittsburgh.

FREEDMAN, P.I. (1983) 'A national sample of multiethnic/multicultural education in secondary schools', *Contemporary Education*, **54**, 2, pp. 130–3.

GOLLNICK, D.M., KLASSEN, F.H. and YFF, J. (1976) *Multicultural Education and Ethnic Studies in the United States*, Washington DC, American Association of Colleges for Teacher Education.

GRANT, C.A. and SLEETER, C.E. (1985) 'Equality, equity, and excellence: A critique' in

ALTBACH, P.G., Kelly, G.P. and WEIS, L. *Excellence in Education: Perspectives in Policy and Practice*, Buffalo, NY, Prometheus Books.

HODGKINSON, H.L. (1985) *All One System*, Washington DC, Institute for Educational Leadership, Inc.

HOLMES GROUP (1986) *Tomorrow's Teachers: A Report of the Holmes Group*, East Lansing, MI, Holmes Group, Inc.

MACRAE, D. JR. and WILDE, J.A. (1979) *Policy Analysis for Public Decision*, North Scituate, MA, Duxbury.

MISSISSIPPI STATE DEPARTMENT OF EDUCATION (1983) *An Opportunity for Excellence: The Education Reform Act of 1982*, Summary; A report of the Task Force for Educational Excellence in Mississippi.

MITCHELL, B. (1985) 'Multicultural education Aviceble component of American Education?' *Educational Research* 937–11.

MITCHELL, B. (1988) *A National Survey of Multicultural Education*. Cheney, WA, Western States Consulting and Evaluation Services.

MITCHELL, D.E. (1984) 'Educational policy analysis: The state of the art', *Educational Administration Quarterly*, **20**, 3, pp. 120–60.

NAGEL, S.S. (1980) 'The policy studies perspective', *Public administration Review*, **40**, pp. 391–6.

NATIONAL COMMISSION ON MINORITY PARTICIPATION IN EDUCATION AND AMERICAN LIFE (1988) *One Third of a Nation*, Washington DC, American Council on Education and the Commission of the States.

NATIONAL COMMISSION ON PRE COLLEGE EDUCATION IN MATHEMATICS SCIENCE AND TECHNOLOGY (1983) Educating American for the 21st century: A Report to the American People and the National Science Board.

NATIONAL CONFERENCE ON EDUCATING BLACK CHILDREN (1987) *A Blueprint for Action II*, Washington DC, Washington Urban League.

NEW YORK STATE DEPARTMENT OF EDUCATION (1990) *A Curriculum of Inclusion*, A summary of the Task Force Report on Minorities: Equity and Excellence.

PETERSON, P.E. (1983) 'Did the commissions say anything?', *The Brookings Review*, pp. 3–11.

SISTRUNK, W.E. (1988) '*A study of the impact of the educational reform movement in Mississippi schools*', paper presented at the annual meeting of the Mid-South Education Research Association Louisville, Kentucky.

US DEPARTMENT OF EDUCATION (1983) *A Nation at Risk: Imperatives for Education Reform, Report of the National Commission on Excellence in Education*, Washington, DC, US Government Printing Office.

US DEPARTMENT OF EDUCATION (1983) *A Nation a Risk: The Imperative for Education Reform*, Report of the National Commission on Excellence in Education, Washington, DC, US Government Printing Office, April.

WARWICK, D.P. and PETTIGEW, T.F. (1983) 'Toward ethical guidelines for social science research in public policy' in CALLAHAN, D. and JENNINGS, B. (Eds) *Ethics, the Social Science, and Policy Analysis*, New York, Plenum.

WHITE, M.J. (1983) 'Policy analysis and management science' in NAGEL, S.S. (Ed.) *Encyclopedia of Policy Studies*, New York, Marcel Dekker.

Notes on the Contributors

Roberta Ahlauist is Professor of Secondary Education at San Jose State University. The area of her research interests is anti-racist multicultural education from an emancipatory perspective. Her research is grounded in what is called 'research as praxis'.

Marianne Bloch is an Associate Professor of Early Childhood Education in the Department of Curriculum and Instruction at the University of Wisconsin-Madison. She is the current Chair of the Elementary Education Program at UW-Madison. Her research has focused on historical and cross-cultural issues related to the development of early education and child care. Her cross-cultural work is best represented by work on women, child care and education in Africa and a current Spencer Foundation grant on improving US minority culture children's achievement through home-school-university collaboration. Her publications include: 'Becoming scientific and professional: Historical perspectives on the aims and effects of early education and child care' in Popkewitz, T. (Ed.) *The Formation of School Subjects: The Struggle for an American Institution*, Falmer Press; a co-edited book (with Anthony Pellegrini), *The Ecological Context of Children's Play*, Ablex; and two volumes in progress (with Gary Price) *Essays on the History of Curriculum in Early Education* and (with R. Tabachnick and J. Beoku-Betts) *Women and Education in Africa*.

Kathryn M. Borman is a sociologist of education whose interest in schools and multicultural education was initiated early in her career. Her first position was teaching social studies to Chinese, White Russian, urban Appalachian, black, Hispanic, Filipino, and Latvian ninth graders in San Francisco's Inner Mission. She has also taught in secondary schools and community colleges in rural New Jersey and inner-city Oakland and Berkeley, California. She has conducted studies of inner-city urban Appalachian and black children's social cognitions and the transition from school-to-work for the 'forgotten half' who enter the work force following high school. Borman is the editor of seven books, many focused on the sociology of childhood, co-author (with Joel Spring) of *Schools in Central Cities*, and author of *The First Job*. She is the author of twenty book chapters and numerous research articles as well as co-editor of *Educational Foundations*. In addition, Borman has recently become editor for the University of Cincinnati's book series on, 'Social and Policy Issues in Education' to be published by Ablex. Currently, Borman is the Associate Dean of Graduate Studies and Research in the College of Education at the University of Cincinnati.

Gena Collins is completing her master's thesis in the Department of Sociology at the University of Wisconsin-Madison. She is examining changes in the racial composition of school districts and the effect of recent policies on those changes.

Robert Crumpton is the Director of the Minneapolis Public Schools/St Cloud State University Partnership Program and Associate Professor of Education. He is on leave from the Minnesota Department of Education where he has held numerous positions including Manager of the Elementary/Secondary Education Section. Dr Crumpton's current research interest focuses on examining the effectiveness of professional ('best practices') development schools which employ multicultural gender-fair instructional strategies.

Zakia El-Amin serves as the Director of Education for the Urban League of Cincinnati. In this position, she conducts research, works with private and public institutions, and organizes minority constituents for systems intervention and coalition building in the educational arena. Her research interest is educational change, specifically in the areas of community and parent involvement. Currently completing the UC Masters program in Educational Administration, Ms El-Amin is a single parent and a native of Selma, Alabama.

Mary Lou Fuller is an Associate Professor in the Center for Teaching and Learning at the University of North Dakota. Her background includes a multicultural doctorate from the University of New Mexico as well as numerous professional experiences in multicultural environments. Her teaching career started on the Navajo Reservation and continued on to a variety of culturally diverse settings, including a barrio in Arizona. She also has a long history of working with Native Americans. Currently, she teaches multicultural education courses as well as doing research and publishing in this area. A common thread that runs through her research and publications is an interest in the mono-cultural pre-service teacher and in developing strategies to help this student become better informed and more culturally sensitive.

Donna M. Gollnick is Vice President of the National Council for Accredittion of Teacher Education (NCATE) in Washington DC. Since 1974, she has followed the development of multicultural education, particularly for the preparation of teachers. Her textbook with Philip C. Chinn, *Multicultural Education in a Pluralistic Society*, is used in many pre-service courses in the United States.

Beverly M. Gordon is an Associate Professor and coordinator of the Curriculum, Instruction and Professional Development Faculty in the Department of Educational Policy and Leadership in the College of Education at the Ohio State University. She has three interrelated areas of emphasis, the theory and practice of emancipatory interests in the curriculum field, teacher education, and African-American epistemology, which inform her teaching, research and writing. She has published in several journals including, *The Journal of Education, The Journal of Negro Education*, and *Urban Review* and has several book chapters. Her current line of research is a longitudinal study of a twelve-year tuition-granting program for economically at-risk gifted and talented youth.

Carl A. Grant is a Professor in the Department of Curriculum and Instruction. Professor Grant was a Fulbright Scholar in England in 1982–1983 studying multicultural education. He was selected in 1990 as one of the top leaders in teacher education by the Association of Teacher Educators. His major professional interests include multicultural education; race, social class and gender and school life; and preservice and inservice education. His article 'Race, class, gender and abandoned dreams' (with Christine Sleeter) published in *Teachers College Record* was selected as one of the three top articles by Educational Press Association of America for 1988. Among his books are *After the School Bell Rings*, Falmer Press, with Christine Sleeter (1986), which was selected by the American Educational Studies Association (AESA) Critics Choice Selection Panel in 1987 as one of the most outstanding books in the area of educational studies; *Turning on Learning*, Merrill Publishers, with Christine Sleeter (1989); *Making Choices for Multicultural Education*, Merrill Publishers, with Christine Sleeter (1988); *Preparing for Reflective Teaching* (1984), Allyn and Bacon; *Bringing Teaching to Life* (1982), Allyn and Bacon; and *Community Participation in Education* (1979), Allyn and Bacon.

Cynthia A. Gray is Assistant Professor at Black Hill State University, Spearfish, South Dakota. Her Ed.D is from the Harvard Graduate School of Education. She teaches courses in educational psychology, methods for elementary and secondary teachers, and the assessment of special needs children. She is also a member of the university's Multicultural Education Committee and the South Dakota Indian Studies Council. She has particular concerns in understanding the history of Native Americans and their integration into curriculum for teacher education. Her interests are in the development of university and school collaboration, the use of video as a tool of communication and change, and action research. She formerly taught at the University of Denver, University of Colorado, and worked with an international teacher outreach project, INREAL. She is a former special education teacher in elementary and secondary education.

Hilda Hernández (PhD, Education, Stanford University) is a Professor in the Department of Education at California State University, Chico. She is Coordinator of the Graduate Program in Education and the Graduate Program in Foreign/Second Language Education. Language and culture provide the focal points for her teaching, research and writing. Recent publications include *Multicultural Education: A Teacher's Guide to Content and Process* (Merrill, 1989). In this text, she presents a unique perspective for bridging theory and practice in multicultural education. She is currently working on a book — *Teaching Second Language Learners: From Theory to Classroom Practice* — addressing the needs of teachers working with students whose primary language is not English. She has conducted research focusing on teacher-pupil discourse in second language classrooms and university tenure and promotion patterns. She also has been actively involved in curriculum development projects integrating multicultural education into teacher preparation. Dr Hernández has taught at the elementary, secondary, community college and university levels, and speaks frequently on issues related to multicultural education and foreign/second language education at regional, state, and national conferences. Many of her university courses have been televised regionally and nationally. Dr Hernández has been a Spencer Fellow with the National Academy of Education and an Administrative Fellow in The California State University Systemwide Program. She has been the recipient of Professional Achievement Honors and Meritorious Performance Awards.

Gloria Ladson-Billings (PhD, Stanford University, 1984) is Assistant Professor of Teacher Education, University of Wisconsin-Madison. Her interests include multicultural education, pedagogical excellence for African-American students, culturally relevant pedagogy, and curriculum development. Her recent publications include, *Treasure in Earthen Vessels: Excellent Teachers of Black Students, Like Lightning in a Bottle: Attempting to Capture the Pedagogical Excellence of Teachers of Black Students, The Teacher Education Challenge in Elite University Settings: Developing Critical Perspectives for Teaching in a Democratic and Multicultural Society* (with Joyce King, forthcoming), *Returning to the Source: Implications for Educating Teachers of Black Students* (forthcoming), and *Coping with Multicultural Illiteracy: The Challenge for Teacher Educators*. She is a recipient of a National Academy of Education Spencer Post Doctoral Fellowship (1988/89) to study successful teachers of black children.

Cora Bagley Marrett is Professor of Sociology and of Afro-American Studies at the University of Wisconsin-Madison, where she has a particular interest in education and equity. She has undertaken research on ethnicity, gender, and mathematics education at the pre-college level. Her publications include 'Male-female enrollment across mathematics tracks in predominantly black high schools' (*Journal for Research in Mathematics Education*, March, 1983), and 'The changing composition of schools: Implications for school organization' (in Maureen Hallinan *et al.*, *Change in Societal Institutions*, New York, Plenum, 1990). She is completing a textbook on racial and ethnic relationships.

Susan Millar, a cultural anthropologist trained at Cornell University, is currently a Research Associate at the Center for the Study of Higher Education at The Pennsylvania State University. In this position, she is working on national studies of post-secondary education. Recently, she was the Associate Director of the Council of Graduate School's national study of master's degrees. In this project she is engaged in an interpretive study of master's level education, using a modified ethnographic case-study methodology.

Yuko Mizuno is a graduate student in the Department of Sociology at the University of Wisconsin-Madison. Recently, she completed a master's thesis on 'The intergroup contact hypothesis revisited'. Her areas of specialization are race and ethnic relations, and research methods.

Martha Montero-Sieburth is Associate Professor in the Teaching, Curriculum and Learning Environments Area of the Harvard Graduate School of Education. She teaches courses in the analysis of curriculum and teaching, bilingual-multicultural education, understanding the transfer of curriculum models, the discourse of cultural literacy, and the intersection of race and curriculum. She is interested in the direct application of cultural anthropology and interpretive research to the development of culturally relevant instructional materials and curricula. Her specific interests involve university-school collaborations, interpretive studies of teachers' knowledge, and the restructuring of urban schools. She is a former secondary school teacher who has also trained parochial and public school teachers in multicultural education.

Gary Glen Price is a professor and the graduate program chair in the Department of Curriculum and Instruction, University of Wisconsin-Madison, where he teaches courses in early childhood education, effects of child-rearing practices on intellectual development, research, and evaluation. His educational background includes Northwestern University (BA, 1968, Philosophy); Boston College (MEd, 1969, Urban Education); University of Lowell (MEd, 1972, Field Studies in Elementary Education); and Stanford University (PhD, 1976, Psychological Studies in Education). His methodological interests have involved him in the Stanford Evaluation Consortium, a nationwide evaluation of Individually Guided Education, assorted consultancies, and occasional publication of methodological and analytic articles. His substantive research, some of it cross-cultural, includes various contemporary problems in early childhood education; but it primarily focuses on processes by which experiences in early childhood affect intellectual development. His research often triangulates between the theoretical base of cognitive science and the empirical base of frequently replicated environment-intellect correlations.

Lourdes Diaz Soto is currently Associate Professor of Bilingual Education with an emphasis on Early Childhood Education at Lehigh University. She chairs the Early Childhood Sig for the National Association of Bilingual Educators and has implemented a Parent Education Program for parents of young bilingual/bicultural learners within the Commonwealth of Pennsylvania. Dr Soto appears in *Who's Who in American Education* and has researched and written about culturally and linguistically diverse young learners.

Beth Blue Swadener is currently an Assistant Professor of Early Childhood Education in the Department of Teacher Development and Curriculum Studies at Kent State University, where she is developing a new graduate emphasis area in social policy. Prior to coming to Kent State, she was Assistant Professor of Early Childhood Education at Penn State University, where she was the coordinator of a mainstreamed child care center on campus and Project Associate with a bilingual childhood teacher education project and with a comprehensive special education and early childhood program. Areas of ethnographic research have included a case study of two mainstreamed, culturally diverse child care programs and, more recently, a case study of a Friends Elementary School, focusing on social problem-solving and consensus decision-making with primary children. Articles reporting on these two projects have appeared in *The Urban*

Review and *Educational Policy's* recent special issue on Early Childhood Education, and are in press. Other research, in progress, addresses pre-primary education policy and teacher preparation in Senegal and The Gambia. Professor Swadener teaches courses in multicultural education, the hidden curriculum, ethnographic research methods, social studies in early childhood, home-school-community relations, and social policy for children and families. She completed the PhD in Curriculum and Instruction from University of Wisconsin-Madison in 1986, and has been involved in children's advocacy work for the past ten years.

Ellen Swartz is the coordinator of the Multicultural Project for the Rochester City School District. She has coordinated the implementation of the multicultural criteria which guides the review and selection of textbooks and educational materials, as well as curriculum and text development. She has authored, co-authored, and edited supplemental textbooks, instructional materials, and audio-visual media published by the district. These materials have been designed to help teachers overcome the omissions, distortions, and misrepresentations of race, class, gender, physically challenged, and other marginalized groups that pervade mass produced materials. Ms Swartz's work is recognized on a statewide (Conference of the Large City Boards of Education) and national level (Council of Great City Schools National Commission on Bias in Textbooks), and she is active in the ongoing dialogue between textbook publishers and educators to bring about change in commercially produced materials. Beyond issues of biased content in instructional materials, Ms Swartz is well able to theoretically explore the current multicultural debate as a wider crisis of representation within Western culture. Ms Swartz has co-authored an article in the *Boston Journal of Education* (1990) and has an article forthcoming in the *Journal of Curriculum Theorizing*.

Patricia Timm (University of Cincinnati) Graduate Research Associate in Educational Foundations is a community organizer and educational activist. Her recent academic work has focussed on the linkages between families and educators, with a special emphasis on the urban Appalachian community. She has presented conference papers on collaboration of community organizations and the university, district desegregation policies and community effect, and multicultural education as policy and practice.

Lois Weis is Professor of Sociology of Education and Associate Dean in the Graduate School of Education, State University of New York at Buffalo. She is interested in the relationship between processes of identity formation and social structure.

Markay Winston is a practicing school psychologist employed with the Cincinnati Public School System. Specifically, she works in the student diagnostic clinic with adolescents referred for emotional and behavioral difficulties. Research interests include home-school relations, self-esteem, multicultural education, the prevention and amelioration of academic and behavioral difficulties experienced by school-aged students.

Index

Index